WALT
DISNEY
WORLD
& ORLANDO
THEME PARKS

YOUR FAMILY GUIDE TO FUN!

ABOUT THE AUTHOR

Jay Fenster, a resident of the Jersey Shore since 1982, is a travel writer, poet, and an author of short fiction. When not hunched over his computer, Jay can often be found performing on local stages, running fantasy sports leagues, or publishing his monthly humor newsletter, the FensterGram.

He first traveled to Orlando at age ten, and has been enthralled with Disney World and Orlando's theme parks ever since.

WE WANT YOUR INPUT!!!

Our goal is to provide you with a guide book that is second to none. There may be some ratings, opinions, or information, however, that you disagree with. Please send me your ideas, suggestions, critiques, or new information so that we can together make this an even better book the next time around. Write to:

Jay Fenster, c/o Open Road Publishing,
P.O. Box 11249, Washington, DC 20008

WALT DISNEY WORLD & ORLANDO THEME PARKS

YOUR FAMILY GUIDE TO FUN!

JAY FENSTER

OPEN ROAD PUBLISHING

YOUR PASSPORT TO GREAT TRAVEL!

To My Parents

Front Cover photo courtesy of Jimmy Shacky; models Stephanie and Melissa
Back Cover photo (top) courtesy of Wet'n Wild
Back Cover photo (bottom) courtesy of Universal Studios Florida

Inside photos courtesy of Sea World, p. 12 and p. 335 (©1993 Sea World of Florida. All Rights Reserved. Reproduced by permission.); Cypress Gardens, p. 30; Universal Studios Florida, p. 41; Busch Gardens Tampa, p. 357; and Kennedy Space Center/Spaceport USA, p. 362. Permission has been granted from the above corporations to use their photographs, but such permission does not imply their endorsement, sponsorship, or any other affiliation with this book.

TABLE OF CONTENTS

NOTE ON RATINGS
Author's ratings are on a scale of 1 to 10, 1 being the worst, 10 being the best. Remember, taste is subjective, and if I don't like a ride, it doesn't necessarily mean that you won't.

INTRODUCTION

A Walt Disney World vacation is a glorious thing. Once you enter the main gate, you leave reality behind. Unlike the real world, everyone here is encouraged to shelve their worries and slip into Fantasyland.

Disney and many of Orlando's great resorts will cheerfully feed you, house you, drive you around, clothe you, entertain you, and equip you with more mouse ears than you can shake a stick at (for a price, of course). They will even arrange to pick you up and drop you off at the airport. However, despite the "we'll do everything for you" attitude, you still need to plan and you still need a fair amount of information so you can make the most of your Orlando vacation.

This book provides you with everything you'll need to turn a good vacation into a *great* vacation. You'll find comprehensive information on hotels and package deals. You'll find all sorts of information on every single attraction inside Walt Disney World, Universal Studios, and Sea World, plus the main attractions at Central Florida's other theme parks, so you can budget your time efficiently. You'll find out what you can do after the sun goes down, from high-tech dance clubs to low-brow comedy spots. You'll learn where the worthwhile attractions off the beaten tourist path are, so even a repeat visitor can find new and different diversions. And when you get hungry, you'll find listings and reviews of restaurants throughout the city in every price range and cuisine, including more than one hundred inside Disney World alone.

And if you're on any sort of budget, you'll appreciate our unique chapter suggesting 64 great ways to save money on your Orlando vacation.

So get comfortable, get psyched, and please remain seated until the book comes to a complete stop!

AUTHOR'S NOTE

Since October 1971, Orlando has grown from a sleepy little Central Florida town with virtually no visitor appeal whatsoever to the biggest tourist draw this side of Mecca. Anyone who visits Orlando and the surrounding towns without the benefit of foreknowledge is likely to find himself confused and blank-faced, standing between Big Thunder Mountain and Grizzly Hall without a clue.

When I first visited Walt Disney World and Orlando, I made all sorts of tourist mistakes and wasted a lot of time and money. My goal here is to prevent you from doing the same.

The object of this book is to make it easier to tour Orlando and its major attractions with the least possible cost and aggravation and the greatest amount of fun.

We believe this to be the most comprehensive Orlando guide available, offering detailed descriptions of the Magic Kingdom, EPCOT Center, the Disney-MGM Studios, River Country, Discovery Island, Pleasure Island, Typhoon Lagoon, Busch Gardens, Sea World, Universal Studios Florida, Cypress Gardens, Spaceport USA, Church Street Station, and many other minor attractions. There are also listings of all WDW hotels, shops, and restaurants; plus selected Orlando nightlife, shopping centers, and eateries, including the city's full lineup of dinner shows.

Keep this book with you throughout your vacation, from the planning stages to the park touring to the return home. So return your seats to the full upright position, buckle up, and get ready to party!

> **All area codes in this book are (407), unless otherwise noted.**

1. OVERVIEW
– EXCITING ORLANDO!

An Orlando vacation's possibilities are bounded only by your budget and your wildest imagination. But with so much to do, where do you begin? In this chapter I'll give you a quick preview of all that Disney World, Sea World, and all the other fantastic theme parks and attractions have in store so you can best plan your stay in Orlando.

DISNEY'S MAGIC KINGDOM

There are three major theme parks and five minor theme parks in Walt Disney World. The first and foremost is the Magic Kingdom, sister attraction to Disneyland in Anaheim, California. Here you'll find a great variety of attractions, ranging from kiddie classics like **Peter Pan's Flight** and the famous **It's A Small World** to intricate, detailed thrill rides.

There are seven themed lands in the Magic Kingdom. The first one, *Main Street USA*, is a replica of a turn-of-the-century town teeming with Americana. *Adventureland* is where you'll find the buccaneer stronghold of **Pirates of the Caribbean**. In *Frontierland*,have yourself an Old West adventure like **Big Thunder Mountain Railroad** and the newest thrill, **Splash Mountain**, plus rowdy, good-time shows like the **Diamond Horse-shoe Revue**.

Liberty Square takes you back to the Colonies for the patriotic **Hall of Presidents** show and the eerie **Haunted Mansion**. *Fantasyland* draws material from Disney movies and includes children's favorites like **Dumbo** and **20,000 Leagues Under the Sea**. *Tomorrowland* has nostalgic and future-themed attractions like the **Carousel of Progress**, **American Journeys**, and a "psychological thrill ride" known as **Space Mountain**. Finally, *Mickey's Starland* is entirely devoted to the celluloid mouse on whom the whole Kingdom is built.

EPCOT CENTER

In 1981, this attraction opened up as sort of a permanent World's Fair. The theme park is twice as big as the Magic Kingdom and has two main sections: *Future World*, where corporate America shows you the possibilities of tomorrow in exhibits like General Motors' **World of Motion** and Met Life's new **Wonders of Life**, where medical science is explored and where you'll find EPCOT's only thrill ride, a flight-simulator adventure called **Body Wars**. Other fields represented indluce agriculture, human imigiantion, the oceans, communications, computers, energy, and more.

The other half of EPCOT, *World Showcase*, has pavilions from eleven nations, each featuring authentic food, merchandise, and entertainment. Wide-screen and 360° films, rides, and shows introduce you to the culture of the country represented. The newest pavilion, **Norway**, feautres a combination boat-ride-film adventure, the **Malestrom**, which has already become one of EPCOT's most popular attractions.

DISNEY-MGM STUDIOS THEME PARK

The newest of the Disney trio, this is a working film, TV, and animation studio. There are four tours of the production facilities in addition to theme park attractions like the unforgettable **Star Tours**, a spectacular flight-simulation ride based on the Star Wars movies, the **Indiana Jones Epic Stunt Spectacular**, a professional stunt show, and **Jim Henson's MuppetVision 4D**, the late Muppets creator's last work.

SEA WORLD

The other Central Florida "World," this is often described as an aquarium, which doesn't really do justice to this beautiful marine theme park – home to Shamu and his aqautic friends. New this year is **Mission: Bermuda Triangle**, which uses flight-simulator technology to teach about this most mysterious part of the Atlantic Ocean.

MAKING FRIENDS AT SEA WORLD

UNIVERSAL STUDIOS FLORIDA

Orlando's newest and largest theme park, Universal boasts what some consider to be the best theme park ride in the state, **Back to the Future ... The Ride!** There's also great attractions based on the Psycho films, King Kong, ET, Jaws, the Hanna-Barbera cartoons, Murder She Wrote, and more.

OTHER ATTRACTIONS

You'll also find within in-depth descriptions of the smaller attractions and theme parks too, like **Pleasure Island**, a Disney nightspot for the over-18 crowd; **Typhoon Lagoon**, a beautiful, high-tech water park with rides for both the daring and the lazy; **River Country**, a huck Finn-style swimmin' hole; **Discovery Island**, a lovely enclave serving as a zoo in the middle of Bay Lake. You'll also find details on **Busch Gardens Tampa**, **Cypress Gardens**, **Kennedy Space Center/SpacePort USA**, **Water Mania**, and the incomparable **Wet'n'Wild**.

ACCOMMODATIONS

In Orlando and environs, there are more than 200 hotels, motels, and inns, 21 of which lie inside Disney World. The best of the hotels are the deluxe **Grand Cypress Resort**; **Disney's Village Resort**; **Holiday Inn Main Gate East**, **Main Gate**, and **Lake Buena Vista**; and the **Sheraton World Resort**.

And you'll sleep a lot easier knowing that you've saved up to 50 percent on your accommodations by using the techniques detailed in Chapter 3, "Discounts, Deals, and Bargains."

SHOPPING

There are a number of malls in the area where you can satisfy your shopping needs and urges, including **Mercado Mediterranean Village** and the **Florida Mall**, and some specialty malls as well, like the Victorian-era **Old Town**. Along US 192 and International Drive you'll see factory outlets and souvenir shops selling everything from t-shirts to jeans to mugs. Although a good deal of the stuff is pure kitsch, there are bargains to be found.

DINING

Orlando is much like EPCOT Center in that it is a cultural melting pot. You can find virtually any cuisine somewhere in the city or its suburbs. From Thai to American to French, I've includedmany of thefine choices available, plus where to go if you're in need of a fast-ffod fix.

Some of the best choices include **Dux** in the Peabody Orlando for elegant Continental cuisine; **Damon's** in Mercado for stellar ribs and chicken; **Ming Court** for non-traditional Asian dishes in a lavish setting, or the fabulous **Fortune Court** in Lake Buena Vista well as the many worthy restaurants inside the Disney complex (more than 100 to choose from). The best here include **Mickey's Village Restaurant** in the Marketplace; **Arthur's 27** in the Buena Vista Palace; and **Restaurant Akershus** in EPCOT Center for the best Norwegian food you'll ever eat south of the 60th parallel.

I also show you ways to have a great meal without morgaging your house!

NIGHTLIFE

There are two major after-dark entertainment complexes: **Church Street Station** in downtown Orlando and Disney's **Pleasure Island**. There are also numerous dinner shows, like the **Mark Two Dinner Theatre** which mounts Broadway plays and musicals with professional actors, the **Hoop-Dee-Doo Revue** at Disney's Fort Wilderness area, and **Medieval Times**, featuring jousting, swordfights, and other crowd-pleasing competitions.

The nightclub scene is fairly extensive, with places like **Cap'n Jack's Oyster Bar**, serving raw seafood and margaritas in Disney Village Marketplace; **Fat Tuesday's**, a frozen-drink bar, and **The Cricketer's Arms**, an English pub, both in Mercado; and **Wolfman Jack's Rock and Roll Palace** in Old Town.

OFF THE BEATEN PATH

Try walking though the Audubon Nature Preserve on the grounds of the Grand Cypress Resort. You can pack a picnic and stroll around, seeing a taste of the real Florida.

Like the King (of Rock 'n Roll, that is)? Old Town houses an **Elvis Presley Museum** licensed by his estate. Like art? The **Orlando Museum of Art** and the **Morse Museum of American Art** offer a fine variety. Like mini-golf? **Pirate's Cove Adventure Golf** gives you miniature golf in an unforgettable setting. Or check out **The Mystery Fun House**, always a good alternative on a rainy afternoon.

SPORTS & RECREATION

Disney World is not generally thought of as a destination for a sports vacation. However, there are nearly 40 tennis courts, 99 holes of golf, dozens of pools, lakes for boat rentals, bike/jogging/exercise trails, water skiing, and more.

EXCURSIONS

From Orlando, you're within easy reach of **Silver Springs**, the Gulf and Atlantic coasts, **Kennedy Space Center/SpacePort USA, Busch Gardens Tampa**, and major league sports in the form of the Orlando Magic (NBA), Tampa Bay Buccaneers (NFL), and Tampa Bay Lightning (NHL).

THE BEST OF DISNEY WORLD AND ORLANDO

Best Ride:	*Star Tours*, Disney-MGM Studios; *Back to the Future ... the Ride!*, Universal Studios Florida
Best Film:	*MuppetVision 4D*, Disney-MGM Studios
Best Live Show/Tour:	*Hoop-Dee-Doo Revue*, Fort Wilderness; *Shamu: New Visions*, Sea World
Best Kids' Attraction:	*Journey Into Imagination*, EPCOT Center
Best Underrated Attraction:	*Horizons*, EPCOT Center
Best Comedy Attraction:	*MuppetVision 4D*, Disney-MGM Studios
Best Thrills:	*Body Wars*, EPCOT CENTER; *Back to the Future ... the Ride!*, Universal Studios Florida; *Humunga Kowabunga*, Typhoon Lagoon
Best Special Effects:	*Indiana Jones Stunt Spectacular*, Disney-MGM Studios; *Body Wars*, EPCOT CENTER; *IllumiNations*, EPCOT Center; *Dynamite Nights*, Universal Studios Florida
BestRomantic Spot:	*France pavilion*, EPCOT Center; *Mercado Mediterranean Village*
BestDinner Show:	*Hoop-Dee-Doo Revue*, Fort Wilderness
Best Pizza:	*Pizzaria Uno*, Lake Buena Vista
Best Buffet:	*Sizzler*, International Drive
Best Chinese:	*Fortune Court*, Lake Buena Vista
Best Burger:	*Jungle Jim's*, Lake Buena Vista
Best Steak:	*Cattleman's Steakhouse*, Kissimmee
Best BBQ:	*Damon's*, International Drive
Best Specialty Mall:	*Mercado Mediterranean Village*
Best Specialty Shop:	*Mickey's Character Shop*, Disney Village Marketplace

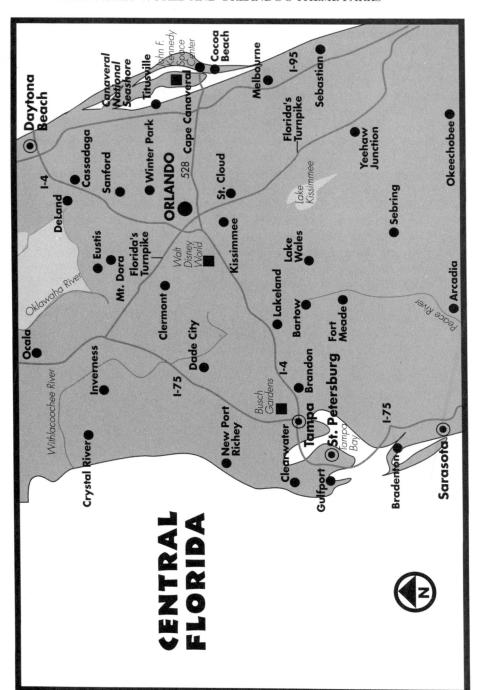

2. PLANNING YOUR TRIP

Alright - you've decided to spend your vacation in Central Florida playing at Disney World and Orlando's other exciting theme parks and attractions. The first thing you'll want to do is some trip planning.

Let's start at the beginning: when to go.

WHEN SHOULD I GO?

This question is one of the first asked by Disney vacationers-to-be, and probably the most vital. This last statement will seem somewhat paradoxical when I tell you that there is no real answer to the question.

There are, however, four factors on which your decision should be based. These are:

- Crowds
- Operating Hours
- Weather
- Special Events.

AVERAGE ATTENDANCE PER DAY, PER PARK	
January and February (excl. President's Week	20,000
President's Week	45,000
March	25,000
Easter/Spring Break	55,000
April and May	35,000
Memorial Day Weekend	40,000
June through August	55,000
September through Thanksgiving Week	30,000
Thanksgiving Week	55,000
Thanksgiving Week/Christmas Week	15,000
Christmas Week through New Year's Day	75,000 & up

On days when under 25,000 people visit each park, you'll pretty much have the place to yourself. Lines will be short or non-existent at most attractions.

At 25,000-30,000 people, the park seems less exclusive, but you've still got a good chance to experience most of the what the parks have to offer. The parks will still be relatively comfortable and waits for popular rides should not exceed a few minutes.

The parks are fairy thronged if you are surrounded by 30,000- 45,000 other visitors. Lines will start to get tricky, so be prepared for a good bit of waiting in lines.

At 45,000-60,000 visitors - a typical summer day - chances of a successful touring day become minute. Crowds queue at all attractions by the gross.

More than 60,000 come during the Christmas season (and a few other times during the rest of the year). These conditions can make first-time touring a living nightmare. Any rookie visitor who considers coming at this time and seeing all the attractions would be well advised to either think again or limit your agenda.

Until the expansion is complete, crowds will seem large at the Disney-MGM Studios because of its unexpected popularity among locals and the small number of attractions inside. On the other end of the spectrum, EPCOT will always seem to be less congested because of the higher number of attractions and the distance between them.

HINT: If your primary concern as far as scheduling goes is avoiding the crowds, the ideal times to visit are September, October, and November; February, March, the second half of April, and May.

HOURS

The hours of operation seem to ebb and flow with the attendance:

SEASONS OF LOW ATTENDANCE

Magic Kingdom	9 AM to	7 PM
EPCOT Center	9 AM to	9 PM
Disney-MGM Studios Theme Park	9 AM to	8 PM

SEASONS OF MODERATE ATTENDANCE

Magic Kingdom	9 AM to	9 PM
EPCOT Center	9 AM to	10 PM
Disney-MGM Studios Theme Park	9 AM to	9 PM

SEASONS OF PEAK ATTENDANCE

Magic Kingdom	9 AM to	Midnight
EPCOT Center	9 AM to	11 PM
Disney-MGM Studios Theme Park	9 AM to	Midnight

NOTE: Low Attendance seasons are January-Easter, excl. President's Weekend and Thanksgiving week until Christmas week; Moderate Attendance seasons arePresident's Week, April, and May (excl. Easter and Memorial Day weeks) and September until Thanksgiving week; and High Attendance seasons are Easter week, June-August,Thanksgiving week, and Christmas week.

During seasons when the parks are not open late, certain shows do not function at all. These are:

- Spectro*Magic   (Magic Kingdom)
- Fantasy in the Sky Fireworks   (Magic Kingdom)
- Sorcery in the Sky Fireworks   (Disney-MGMStudios)

HINT: If you call the WDW Information line, they will always tell you that the parks open at nine o'clock. However, in reality, they will usually open the parks earlier. How much earlier depends on the attendance, but as a general rule of thumb, arrive a half-hour early during off-seasons and an hour in advance for peak seasons. On selected days, ususally during the summer, Walt Disney World Resort guests are given admission to the Magic Kingdom an hour earlier than the general public.

For exact times, call about a week in advance at 824-4321.

WEATHER

Central Florida weather is unpredictable at best. In an attempt at predicting the erratic, here are some guidelines. Just don't hold me to them ...

	HIGHS (f)	LOWS (f)	PRECIP. (inches)
January	70	50	2.28
February	72	51	2.95
March	76	56	3.4
April	82	62	2.72
May	87	67	2.94
June	89	71	7.11
July	90	73	8.29
August	90	73	6.73
September	88	72	7.20
October	82	66	4.07
November	76	57	1.55
December	71	51	1.90

From June to September, there are more than six and a half inches of rain per month, usually in the form of thunderstorms and short-lasting deluges that occur during the afternoon. And in three successive years, daytime temperatures during the first week of November have varied from the sixties to the upper eighties.

In the event that it does rain on days when you plan to visit the parks, don't worry about it. The rain will serve to drive away some of the crowds as well as cool off the air. Besides, almost all of the attractions are indoors or under shelter, and the same can be said for most of the lines. And few and far between is the Florida thunderstorm that lasts more than a few minutes.

The weather most favorable to park touring occurs in February, March, April, October, and November.

SPECIAL EVENTS

There are happenings throughout the year that may influence your decision of when to go. They are arranged on the following pages by chronological order and sub-divided by alphabetical order.

January

CITRUS BOWL: This college football tradition kicks off at Orlando Stadium on New Year's Day. Call 423-2476.

RESIDENT SALUTE: This is a program that offers a discount on WDW admission to Florida residents.

SCOTTISH HIGHLAND GAMES: Fun at the Central Florida Fairgrounds, this includes Highland dancing, caber tossing, and bagpipes. Scottish shops are also put up for the occasion. More information is available by contacting the Scottish-American Society, Box 2149, Orlando, FL, 32802. Or call 422-8226.

February

BASEBALL SPRING TRAINING: Eighteen major league ballclubs play from late February until early April in the Grapefruit League. The nearest sites are the Astros in Kissimmee, the Royals at Haines City, the Red Sox in Winter Haven, the Tigers in Lakeland, and the Reds in Plant City. For more information, see the section on spring training in Chapter 11.

CENTRAL FLORIDA FAIR: Held annually at the Central Florida Fairgrounds in Orlando. Call 295-3247.

DAYTONA SPEED WEEK: The NASCAR's marquee names are here en force for a whole week of racing, culminating with the Daytona 500. Contact Daytona International Speedway, Daytona Beach, FL 32115-2801. Tel. (904) 254-6767.

DISNEY VILLAGE WINE FESTIVAL: Over sixty wineries from the U.S. and Europe participate in this annual event at the Marketplace. Details: Special Events: Disney Village Marketplace, Box 10150, Lake Buena Vista, FL 32380-1000. Tel. 824-4531.

GASPARILLA DAYS AND GASPARILLA INVASION: Five hundred members of a local club dress as the crew of the famed pirate Jose Gaspar set sail in Tampa Harbor and claim the city for themselves and then parade (a la Pirates of the Caribbean) through the streets to celebrate Tampa's piratic past. Two weeks later, a nighttime parade brings the event to its finale. For more information, contact Ye Mystic Krewe of Gasparilla at Box 1514, Tampa, FL 33601, tel. (813) 228-7338.

GOLDEN HILLS ACADEMY INTERNATIONAL CHARITY HORSE SHOW: This show, considered one of the top hunter and jumper competitions, is part of the Winter Equestrian Festival.

GRANT SEAFOOD FESTIVAL: On the third weekend in February, this small town on the east coast serves up fresh Indian River seafood. A very big deal to locals. Information: Seafood Festival, Box 44, Grant, FL 32949. Call 723-8687.

SILVER SPURS RODEO: A Kissimmee tradition since 1944, this biannual competition draws cowboys from all across the country to vie for thousands of dollars. The rodeo lasts four days. Information: Kissimmee — St. Cloud Convention and Visitor's Bureau, Box 422007, Kissimmee, FL 34742-2007 or call 847-5000.

YBOR CITY FIESTA DAY: Part of the Gasparilla Days celebration, this features a raid similar to the one on Tampa plus Latin music, costumes, dancing, art, and Cuban bread, Spanish bean soup, and Cuban coffee at the Fiesta Sopa de Garbanzo.

March

MEDIEVAL FAIR: Hundreds of people participate in events such as a human chess match, jousting, singing and dancing, processions, and the like at the Ringling Museum complex. Food, drink, and speech carry the theme seamlessly. And for that truly feudal experience, you can try the turkey legs, pot pies, and tankards of ale offered by the participants. More information is available by writing Ringling Museums at 5401 Bayshore Road, Sarasota, FL 34243, or by calling (813) 355-5101.

NESTLE INTERNATIONAL: Arnold Palmer's Bay Hill Club in the suburb of Windermere, about ten minutes from WDW, hosts this major PGA event every year. Information: Tournament Office: Bay Hill Club, 9000 Bay Hill Blvd., Orlando, FL 32819, tel. 876-2888.

ST. PATRICK'S DAY STREET PARTY: Church Street Station, Orlando's longtime favorite nightclub complex, plays host to this popular bash each year. Information: Church Street Station, 129 West Church Street, Orlando, FL 32801. Phone: 422-2434.

WINTER PARK SIDEWALK ART FESTIVAL: Held every year on the third weekend of March in a scenic little park full of moss-covered trees, this show of crafts, pottery, etchings, sculpture, paintings, and other art draws locals to the trendy community of Winter Park. Information: Box 597, Winter Park, FL 32790. Tel. 623-3234.

EASTER IN ORLANDO

EASTER SUNRISE SERVICE: Presented at the Atlantis Theater in Sea World. Information: Sea World, 7007 Sea World Drive, Orlando, FL 32821. Tel. 351-3600.
WALT DISNEY WORLD EASTER PARADE: Festive floats are captured on national television as they wind their way down Main Street. The parks are open late this time of year, but it is VERY, VERY crowded.

April
   MINOR LEAGUE BASEBALL: Several teams play in the area, including affiliates of the Houston Astros, Kansas City Royals, and Chicago Cubs. See Chapter 11 for details.
   GREAT INDIAN RIVER FESTIVAL: A weekend of carnival rides, arts and crafts, entertainment, food, a car show, a boat show, culminating in the Great Indian River Raft Race, where homemade crafts compete for the title. This annual event takes place near Kennedy Space Center. Contact the Titusville Area Chamber of Commerce, 2000 Washington Ave., Titusville, FL 32780, 267-3036.

May
   ANNUAL UP, UP, AND AWAY AIRPORT ART SHOW: The Orlando International Airport is decked out for the occasion. Call the airport for information at 826-2055.
   GRAD NITES: On two weekends, rock entertainment is staged and the Magic Kingdom is open from 11 PM until 5 AM for graduating high school seniors, who may buy discounted tickets. For more information, contact the Grad Night Office at Box 10000, Lake Buena Vista, FL 32830.
   RESIDENT SALUTE: Same as in January.

July
   FIREWORKS AT WDW: Fireworks are set off over Cinderella Castle and Seven Seas Lagoon as well. The parks are open late and are packed to their limits.
   SILVER SPURS RODEO: Same as in February. Held on Fourth of July Weekend.

September
   OKTOBERFEST: Yet another celebration hosted by Church Street Station, this features oompah bands, German folk dancing, German food, and lots of beer. Contact Church Street Station, 129 West Church Street, Orlando, FL 32801. Phone: 422-2434.

October

BOAT SHOW: At the Disney Village Marketplace, boats are displayed not only on the grounds of the Marketplace but also in Buena Vista Lagoon. This is one of the area's largest boat shows, with over 200 boats from manufacturers across the country.

FLORIDA STATE AIR FAIR: A two-day agenda of airborne activities including a show of old military planes (on the ground), aeronautical displays, and demonstrations of acrobatics in the sky. Information: Rotary Club of Kissimmee, Box 422185, Kissimmee, FL 34742-2185. Tel. 896-3654.

HALLOWEEN PARTY AT DISNEY VILLAGE: Local youngsters dress up for a costume contest, and the atmosphere is spiced up by "halloween-ifying" the Captain's Tower with cobwebs, Halloween merchandise, and the presence of villains from Disney flicks.

HALLOWEEN STREET PARTY: Held at Church Street Station, this Halloween party is favored by the over-21 set. Contact Church Street Station, 129 West Church Street, Orlando, FL 32801. Phone: 422-2434.

PIONEER DAYS FOLK FESTIVAL: Over two days, this includes bluegrass music and crafts demonstrations. Information: Pine Castle Folk Art Center, 6015 Randolph Street, Orlando, FL 32809. Tel. 855-7461.

TAMPA BAY LIGHTNING: The new NHL franchise did so well it surprised everybody during its maiden season in 1992. Located about sixty-five minutes from WDW.

WALT DISNEY WORLD/OLDSMOBILE GOLF CLASSIC: This stop on the PGA tour draws pros and amateurs alike. Most of the Tour's top players enter. However, if you plan on golfing at one of the Disney courses during your vacation, AVOID GOING THIS WEEK. Playing will become well-nigh impossible unless you are a member of the Classic Club. Information: 828-2255.

YOUNG AT HEART DAYS: Florida residents aged 55 or older get special, low-cost admission to the Magic Kingdom, EPCOT Center, and the Disney-MGM Studios from October 1 to December 15.

November

NOTE: For more detailed information on goings-on in the time between Thanksgiving and New Years, see the "Holidays" section in this chapter.

FESTIVAL OF THE MASTERS: This is one of the biggest events of the year at the Marketplace, and the hype is decidedly worth it. This art show draws award-winning artists from around the country and is attended by locals and tourists with equal and ample enthusiasm, as one can see from the parking lot, packed to capacity.

LIGHT UP ORLANDO: A weekend in early November featuring a street party, an illuminated parade, and fireworks in the downtown area. Live entertainment. This is one celebration that is almost completely overlooked by tourists; it's a good way to see just how a Floridian parties. Information: 648-4010.

ORLANDO MAGIC: Led by seven-foot center Shaquille O'Neal, the NBA's latest expansion team has become the city's darling. They play downtown at the new Orlando Arena (called the O-rena by locals) from November to April. If you hope to see them in action, though, get your tickets in advance. The team is **very** popular with the locals and tickets, thus, are difficult to come by. Tickets and schedules are available by calling the Orlando Arena at 896-2442 or write them at 600 West Amelia, Orlando, FL, 32802.

December

ANNUAL HALF-MARATHON: A thirteen-mile race that departs from Lake Eola Park in the downtown area. Information: 898-1313.

CHRISTMAS AT WDW: Of course, WDW does not have a monopoly on this event — an atmosphere of happiness pervades the whole city — but its celebrations at the Magic Kingdom are noteworthy. In Town Square on Main Street, USA, a huge Douglas fir Christmas tree is erected, and the cast becomes festive, as is the atmosphere in all the lands: Christmas as only Disney can do it. There are also shows, carollers, Mickey's Very Merry Christmas Parade, and a brilliant nativity pageant in the Village. The parks are open late during this season. See the end of this chapter for more information.

CITRUS BOWL PARADE: Occurs every New Year's Eve. Information: 423-2476.

JOLLY HOLIDAYS JOYOUS CELEBRATION DINNER SHOW SPECTACULAR: Put on at the Contemporary Resort Convention Center every December. Information: 934-7639.

NEW YEAR'S EVE CELEBRATIONS: The parks are open late (until 2 AM) and the excitement is intense. There are fireworks displays commencing on the stroke of midnight. The atmosphere is party-like across the parks. The standout celebrations are those on Pleasure Island and in the Contemporary Resort, although you can also find parties at the Polynesian and Fort Wilderness.

GATHERING INFORMATION

As I stated earlier, the key to a successful WDW vacation is planning. Here are some sources to go to to acquire the information you'll need. The **Florida Department of Commerce's Tourism Division**, Visitor Inquiry Section will send you a free publication, the *Florida Vacation*

Guide. Just contact them at 126 Van Buren Street, Tallahassee, FL, 32339-2000 or call them at 904/487-1462, tell them where you want to go and what you want to do and they'll try to oblige you.

The **Orlando Tourist Information Center** (8445 International Drive, Orlando, FL 32819) offers the *Official Visitors' Guide* and *Official Accommodations Guide*, two books listing hundreds of lodging, entertainment, and dining options. The Center has brochures from virtually all area attractions and hotels, and offers discount attraction tickets. It is open from 8 to 8 daily and is located in the Mercado Mediterranean Village (363-5871). Upon arrival, you might want to make this your first strop. Pick up all the magazines you can, they are loaded with coupons and special offers. Doing this can save hundreds of dollars over the course of a vacation.

Also, try the **Kissimmee/St. Cloud Convention and Visitors' Bureau** (1925 E. Spacecoast Parkway, Kissimmee, FL 32742) for brochures. Call 874-5000. From Florida, call 800/432-9199, or from the rest of the U.S., 800/327-9159. The **Orlando/Orange County Convention and Visitors' Bureau** is also good for info. Write (7204 Sand Lake Drive, Suite 301, Orlando, FL 32819) or call them at 345-8882.

For information on restaurants, attractions, entertainment, and more, call the **Sentinel Source Line** at 872-7200 or 800/775-7202 from any touch-tone phone. For instructions on how to use the system, press 9930. For lists of various articles of interest, you press a four-digit code. For example: weather (5000), Orlando area restaurants (7010), Kissimmee area restaurants (7490), International Drive restaurants (7600), Lake Buena Vista area restaurants (7340), dinner shows (8030), golf courses (8175), museums (8055), nightlife (8070), pari-mutuels (8085), theme parks (8125), water activities (8145), and water trips (8165).

If you are driving to WDW, it would aid you immeasurably to have a *Traveler Discount Guide*, published by Exit Information Guides. They can be had in the Tourist Information Center, but they don't do much good once you're already there, so to get one in advance, send your name, address, travel dates, and the states in which you'll be travelling to Exit Information Guide, Inc., 3014 NE 21st Way, Gainesville, FL, 32609. The cost for postage is $2 for one guide, $5 for three, or $10 for all nine guides.

The Florida guide tells you what lodgings, restaurants, and gas stations are in close vicinity to highway exits in these states as well: I-95 from the Florida state line to the Canadian border, I-24 in Tennessee, and I-75 in Tennessee and Georgia.

Several other independent publications offer coupons and information and are definitely worth a look, since they can save you anywhere up to 62% on hotels, plus get you free or discounted meals at restaurants, in addition to getting you reduced admission rates to Orlando's myriad playgrounds. They can be acquired at the Tourist Information Center.

Listed below are the different publications and if and how they can be attained before you leave:

- **Best Read Guide Kissimmee** and **Best Read Guide Orlando**, 64 pgs each. Coupons, maps, and ads, but more articles than other guides. Also published monthly, this is found in more places than other guides. Free wherever you can find them. You can also order single issues or subscriptions for $2 and $20, respectively. Write to Best Read Guides, 7676 Municipal Drive, Orlando, FL, 32819 or call at 363-3600. Be sure to specify the Orlando and/or Kissimmee editions.
- **Central Florida Magic**, 20 pgs. Ads, coupons. Available at various locations. Lots of maps. Not available by subscription.
- **Central Florida Travel Guide**, 36 pgs. Ads, coupons, and lots of maps. More hotel- than attraction-oriented. Published quarterly. Single copies are available for $3 for postage and handling, subscriptions for $10 by writing Kenney Communications, Inc., 4303 Vineland Road, Suite F15, Orlando, FL 32811. Call them at 422-8333 or 847-3357.
- **Dining & Entertainment**, 24 pgs. Coupons, maps, and ads. No articles, only available at Tourist Information Center and other brochure racks.
- **Enjoy Florida Magazine**, 56 pgs. Coupons, ads, lengthy profiles on several local attractions or restaurants, WDW tips and operating schedules. Also, dining guide, maps, attraction guide, Single copies are available for $3. A one-year, twelve-issue subscription is available for $10 from the publishers, Kenney Communications (see above).
- **Florida on the Go**, 80 pgs. Ads, coupons, and maps from attractions, hotels, restaurants, and shopping areas all over Florida.
- **Good Times Orlando**, 32 pgs. Ads, coupons, lots of maps. The restaurant and attraction listings in here are very extensive and printed in English, Portuguese, German, Spanish, French, and Italian. Some articles of interest.
- **International Drive Bulletin**, 52 pgs. Ads, coupons, attraction listings, shopping directories, and dining options. Some articles. Available up and down International Drive, or by subscription, $9.54 for twelve issues by calling 351-1573.
- **See Orlando**, 88 pgs. Includes lots of coupons, maps, and advertisements, including maps of all five major area theme parks and the Orlando area. It is published monthly, and they are free at the Tourist Information Center. To have them mailed to you in the U.S., it costs $1.50 for a single issue, $7.00 for a one-year subscription. For copies or subscriptions, write SEE Magazines, 5728 Major Blvd., Suite 200, Orlando, FL 32819. Tel. 363-7977.
- **Orlando Magazine**, 104 pgs. This monthly publication tells about the lifestyle of the citizens of the city. Along with articles on Orlando

personalities and events, there are monthly features on attractions and restaurants. So useful is this magazine that many relocation packages include a copy. Subscriptions and single issues are available by calling 539-3939.

WHAT TO PACK

This is another item of vital importance which can keep a good vacation from being great, regardless of where you go. In WDW, the rule of thumb is to dress comfortably. T-shirts and shorts or blouses and skirts are the norm most of the year. However, as it grows colder, clothes grow thicker and longer. But above all, wear comfortable sneakers. As you will be doing a lot of walking at any of the theme parks, this cannot be stressed enough. If you forget your sneakers, purchase a pair. Otherwise, your feet'll be screaming bloody murder by your second day of touring.

As for restaurants, only a few in WDW or the Orlando area require a shirt and tie or a dress. Otherwise, dress is casual.

A bathing suit is a given necessity regardless of the time of your visit. On winter nights, temperatures can dip into the 40s, so a sweater or jacket is a good idea. It's even a good idea to bring a light jacket in the 100-degree heat of July because most Florida hotels have air conditioning. Other items that you may want to bring include: cameras or camcorders, film (often forgotten), sporting equipment, or anything else you feel a need to bring.

HOLIDAYS IN ORLANDO AND DISNEY WORLD

Earlier in this chapter, I listed the main events throughout the year. Below you'll find more detailed information on the holiday and special events in the area. Programs are subject to change without notice.

18TH ANNUAL NEW YEAR'S EVE STREET PARTY: Orlando's original nighttime entertainment complex, Church Street Station, rings in each new year in style, with a gala including noisemakers, party favors, and a free champagne toast at midnight. Past New Year's Eve performers include the likes of classic rockers Rare Earth. For information, ring Church Street at 422-2434 or Ticketmaster at 839-3900.

30 YEARS OF ROCK'N'ROLL NEW YEAR'S EVE PARTY: At the Disney-MGM Studios Theme Park, rock into the new year with musicians like Otis Day and the Nights, Mitch Ryder, Pat Upton, Mickey Dolenz, and Mike Harvey of radio show Super Gold.

CHRISTMAS BOAT PARADE: A lighted parade on Kissimmee's lakefront, held in the middle of December. Information: 847-2033.

CHRISTMAS TREE LIGHTING CEREMONIES: In EPCOT Center, every night starting the first week of December at 6 PM (Christmas Eve at 5:45), the Voices of Liberty Choir visit Showcase Plaza to light the tree.

In the Disney Village Market place, from Dec. 1 to Christmas Eve, the lights go on at 5:45 PM.

DICK CLARK'S "ROCKIN' NEW YEAR'S EVE": For three years now, Universal Studios Florida's guests have been invited to celebrate the end of the year with eternal teenager Dick Clark at the "largest street party outside of Times Square." Future shows will ber hard pressed to top the 1992 affair, because, well, The Village People just can't be beat.

EXPLODE INTO THE NEW YEAR: EPCOT Center's celebration includes musicians of varied styles, such as Kool and the Gang, Mickey Finn and his Dixie Land Band, and Frankie and the West End Boys, plus a special Illuminations display at midnight.

FLORIDA CITRUS BOWL: Two top-ranked college football teams clash in this annual, nationally-televised event at the Florida Citrus Bowl Stadium. Tickets, available through Ticketmaster (839-3900), cost $37.75.

FLORIDA POST-GAME BOOLA BOWL STREET PARTY: Two parties in two days! Church Street Station hosts this event with post-game celebrations, pep bands, cheerleaders, entertainment, and the presentation of the Most Valuable Player trophy. For tickets, call 423-2476.

THE GLORY AND PAGEANTRY OF CHRISTMAS: This live nativity scene, staged at the Disney Village Marketplace, certainly lives up to the "glory" in its name. Performed from the second week of December until Christmas Eve at 6:00, 7:00, 8:30, and 9:30 PM (no 9:30 show on Christmas Eve).

HOLIDAY POPS: The Florida Symphony Orchestra kicks off the holiday season with their annual Holiday Pops concert in the Carr Centre in downtown Orlando. Tickets cost $18 to $34 and can be purchased through Ticketmaster (839-3900).

HOLIDAY WINTERFEST: An arts and crafts festival held during the last week of November, held on the shores of Lake Tohopekaliga.

JINGLE BELL JUBILEE: The Odyssey Restaurant plays host to a Christmas show starring favorite Disney characters. Presented throughout December at 11:00 AM, 3:00, 4:30, and 5:45 PM daily.

JOLLY HOLIDAYS DINNER SHOW: Presented from the end of November to the end of December at the Contemporary Resort Convention Center, this show features a cast of over 100 singers and dancers who perform a montage of holiday classics. Call 872-7200 for details.

LIGHTING OF THE GREAT AMERICAN CHRISTMAS TREES: At Church Street Station's Orchid Garden Ballroom, this event includes a sing-along, entertainment, and free refreshments.

MACY'S NEW YORK CHRISTMAS: The 6-story tall balloons made famous in the Macy's Day Parade come to their winter home on the New York Street on the backlot of the Disney-MGM Studios Theme Park. On display throughout December.

MICKEY'S VERY MERRY CHRISTMAS PARADE: A Magic Kingdom classic, starring Santa Claus, favorite Disney characters, and traditional yuletide personalities, this parade runs the first two weekends of the month and daily starting around Dec. 19.

MICKEY'S VERY MERRY CHRISTMAS PARTY: Prepare the coffee! Pack the Vivarin! You can purchase a specially-priced admission ticket giving you the opportunity to run through the Magic Kingdom three nights during the month, from 8 PM until 1 AM.

MISS MINNIE'S COUNTRY CHRISTMAS AND FANTASY FAIR: Minnie finally gets her own Christmas show, guest starring Melvin the Moose and the Country Bears. Performed throughout December in the Magic Kingdom.

NEW YEAR'S CITRUS EVE: In honor of the next day's college bowl and the coming year, Sea World's Citrus Eve party included acts such as comedian Dan Riley and a C&W concert that has featured Suzy Boggus and Diamond Rio. Discounted tickets are available for all-day admission, admission to party, and admission to the party and concert.

NEW YEAR'S EVE IN THE DISNEY RESORTS: The South Seas Spectacular at the Polynesian Resort features either a five-course dinner at the Papeete Bay Verandah, specialty desserts, dancing, and unlimited drinks ($130 per person) or in Luau Cove, a dinner show including specialty drinks and champagne ($75 per person). The Contemporary Resort's *Top of the World Supper Club* hosts the Broadway at the Top Revue, followed by a cocktail reception, champagne in a keepsake glass, souvenir program, and photo ($150 per person). The Grand Floridian offers an elegant seven-course dinner show, unlimited cocktails and wine, dancing, midnight champagne, and a continental breakfast ($150 per person). The *Hoop-Dee-Doo Musical Revue* at Fort Wilderness puts on a special show and throws in unlimited cocktails and non-alcoholic beverages, party favors, a souvenir photo, and a C&W band ($95 a head, $80 per person under 21). On the Empress Lilly in the Marketplace, there's a four-course dinner in the Steerman's Quarters or Fisherman's Deck, strolling entertainment, and champagne or wine ($60 per person, $40 per person under 21). For an extra $20 per person, you can add admission to the party in the Baton Rouge Lounge with a midnight champagne toast, party favors and name entertainment. For information or reservations, call 934-7639.

NUTCRACKER BALLET: For 100 years now, each winter has seen the tale of Drosselmeyer and Clara in the Christmas world of make-believe. This winter is no different, as the classical piece is performed at the Bob Carr Performing Arts Centre downtown. Tickets are $26 for adults, $18 for kids 6 to 12, and $5 for kids under 6. Call Ticketmaster at 839-3900.

OLD-FASHIONED CHRISTMAS PARTY: One thing you don't

expect during an Orlando vacation is the opportunity to build a snowman or go careening down a mountain of snow. Well, on two weekends in December, the Winter Carnival comes to Universal Studios Florida. Also, Delancey Street is decked out with carollers and chestnut vendors. Hollywood Boulevard is beautifully illuminated, including a fifty-foot tree. Free gifts are given out, including hot cocoa, cookies, and gifts from E.T. There is also an outdoor ice show, a Yuletide Yacht Parade, fireworks, Santa's house, and a magical Santa's flight.

WARBIRD WEEKEND: A combination airshow and museum exhibit, this event features aerial demonstrations, static displays, and vintage aircraft and military vehicles. Information: Flying Tigers Warbird Museum, 933-1942.

JUST ANOTHER WACKY WATER-SKIING BIRTHDAY CAKE ROUTINE AT CYPRESS GARDENS

PACKAGE DEALS

The vast diversity of central Florida packages makes this an option well worth exploring. You can stay anywhere from low-budget chains to one-of-a-kind luxury hotels. There are bus packages, air packages, drive packages all options are covered.

If you decide that you want a package, you can get all the appropriate literature from your local travel agency. Shop around. Different chain agencies will sometimes offer their own packages. When you are deciding on your package, it is crucial that you find out exactly what is included in it. Some packages include airfare and hotel only, others come with transfers or rental cars, admissions, meals, tips, taxes, and entertainment. Bear in mind that although things like nightly cocktails or coffee and juice in the morning sound nice, but you're probably paying for it.

Also, beware of packages that offer as selling points options available to all Disney guests, i.e., use of transportation in WDW.

Evaluating Cost Efficiency

Trying to find the best value in a package can be difficult, to say the least. There are some packages which are cheaper than if you had made all the arrangements yourself. Other times, the opposite is true. To determine whether a package is viable, find out the cost of all the components of the package, if purchased separately, and compare that total to the package cost. When calculating value for plans that include meals, figure on a per person cost of $5 for breakfast, $8 for lunch, and $12 for dinner.

With plans that include airfare, it's slightly more complex. You can figure it out by adding up the package's components excluding airfare. If you can't get airfare for less than the difference, the package is a good deal. For example, Package A costs $1200. Its components, less airfare, cost $900. If you can't get airfare for $300 or less, the package is worthwhile.

Three of Disney's plans include unlimited recreational use, and for these plans, figure out the price of all the components excluding the recreation and then decide if you will rack up enough bills in recreation to make up the difference. If you plan to spend more than the difference, the package will save you money. But beware of paying for materials and services you won't use.

Disney Package Deals

These are the packages offered by the Walt Disney Travel Company. All prices are per adult, double occupancy. Juniors are ages 10 to 17, children are those 3 to 9. Kids under 3 are free. Unless otherwise noted, packages run from four to seven nights and include transportation within WDW, choice of transfer, rental car or a drive plan, a guidebook, and a Magic Morning breakfast feature inside the park.

The **Grand Plan** includes accommodations at the Grand Floridian, unlimited admission and use of recreational activities and facilities, the Wonders of Walt Disney World learning programs, breakfast, lunch, and dinner daily, gratuities for baggage handling at the hotel, room service, six hours' daily babysitting in-room and at the Mousketeer Clubhouse, special room amenities, private golf and tennis lessons, use of St. John's Health Club, valet parking at the hotel, stroller and wheelchair rental, use of a rental video camera in the theme parks, and an exclusive framed Disney Classic Art lithograph. Rates per adult start at $1,315 for four nights, $1,594 for five, $1,872 for six, and $2,150 for seven. Juniors cost $622 to $997, children are $401 to $581.

The **Admiral Plan** includes accommodations at the Yacht and Beach Club Resorts, unlimited admissions and use of recreational activities and facilities, Wonders of Walt Disney World learning programs, breakfast, lunch, and dinner daily, gratuities for baggage handling at the hotel, room service, six hours' daily babysitting in-room and at the Sandcastle Club, special room amenities, private golf and tennis lessons, use of the Ship Shape Health Club, valet parking at the hotel, stroller and wheelchair rental, use of a rental video camera in the theme parks, and an exclusive framed Disney Classic Art lithograph. Rates per adult start at $1,326 for four nights, $1,607 for five, $1,888 for six, and $2,169 for seven. Juniors are $622 to $997, children are $401 to $581.

The **Disney Deluxe Magic** package includes accommodations at the Grand Floridian, Yacht and Beach Club, Polynesian Resort, Contemporary Resort, Disney Inn, Village Resort, or Fort Wilderness Resorts, unlimited admission and use of recreational activities and facilities, Wonders of Walt Disney World learning programs, breakfast, lunch, and dinner daily, gratuities for baggage handling at the hotel, and an exclusive framed Disney Classic Art lithograph. Adult rates start at $971 for four nights, $1,235 for five, $1,374 for six, and $1,576 for seven. Juniors are $532 to $856, kids are $307 to $469.

The **Resort Magic** plan offers accommodations at the Grand Floridian, Yacht and Beach Clubs, Disney Vacation Club, Polynesian Resort, Contemporary Resort, Disney Inn, Village Resort, and Fort Wilderness Resort, and unlimited admission. Adult rates begin at $571, $686, $798, and $902 for four, five, six, and seven nights, respectively. Juniors pay $201 to $252, kids pay $158 to $200.

Disney's **Festival Magic** plan includes accommodations at the Caribbean Beach, Port Orleans, or Dixie Landings Resorts and unlimited admission. Adult cost is $404 for four nights, $480 for five, $553 for six, and $618 for seven. Juniors pay $201 to $252, kids pay $158 to $200.

The **Disney Honeymoon Magic** plan includes accommodations at the Grand Floridian, Yacht and Beach Clubs, Polynesian Resort, Contemporary Resort, or Disney Inn, unlimited admissions, three to six special continental breakfasts for two delivered to your room, and one dinner for two. Rates per couple start at $1,383 for four nights, $1,650 for five, $1,908 for six, and $2,153 for seven.

The **Swan & Doplhin Magic** plans include accommodations at the Walt Disney World Swan or Dolphin, unlimited admissions to the major parks and Pleasure Island, one dinner, and one Pleasure 'n Play coupon (five and six night plans) or two Pleasure 'n Play coupons (seven night plan) good for admission to Typhoon Lagoon or both River Country and Discovery Island or lunch. Adult rates start at $626 for four nights, $772 for five, $898 for six, and $902 for seven. Juniors are $219 to $299, kids are $154 to $221.

The **Village Magic** plan includes three to seven nights' accommodations at the Buena Vista Palace, Guest Quarters Suite Hotel, Hilton, Grosvenor Resort, Hotel Royal Plaza, Travelodge Hotel, or Howard Johnson Resort, unlimited admission to the major parks and Pleasure Island, and one Pleasure 'n Play coupon (four through seven night plans) good for admission to Typhoon Lagoon OR both River Country and Discovery Island or lunch. Rates begin at $290 for three nights, $370 for four, $440 for five, $506 for six, and $561 for seven. Juniors cost $161 to $246, children are $126 to $191.

The **Vacation Magic** plan includes three to seven nights' accommodations at the Orlando Marriott, Embassy Suites Plaza International, Hampton Inn Maingate, Howard Johnson Maingate West, Howard Johnson Park Square Inn & Suites, Holiday Inn Maingate, Holiday Inn Lake Buena Vista, Radisson Inn Maingate, Sonesta Villa Resort Orlando, Sheraton Lakeside Inn, Homewood Suites Maingate, Sheraton World Resort, Hyatt Orlando, Stouffer Orlando Resort, Doubletree Club Hotel, Holiday Inn Maingate East, Hawthorn Suites Hotel Orlando, Parc Corniche Condominium Resort Hotel, or Embassy Suites Resort Lake Buena Vista.

This plan also includes admission to the major parks for four days (three and four night plans) or five days (five, six, and seven night plans), one Pleasure 'n Play coupon (three and four night plans) good for admission to Typhoon Lagoon or both River Country and Discovery Island or lunch, admission to Typhoon Lagoon, Pleasure Island, River Country, and Discovery Island for five days (five, six, and seven night plans), four or five round trip transfers between hotel and Magic Kingdom, EPCOT Center, or Disney-MGM Studios Theme Park, or, with rental car and drive plans, four or five days' parking in the Magic Kingdom, EPCOT Center, or Disney-MGM Studios Theme Park parking lots, one admission to Pleasure Island per person (three and four night packages), and one admission to Sea World per person (six and seven night packages), including transfers from hotel with transfer plan. Rates start at $264 for three nights, $296 for four, $337 for five, $390 for six, and

$421 for seven. Juniors pay $214 to $265, children pay $174 to $212.

Other Tours and Packages

Domenico Tours (751 Broadway, Bayonne, NJ 07002, phone 201/823-8687 or 800/554-TOUR) offers tour packages including travel by air or bus. **Globus Gateway/Cosmos** (150 South Los Robles Ave., Pasadena, CA 91101, phone 818/449-0919 or 800/556-5454) has extensive eight-day packages including WDW admission. In addition to the agencies listed below, local travel agencies may have their individual packages.

Including WDW Hotels

American Express (Box 5014, Atlanta, GA 30302, tel. 800/637-6200) is one of the few groups that offer accommodations in Disney-owned, Disney-operated hotels. **Delta**, the official airline of Walt Disney World, offers Delta Dream Vacations which include everything you need, from admissions to airfare, from accommodations to rental car. Call 800/872-7786 for details.

Including Off-Premises Hotels

American Fly AAway Florida (800/355-1234 or 800/433-7300) offers some packages that don't include WDW admission. **GoGo Tours** (69 Spring St., Ramsey, NJ, 07446, phone 201/934-3500 or 800/821-3731) and **SuperCities** (7885 Haskell Ave., Van Nuys, CA 91406, 818/988-6774 or 800/556-5660) present tours that include accomodations, admissions, rental cars, and admissions to area attractions.

3. DISCOUNTS, DEALS, AND BARGAINS: 64 GREAT MONEY-SAVING TIPS

Even with the best of intentions, you can spend a lot more money in Orlando than you need to. If you follow the 64 tips and suggestions listed in this chapter, you'll find some great ways to stretch your hard-earned dollars!

BEFORE YOU GO

1. If you can swing it, plan your vacation for an "off-season" period, i.e. anytime except summer and holidays.

2. Order an **Orlando Magicard** and **Official Visitors Guide** from the Orlando Convention and Visitor's Bureau (363-5871), and if you are planning your visit in fall or winter, call the Kissimmee-St. Cloud Convention and Visitor's Bureau (800/327-9159) and order a **Visitor's Guide** and the **Great Fall-Winter Getaway** brochure. The Getaway brochure and Magicard offer discounts at hotels, attractions, restaurants, and shops all around the area.

3. Contact area travel agents for information about available packages.

4. Call Exit Information Guides (904/371-3948) and order a **Traveler Discount Guide** for Florida plus any states you are planning to drive through, if planning to drive. This book, published every 90 days, has 100+ pages of coupons for hotels and restaurants just off major highways.

5. Remember video tape, film, aspirin, Pepto-Bismol, sunscreen, and other sundries. They are *waaaaay* overpriced in Orlando.

6. If you're taking advantage of the Premier Cruise and Disney Week vacation, membership in the Magic Kingdom Club will cut 10% off your price.

ACCOMMODATIONS

7. For Disney hotels, join the **Magic Kingdom Club**. It is a fringe benefit for some companies, but if you aren't already a member, you can join for $49. MKC members receive special vacation packages plus discounts of up to 30% at Disney hotels.

8. For Disney hotels, AAA members have been offered special discounts of 15% on nightly rates or 20% on packages.

9. Disney runs an information booth on I-75 in Ocala, and a percentage of rooms are sold from here at discounts up to and above 40%. However, this is a very risky way to go about getting accommodations. You can inquire about room availability by calling 904/854-7040.

10. AAA members receive discounts of up to 25% at chain hotels including Days Inn, Holiday Inn, and more.

11. When calling hotels, ask for the room rate for whenever you want to go. Then ask for the best rate available. There may be a substantial difference. Also, if you are a senior, student, AAA member, or veteran, inquire about special rates for your own group.

12. Many frequent-flyer plans have tie-ins with hotel chains. This may entitle you to earn miles or spend the miles for free nights, room upgrades, etc.

13. Non-profit associations often sell thick Entertainment books as fundraisers. The back of these books contain listings of villa accommodations and hotels offering Entertainment cardholders 50% discounts.

14. The **Vacation Accommodations Directory** offers listings of villa and hotel accommodations all over the world, and in every price range. To order, call 800/237-7700.

15. For large families that would otherwise be forced to rent multiple rooms, villas offer a cost-effective alternative, and as an added bonus, many have kitchens.

16. In 1991, Conde Nast Traveler did a study of chain hotel rates quoted by the central reservations office and the individual hotels themselves, and they found some discrepancies. If you are thinking about staying at a chain, call both numbers.

17. The farther from Disney World a hotel is, the less you can expect to pay for it. There are exceptions to the rule, but for the same price as an average Days Inn on Sand Lake Drive, you can stay at a quieter, nicer hotel in a surrounding area.

18. If you are staying in an on-site Disney hotel, it is unnecessary to rent a car. However, this locks you on Disney turf for the duration of your trip.

19. You can save a couple of bucks by staying at a hotel that includes a daily continental breakfast or breakfast buffet. These are mainly all-suite or budget establishments.

20. Many hotels have no extra charge for children under 18 in the same room as their parents. Check the cut-off age.

21. If at all possible, choose a hotel that offers free local phone calls. If your accommodations do not, bring your telephone calling card. Some establishments charge high "service fees" for even toll-free calls.

22. Ask about corporate rates and how to qualify for them.

AIRFARE

23. Check into benefits of frequent flyer plans you are a member of. If you are not a member, join one of the plans. Some offer discounts on hotels and car rentals.

24. Fly when nobody else does, rates may be much lower.

25. Look into bucket shops, agencies that resell tickets at deeply discounted prices.

26. Entertainment books offer coupons for discounts on airline tickets.

27. If you include a Saturday in your trip, you may be eligible for a special Excursion Rate, designed to exclude business travelers from low rates.

28. Some travel agencies subscribe to a service that keeps an eye out for airline prices and can be used to get the lowest price available for any given flight.

29. Magic Kingdom Club members receive a 10% discount on Delta flights to Orlando.

DRIVING TO AND AROUND ORLANDO

30. As with hotels, ask for the rate for whatever kind of car you want and then ask for the best rate.

31. AAA, AARP, and other clubs often are offered car rental discounts as well.

32. If you pay for a rental car with certain credit cards, a collision damage waiver (CDW) may not be neccesary, as any damage would be insured by the card.

33. Instead of stopping at a roadside fast-food joint while en route, pack homemade sandwiches or snacks in a cooler.

34. The closer to WDW you are, the more gas will cost you.

35. Magic Kingdom Club members receive a discount on cars from National InterRent, up to 30% off.

EATING

36. Make your main meal of the day lunch, instead of dinner. The same meals are often much cheaper then.

37. Instead of eating a fast food lunch in the parks, you might consider leaving for one of the better-quality chain or buffet restaurants on U.S. 192 or S.R. 535, depending on how tight your schedule is.

38. Guests at hotels with kitchens or kitchenettes can save a substantial amount of money by cooking their own meals.

39. If you don't have a kitchen, you can save time and money by purchasing breakfast the night before. Bottled juices and baked goods are a good choice.

40. Buffet restaurants in the tourist strips offer hearty eaters the chance to fill their tanks for one low price.

41. Magic Kingdom Club members receive a 10% discount on WDW dinner shows.

42. Not a Magic Kingdom Club member? Pay for your dinner show ticket with the American Express card and receive the same 10% discount.

43. In the theme parks, you can save both valuable time and money by getting lunch from one of the carts traveling the park. Especially good are the title items at the Turkey Leg Wagon in the Magic Kingdom's Frontierland and the foot long hot dogs at the American Adventure in EPCOT and by the Great Movie Ride in the Disney-MGM Studios.

44. In visiting Disney's water parks, pack a picnic lunch. It's cheaper and better than the stuff you can get there.

45. Some hotels have promotions that allow kids to eat free in the hotel's restaurant.

SHOPPING

46. Allot a certain amount of time and money for souvenirs, and stick to the limit.

47. Comparison-shopping inside Walt Disney World is useless. The same items have the same prices in all shops.

48. However, if you are a member of the Magic Kingdom Club, you might want to make any souvenir purchases in the Disney Village Marketplace and Pleasure Island stores, as your card entitles you to a 10% discount.

49. Orlando and Kissimmee are home to hundreds of factory outlet stores, all of them a good bet for getting brand-name merchandise at cut-rate prices.

50. Visitor information centers often have vouchers for coupons at area malls like the Mercado, Old Town, and Belz Factory Outlet World.

51. If you get a kick out of "I'm with Stupid" t-shirts and hokey sayings on mugs, cruise U.S. 192 and International Drive. Most of the merchandise is pretty tacky, but there are good buys to be found.

ATTRACTIONS

52. If you are planning to spend several days in Disney World and are staying at a WDW-owned hotel, look into the **Be Our Guest Pass**, which includes admission to all Disney parks from check-in until the end of check-out day.

53. If you are not staying on-site and wish to experience the minor parks, the **Five Day Super Duper Pass** is probably your best bet.

54. Magic Kingdom Club members recieve small discounts on admission media to WDW.

55. Coupons to many area attractions can be found in magazines like **Best Read Guide**, **Enjoy Florida**, and **SEE Orlando**. These magazines are available from visitors' bureaus and area businesses.

56. If you work for one of the corporations that sponsors an attraction in WDW or Universal (i.e. AT&T, Texaco, General Electric), you may be entitled to special discounts, in addition to access to lounges not open to the general public.

57. AAA, AARP, and other groups often are offered discounts. Veterans, seniors, and Florida residents have been offered discounts at WDW in special annual programs.

58. Many water parks offer discounted admission after a certain time in the afternoon, usually between 3 and 6 PM, dependent upon the season.

SPORTS

59. Inside WDW, golf is cheaper at the Lake Buena Vista, Palm, and Magnolia courses than at the new Eagle Pines and Osprey Ridge courses.

60. The **Disney Inn's Oak Trail** is a par-36 executive golf course, with 9 holes measuring 2,913 yards. The cost of 18 holes (par 72, 5,826 yards) is $25, compared to $85 for the new courses.

61. If you want to play tennis in WDW, it's free at Fort Wilderness, the Disney Village, the Disney Inn, and all the other resorts EXCEPT at the Grand Floridian ($12) or Contemporary Resort ($10).

62. The **Florida PGA Passport** allows discounted play at over 250 of the state's top-rated courses. For more information on the Passport, call 894-4653.

63. *Tee Times Magazine* offers a multitude of listings and coupons for golf courses around the area. Call 895-GOLF or 800/833-7421. For a complete listing of all Florida's golf courses, consult Jimmy Shacky, **Florida Golf Guide**, published by Open Road Publishing ($14.95), available in bookstores. Or, order directly from the publisher at P.O. Box 11249, Cleveland Park Station, Washington, DC, 20008; enclose $2.00 for shipping and handling.

64. Resort golf is generally more expensive than public or municipal courses.

4. BASIC INFORMATION

For your convenience, I've listed below in alphabetical order some of the basic information you may find handy during your Orlando vacation.

Convenience Stores – There are Cumberland Farms and 7-Eleven stores around every corner in Orlando and its environs.

Drinking laws – You must be 21 to be served alcohol. However, you are allowed in bars if you are over 18.

Driving laws – Right turns on red permitted unless otherwise indicated. Seat belts are mandatory for driver, front-seat passenger, and children under 6. All drivers suspected of driving under the influence face an automatic one-year license suspension if they refuse a Breathalyzer test. During rain, low-beam headlights must be used.

Emergencies – To reach the fire, police, or an ambulance, dial 911.

Media – The primary newspaper in Orlando is the Orlando Sentinel (tel. 420-5000). The daily, founded in 1876, is now the nation's 33rd largest paper. On Fridays, there's the Calendar insert, giving information on local eateries, nightlife, festivals, concerts, and other entertainment. It's an extremely comprehensive way of finding out what's up. Many hotels also offer national and out-of-town papers. As for the boob tube, CBS's affiliate is WCPX, Channel 6. NBC hangs out as WESH on Channel 2, and you can find ABC programming on Channel 9, WFTV. The FOX network occupies WOFL, Channel 35, and PBS is on Channel 24, WMFE.

Your hotel room may have more and/or different channels, but there is usually a station guide in the room. Or, call the front desk. In Walt Disney World Resorts, the televisions receive two radio stations: WCBS Newsradio out of New York City, and Chicago's superstation WGN, so residents of those two metropolitan areas can keep up with hometown events.

Sundries – Buy them before you arrive in Orlando, they get more expensive the closer you get to Walt Disney World.

Supermarkets – There are Gooding's supermarkets at the Marketplace (Dr. Phillips Blvd. at Sand Lake Drive), Goodings Interantional Plaza, and Crossroads of Lake Buena Vista shopping center. All are open 24 hours a day. There's a Publix on Vine Street in Kissimmee.

Taxes – Florida state sales tax is 6% on most items, including hotel rooms. There is an additional 4% local tax on hotel rooms, 5% in Kissimmee.

Telephone – Orlando, Kissimmee, and Walt Disney World are part of area code 407. The area south and west of Orlando (including Tampa) is area code 813. North and east of the city, it's area code 913. Orlando and Orange County's local telephone service is carried by Southern Bell. Local calls from pay phones cost 25¢.

Time – All of Central Florida lies inside the Eastern Time Zone.

Tropical Storms – Since Orlando is landlocked, tropical storms don't really pose much of a threat. However, when a hurricane the caliber of August 1992's Andrew hits, Orlando gets quite a bit of rain dumped on it. Most attractions stay open unless there is a full-blown hurricane bearing down on them. If there is, tune in to one of the local television or radio stations for instructions.

Weather – Call 851-7510.

THE GANG AT UNIVERSAL STUDIOS FLORIDA

5. ARRIVALS & DEPARTURES

GETTING THERE & LEAVING ON YOUR OWN

There are nearly as many ways to get to WDW as there are to skin a cat. You can come by plane, bus, car, ship, or train. In addition, there is the matter of getting around the town once you arrive in Orlando. WDW itself has an intricate system of internal transportation, including buses, boats, monorails, and 123 miles of roads. Orlando has a mass-transit system also, but the most popular option is car rental. All of this will be discussed in the next chapter, "Getting Around."

BY CAR

For many a family living in the Eastern Seaboard or deep South, driving to Orlando is by no means an unreasonable or inconvenient choice, and for some families it can save over a thousand dollars. The major routes leading into Orlando are I-4 leading from Tampa to Daytona Beach and the Florida's Turnpike from Ocala to Miami. Listed are some routes from major cities around the east.

Atlanta, Chicago, Cincinnati, Dallas, Indianapolis, Louisville, Minneapolis, Ocala: Take I-75 to U.S. 27, U.S. 27 to U.S. 192.

Baltimore, Boston, Buffalo, Cleveland, Jacksonville, Montreal, New York, Philadelphia, Pittsburgh, Richmond, Toronto, and Washington D.C.: Take I-95 south to I-4 west.

Miami and points southeast: Florida's Turnpike or I-95 north to I-4 west (Exit 259 from the turnpike).

Daytona Beach, St. Petersburg, Tampa: Use I-4.

It is wise to join **AAA**, the American Automobile Association, before going anywhere. If nothing else, join for their Triptik service, which plans out a map for you to follow to your destination. Another advantage of joining is the special (and sometimes sizeable) room discounts at chain hotels across the country.

AAA estimates that the average cost of a day of driving for two adults and two children is $173 for lodging and meals, and $8.40 in car expenses every hundred miles. Your costs may be higher or lower, depending on variables.

About 70 miles north of Orlando, on I-75, sits a Disney-operated information and welcome center. Here you can procure passports, make hotel reservations, or buy souvenirs. Welcome stations, filled with helpful workers and informative brochures, can be found as you enter the Sunshine State in Yulee (I-95), Jennings (I-75), Pensacola (I-10), Hillyard (U.S. 1/301), and Campbellton (U.S. 231).

HINT: One important thing to remember if you've got a long drive ahead of you: hunger pangs are not synchronized with freeway exits. So it's wise to pack a few snacks or stop for them at gas stations when you go for gas and a bathroom stop. Also, it is much easier to retain your sanity if you bring books, magazines, or tapes for use in the car.

From the airport or Kennedy Space Center, take the Beeline Express-way (S.R. 528) west to I-4. From there, go east on I-4 for downtown Orlando, International Drive, Sand Lake Drive, and Universal Studios. Go west to get to WDW, Kissimmee, Lake Buena Vista, and Tampa. Traveling in the Orlando area will be discussed later in this chapter.

BY PLANE

Orlando International Airport is clearly not a Mickey Mouse facility, although he can be found all around the spot.

If you haven't been to the airport recently, you would have a hard time recognizing it. Recently completed overhauls have modernized and expanded it with more renovations than you would expect anyone to pour into a ten-year old building.

The main facility is composed of three levels. The lower level has parking and rental car drop-off/pick-up areas. Level two has baggage claim areas, rental car agencies, direct phone lines to hotels, and pick-up stations for taxis, buses, and limos. The upper level has the ticket counters and check-ins, restaurants, snack bars, newsstands, a bank, information counters, a chapel, a USO office, duty-free shops, and the second-most famous monorail in central Florida. This grand-circle tour of the airfield connects the main facility and the terminals.

Among the changes in the $700 million renovations are a third 24-gate terminal, a third runway, a doubling of the size of the main facility, and expansion and enrichment of the monorail and airport roads. Still more is planned: a fourth terminal, a full-service Hyatt Regency Hotel and a large, multi-level parking garage. At last count, there were approximately 25 airlines flying in and out of Orlando International Airport, offering direct service to over a hundred cities nationwide and also to major cities in Europe, South and Central America, and Canada. **Delta Airlines** (800/872-7768), the official airline of Disneyland and Walt

Disney World, has 70 flights in and out of Orlando daily.

DOMESTIC AIRLINES SERVING ORLANDO			
American	425-8098	Continental	295-6000
Delta	849-6400	Northwest	351-3190
Pan Am	800/221-1111	TWA	351-3855
United	800/241-652	USAir	874-5040

The international airlines operating out of Orlando International include Air Canada, Air France, BahamasAir, British Airways, Icelandair, KLM, Mexicana, Nordair, Northwest Orient, QuebecAir, TransInternational Airlines, Virgin Atlantic, and Wardair Canada.

Need to send someone a package? Several all-cargo airlines also operate from the jetport. If you've got time on your hands at the airport and you think that all there is to do is sit and idly people-watch, think again!

Some things to do at the airport include spending time at a chapel, or visiting the mall, where books, gifts, souvenirs, and citrus fruits can be purchased. You can exchange currency at the bank. Or use the ATM. Visit the post office or the USO. Or go to the tourist information center or the kiosks around the terminal and bone up.

Or for those growling stomachs, try the **Orlando Marketplace**, a pleasant food court where you can get sandwiches from **Mort's Deli**, seafood from **Snapper's**, or pizza, pasta, Oriental, pastries, fruit, and ice cream. At **Chirp's,** you can enjoy a cold one or a mixed drink while gazing at the aviary or fountains. More elegant dining can be found upstairs at **Beauregard's Restaurant and Bar**. In this waitress-service establishment, you can sample Florida delicacies like conch chowder and gator tail. Or for the less adventurous, prime rib and seafood.

BY BUS

This method of travel is not used very often by WDW vacationers because it takes the longest. However, it is usually fairly inexpensive. Bus travel is only a feasible selection if you live a short distance away; if you have plenty of time; or if cost is the biggest item taken into account.

The nation's biggest bus line, **Greyhound/Trailways** (phone 843-7720 for Orlando or 847-3911 for Kissimmee) can get you there from most of the continental forty-eight, but it'll be a long ride. The Kissimmee station offers shuttles to the WDW theme parks. They also offer packages. One, a one-day jaunt from Ft. Lauderdale, costs $78 ($58 for kids) and includes transportation, admission, and breakfast. The excursion leaves at 6 AM and returns at midnight.

Also worth investigation are the plans offered by **Gray Line** (tel. 422-0744), the company that runs most of Orlando's shuttle buses.

BUS TRAVEL TIMES FROM SELECTED CITIES			
Jacksonville, FL	3 hrs.	Washington, DC	24 hrs
Tallahassee, FL	7 hrs.	New York, NY	28 hrs.
Atlanta, GA	13 hrs.	Los Angeles, CA	72 hrs.

BY TRAIN

This is another of the less popular ways to get to WDW, but it's a good way to see America and it saves you the hassle of air travel or driving. Amtrak's **Silver Meteor** and **Silver Star** trains travel southward from New York's Penn Station daily.

The Silver Star leaves at 9 AM and arrives at Kissimmee the next morning. The Silver Meteor leaves at 4:30 and arrives around the middle of the next day. The major stops on the route, followed by both trains, include Newark (NJ), Trenton, Philadelphia, Wilmington, Baltimore, Washington, Richmond, Raleigh, Columbia (SC), Savannah, and Jacksonville. Fares for the run are $145 one way, $174 to $290 round trip. Like many airlines, Amtrak offers lower prices for special groups: military, seniors, families, students. There's probably one that fits you.

Europeans visiting the United States can exclusively buy a **USA Railpass**, which entitles the user to 45 days of unlimited train travel across the entire nation. It sells for $299. For those 2 to 11 years old, $150. Major travel companies like Thomas Cook, Kuoni, and American Express can get these for you. Amtrak's All Aboard America plan allows all travel in one of four regions of the country, i.e. Miami to Washington, for a single fare. At press time, the cost was $189.

Another option, one that allows travel all along the eastern half of the country, is the **Eastern Region Pass**, good for unlimited travel and stopovers east of the Mississippi, setting you back $179.

As with other modes of transport, Amtrak offers numerous packages. For information, call 800/USA-RAIL or write Amtrak at Box 7717, Itasca, IL 60143.

One of Amtrak's most popular services is the **Auto Train**. Put simply, it's the only way to drive two thousand miles without moving your odometer. Just drive your car onto the train at one of its two stations: one in Lofton, VA, just south of Washington; and the southern terminus in Sanford, FL, about 20 minutes north of Orlando. Park the car and settle into your seat or compartment (sleepers from $179 to $358); at 4:30 you're off, at 9 AM tomorrow, you're there!

A round-trip costs $298 to $490 per car, $169 to $280 per adult, less for children and singles. Costs are mainly dependent on the season that you're visiting the area. Like the Star and Meteor, lower rates than those quoted above can be acquired. Ask a lot of questions and inquire about their off-peak excursion rate. All you must do to qualify is travel between October and May and stay for no more than forty-five days. For more information on the AutoTrain, call the Amtrak number above or the Sanford station at 323-4800.

HINT: Train travel as a whole is not advisable because it costs as much as flying and takes as long as driving. So depending on which is more important to you — time or money — choose one of the other options.

BY CRUISE SHIP

Premier Cruise Lines (800/327-7113 or 800/327-7714) offers Disney packages including three- or four-day cruises aboard the Big Red Boats, the StarShips Atlantic, Oceanic, and Majestic and immediately before or after your cruise, an all-inclusive WDW vacation for three or four days to equal a week's vacation. The land portion of the trip includes rental car, a three- or four-night stay at a Disney resort (if you book 6 months in advance) or an Orlando hotel, a tour of SpacePort USA, three days admission to WDW, and airfare.

Premier, as the official cruise line of WDW, is the only cruise line whose packages include lodging inside Walt Disney World at Disney-owned hotels and resorts. Premier has been commended throughout the cruise line industry for being one of the first lines to offer staterooms that can accommodate five people, as well as making special arrangements for single-parent families.

While on board, you can enjoy up to 8 meals a day, marquis entertainment, and activities all day long. The ports of call for the Bahamas/Salt Cay cruise are Nassau and Salt Cay. For the Out Island cruise, Green Turtle Cay, Great Guana Cay, Man-o-War Cay, and Treasure Cay. Both routes run a three- and a four-day cruise every week. All of the different itineraries go for the same cost ($795 to $1,490 in the cheapest season, $895 to $1570 in the most expensive season) and include everything but alcoholic beverages, soft drinks, port charges, taxes, tips, and onshore excursions. Third, fourth, and fifth passengers in the same stateroom are $580 to $645. All prices are $200 less without airfare.

Not letting WDW get the monopoly on "official" cruise lines, Universal Studios Florida offers admission as part of a pre- or post-cruise package available thanks to **Norwegian Cruise Lines**. Their packages are more limited in nature than Premier's, though. Their three- and four-night Universal packages include rental car, admission, and lodging at the Comfort Suites Hotel.

Furthermore, they offer four- and five-night packages that add admission to WDW, a car or transfers and use of the transportation system, and choice of accomodations at the Grosvenor Resort at Disney Village Hotel Plaza, Sheraton Lakeside Inn, Hyatt Orlando, or Howard

Johnson Lake Buena Vista. NCL's cruises departing from Florida include ports of call such as St. John, St. Thomas, St. Maarten, San Juan, Ocho Rios, Grand Cayman, Playa del Carmen, Cozumel, Nassau, Freeport, and Key West.

Other cruise lines similarly offer Central Florida packages. They include **Carnival Cruise Lines**, who offer five-, six-, and seven-day cruise and tour packages. You can mix and match a three- or four-day cruise with a tour from two to four days. The package deals all include a cruise aboard either the Mardi Gras or the Carnivale, airfare from 130 cities or rail travel from the east, an Alamo rental car for the duration of the package, accomodations at the Orlando Marriott, Ramada Resort Maingate East, or Comfort Suites Hotel, for two to four nights, a guided tour of Spaceport USA, and for seven-night packages, three or four days admission to WDW.

The cost of the packages start at $575 for five days, $650 for six days, and $825 for seven days, including Disney admission. For more information, call Carnival at 800/327-7373, 800/325-1214 in Florida.

Holland America Cruise Line, winner of the Best Cruise Line Award in the 1990 Traveler Magazine Readers' Choice Poll, offers two pre- or post-cruise packages. The first one, the three-night EPCOT package, includes three nights at either the Buena Vista Palace, Hyatt Orlando, or Howard Johnson Park Square Inn, three days admission to Walt Disney World, and either a Buick Regal for three days and parking for three days OR Orlando airport to hotel transfer, shuttle to the parks, and transfer from your port city to Orlando.

They also offer a seven-day Florida Drive Yourself package that is included in some off-season sailings. This consists of a Buick rental for seven days, five nights at the Delta Orlando Resort and two nights at a hotel in your port city — Ft. Lauderdale or Tampa. On sailings where the package is not gratis, it sets you back $325 to $405 per person, double occupancy. The price tag for the week-long cruises that include it runs from $1,359 to $2,659. For more information, write Holland America at 300 Elliot Avenue West, Seattle, WA 98819, or call your travel agent.

Royal Caribbean also has several packages available to cruisers. These include air transportation from Miami to Orlando, transfer to the hotel, accomodations for two or three nights, and one day WDW admission per person per night. The hotels at which you can stay include the Hilton at Disney Village Hotel Plaza, Sonesta Village, Orlando Marriott, Hyatt Orlando, and Hyatt Regency Grand Cypress. Prices run from $163 to $373 for the two-night package. The three-nighters go for $204 to $514. More information is available, call 800/327-6700 or 800/432-6559.

6. GETTING AROUND

BY BUS

If you're headed to downtown Orlando, public buses will take you to the **Tri-County Transit Authority** main terminal on Woods Avenue. From there you can transfer to other buses crossing the area. Cost is $.75, a dime for transfers. This, however, is a time-consuming option and viable only if you are headed to the O-rena, Tinker Field, Orlando Stadium, Church Street Station, or the downtown hotels.

Three routes of interest to tourists are:
- **BUS 1:** Connects downtown and the airport.
- **BUS 8:** Connects downtown and International Drive.
- **BUS 41:** Connects the airport and Altamonte Mall via S.R. 436.

For more information and an up-to-date schedule, call them at 841-8240.

BY CAR
Renting a Car

When you plan your trip to WDW, you need to decide whether or not you will rent a car once you get there. You may ask, "Well, do I need to rent a car?" The answer is absolutely, positively, definitely, "sort of."

It is by no means necessary to rent a car when you are in central Florida. If you are staying at a WDW hotel, transportation throughout the property is complimentary and convenient. If you are staying off-property, shuttles are usually available.

However, with no car, there is no way other than taxi to get to attractions or restaurants outside of WDW and off the beaten path. Even if you intend to stay inside the Vacation Kingdom for your entire vacation, a car will save you some time. If you are staying in one of the Village Area Resorts, a car will save you as much as a thirty minute wait on both ends of your commute.

HINT: A pleasant surprise: rates for car rental in Orlando are amongst the lowest in the country, possibly due to itspopularity. Competition is rampant, and the winner is always the consumer.

Remember that in a worst-case scenario, a collision damage waiver (CDW) can insure against trouble, expense, and hassle later. However, if you pay with a credit card, you already may be insured for it. If you do decide to rent a car, proceed to the second level of the main passenger facility. Each of the firms listed below either has an office in the airport or close to it — in which case, a direct line to the airport will alert them to your arrival and they will pick you up.

MAJOR RENTAL CAR AGENCIES	
Alamo	855-0210 (800/327-9633)
Auto Host	857-4848 (800/448-4678)
Avis	851-7600 (800/331-1212)
Budget	850-6700 (800/527-0700)
Dollar	851-3232 (800/421-6868)
Dolphin	851-0255 (800/553-6574)
Hertz	859-8400 (800/654-3131)
Lindo	855-0282 (800/237-8396)
Major	859-1240 (800/34-MAJOR)
National	855-4170 (800/227-7368)
Payless	825-4400 (800/729-5377)
Superior	857-2023 (800/237-8106)
Thrifty	380-1002 (800/367-2277)
Value	851-4790 (800/327-2501)

Parking

Travelers who have visited New York or Washington often grumble about the city's parking (or lack thereof). If you are visiting Orlando, though, there's only one place where you may have any trouble finding a parking spot, that area being the downtown area.

Parking can also be tricky if Church Street Station is hosting a special event. All three WDW theme parks have a colossal parking lot. You can park there for $4, free for WDW resort guests. The Magic Kingdom's parking lot can hold 12,156 vehicles. EPCOT Center's can hold 11,391. The Disney-MGM Studios' parking lot can hold 6,500 vehicles.

HINT: If you are planning to leave the parks and return later, get your hand stamped before you leave the parks and hang on to your parking pass, so you can return without having to pay another $4. Also, write down the section in which your car is parked, or you'll have a hell of a time trying to find it. The last thing you want to do at the end of a long, tiring day is to have to wait for all the other cars to pull away before you find yours.

Typhoon Lagoon, the Disney Village Marketplace, and Pleasure Island complex all have ample, convenient, and free parking. However, the Fort Wilderness lot costs $4 per car, and River Country is connected to the parking lot via a rather lengthy tram ride. Universal Studios Florida has two lots totalling 7100 spaces. The fee is $4. Be sure to note your row and slot.

If you do manage to lose your car, an attendant will help you find it if you can tell them when you arrived. Sea World's parking lot now charges, and is still big enough to give headaches to those who forget where they parked.

Main Roads

If you are planning to drive around central Florida, it helps to have a general idea of the main traffic arteries on which you'll be travelling. The foremost highway in central Florida is Interstate 4. It runs from I-95 at Daytona Beach in the east to Tampa on the west coast. Coming east from Tampa, here are the major exits of tourist interest.

Exit 23 puts you on U.S. 27, on which Cypress Gardens, the Baseball City Stadium, and the Bok Tower Gardens are located.

Exit 25A puts you on U.S. 192, the W. Irlo Bronson Memorial Highway, in the direction of the Osceola County Stadium, Old Town, Medieval Times, Fort Liberty, Arabian Nights, Water Mania, the Tupperware Center, and downtown Kissimmee.

Exit 25B puts you on U.S. 192 West to the main entrance of Walt Disney World, convenient to the Magic Kingdom and the Magic Kingdom Resort Area.

Exit 26A puts you inside Walt Disney World, close to the Disney-MGM Studios, the Caribbean Beach Resort, EPCOT Center, and the EPCOT Resort Area.

Exit 26B is closest to the Disney Village Resort Area, Disney Village Hotel Plaza, Pleasure Island, Typhoon Lagoon, Bonnet Lakes Golf Club, the Lake Buena Vista Club, Crossroads of Lake Buena Vista Palace, and Disney Village Marketplace.

Exit 27 puts you on S.R. 535, just outside of WDW, next to Crossroads and close to the Grand Cypress Resort, a lavish property with 45 holes of golf, tennis, equestrian, and racquetball facilities. It is also close to many dining, lodging, and shopping options; including Vista Centre and the Disney Village. 535 will also take you to Apopka-Vineland Road, and then to Bay Hill and Windermere.

Exit 27A puts you on Westwood Blvd., close to Sea World, the International Golf Club, and International Drive.

Exit 28 puts you on the Bee Line Expressway, S.R. 528, and the southern part of International Drive. It is close to the Convention Center, Sea World, and Mercado.

Exit 29 puts you on Sand Lake Drive, one block away from International Drive and Turkey Lake Road. This exit is convenient to Universal Studios Florida, Mercado, Wet'n'Wild, the Convention Center, and the Florida Mall.

Exit 30A puts you right at the northern end of International, right by the Belz Factory Outlet Mall and a profuse number of hotel and restaurant options.

Exit 30B is where you want to get off for Universal and Kirkman Road.

Exit 31 is an interchange for the Florida's Turnpike, which crosses Florida from Ocala to Miami.

Other main routes are U.S. 441-17-92, more commonly referred to as the Orange Blossom Trail. The Gatorland Zoo, the Florida Mall, and the Tupperware Center are on this road. S.R. 535, also known as Apopka-Vineland Road, goes from Conroy-Windermere Road to U.S. 192 and accesses the Marketplace, Sand Lake Drive, Dr. Phillips, Arnold Palmer's Bay Hill Club, Disney Village, Crossroads of Lake Buena Vista, and Vista Centre.

U.S. 192 is Kissimmee's main highway, and oft-traveled by guests going from I-4 to WDW's main gate and back. The road provides access to Medieval Life, Medieval Times, Fort Liberty, Arabian Nights, Old Town, and Water Mania.

International Drive is another main tourist drag, anchored on the north by the Belz Factory Outlet Mall and on the south by Sea World. In between, there's Mercado Mediterranean Village, Wet'n Wild, King Henry's Feast, and the Orange County Convention/Civic Center.

BY SHUTTLE AND LIMO

For those of you choosing not to rent a car, several shuttle and limousine services are available from the airport and major hotels every half hour, one an hour for less-frequented places. One of the most popular modes of shuttle transit is **Mears Motor Shuttle** (tel. 423-5566), whose large yellow vans can be seen in tourist-laden areas of Orlando's environs. Prices start at $11 ($8 for kids under 12) for a trip to Kisimmee or International Drive hotels. Prices are higher to other locales. For a large family, this can be expensive. Various hotels offer private, free shuttles. You can even call them from the airport on a direct line in the baggage claim area.

Limos take you where you want to go for about $4 more than a taxi. Cheaper rates can be obtained for large groups or round trips. **Carey Limousine** (tel. 855-0442) will pick you up in either a Caddy or presidential stretch limo and take you to your destination for between $60 and $90. This could save some money if you're travelling in a large group.

It's almost as if every other vehicle in Central Florida is a shuttle bus. Most hotels have a shuttle bus stopping in front of it and other area hotels, some have their own private buses, going to major attractions at regular intervals. Prices can be as much as $4 each way. For details, call the front desk of your hotel or **Grey Line** (422-0744), **Phoenix Tours** (859-4211), or **Rabbit** (291-2424).

BY TAXI

Taxis are plentiful in Orlando and its suburbs. However, cheap they are not. There are only a few cab companies licensed by the city of Orlando to pick up passengers at the airport. As a rule of thumb, expect a tab of about $22 for a drive downtown or to International Drive, $28 to Lake Buena Vista; and about $35 to go to Kissimmee.

The cabs whose lines are listed below are inspected, metered, operate 24 hours a day, and generally have their rates posted on the side. The only lines permitted to pick up at the airport are **Ace Metro Cab** (855-1111) **Yellow Cab** (699-9999), and **City Cab** (422-5151). Expect prices to run about $2.25 for the first mile, $1.30 each additional.

DISNEY TRANSPORTATION

If you are staying at a resort on WDW property, you don't have to worry about getting around. Everything is arranged for you by the Disney folks.

Their system of buses, elevated monorails, and watercraft is nothing short of ingenious. The buses have a color-and-letter-code system printed on the front and side of the bus, as well as an electronic display that flashes all the stops on the route.

The Monorail

SPECIAL NOTES: For the TTC to Magic Kingdom route only: The ramp accessing the platform can be treacherous to wheelchair-bound guests if the line extends onto it. Also, if there's much of a line at all, the ferry will be quicker.

This is by far the most famous mode of Disney conveyance. The monorail runs in two loops on three tracks, arriving at each stop at a fifteen-minute interval from 7:30 AM to 11 PM or 1 hour after the Magic Kingdom closes, whichever is later.

Loop A runs on two separate tracks around Seven Seas Lagoon. Track 1 is for day guests and those staying off the property. It stops at the TTC and the Magic Kingdom. Track 2 is for those staying at on-property hotels, or so Disney people will tell you. However, you can almost always get on these without hotel ID.

Its stops are the TTC, Contemporary Resort, Magic Kingdom, Grand Floridian Beach Resort, and the Polynesian Resort (sometimes when closing is nearing, monorail attendants ask for resort identification. This policy, though designed to give an advantage to the people who shell out the extra cash for Disney hospices, can be aggravating).

Loop B of the monorail swings from the TTC down to EPCOT Center's main (Future World) Entrance.

The advantages of taking the monorail are plentiful. Its air conditioning is a godsend on summer days. Also, it's a fun way to travel and a small glimpse of how we might get around in the future. The best time can be had by sitting up in the nose cabin, where the driver and his crew are situated. Between the 200-degree panorama and the conversation of the driver, this is an experience you won't want to miss. To sit up front, ask any attendant at the station and he or she will escort you to a private waiting area. Talk about service!

There are drawbacks to the monorail, though. It is notorious for delays during busy seasons due to overcrowding and mechanical problems.

HINT: Most people take the monorail to the park in the morning and relax on the ferry on the way back. If you want to avoid the crush, do the opposite.

Watercraft

SPECIAL NOTES: This is the exception to the rule — attendants here usually **do** check for the proper ID.

Walt Disney World has one of the largest navies in the world, with a fleet of over 750 ships. The most widely-known part of the "navy" is the ferry that transverses Seven Seas Lagoon from the TTC to the Magic Kingdom. The trip takes about five minutes and runs every twelve. If there's a line at the monorail, this is quicker.

There are two routes for the **water taxis**, the same FriendShip boats found crossing World Showcase Lagoon at EPCOT Center. The first route connects EPCOT Center's International Gateway, the WDW Dolphin, the WDW Swan, the Beach and Yacht Club Resorts, and the Disney-MGM Studios Theme Park. The second route of canals connects the Disney Vacation Club, Pleasure Island, the Disney Village Marketplace, the Dixie Landings Resort, and the Port Orleans.

Motor launches depart every fifteen to twenty-five minutes from ports on Bay Lake and Seven Seas Lagoon. There are three different routes. Take notice that routes servicing Discovery Island only do so while the park is open.

Blue-flagged boats connect the Contemporary Resort, Discovery Island, and Fort Wilderness. This line operates from 9 AM to 10 PM. Gold-flagged boats link the Grand Floridian, Magic Kingdom, and Polynesian Resort. These operate from 8:30 AM until the park is cleared, with pickup only from the Magic Kingdom after it closes.

Green-flagged boats go between the Magic Kingdom and Fort Wilderness, stopping at Discovery Island. This line also runs from 8:30

until the Magic Kingdom clears.

Disney Buses

The buses have a color-and-letter code. Listed below are the routes. **NOTES:** (1) denotes route beginning at 6 PM. (2) denotes route stopping at Pleasure Island after 6. (3) denotes route that stops at TTC instead of the Magic Kingdom outside of its operating hours.

HINT: If you wish to visit Pleasure Island before 6 PM, go to the Disney Village Marketplace and follow the footpaths from there.

MAGIC KINGDOM RESORTS – Blue-flagged buses link Fort Wilderness and the Ticket and Transportation Center (TTC). A gold-flagged bus goes from the Contemporary Resort to TTC, the Polynesian Resort, and the Grand Floridian. Gold-and-black-flagged buses (2) marked STE go from the Contemporary Resort and Fort Wilderness to the Disney-MGM Studios and Pleasure Island. Those marked STW link the Polynesian, Grand Floridian, and Disney Inn to the Disney-MGM Studios and Pleasure Island. The green-flagged bus takes guests from the Disney Inn to the Polynesian, TTC, and Magic Kingdom.

DISNEY-MGM STUDIOS THEME PARK – Blue-and-white-flagged buses marked EC connect EPCOT Center and the Disney-MGM Studios Theme Park. The blue-and-whites with a MK link the Magic Kingdom and the Studios.

WDW VILLAGE HOTEL PLAZA AND MARKETPLACE – The red-flagged bus (2) connects the TTC, the Marketplace, Pleasure Island, Typhoon Lagoon, and EPCOT. Red-and-white-flagged buses hit all the hotels of the Plaza, and then head on to these destinations: EC, EPCOT Center; MK (3), Magic Kingdom; ST, the Disney-MGM Studios; and V (1), the Marketplace and Pleasure Island.

DISNEY'S VILLAGE RESORT – Guests at this resort get around by green-and-gold-flagged buses. The one marked ECV stops at EPCOT Center and the Marketplace. The MK (3) bus stops at the Magic Kingdom. Last, the bus labeled STV (2) stops at the Disney-MGM Studios, Disney Village Marketplace, and Pleasure Island.

PORT ORLEANS, DIXIE LANDINGS, AND VACATION CLUB RESORT – These new resorts are linked to the rest of the World by pink-and-green-flagged buses. The bus marked EC connects the resorts to EPCOT Center. The MK bus (3) goes to the Magic Kingdom. The ST bus hits the Disney-MGM Studios Theme Park. The V (2) line will take you to Typhoon Lagoon, the Disney Village Marketplace, and Pleasure Island.

CARIBBEAN BEACH RESORT – This resort uses orange-flagged buses for internal circulation and orange-and-white-flagged buses, the EC for EPCOT Center, the MK (3) for the Magic Kingdom, the ST for the

Disney-MGM Studios, and the V (2) for Typhoon Lagoon, the Disney Village Marketplace, and Pleasure Island.

EPCOT RESORT BUSES – For all intents and purposes here, the EPCOT Resorts are only the Boardwalk, Dolphin, Swan, and the Yacht and Beach Club Resorts, as the Caribbean has its own buses. The purple-and-gold-flagged buses marked MK (3) go to the Magic Kingdom, and the V (2) takes guests to Typhoon Lagoon, the Disney Village Marketplace, and Pleasure Island.

FORT WILDERNESS RESORT – This resort/campground is so big that it needs three internal circulation routes: the brown-flagged bus, connecting the Settlement Transportation Circle, the trailer loops, the camping loops, and the Recreation Outpost. The orange-flagged bus connects River Country and the day visitors' parking area. The silver-flagged bus follows the path between the Settlement Transportation Circle, Camping Loops, and Creekside Meadow.

BONNET LAKES COUNTRY CLUB – Call your hotel's Guest Services desk in advance and they will arrange for shuttle transportation from your resort. This is done to avoid cluttering buses with golf clubs. If you're unsure about a route, contact the front desk of your hotel or ask any cast member, they can usually help you out. For more information, call 824-4321 or 824-4457.

Identification

The rule says that to avail oneself of the forementioned transportation system, you must have some sort of "proper identification" before you board. However, enforcement of this rule is usually somewhat lax. Bus drivers don't check at all (in the interest of time) and monorail attendants only do sporadically. The boat attendants do check most of the time, however, so you must have the needed ID. Accepted ID include:

WDW RESORT IDENTIFICATION CARD – You receive this on check-in if you are staying at a WDW resort. It allows you unlimited use of the entire WDW transportation system up through the date printed on it.

DISNEY VILLAGE HOTEL PLAZA ID CARD – Also received on check-in, this allows use of the bus system only.

MAGIC KINGDOM TICKET – A one-day Magic Kingdom ticket allows transportation by ferry or monorail to the Magic Kingdom only. A one-day Disney-MGM or EPCOT Center ticket does not include transportation.

ACTIVITY TICKET – A ticket to Pioneer Hall, Discovery Island, or River Country includes all the transportation necessary to get there, including boats from the Magic Kingdom and buses or boats from the MK Resorts.

PASSPORT – A valid four-day or one-year All Three Parks World Passport, a five-or six-day Super Pass, or a valid Be Our Guest Pass or MagicPass allow for unlimited travel for the duration of the ticket.

TRANSPORTATION TICKET – Sold for about $2.50, this allows unlimited transportation across the property for a day.

7. WHERE TO STAY

Since Disney's arrival on the Orlando scene in October 1971, the number of hotel rooms in the city and its surrounding municipalities has soared from 5,922 to nearly 80,000 today. A good percentage of these are in WDW itself, and several thousand in plain sight of one of the three theme parks. Outside WDW, there are several main concentrations of hostelries. They are found mainly in the following areas: the US 192 area in Kissimmee, the SR 535 area in Lake Buena Vista, and the International Drive, Sea World, and Universal Studios areas. Of course, many hotels are located elsewhere in the greater Orlando area.

WALT DISNEY WORLD® RESORTS

There are currently twenty hostelries in the land of the Mouse and between them, they pepper the Vacation Kingdom with over 14,000 rooms, suites, villas, and campsites. The WDW owned-and-operated hotels are generally more expensive than comparable inns on the other side of the WDW border. The exceptions are the Caribbean Beach, Dixie Landings, and Port Orleans Resorts (three large, moderately priced complexes). The hotels cost more, but the added conveniences are worth the extra cost.

First of all, there's a big psychological thing of staying inside Walt Disney World. This appeals to children most, but it warms all but the staunchest heart and whets appetites for what lies inside the admission gates. Second, there's the not-insignificant advantage of being able to charge purchases with your room tab with your helpful resort identification card. The only exceptions are theme park fast food and Magic Kingdom purchases. The third, and probably the biggest advantage is the unlimited, free use of the WDW transportation system for the length of your stay.

Other advantages of staying at WDW resorts are listed below:
• Guaranteed admission to the parks even when they're full.
• Two closed-circuit TV channels; one an information channel giving continual weather reports, hours, and listings of special events inside the World, the other a video journey across the World, showcasing each park and hotel in turn.

• Reservations at Disney-MGM and EPCOT restaurants can be made up to 2 days in advance for WDW hotel guests.

• Tee-off times for the five golf courses can be made up to 30 days in advance.

• Seats at dinner shows can be reserved as soon as your hotel booking is confirmed.

• Free guides to all three theme parks.

Rooms can can accommodate five to a room except at the Dolphin, Swan, Caribbean Beach, Port Orleans, and Dixie Landings Resorts. Most rooms have either patios or balconies and many offer nice views, even if only across a small planting. Reservations can be made by calling the **Central Reservations Office** at W-DISNEY. For people who speak French or Spanish, 824-7900. The office is open from 8:30 AM to 10 PM daily. The best times to call are after 6 PM and on weekends.

HINT: Don't worry if your call is not answered for several minutes when calling the CRO. To keep long-distance callers from accumulating sizeable phone bills, Disney does not put callers on hold, instead, they organize the calls and answer them in the order they were received.

For peak holiday seasons, you might want to reserve your room up to one or two years in advance. For a mid-summer trip, 6 months will suffice. For other times, reservations can be made as little as two weeks in advance.

The hotels are divided into three areas inside WDW. These are the Magic Kingdom Resort Area, EPCOT Resort Area, and the Village Resort Area. Unless otherwise stated, check-in is at 3 PM and check-out is at 11 AM. The town and zip code of all Walt Disney World hotels is Lake Buena Vista, FL 32830.

MAGIC KINGDOM RESORT AREA

THE DISNEY INN

Address: 1 Palm Magnolia Drive(824-2200). *FAX:* 824-3299. *Rates:* Rooms, $180 to $215; suite, $460 to $500. *At a Glance:* Among the quietest of the Disney hotels, the Disney Inn boasts 63 holes of golf interspersed with three-story motel wings. *Ratings:* Room Comfort 8; Amenities 10; Eateries 6; Shopping 6; Convenience 7; Decor 8.

The excitement of the Vacation Kingdom's glitzier hotels like the Contemporary is replaced here by a relaxed, laid-back feeling. Mind you, the **Disney Inn** is far from boring. The hotel only contains 288 rooms, the smallest of the Disney properties, but boasts a good chunk of the Vacation Kingdom's recreational facilities. This hotel was built originally to serve as a golf clubhouse, hence its original moniker of the Golf Resort. However, non-golfers shied away from this hotel. To solve this problem,

Disney in the mid-80s changed the hotel's name to the Disney Inn and occupancy jumped.

The Disney Inn is the most relaxing of Disney lodging choices, because all of the rooms look out on either a pool, golf course, or forest.

Rooms

The rooms at the Disney Inn are contained in two 3-story wings flanking the lobby. Here, rooms are larger than in any of the other Magic Kingdom Resorts, almost seeming like small suites. All of the rooms have either a balcony or a patio boasting views of forests, courtyards, pools, or the golf courses. All rooms can accommodate five persons on two queen beds and a sleep sofa. Guestrooms have dividers between the bedroom and the sofa and table, and furniture of light oak. The rooms are decorated with floral accents and quilts, giving each room a look of a country inn. The hotel's one suite can sleep seven people.

Dining Options

A snack spot called **The Diamond Mine** offers the usual fare: sandwiches, salads, and beverages. The **Garden Gallery** is the only full-service restaurant at the Disney Inn. The eatery is bright and airy, and best of all, rarely crowded. The menu is loaded with American specialties. Seafood, steak, poultry, a breakfast buffet, and a salad bar comprise a good part of he menu. There is also a children's menu. The **Sand Trap** is a poolside snack bar serving hot dogs, sandwiches, chips, and continental breakfasts.

Watering Holes

The **Back Porch** is the only lounge at the Disney Inn. This spot adjoining the Garden Gallery serves, in addition to specialty drinks, a light menu of sandwiches and appetizers.

Shopping

At **Disney Inn Gifts and Sundries**, souvenirs, reading material, toiletries, film, liquor, tobacco, and other items can be bought. The **Disney Inn Pro Shop** stocks golf equipment and fashions, some of which wear Mickey and Minnie's faces. Tennis goods can also be had.

Recreation

There are two small gamerooms at the Disney Inn — the **Mine Arcade** in the lobby and the **Diamond Mine Arcade at Happy's Hollow**.

Golf is the main attraction here, golf, golf, golf, and just when you think any more golf will send you to an institution, golf. There are two par-72 courses here designed by Joe Lee. One, the Magnolia, is peppered with trees and ranges from 5,414 to 7,190 yards. The other, the Palm, has nine water hazards and tighter, wooded fairways. The latter course runs from 5,398 to 6,957 yards. Both courses are in the *Golf Digest Magazine* Top 100 list. There is also the nine-hole, par-36 Executive Course, a 2,913 yard set of links designed specifically for the beginner. The two 18-hole courses each have a driving range.

The hotel's health club, the Magic Mirror, boasts a selection of Nautilus machines, weights, stationary bikes, treadmills, weights, and aerobics. There are two swimming pools here. Two lighted tennis courts are hidden behind the hotel. They are open from 8 AM to 10 PM.

DISNEY'S CONTEMPORARY RESORT, A MONORAIL HOTEL

Address: 4600 North World Drive (824-1000). *FAX:* 824-3439. *Rates:* Rooms, $190 to $260, suites, $640 to $1,430. *At a Glance:* A 15-story, 1,052-unit complex consisting of an A-frame hotel and 2 three-story extensions, 6 shops, 5 eateries, 2 lounges, and a tennis complex, along withother amenities. *Ratings:* Room Comfort 7; Amenities 8; Eateries 8; Shopping 9; Convenience 10; Decor 8. *NOTE:* The handicapped can not board the monorail here.

This resort gets a decidedly split rating from those who spend their vacations here. There are a few visitors who don't care for the place at all because of future shock. Another major turn-off is that some people think of the white, concrete structure as bleak and sterile. However, this is the favorite of many because it has the most hustle and bustle, which, ironically, is another turn-off to some.

HINT: Artist Mary Blair created a towering, 90-foot mural on one of the walls at the Grand Canyon Concourse. The floor-to-ceiling mosaic is composed of over 18,000 hand-painted tiles. The designs, including Indian families, flowers, trees, and a five-legged goat, are inspired by native American art of the Southwest. It is one of the World's more intriguing pieces of art, so you might wan to check it out, if you happen to find yourself here.

HINT: The hotel is currently undergoing a $100 million renovation, which will be finished in 1993. Areas slated for refurbishment include all guestrooms, the lobby, public halls, and the existing convention space.

Rooms

The fifteen-story Tower, the most recognized part of the Contemporary, holds about half of its 1,052 rooms. This is the more expensive section of the hotel, these rooms at a premium because they have the best views. The higher up the structure you go, the finer the view, the bigger the bill. Those on the west side of the Tower overlook the Magic Kingdom, and make a great vantage point for the fireworks, whereas the windows of the more easterly rooms make great panoramas of Bay Lake with Discovery Island and Fort Wilderness as a backdrop. The downside to staying in the Tower is the speed of the elevators, or more accurately, the lack thereof. The North and South Garden Wings, formerly known as the Bayfront Wings, do not boast such striking views and thus, do not boast such striking tabs. However, those rooms in the Garden Wings farthest from the Tower have stunning views of a white-sand beach and Bay Lake. These vistas rival those from any room in the Tower. Garden View rooms have more of an away-from-it-all and relaxed feeling than those in the Tower.

HINT: The Garden Wing rooms listed as offering a "Magic Kingdom view" do look towards the Magic Kingdom, but across the vast parking lot of the hotel.

Rooms in both the Tower and Garden Wings share some common features. The rooms in both sections are fairly large and can accommodate five. All the rooms have a day bed plus either a king or two queen beds. Most have a small terrace or balcony. The bathrooms are large too, and nicely laid out. They each contain double sinks, a bathtub with a shower head, or a bathtub with a separate shower stall.

Suites

The 14th floor is the Contemporary's concierge floor. A variety of suites is available, each sleeping from 7 to 12 people. Their concierge package includes free valet parking, fruit and juice in the morning, wine and cheese in the evening, and a nightly turndown service, complete with milk and cookies. The prices for this run from the expensive ($640) to the mortgage-your-house exorbitant ($1,430).

Dining Options

On the fourth floor is the **Concourse Grill**. All three meals are served. Fare includes such staples as eggs and pancakes for breakfast, soups, salads, and sandwiches for lunch, and fish, steak, chicken, and ribs for dinner. Reservations are accepted, though not required. The **Contemporary Cafe**, also on the fourth-floor Concourse, features an all-you-can-eat character buffet for dinner and a daily character breakfast buffet. Considered one of the best buys in the World. No reservations.

The **Dock Inn**, a snack bar by the marina, offers light stuff during peak seasons only. If you get the munchies at 3:48 AM or any other desolate (or not-so-desolate) hour of the day, head on over to the **Fiesta Fun Center Snack Bar** on the first floor.

At the top of the World is the aptly-named **Top of the World Supper Club**. Fifteen stories above Bay Lake, the view is absolutely breathtaking.

On Sundays, there's an all-you-can-eat brunch, on other days, a buffet breakfast. Each evening, the **Broadway at the Top** dinner show, diners choose items from an a la carte menu while revelling in the view and listening to tunes from Broadway musicals. Reservations for the dinner show are made through W-DISNEY. For brunch or Sunday breakfast, call 824-3611.

Watering Holes

On the Grand Canyon Concourse is the **Outer Rim Seafood and Cocktail Lounge**. This appealing bistro serves sandwiches, seafood, and specialty drinks. Next to the marina, the **Sand Bar** serves mixed drinks. Adjoining the Top of the World Restaurant is the **Top of the World Cocktail Lounge**. This is a great spot to watch the sunset, the nightly Fantasy in the Sky fireworks, or the Electrical Water Pageant with a cool drink in your hand.

HINT: For the best vantage point for the Water Pageant, head to the easternmost of the observation decks at about fiveminutes after ten.

Shopping

Bay 'n Beach is a character merchandise outlet. **Bay View Gifts** has a misleading name. From the title, you would think that this is one of the hundreds of Disney-themed merchandise outlets found in and around Walt Disney World. Not so. This shop features Southwestern and Native American-themed objects, including silk flowers and pottery. The bright, airy, atmosphere and skylights make this a pleasant place to browse.

If you don't want to head to one of the lounges but you still want a drink or a snack, visit the **Concourse Spirits and Sundries** shop on the Concourse, next to Fantasia. They sell newspapers, magazines, snacks, and liquors, as well as soft drinks. Here, you can get all you need for a cocktail party or a quick nibble. Two adjoining shops on the other side of the Concourse are **Contemporary Man** and **Contemporary Woman**. These two shops have no clear boundary, and with today's fashions, that line is even more blurred. The men's store sells casual and beachwear, and rents tuxedos. The women's store sells upbeat fashions and swimsuits.

Fantasia is one of Disney's best-loved films and also the largest shop in this futuristic lodging. This is one in a genre of shops that Disney people refer to as "character shops" — shops that sell Disney merchandise and WDW souvenirs, and has probably the best selection of the merchandise outside the parks and shopping village. Of particular interest is the fiberoptic display on the back wall of the store, depicting the WDW logo, Mickey Mouse, and fireworks. As far as the wares are concerned, t-shirts, postcards, stuffed animals, figurines, and other Disney memorabilia are available.

Kingdom Jewels, Ltd. is across from Concourse Spirits and Sundries and next to Contemporary Man. Here, baubles of precious stones and things that glitter tantalize both men and women. The **Racquet Club** sells character merchandise, sports apparel, and specialty items.

Services

The **American Beauty Shoppe** is located on the third floor of the Tower. Here, among the list of available services are manicures, shampoos, setting, coloring, and waving. Also on the third floor of the Tower is the **Captain's Chair** barber shop.

In the first-floor lobby is the **Contemporary Resort Ticket Counter**, which is recommended for any resort guest who doesn't already have his tickets. It saves the hassle and time of waiting at the parks and offers an admission option not seen elsewhere, a Six-Day Super Pass. It has all the qualities of a Five-Day Super Pass but allows an extra day's admission to the three major parks.

HINT: You need WDW Resort ID to buy tickets at resort ticket offices or guest services desks.

Recreation

Boat rentals are available at the marina next to the beach. Water Sprites, sailboats, flote boats, and pedal boats are available. At the marina are situated a small taproom and a snack bar, both seasonal.

Kids go into fits of ecstasy when they see the **Fiesta Fun Center**, and even grown-ups tend to sneak down there. More than just a game room, this entertainment complex boasts not only standbys such as pinball and air hockey, but new arcade favorites like Teenage Mutant Ninja Turtles and NeoGeo systems. The rule here is variety. You can find pretty much any game you want to play here. Also, for those without the penchant for video games, this complex offers a movie theater and a snack bar. The facility is open 24 hours a day, and is jumping for a sizable portion of them. All kids staying here will insist a trip here, and most consider it well worth the trip. If you're in the mood for seeing movies, there is a theatre in the Fiesta Fun Center showing Disney flicks three times nightly. A great place to get off your feet for a while.

Those who prefer their entertainment more vigorous can head to the **Olympiad Health Club** on the third floor of the Tower. This facility is complete with Nautilus gym equipment, saunas, personal whirlpools, and everything else necessary for a decent workout. The cost is $5, an additional $5 for use of the whirlpools. The club is open to both resort and day guests, and its hours are 9 AM to 6 PM Monday through Saturday. Call 824-3410 for more information.

There is a playground Located near the North Garden Wing and the wading pool. Swimming opportunities prevail at the Contemporary. There are two swimming pools. One, a 20' by 25' rectangular pool, one of the best-suited WDW pools for lap swimming. The other is a smaller, round pool, deep in the center and shallow in the fringes. There is also a wading pool near the North Garden Wing. On Bay Lake is a small, pleasant white-sand beach. Swimming is allowed in the roped-off areas only and when a lifeguard is on duty.

Just north of the Tower are the Contemporary's six tennis courts. This is the World's major tennis facility, boasting in addition to the courts, three backboards, an automatic ball machine, and a tennis clinic program. The cost for use of the courts is nonexistent for WDW resort guests and $10 an hour for day guests. Reservations can be made 24 hours in advance by calling 824-3578.

There are also volleyball nets set up on the beach. For the adventurous, water skiing can be done here. Rentals include boat, driver, and equipment.

Babysitting

For a fee, parents can leave their kids at the **Mousketeer Club** and head to Pleasure Island or any other nightspot.

DISNEY'S FORT WILDERNESS RESORT AND CAMPGROUND

Address: 4510 North Fort Wilderness Trail (824-2900). *At a Glance:* A 780-acre campground, complete with 827 campsites and 407 Fleetwood trailers. Thisis a bona fide resort — complete with a beach on Bay Lake, horses, bike trails, and organized recreation. *Ratings:* Room Comfort 8; Amenities 10; Eateries 5; Shopping 3; Convenience 8; Decor 6. *Rates:* $30 to $48 for campsites, $160 to $175 for Fleetwood Trailers. *Check-in:* 1 PM for campsites, 3 PM for trailers.

This 780-acre tract is only a stone's throw from the Magic Kingdom, but it seems a million miles away. Many visitors to **Fort Wilderness** are either are unaware of its existence or believe it to be associated with Frontierland in the Magic Kingdom.

The resort is set amid cypress and pine, its campsites and trailers nestled along placid canals or on the fringes of majestic forest. And while camping out can have a negative connotation to some, "roughing it" here can be completely pleasant, given the wealth of recreational facilities available at Fort Wilderness. Or, for those of you who would rather not be such a close partner with the Great Outdoors, trailer homes with accomodations not unlike those at the Village Resort are available for about the same price as Club Suites at the Village.

Campsites

The 21 camping loops at Fort Wilderness contain 827 campsites. The size of the sites ranges from 25 to 65 feet in length. The sites are rented to either tenters or RV users. Each site has a 110/220-volt electrical outlet, barbecue, and a picnic table. The majority of the sites have hookups for sanitary-disposal units. But all of the loops has a comfort station with restrooms, showers, phones, ice machines, and laundry facilities. Each site can accommodate up to 10 people for a single fee.

The loops are indicated by number: 100 to 500 are closest to the beach, Settlement Trading Post, and Pioneer Hall. Loops 1700 to 2100 are in the deeper concentrations of forest and have much more privacy.

Fleetwood Trailers

Non-campers are accommodated at Fort Wilderness just as easily as the outdoorsmen. For those who would like all the advantages of a hotel plus the serenity of a campground, Disney offers 407 rental **Fleetwood Trailer Homes**. Not what you would expect, these are very similar in size and furnishings to a villa at Disney Village Resort.

There are two varieties of trailers: the first can hold four people in a double bed in the bedroom and a sofa bed in the living area. The other trailers can accommodate four adults and two children in a double bed, a bunk bed, and a pulldown. The trailers all have a good-sized living room and a bathroom laid out like at the villas.

A major advantage of staying here is the presence of kitchens in every trailer, complete with dishes, cookware, and other equipment. The trailers are also equipped with color TV and have daily maid service. The kitchens here offer the option of being able to cook your own meals. This saves time and money, and you can usually have somewhat better food than at the parks. *HINT:* Because of their size and reasonable price, these make good choices for families who want something more than the typical-sized hotel room.

Dining Options

Most of the Fort Wilderness patrons choose to cook their own food, especially those staying in the trailers. However, if you don't want to cook, there are several places you can visit for edibles.

The **Beach Shack**, located on the Bay Lake coastline, sells chips, sandwiches, ice cream, and other snack fare. **Crockett's Tavern** is one of the two full-service restaurants in Pioneer Hall. It serves steaks, ribs, chicken, and appetizers in a rustic atmosphere filled from wall to wall and floor to ceiling with Davy Crockett memorabilia.

The **Hoop-Dee-Doo Revue** is one of Disney's best-loved dinner shows. There are three shows daily, at 5, 7:30, and 10 PM. The food is unlimited ribs, chicken, corn on the cob, and strawberry shortcake. The entertainment is top-notch, a dazzling production full of humor, song, and dance. In the Meadow Recreational Complex is the **Meadow Snack Bar**, a seasonal establishment serving the usual array of snack fare.

Groceries are available at the **Meadow** and **Settlement Trading Posts**. Also, deli sandwiches and snacks are sold here for take-out. Fort Wilderness's foremost eatery is the **Trail's End Buffet**, also inside the confines of Pioneer Hall. It serves large breakfasts, some of the breakfast items Western staples like grits and biscuits and gravy, as well as country fare, pot pies, and fish the other two meals. Pizza is served here nightly starting from 9 PM until 11. They host a seafood buffet on Fridays and an Italian buffet Saturday nights.

Shopping

Sundries, souvenirs, character merchandise, specialty items, and groceries can be purchased at the **Meadow** and **Settlement Trading Posts**. Both are open from 8 AM until 10 PM, 11 PM in the summer.

Recreation

There are a few baseball/softball diamonds near the bike barn. These are open to WDW resort guests only. Equipment is not provided, you must bring your own.

Basketball courts are scattered throughout the camping loops. These are available at no cost and solely to WDW resort guests.

Different sorts of bicycle are available for rental: tandems, dirt bikes, and others. Visit the **Bike Barn** to charter one.

On Bay Lake at the north end of the campground is situated a large marina, offering boat rentals, specifically, Water Sprites, pontoon boats, flote boats, pedal boats, and sailboats.

Near the Meadow Trading Post, a nightly campfire program omplete with Disney movies, cartoons, sing-alongs, and an appearance of Chip and Dale. Free, available to WDW resort guests only.

Canoes can be rented for use rowing down the serene Fort Wilderness canals at the Bike Barn. The large beach on Bay Lake is a great spot to view the **Electrical Water Pageant**. It passes around 9:45 PM nightly.

Guided excursions into Bay Lake for fishing are available. The trips are two hours long and include gear, refreshments, boat, and guide. Note that fishing on your own is not allowed in Bay Lake. However, it is permitted in the canals of Fort Wilderness without a guide. Largemouth bass are the catch in both places. Those with a ken to fish in the canals but no equipment can purchase it at the Trading Posts or rent the poles and lures at the Bike Barn. No license is required.

Fort Wilderness boasts a fitness and jogging trail, 2.3 miles long.

There are exercise stations situated at a rate of about one every quarter mile. This is a draw for guests at all the Magic Kingdom resorts. *HINT:* The best time to use the facilities is early in the morning or around dusk.

Fort Wilderness possesses two gamerooms — named after the two greatest frontiersmen of all time. **Daniel Boone** has his arcade in Pioneer Hall, while **Davy Crockett's Arcade** can be found at the Meadow Trading Post.

If you're one of those poor, deprived souls who hasn't been on a hayride recently, here's your chance. The wagon departs from Pioneer Hall and heads to Bay Lake before returning. The trip takes about an hour and tickets are available from the host. Allergy sufferers are exempt.

Ever been told to take a hike? This is among the best places in the World to do so, on the **Wilderness Swamp Trail**, a mile-and-a-half-long path that offers picturesque views of Bay Lake and a huge forest of cypress. The trail is located near **Marshmallow Marsh**, at the northern end of the campground.

Horseback riding enthusiasts also get what they want here. Organized trips through the campground leave from the center of the campground four times in the morning and early afternoon hours of each day. The rides are slow-paced (sorry, no galloping) and offer great vistas of the Florida wilderness. Riding knowledge is not required.

Facilities for a round of horseshoes are scattered throughout the property.

One of the nightly events at the Fort Wilderness Resort (only during the summer, though) is the **Marshmallow Marsh Excursion**, an event including a marshmallow roast, a canoe trip down one of the canals, and a hike to the beach, where the Electrical Water Pageant can be seen. Mosquito repellant is a must.

Near Pioneer Hall sits a small petting farm, which houses animals such as goats, a miniature bull, rabbits, sheep, and chickens. If you arrive at the Hoop-Dee-Doo Revue early, you might want to pass a little time here.

Swimming options are plentiful here. There are two swimming pools for starters, plus a beach on Bay Lake 175 feet wide and longer than a football field. Swimming is allowed in the roped-off areas only. Fort Wilderness also plays host to **River Country**, WDW's older, smaller, but more aesthetic swimming park. This, however, requires a separate admission fee.

Recently, two tennis courts were added to the list of amenities of Fort Wilderness. They are lit at night, and are located at the Meadow Recreation Complex, behind the Meadow Trading Post.

Tetherball and volleyball courts are scattered throughout the resort. Water skiing can be done out of the Fort Wilderness marina but you must call the Contemporary's marina and make reservations 2 to 3 days in advance.

Fort Wilderness even has a zoological park called Discovery Island, a landfall in Bay Lake filled with birds, turtles, and other animals. Some endangered species have representatives here. This, like River Country, has an admission fee.

HINT: Fort Wilderness, located in the thick of Central Floridian nature, has quite a few sights that are not sufficient enough to lure many visitors on their own, but are worth a look if you're in the area.

The horses of Walt Disney World get their footwear at the blacksmith shop here. The blacksmith is usually on hand for a time every day to answer questions and speak abou t this profession. Occasionally, you will be able to watch him shoe the animals' hooves.

The canals of Fort Wilderness hold a particular beauty to them, a very different kind of beauty than what Disneydishes up in the parks.

Something called the **Lawn Mower Tree**: A tree that managed to somehow tangle itself up in the workings of, well, a lawn mower. Or possibly the other way around... In any case, it has kept on growing (the tree, not the lawn mower) since then and is one of Fort Wilderness's oddities. You can see it as you walk towards the marina. A poem sits by the tree. It reads:

Too long did Billy Bowlegs
Park his reel slow mower
Alas, one warm and sunny day
Aside a real fast grower.
Strange. Very strange.

The horses who pull trolleys up Main Street in the Magic Kingdom are kept at the **Tri Circle D Ranch** here on their days off. You might happen to see a horse with its colts if you're lucky.

DISNEY'S GRAND FLORIDIAN BEACH RESORT, A MONORAIL HOTEL

Address: 4401 Floridian Way (824-3000). *FAX:* 824-3186. *Rates:* Rooms, $230 to $440; suites, $340 to $1000. *At a Glance:* A Victorian hotel that evokes thoughts of Palm Beach luxury hotels of Florida at the turn of the century. *Ratings:* Room Comfort 7; Amenities 7; Eateries 10; Shopping 7; Convenience 10; Decor 10.

Walt Disney's father came to Florida around the turn of the century and opened up a hotel in Daytona Beach. That Victorian failed. Walt Disney's company came back and in 1988, opened up a hotel on Seven Seas Lagoon. This Victorian will not fail.

The **Grand Floridian** was the first part of the intense expansion of

WDW's guest areas, opening its doors in August '88. The facilities offer all the pleasant little quirks of the hotels of Florida's heyday, such as wide verandahs, wicker chairs, ceiling fans, latticework, red-gabled roofs, brick chimneys, turrets, and towers. A white-sand beach is touched on the east by the Seven Seas Lagoon.

But Disney is not living in the past. That's obviously demonstrated by the presence of a monorail station. It's also noticeable during the summer months from the cool air being piped in through the air conditioning system. This hotel also plays host to restaurants, lounges, a health club, and other modern amenities. In the main building is the Grand Lobby, a 15,000 square-foot area, five stories high. This structure houses stained-glass domes, an aviary, potted palms, and sparkling crystal chandeliers. A vintage open-cage elevator links the main level with the shops and eateries on the second floor.

Rooms

The 901 rooms reflect the fact that this is the Vacation Kingdom's most costly resort. They are decked out lavishly, with light oak armoires and furnishings, Victorian woodwork, ceiling fans, and marble-topped sinks. The walls are painted in delicate green and salmon.

The main building embodies 61 concierge rooms and 34 suites. Five lodge buildings surround it. Each is four or five stories high, and all told, they contain 624 standard-sized rooms and 176 smaller "attic" rooms. The standard rooms measure about 400 square feet, about the size of a two-car garage. Each of the rooms has a pair of queen beds and a sofa bed, and most of them have terraces.

Suites and Concierge Rooms

All of the suites and concierge rooms are located on the third, fourth, and fifth floors of the main wing. They can be reached by way of private elevator. However, access to the third story and up is limited solely to those staying on those floors.

The suites have a parlor and one to three bedrooms. Located in the turrets of the third through fifth floors are honeymoon suites, each of which boasts views out five windows.

The third through fifth floors are the concierge levels. Among the amenities exclusively available to those staying on these levels are wet bars in each room; a concierge desk offering services such as rapid check-in and check-out, information, and reservations; access to the private fourth floor sitting area, serving daily continental breakfast; and the private lounges on the fourth and fifth floor.

The concierge rooms cost $340 to $395, the suites go for $340 to $1,000.

Dining Options

The Floridian is home to several of WDW's best restaurants. Atmosphere at the Grand Floridian's restaurants is particularly faithful to the hotel's elegant theme and draws guests from around the World.

The hotel's largest restaurant, **Flagler's**, offers food with splashes of French and Italian influence. All meals are kicked off by a complimentary appetizer. The restaurant overlooks the marina and serves elegant seafood and beef dishes. If you're lucky, you'll be here when the waiters and waitresses break into song, which has been known to happen on occasion.

Next to the pool is the **Gasparilla Grill and Games**, a take-out, self-service snack bar by pool. Continental breakfast is served here in the morning, hot dogs, burgers, and chicken the rest of the day. Open 24 hours. The **Grand Floridian Cafe** also serves a character breakfast with Mary Poppins. However, while offerings at 1900 Park Fare are staid, tried-and-true, well-known (if somewhat unimaginative), and all-American, the fare here is pure South. Lunch and dinner choices include catfish fillet with bell pepper relish, Cajun burgers, and honey-dipped fried chicken.

Narcoosee's is an interesting restaurant, to say the least. The place is octagonal and located right on the fringe of the sugar-sand beach. The kitchen is open and airy, and the fare focuses on seafood, but also includes steak, lamb chops, veal chops, and grilled chicken. There is nightly entertainment. The biggest attraction of **1900 Park Fare** is not the food but the surroundings in which patrons dine. The centerpiece is Big Bertha, a century-old band organ. Mary Poppins and her friends preside over the character breakfast, and at dinner, Chip and Dale's Rescue Rangers entertain. The food is utterly American... seafood, salads, vegetables, breads, pork, lamb, and sirloin. The menu changes weekly.

The finest foodstuffs in Walt Disney World can be savored at the Grand Floridian — at **Victoria and Albert's**. This dining room has won its share of awards, including being named to the list of Florida's Top 100 Restaurants, one of three WDW establishments to achieve that distinction. This restaurant has a prix fixe policy, a tab of $75 per person (excluding gratuity and alcohol). Another interesting thing about Victoria and Albert's is the lack of printed menus. The specialties change daily, and usually include entrees of veal, red meat, fish, lamb, and fowl. The dinner includes choice of soups, salads, and desserts, all of the latter sinfully delicious, including souffles of chocolate or berries. There is a lengthy wine list. Only dinner is served, reservations and jackets are necessary.

Watering Holes

Overlooking the garden and pool is the **Garden View Lounge**, a pleasant dive serving specialty drinks and afternoon tea. The bar called

Mizner's Lounge pays homage to the father of Palm Beach architecture. Quiet and friendly. **Narcoosee's** (see above) serves beer in an unusual fashion: in mugs, half-yards, and yards (as in three feet!). The name of this peculiar form of drink service is Yards of Beer. The **Summerhouse** is the Floridian's pool bar.

Shopping

On the second floor, **Commander Porter's** sells menswear. Also on the second level is **M. Mouse Mercantile**, a character shop. And you can guess what the "M" stands for. **Sandy Cove**, located on the first floor, is a good place to pick up sundries and souvenirs. Women can purchase articles of clothing and jewelry at **Summer Lace**.

Recreation

An arcade is here as the latter part of Gasparilla Grill and Games.

The Floridian's marina, the **Captain's Shipyard**, offers all sorts of boats for rent. Near Gasparilla Grill and Games sits a playground.

The hotel has a health club, **St. John's**. It offers an exercise room complete with the latest equipment, steamrooms, lockers, and massages.

There is a nicely landscaped, 275,000 gallon swimming pool here, as well as a powder-sand beach on **Seven Seas Lagoon**. Water skiing can be done here as well.

The Floridian has two clay tennis courts.

Babysitting

The **Mousketeer Club** program is available here, near the Gasparilla complex.

DISNEY'S POLYNESIAN RESORT, A MONORAIL HOTEL

Address: 700 South Seas Drive (824-2000). FAX: 824-3174. *Rates:* Rooms, $190 to $290; suites, $540 to $860. *At a Glance:* A South Seas-themed 855-room resort complex complete with restaurants, lounges, and stores carrying out the Pacific theme. *Ratings:* Room Comfort 8; Amenities 7; Eateries 7; Shopping 10; Convenience 10; Decor 9.

This hotel's kitschy motto, "Aitea-Paitea," means "Tomorrow will be another day just like today." Few would take objection to that sentiment. This hotel has the greatest popularity among repeat visitors. That, combined with its convenience and the contented air that pervades the hotel, makes this one of the first Disney hostelries to sell out.

As is the case with Disney, lobbies here are not really lobbies. This one is known as the Great Ceremonial House. Most of the hotel's public areas are located here, and as you might expect, this is the focal point of the resort. Disney grabs your attention the minute you walk into any of their lobbies, and they certainly accomplish that here. Most of the Poly's lobby is covered by a vast, three-story garden. Amid 250 square feet of indoor rainforest are orchids, trees, ferns, and in the center, a fountain themed after a waterfall. Volcanic rocks and tropical plants rim the wellspring, and the climate of the lobby allows the lush vegetation to be in bloom, regardless of when you visit.

Situated on either side are the eleven two- and three-story "longhouses" where the hotel's rooms are located. The longhouses are identified by names of Polynesian islands.

HINT: About 60% of the Polynesian's guests have stayed there before. This should tell you something about the hotel.

Rooms

The 855 rooms are located in eleven longhouses, all of which lie alongside the Great Ceremonial House. Most of the rooms have either a patio or balcony, offering varying panoramas. The rooms are priced according to view, and the scale goes from longhouse view (least expensive), monorail, garden, and pool to marina view (most expensive).

Features shared by all the guest rooms are two queen-sized beds and a sleep sofa, which accommodate five. The largest of the rooms are in the Oahu longhouse. Non-smoking and adjoining rooms are available upon request.

Suites and Concierge Rooms

The Polynesian Resort offers a concierge program similar to the one at the Contemporary, called **Royal Polynesian**. The service includes free valet parking, special check-in and check-out privileges, juice and coffee in the morning, soft drinks and snacks in the afternoon, and a special concierge on duty to serve the concierge guests between 8 AM and 9 PM. These are located in the Tonga, Moorea, and Samoa longhouses. In the Bali Hai are the Poly's 14 suites, which can host up to six persons on a king-sized bed and two queens. Some suites even have big-screen TVs.

Dining Options

On the lobby level of the Great Ceremonial House is **Captain Cook's Snack and Ice Cream Company**. This small establishment serves continental breakfasts and burgers, hot dogs, snacks, and ice cream later on. The **Coral Isle Cafe** is located around the corner from Papeete Bay Verandah on the second floor of the Great Ceremonial House. This is pretty much a customary coffee shop, serving good, unpretentious meals. Edibles purveyed here include old breakfast standbys: eggs, omelets, and cereal, salads, sandwiches, and hot entrees for lunch and dinner. Some

Polynesian specialties are also served. Bustling and popular. Disney never misses a trick. Here, at the **Luau Cove**, they take advantage of the fancy-tickling atmosphere of the Polynesian and blends it with dancing, music, and those omnipresent Disney characters to create two of the World's most popular dinner shows, Mickey's Tropical Revue and the Polynesian Revue (also called the Luau). The entertainers, many of whom have studied at the Polynesian Cultural Center in Hawaii, are top-notch and the food, although less than authentic, is tasty.

The Poly's largest feasting hall is the **Papeete Bay Verandah** on the second floor of the Great Ceremonial House. This restaurant offers Minnie's Menehune Breakfast Monday through Saturday and a character buffet on Sunday, in addition steak and seafood, more exotic Polynesian fare. During the evenings, the view across the Seven Seas Lagoon is absolutely breathtaking. The **Snack Isle** is a small snack bar near the East Pool, serving burgers, hot dogs, and submarines. On the eastern fringe of the property, next to the Oahu longhouse, is the **Tangaroa Terrace**, a nice establishment renowned for its banana-stuffed French toast at breakfast. It also serves a dinner buffet.

Watering Holes

Next to the Swimming Pool Lagoon is the **Barefoot Bar**, which is open from 11 AM until 5 PM (or 10:30 during the summer). Soda, beer, and mixed drinks are served here. The **Tambu Lounge** is a cozy bistro adjoining the Papeete Bay Verandah. You can get Polynesian-style drinks and appetizers here from 11 AM until 1:30 AM. Entertainment nightly.

Shopping

Crusoe and Sons' sells mens' and boys' swimwear and casuals. Guests can find a nice assortment of childrens' clothing and accessories at **Kanaka Kids**. Sundries and supplies are available at **News from Civilization**, on the first floor of the Great Ceremonial House. Here, in addition to tobacco, film, newspapers, magazines, and gifts, you can buy a grass skirt or Florida conch shells. Interesting.

Outrigger's Cove is the Polynesian equivalent of Bay View Gifts. Items with a South Seas flair are sold here, including gifts and souvenirs. For women, **Polynesian Princess** is the place to stop for bathing suits, resortwear, and accessories. Food, beer, wine, and spirits can be purchased at **Trader Jack's Grog Hut** on the first floor. **Village Gifts and Sundries** is the place for Disney merchandise and gift items.

Services

The **Alii Nui Barber Shop** and **Pretty Wahine Beauty Shop** are located on the first floor of the Great Ceremonial House.

Recreation

Boat rentals are available at the Polynesian's marina on Seven Seas Lagoon. Sailboats, Water Sprites, pedal boats, flote boats, and outrigger canoes can be rented.

Next to the Tangaroa Snack Isle is the hotel's gameroom, **Moana Mickey's Fun Hut**. This facility is smaller than the Fiesta Fun Center, but is still a formidable diversion for the younger set.

Jogging and exercise trails, at Fort Wilderness and the Disney Inn, are just a short jog away. There is a large and well-planned playground by the Great Ceremonial House.

The Polynesian has one of the World's nicest swimming areas: the **Swimming Pool Lagoon**. This lushly landscaped, free-form pool is bordered by a set of boulders that join to form a waterslide. A pathway crossed by a waterfall leads to the top of the slide. Also, the **East Pool**, which is by the Oahu, Tonga, Hawaii, Bora Bora, and Maui longhouses; and the beach on Seven Seas Lagoon offer opportunities for those with water on their minds. Water skiing boats, equipment, and drivers can be hired here.

Babysitting

The **Neverland Club** is a dinner attraction just for kids 3 to 12 years old, and no adults — by order of Peter Pan. Kids dine on a buffet of pasta, hot dogs, and chicken. Entertainment includes Disney movies, free arcade, video games, a live bird show, and a visit from Goofy, all in a setting that looks like it's borrowed from Captain Hook's ship and the Lost Boys' hideout.

EPCOT CENTER RESORT AREA

DISNEY'S BOARDWALK RESORT – Scheduled to open in early 1994, this creation of Robert A. M. Stern (Disney's Yacht and Beach Club Resorts) will be integrated with the **Boardwalk Entertainment Complex**. The hotel and surrounding area will pay tribute to the Atlantic City boardwalk as it looked in its glory days.

The centerpiece of the 30-acre project will be a 530-unit, all-suite hotel. The rest of the entertainment complex will include three dinner shows, an antique carousel, a Ferris wheel, midway games, cotton candy vendors, and two night clubs. When completed, the project will serve as another nighttime entertainment complex, like Pleasure Island and Church Street Station.

DISNEY'S CARIBBEAN BEACH RESORT

Address: 900 Cayman Way (934-3400). *FAX:* 827-5990. *Rates:* $87 to

$114. *At a Glance:* One of the largest in the U.S., this resort is the first Disney hotel catering to those who can't afford the more expensive hotels. *Ratings:* Room Comfort 7; Amenities 7; Eateries 6; Shopping 6; Convenience 7; Decor 10.

The **Caribbean Beach Resort** is Disney's first venture into the moderately-priced hotel pool, and it is certainly impressive for a freshman entry. There are 200 acres, including a 42-acre lake in the center of the resort. The lake is the focus of the resort, and five villages with about 400 rooms apiece surround it.

The main guest facilities are located at **Old Port Royale** and the **Custom House**. The former features stone walls, pirate flags, cannons, tropical birds and flowers and houses the resort's restaurants and shops. The latter is the reception building. Both public buildings are decorated in Caribbean fashion.

I stated that this hotel is too big for its own good. Let me explain. The hotel's food court, located at Old Port Royale, can seat a maximum of 500 people at any given time. The hotel has 2,112 rooms. Four people a room, if 10% of the hotel's guests (during peak season) visit at the same time, visitors will have to endure sizable waits for a meal. Another disadvantage of this hotel: rooms can only accommodate four people each. If you have more than that in your family, the least expensive Disney lodgings with room for five or more would be the Village Resort's Club Lake Suites or the trailer homes at Fort Wilderness.

Rooms

The 2,112 rooms here are located in five villages surrounding the lake, each named after a Caribbean island —Martinique, Barbados, Trinidad, Aruba, and Jamaica. Each village contains several two-story buildings containing the rooms, laundry facilities, a pool, and a section of beach on the lake.

The buildings housing the rooms are soft pastels, the roofs brighter colors — crimsons and jade greens. Deeply painted towers look over each village. Each village is designed slightly differently, to give them a slight feel of their namesake islands.

All of the rooms are the same in terms of size and amenities. The only thing differentiating the different-priced rooms is the view. The units here are about 400 square feet, smaller than the rooms at other Disney hotels. The rooms are decorated in soft, light pastels. The beds are covered in pinks and blues, the furniture is oak. Bathrooms here are large and comfortable. Each room has a portable coffee-maker.

Dining Options

All of the restaurants here are located in the food court at **Old Port Royale**. Diners at all six counter-service restaurants eat in the 500-seat commons. Each offers children's and health-conscious meals. Reggae music plays in the background and there's a lake view.

Bluerunner Pizza is the only Caribbean Beach eatery outside the food court. Pizza delivery is available. The **Bridgetown Broiler** serves chicken fajitas, rotisserie-grilled chicken, and taco salad. For the sweet tooth, the **Cinnamon Bay Bakery** sells continental breakfasts, fresh croissants, rolls, and other pastries. Cookies and ice cream are also served here. Soups, salads, and deli sandwiches are sold at **Montego's Market**.

Yearnings for Chinese cuisine can be satisfied at **Oriental Cargo**, a counter offering soup, spare ribs, lo mein, egg rolls, and entrees. A buffet is held here at breakfast and dinner. The menu at **Port Royale Hamburger Shop** features hot dogs, chicken, burgers, hot sandwiches, and soft drinks. The **Royale Pizza & Pasta Shop** offers pizza by the slice or the pie plus a medley of pasta dishes. A full selection of breakfast dishes is also available.

Watering Holes

Next to the pool at Old Port Royale is **Banana Cabana**, a pool bar where drinks and snacks are served. The largest lounge in the resort is the **Captain's Hideaway**, a 200-seat bistro in Old Port Royale. Beer, wine, mixed drinks, and tropical cocktails are purveyed here.

Shopping

Items sold at the **Calypso Straw Market** include island-themed gifts and Caribbean Beach logo items. The **Calypso Trading Post** stocks a good variety of sundries as well as character merchandise and souvenirs.

Recreation

Bicycles can be rented at the **Barefoot Bay Bike Works and Boat Yard**. Trails for biking or walking meander across the property and around the lake. Also available at the Barefoot Bay Bike Works and Boat Yard are boat rentals — the usual array of Water Sprites, sailboats, and pedalboats.

A gameroom, **Goombay Games**, is located at Old Port Royale. There is about a mile and a half of jogging to be had in the form of a promenade circumnavigating the lake. Nature walks are held on Parrot Cay Island, in the middle of Barefoot Bay. There are six swimming pools here — one at each of the five villages and another at Old Port Royale. The pool at Old Port Royale is a work of art: concrete bridges transverse the waters and cannons loom over the water. Also worked into what seems like a recreation of a pirate stronghold are several waterslides. Also, each village sits on a stretch of white sand on Barefoot Bay, where swimming can also be done.

DISNEY'S YACHT AND BEACH CLUB RESORTS

Address: Beach Club: 1800 EPCOT Resort Boulevard (934-8000). *FAX:* 934-3850. Yacht Club: 1700 EPCOT Resort Boulevard (934-7000). *FAX:* 934-3450. *Rates:* Rooms, $205 to $370; suites, $215 to $650. *At a Glance:* A dual resort that evokes images of New England around the turn of the century. Though connected, each hotel has its own distinct flavor and personality. *Ratings:* Room Comfort 8; Amenities 8; Eateries 10; Shopping 5; Convenience 9; Decor 9.

These two hotels, designed by Robert A. M. Stern, sit next to each other just outside the new International Gateway entrance of EPCOT Center and a boat ride away from the Studios. These resorts are convenient choices for those who plan on spending a lot of time at the Studios or EPCOT.

The hotel complex, which totals 1,215 rooms (635 rooms at the Yacht Club, 580 at the Beach), features a central recreation and dining area where most of the resorts' public areas are located. Also, three restaurants and two lounges are located at each resort. The centerpieces of the resort are a 25-acre lake and a 3-acre swimming lagoon, called Stormalong Bay.

The **Yacht Club's** architecture is designed as a New England beach resort, circa 1880, with gray clapboard and flags poking up from the roof, five stories up. A pier and a lighthouse carry the nautical theme here, as do the rooms and restaurants. The **Beach Club** is decorated nicely, its blue and white stick house architecture blends amiably with its sister hotel, the Yacht Club. The staff here is decked out in period costumes that echo the beach theme found in all the hotel's areas.

Rooms

At the Yacht Club, the rooms are designed with a nautical flair. The rooms are bright and airy, the appointments are faithful to the motif — rose and cobalt blue linens and carpet. The furniture is painted a fresh white, as are the walls, which are accented by blue trim where they meet the ceiling. The bathrooms are large and feature double sinks and brass-trimmed mirrors. Rooms are also highlighted by color TVs, ceiling fans, a minibar, a table (that doubles as a checkerboard) and chairs, and chess and checkers sets. The rooms here are quite spacious.

The rooms at the Beach Club are laid out similarly to the ones at the Yacht Club, but reflect more of a beach attitude in their decor. These rooms are apparelled in coral and sea green, with a splash of robin's-egg-blue. Furniture here is in natural tones, and the rooms contain two double beds, ceiling fans, and other amenities similar to those in the Yacht Club's rooms.

Suites and Concierge Rooms

Concierge rooms and suites sleeping five to ten persons are available at both resorts.

Dining Options

Ariel's is the signature restaurant of the Beach Club. Serving breakfast and dinner, this restaurant is a pleasant place to dine. A 2,500-gallon saltwater aquarium is situated at this eatery named for The Little Mermaid, but the seafood served at this establishment comes from sources other than the fish tank.

The **Beaches and Cream Soda Shop**, in the area shared by the two hotels, is a turn-of-the-century ice cream parlor, the menu is the epitome of American cuisine, featuring sundaes, floats, shakes, cones, ice cream sodas, and the Fenway Park Burger, which is available in four forms, (what else?) the single, double, triple, and grand slam.

A song in the Rodgers and Hammerstein classic Carousel proclaims "It was a real nice clambake, and we all had a real good time." Well, that statement rings true in the **Cape May Cafe**, one of the Beach Club's restaurants, where an indoor New England clambake is held each evening. Food is steamed in a cooking pit in full view of the patrons, making for an interesting atmosphere. The spread includes clams, lobster, shrimp, mussels, oysters, chicken, and stews. A character breakfast buffet and a buffet lunch are also held here.

Hurricane Hannah's Grill is another of the shared restaurants. The bill of fare here is light and features American favorites. Sandwiches, fries, and ice cream are served and there is a full bar. Near the smaller pool at the Beach Club is the **Portside Snack Bar**. Fast food such as sandwiches, salads, and hot dogs is served, along with beer, wine, and specialty drinks.

The Yacht Club's pool area boasts the **Sip Ahoy Snack Bar**, the counterpart of Portside at the BC. Burgers, dogs, sandwiches, soft drinks, and liquor are served here. The **Yacht Club Galley** features a buffet at breakfast and dinner, and an a la carte menu at lunch. The dinner buffet features dishes that represent New England cuisine. Also located at the Yacht Club is the **Yachtman's Steakhouse**. Like the Cape May Cafe, diners can watch the chef as he chooses cuts of meat and then prepares them in an open kitchen. Steak, chicken, and seafood are the standards here.

Watering Holes

The **Ale and Compass Lounge** is located in the lobby of the Yacht

Club. The lounge is open until 1 AM each night and serves specialty drinks, including ale and coffee. Next to the Yachtman's Steakhouse is the **Crew Cup Lounge**. This "pub" is a pleasant spot for a dinner aperitif.

The **Martha's Vineyard Lounge** is situated at the Beach Club, right next to Ariel's. The lounge's drawing card is its extensive wine list, featuring wines from Martha's Vineyard, California, Long Island, and Europe. The **Riptide Lounge**, the Beach Club's chic lobby bar, serves California wines, specialty drinks, and wine coolers. Open 'til 1 AM.

Shopping

Atlantic Wear and Wardrobe Emporium at the Beach Club and **Fitting and Fairings' Clothes and Notions** at the Yacht Club sell similar merchandise: sundries, souvenirs, character merchandise, and items that follow the nautical and beach themes.

Services

The **Periwig Salon**, in the hotels' common area, is a barber shop/ beauty parlor for men and women. Open from 9 to 5 daily.

Recreation

The 25-acre lake here is a prime location for boating, and watercraft can be rented at Bayside Marina. Boats available include Water Sprites, sailboats, flote boats, pedal boats, and row boats.

Ever wanted to play croquet? This is the place to do it. There is a grass court on the Beach Club side. But you don't have croquet equipment? It's not a problem. Disney loans the equipment out at the health club — and it's free.

There are about 40 video games and pinball machines at the twin resorts' shared gameroom, the Lafferty Place Arcade. Also located in the central area is the **Ship Shape Health Club** offering exercise machines, aerobics classes, massage rooms, spa, steamroom, and saunas.

Swimming is a major attraction here. Both hotels have their own pool and a section of lakeside beach, plus the centerpiece of the resort: **Stormalong Bay**. This 3-acre swimming complex features a 750,000 gallon main pool, next to another pool with a pair of waterslides coming off a shipwreck, a snorkeling lagoon complete with aquatic life, an active lagoon with bubbling jets of water and whirlpools, and yet another lagoon for the sedentary.

On the Beach Club side of the resort are two lit tennis courts. Rental equipment is available at the health club. There is a volleyball court on the sand of the Beach Club. Equipment is loaned out at the Ship Shape Health Club.

Babysitting

The **Sandcastle Club**, a youth program at the resorts, keeps kids entertained while the parents can go for a night out. Disney videos, games, toys, and Apple computers keep children occupied, while juice, milk, and snacks keep their stomachs happy.

THE WALT DISNEY WORLD DOLPHIN

Address: 1500 EPCOT Resort Boulevard (934-4000). *FAX:* 934-4099. *Rates:* Rooms, $179 to $350; suites, $450 to $2,750. *At a Glance:* A 27-story tower rising off the 14-story main building. Two dolphin statues balance on either side of the tower. Eccentric won't even begin to describe this hotel. *Ratings:* Room Comfort 7; Amenities 7; Eateries 10; Shopping 7; Convenience 9; Decor 5.

This hotel (operated by Sheraton), an odd creation of Michael Graves, was recognized by *Progressive Architecture* magazine for "its striking post-modern design." The tallest hotel in WDW and the strangest, it can be recognized by the twin dolphin statues that stand guard atop either side of the 14-story main building. The 55-foot high statues overlook lush landscaping, grotto pools, and Crescent Lake, which connects the Studios and EPCOT. The exterior of the hotel is done in oranges, greens, and blues, while the public areas are an eccentric melange of all the colors of the spectrum. The hotel is a new genre of structure called "Entertainment Architecture," as is the Swan Hotel.

By the entrance, a waterfall trickles down through a series of shell-shaped fountains propped up by dolphin statues. From here, trams depart to the new International Gateway entrance to EPCOT Center, to which it is very convenient. Keep your eyes open as you travel the Dolphin, or you may miss an intricate detail, like a dolphin carved into a bench, or a monkey hanging from a chandelier. VERY STRANGE!!!

Rooms

The Dolphin's 1,369 rooms are just as outlandish as the hotel's brash exterior. As they reflect the tropical theme, the rooms are all decorated in soft, light pastels. Palm trees are etched on the furniture, while the bedcovers are striped in coral and blue. Common features here include clock-radios, mini-bars, cable TV, newspaper, and voice mail.

Suites and Concierge Rooms

The Dolphin's tower houses seven concierge floors (12 through 18), which offer amenities above and beyond those at the everyday units. The rooms, called Dolphin Tower rooms, go for $250 to $325 each. Suites, ranging in size and luxury from lavish to profusely extravagant, are also available. Tabs for a suite run from $450 to $2,750 (!) and offer spectacular views of the Studios and EPCOT.

Dining Options

At poolside is the **Cabana Bar & Grill**, a snack bar serving burgers, chicken, sandwiches, yogurt, and fruit. The Dolphin has its own 24-hour eatery: the **Coral Cafe**. Buffets are offered here for breakfast and dinner, while those who prefer a la carte dining can do so at all three meals. Wednesdays and Sundays offer character breakfasts, and on Sunday, a buffet brunch.

The **Dolphin Fountain** is the place for exotic flavors of ice cream. The frozen treats are served as sundaes or in waffle cones. Breakfast offerings are somewhat limited, but include muffins and cereal. Sandwiches and burgers are purveyed here also. The staff at this establishment will start singing and dancing when the urge strikes.

Harry's Safari Bar & Grille is one of the restaurants in WDW that has characters and a story surrounding it. This particular anecdote features Harry, a barkeep-cum-world traveler. The fare here reflects his taste for the exotic and includes chicken, beef, and seafood with seasonings found by Harry during his journeys. The atmosphere is rich and jungle-like, the carpets tiger-striped patterns, the walls cloaked in tropical murals and stuffed animals. The friendly staff here dresses in safari gear. Very interesting indeed.

The hotel's most festive eatery, **Ristorante Carnevale**, is a lot of fun, in addition to being one of WDW's finer Italian restaurants. The house specialties include a borchette of veal, sausage, and quail and a seafood risotto. A wide variety of Asian dishes can be sampled at **Sum Chows**. Ambitious dinners are served here in a laid-back yet chic Oriental atmosphere. The menu is quite extensive and non-traditional.

Tubbi Checkers Buffeteria is a cafeteria-service restaurant with an unusual checkerboard setting. This is a good bet for when you want a quick, hot meal.

Watering Holes

Adjacent to Ristorante Carnevale is the **Carnevale Bar**, a taproom to which the festive attitude of the neighboring eatery radiates. A nice place to visit if you want a taste of the Carnevale's atmosphere but not a taste of its food. **Copa Banana's** tabletops are shaped like slices of fruit. The food and drink served here reflect the tropical theme of the hotel. Entertainment nightly.

Any voyager has a story to tell. That includes "Harry" of **Harry's Safari Bar** here. The **Lobby Lounge** is an affable place to sit with a cool drink and an appetizer and people-watch.

Shopping

Brittany Jewels offers a good selection of Cartier gems. **Daisy's Garden** is this hotel's combination character and sundry outlet. If you're a chocoholic or just someone who appreciates an occasional sugar rush, **Indulgences** is the place for you. Resortwear for both men and women can be purchased at **Signatures of Fashion**.

Recreation

A selection of boats are available for rent at the marina, near the grotto pool.

Near the pool is the hotel's health club, a branch of the chain **Body by Jake**, run by Jake Steinfeld. The equipment is top-rate, and available benefits include saunas, steamrooms, whirlpools, and personal trainers.

Near the Camp Dolphin area is a gameroom.

Swimming here is quite pleasurable, and just sitting back and watching is a enjoyable pastime. There is a rectangular pool, great for laps, and a grotto pool featuring waterfalls, a waterslide, bridges, and mountains. Also, swimmers can partake in the waters of Crescent Lake. The Dolphin and her sister property, the Swan, share eight lit tennis courts.

Babysitting

A supervised children's program, **Camp Dolphin**, is available for resort guests. Here, kids from 4 to 12 can participate in many activities.

THE WALT DISNEY WORLD SWAN

Address: 1200 EPCOT Resort Boulevard (934-3000). **FAX:** 934-4499. **Rates:** Rooms, $180 to $335; Suites, $425 to $1,540. **At a Glance:** The Dolphin's smaller sister hotel. 758 rooms on Crescent Lake, in the EPCOT Resort Area. Also the brainchild of Michael Graves. **Ratings:** Room Comfort 8; Amenities 6; Eateries 7; Shopping 5; Convenience 9; Decor 5.

The theme at **The Walt Disney World Swan** (operated by Westin) is oceanic, as the turquoise and coral designs of the building suggest a tropical resort hotel. The Swan's namesakes are represented in the form of two 45-foot high, 14-ton statues on either end of the hotel. Facing the Dolphin, this hotel is just as convenient as her sister. Like the Dolphin, this is an example of "Entertainment Architecture." In fact, most of the Swan's features are shared by the sister property, the Dolphin.

The guestrooms are located in the 12-story main building and a pair of seven-story wings. The hallways are adorned in patterned carpeting, murals covering the walls. Chandeliers in the halls are shaped like seahorses. This is only slightly less weird than the Dolphin.

Rooms

The motif here is mainly the same as that of the Dolphin, the rooms in the same turquoise and coral as the exterior. The units have amusing little touches that help to enforce the waterfront semblance of the hotel, touches like pineapples painted on the headboards and parrot-shaped lamps. Amenities of the rooms include safes, clock-radios, voice mail, cable TV, mini-bars, bathrobes, hair dryers, and newspaper delivery each morning.

Suites and Concierge Rooms

A variety of suites, from junior suites ($310) to two-bedroom presidential suites ($1,540) are available. Also, there are 45 concierge "Royal Beach Club" rooms ($310 to $330) located on the eleventh and twelfth floors.

Dining Options

The **Garden Grove Cafe** is a 24-hour spot where the "greenhouse effect" can be experienced. That's probably because of the location: inside a airy, high-ceilinged greenhouse. The walls are ornamented with topiary depiction, making for a very casual atmosphere. Fresh Florida seafood is the feature presentation here. The pastry kitchen is glassed in, so diners can watch as delightful goodies are prepared. The desserts here are advertised as "the most sinful pastries in town." It may or may not deserve that designation, but in any case, the pastry offerings are delicious.

A nice Italian bistro, **Palio**, features stellar homemade pizza made in a wood-burning oven and six ambitious, homemade pasta dishes. Named after the town of Sienna's famed horse race, Palio's surroundings feature authentic banners representing the Italian counties who participated in the race. Guitarists promenade through the restaurant nightly. The restaurant calls itself casual, but the price tags seem to suggest otherwise. At the **Splash Grill**, light snack fare is served for breakfast and lunch. Snacks and drinks are also served.

Watering Holes

Kimono's is a surprising lounge. There's a likable Japanese environment here, and drinks and sushi are served. There are sofas and chairs throughout the Lobby Court Lounge for visitors to sit with a drink in hand and watch life's parade passing by.

Shopping

Located in the lobby, **Swan Disney Cabana** sells sundries, souvenirs, and character merchandise. The **Swan Fashion Cabana** sells men's and women's resortwear plus jewelry.

Recreation

Boat rentals are available at the marina between the Dolphin and Swan. Near the pool is a small gameroom. The hotel possesses a small health club, featuring aerobics classes and exercise equipment.

Swimming can be done in the hotel's large, rectangular pool or in Crescent Lake. Between the two hotels are eight lit tennis courts.

Babysitting

The Swan has its own children's program, **Camp Swan**. The details of it are similar to those at the Dolphin.

DISNEY VILLAGE RESORT AREA

DISNEY'S DIXIE LANDINGS RESORT

Address: 2201 Orleans Drive (934-6000). *Rates:* Rooms from $87 to $119. *At a Glance:* A large resort featuring two distinctive types of structure, the Plantation and Bayou buildings, which combined, hold over two thousand rooms. *Ratings:* Room Comfort 7; Amenities 7; Eateries 7; Shopping 5; Convenience 8; Decor 9.

The resort is composed of 2,048 rooms (bigger than all the WDW resorts but the Caribbean)builtin two distinct architectural styles, **Bayou** and **Plantation**. The Plantation rooms, closer to the entrance, are dignified and stately, while Bayou rooms have a decidedly rugged feel to them.

The main pubic facilities are located in the Colonel's Cotton Mill, a building designed as a steamship. Among the facilities here are the registration, restaurant, food court, and gift shop. The centerpiece of the recreational facilities is **Ol' Man Island**, a 3 1/2 acre amusement island with a pool, playground, and fishing hole.

Rooms

The rooms are all the same in terms of size and comfort, only the architecture and decor differ. Rooms at both types of structure share common features in terms of amenities but everything from the carpeting to the beds to the ceiling fans has its own specific flavor.

Magnolia Bend Plantation rooms are found in elegant estate homes with cream-colored siding and pale grey-shingled roofs. Brick chimneys and hanging flowers accentuate the Southern feel. Balconies with elaborate railings and porches with wooden benches give an impression of lazy satisfaction.

The Alligator Bayou buildings are rugged and scruffy in their appearance, their tin roofs and weathered wood siding a sharp foil to the elegance of the Plantation. Furnishings here carry a distinct bayou flavor, the walls a simple ivory with wood trim, wood and tin armoires, and tin lamps. The bedposts are textured and colored like logs. The bathrooms have ample space, and the double pedestal sinks are a nice touch.

Dining Options

Outside the cotton mill in which the food court and restaurant are located is a bona fide water wheel. It powers the working cotton press inside the building. The food court, the **Captain's Cotton Mill**, seats 480.

A food court with five options is located here. The first of the restaurants is **Acadian Pizza 'n' Pasta**, offering fresh pizza with an assortment of toppings. Pasta dishes are also sold here. If you wish, pizza is available for delivery. **Bleu Bayou Burgers and Chicken** sells a variety of burgers as well as fried and grilled chicken. The hotel's full-service eatery, **Boatwright's Dining Hall**, was fashioned after a boatmaking warehouse. The table-service restaurant features Cajun specialties and Southern dishes. If you'll notice, the carpeting was custom-made to look like wood chips. The **Cajun Broiler** serves Cajun dishes and broiled chicken. The **Riverside Market and Deli** serves delicatessen fare and snack food. Pastries, fresh breads, and sticky buns are available at **Southern Trace Bakery**.

Watering Holes

The **Cotton Co-op** is modeled after a cotton exchange and serves specialty drinks and hors d'oeuvres. Next to the pool at Ol' Man Island is **Muddy Rivers**, a poolside lounge serving snacks and drinks. Open during pool hours.

Shopping

Located in the Colonel's Cotton Mill, **Fulton's General Store** offers character merchandise, sundries, and souvenirs.

Recreation

You can bike along the footpaths connecting the parishes. Rentals are available at the Dixie Levee.

Boat rentals are available at Dixie Levee. On Ol' Man Island is a fishing hole, stocked with catfish.

A gameroom, the **Medicine Show Arcade**, is located at the Colonel's Cotton Mill, offering a small selection of electronic games. Jogging can be done on the footpaths between the parishes. A playground is located on Ol' Man Island.

There are five swimming pools scattered between the parishes, as well as Ol' Man Island, which possesses a themed pool, a spa, and a wading pool.

DISNEY'S PORT ORLEANS RESORT

Address: 1661 Old South Road. (934-5000). FAX: 934-5353. *Rates:* $87 to $119. *At a Glance:* This resort has all the romance and charm of the historic French Quarter of New Orleans. This is the second moderately-priced Disney resort. *Ratings:* Room Comfort 7; Amenities 7; Eateries 7; Shopping 5; Convenience 8; Decor 10.

This 1,008-room resort reeks of the Delta City, with its wrought-iron railings and ubiquitous plantings. The entrance driveway leads to the center of the resort, Port Orleans Square. Located here are the main building (the Mint), the food court (Sassagoula Floatworks and Food Factory), the Bonfamilles Cafe, and a shop.

The Mint, whose architecture was actually based on that of a mint (circa 1900), has a vaulted ceiling under which all the check-in and check-out facilities are located. The desks are designed like antiquated bank teller windows. Visible behind the reception desk is a mural depicting a Mardi Gras street scene. The hotel has a more urban feel to it than the Dixie Landings, and the property is transversed by streets, complete with road signs, black street lanterns, and tightly packed garden areas and brick and wrought iron gates.

Rooms

Located in seven three-story buildings are the 1,008 rooms of the Port Orleans Resort. The structures housing the units are all different, their hues range from cream, pink, and yellow to purple and blue. The wrought iron railings surrounding each building vary in design. The rooms themselves are nice, the walls bright and undistinguished. Two double beds in each room sleep up to four people. Some king-size beds are also available. The rooms are all the same otherwise in terms of space and comfort, the rate system is based on view.

Dining Options

The food court here is located in the Sassagoula Floatworks and Food Factory, which seats 300. **Basin Street Burgers and Chicken** sells a varied selection of burgers, plus deli items and batter-fried chicken. The **Bonfamilles Cafe**, located near the Sassagoula Floatworks and Food Factory, serves steak, seafood, and Creole dishes in a relaxed, table-service atmosphere. The casual setting is achieved thanks in part to the presence of courtyards, paddle fans, brick, wood, tile, and colorful fabrics. Specialties of the house include a Creole skillet breakfast, a Mardi Gras combo, shrimp and crawfish remoulade, and barbecue oysters.

Jacques Beignet's Bakery, another food-court location, serves ice cream, pastries, and "Nawlins-style" beignets. One of the World's better selections of Creole fare, the King Creole Broiler serves spit-roasted chicken with jambalaya and other Cajun dishes. Pizza and pasta, as well as other Italian specialties, are available at the Preservation Pizza Company. Delivery is also available.

Watering Holes

Mardi Grogs is a poolside bar serving specialty drinks and popcorn, hot dogs, and pretzels. The **Scat Cat's Club** is a customary barroom serving drinks and hors d'oeuvres.

Shopping

At Port Orleans Square is the resort's only shop, **Jackson Square Gifts and Desires**, which sells character merchandise, clothing, and sundries.

Recreation

Boat rentals including pedal boats, rowboats, canopy boats, and flote boats are available at **Port Orleans Landing**. Also located at Port Orleans Square is a gameroom, **South Quarter Games**.

The Port Orleans' themed swimming pool, **Doubloon Lagoon**, is a beguiling place. Scales, the sea serpent whose body pokes out of the ground in several places and whose tongue serves as a waterslide, apparently has an infatuation with jazz music, and is entertained by his buddies, the alligator musicians performing on the clamshell in the center of a nearby fountain.

DISNEY VACATION CLUB RESORT

Address: 1510 North Cove Road (560-5680 or, for the info line, 800/800-9100). *Rates:* $170 to $335. *At a Glance:* Disney's first venture into timeshares,villas and suites not being used by vacation owners will be rented out as hotel units. *Ratings:* Room Comfort 8; Amenities 7; Eateries 5; Shopping 3; Convenience 7; Decor 8.

This is the first venture by Disney into the timeshare business, which it calls "vacation ownership". The timeshare industry has been somewhat tarnished over the years, but when Disney puts its prestige behind something, it's reputable.

Units range from studios that sleep four to three-bedroom Grand Villas that can lodge up to twelve. When these units are not being used as timeshare properties, they will be rented out as hotel rooms. The **Vacation Club program** features a point system that offers greater flexibility than other timeshare programs. For about $12,000, prospective vacation owners can purchase 230 points, which can be traded for either three or four days in a three-bedroom villa during busy season, a one-week stay in a two-bedroom unit during the mid-season, or a three-week stay in a studio during the off-season. The plans include admission to the theme parks and personalized travel services. Ownership lasts for fifty years.

The program also allows owners to trade their Vacation Club vacations to any of 125 domestic or foreign resorts through Resorts Condominiums International (RCI). For more information on membership, call 939-3100.

Rooms

The exteriors of the buildings are done in grays and pastel greens, with tin roofs, back porches, gazebos, gingerbread, and latticework abounding. Its architecture is somewhat reminiscent of the Yacht Club Resort.

The one, two, and three-bedroom vacation homes are all decorated in a whimsical Key West motif, pinks and light greens dominating the color schemes here, the furniture bleached wood. Amenities of the units include ceiling fans, full kitchens (including microwave oven, china, flatware, and cookware), TVs with VCR, hardwood floors, whirlpool tubs in the master suite, and full-sized washers and driers. Windows are large and take advantage of the environment: each room has a view of either the forest, water, or golf course.

An original feature of the Resort, the DVC **Clubhouse**, is themed after a Key West retreat, with hardwood floors, historical photos, and Papa's Den: a comfortable reading room with bookshelves filled with the works of authors who once inhabited Key West.

Dining Options

The poolside snack bar **Good's Food to Go** offers the usual lineup of fast food, but the house specialty is conch fritters. **Olivia's Cafe** features dining indoors and outdoors on a terrace and offers Key West specialties like conch fritters, homemade French fries, and Key Lime white chocolate mousse. The cuisine here is seasoned with spices straight from the restaurant's herb garden. A benefit for Vacation Club members is the **World of Dining** program which allows guests to purchase for one price, a dining card that covers the cost of dining for the entire stay.

Watering Holes

Overlooking the island-themed swimming area is **The Gurgling**

Suitcase, an open-air bar serving a variety of mixed drinks, beer, and wine.

Shopping

There is a well-stocked general store here.

Recreation

Bicycles can be rented at **Hank's Rent'n'Return**.

Boat rentals are also available for use on the canals connecting the Vacation Club Resort to the Buena Vista Lagoon. The marina, Hank's Rent'n'Return, is pleasant and extensive, and a lighthouse sits on the rocky shore to serve as a beacon for seafaring guests.

The younger set seems to gravitate to the **Electric Eel Gameroom**.

For those so inclined, the **Lake Buena Vista Golf Course** winds through the resort. The World of Golf program allows members reduced greens fees at the five WDW courses.

There is a library featuring the works of authors who lived in Key West at one time. Known as **Papa's Den**, this is a cozy little spot at the Clubhouse. There are shuffleboard courts here as well. **Slappy Joe's** is a health club complete with massage, free weights, exercise equipment, and sauna. An island-themed swimming pool is located here. Two tennis courts are available for use. Volleyball can be played at poolside.

DISNEY'S VILLAGE RESORT

Address: 1901 Buena Vista Drive (827-1100). FAX: 828-8938. *Rates:* Club Suites from $190 to $270. Vacation Villas from $220 to $290. Fairway Villas from $315 to $335. Treehouse Villas from $295 to $315. Grand Vista Suites from $725 to $800. *At a Glance*: One of Disney's best-kept secrets, the quiet resort features tennis, golf, and shopping. Also, this is one of WDW's less expensive resorts, yet has the most space per unit. *Ratings:* Room Comfort 10; Amenities 8; Eateries 8; Shopping 8; Decor 10; Convenience 8. *Check-in:* 4 PM.

The **Disney Village** is a 4,000 acre entertainment, dining, shopping, and lodging complex sandwiched between S.R. 535 and EPCOT Center. **Disney's Village Resort** is the centerpiece of the complex.

Modeled after a country club resort, the Village Resort is the World's least expensive option for larger families. The smallest accommodations here, the Club Suites, provide ample space for a family of five. The largest quarters, the four Grand Vista Suites, were originally designed as model homes. One thing that guests here miss out on that other Disney resort invitees can enjoy is a specific theme of the hotel. The Village Resort has no specific geographic or ethnic flavor, but the rooms are as pleasant and tasteful as those in any Disney hotel.

All guests (except conventioners) check in at the new Reception Center next to the Marketplace. The Reception Center is airy and open with benches and trees in the center of the skylighted room. It also houses a guest services desk, a cashier, a telephone to National Car Rental, and other services.

Club Suites

There are 316 regular Club Suites and eight full suites situated on either side of Club Lake. These are particularly convenient to the Lake Buena Vista Clubhouse and the Disney Village Marketplace. These suites are delightful, decorated in reds and blues. The walls are adorned with lithographs of WDW landmarks. Disney Imagineers designed the suites with conventioners in mind, but the Club Suites have gained popularity with families at a steady rate.

As you walk into the suite (from a landscaped courtyard), you have a view of either Club Lake or a parking lot through a sliding-glass door. Outside is a small patio with a deck chair or a balcony. In the entry room is a convertible sofa, loveseat, television, table and chairs, and a mini-kitchen complete with a sink, microwave, and a small refrigerator. Tucked away in a cabinet is a coffee-maker with coffee, tea, and hot chocolate mix. The rooms are L-shaped, so you hang a turn to enter the bedroom, where furnishings include two double beds and another TV, a night table and dressers. The one weakness of the club suites is the small size of the bathrooms.

Deluxe Club Suites are larger than the regular Club Suites, sleep six on two queen beds and a sleep sofa, and have bigger bathrooms and jacuzzi.

Vacation Villas

These 119 one- and two-bedroom villas are located between the LBV Clubhouse and the Marketplace. These are not all that much bigger than the Club Suites, but they have full kitchens. The one-bedroom villas can sleep four, the two-bedrooms six. Each bedroom has a king bed, and the living rooms feature Sico beds and cathedral ceilings. The Vacation Villas were refurbished in 1986.

Fairway Villas

These 64 units straddle the 10th, 17th, and 18th fairways of the Lake Buena Vista Golf Course. They are among the nicest of WDW's hotel rooms, with cathedral ceilings. The windows are large and panoramic, the furniture fresh and modern. The exteriors resemble that of the Club Suites, but the appointments are much more elegant.

There are two double beds in one bedroom, a queen in the other, and a double convertible in the living room. Overall, these are spacious enough to sleep six (plus 2 children under 12).

Treehouse Villas

To get to the **Treehouses**, you pass the golf course and head down a narrow, winding road through the most dense woodlands outside of Fort Wilderness. There, amongst the scrubby pines and cypress are 60 odd-looking, octagonal villas suspended above the ground by stilts. Some are surrounded on one side by the 17th fairway of the Lake Buena Vista course and on the other by the pinelands on the other. These particular Treehouses are my pick as the most enchanting accommodations in the World. The treehouse villas are not connected to one another like the other accommodations, but are separated by twisting roadways and thick forestland. Downstairs is a study with a double bed and a laundry room, while ten feet above, a kitchen, a living room, two bedrooms, and two bathrooms. The living room holds a sleep sofa and a TV. Each bedroom has a queen-sized bed. the whole second floor is flanked by a cedar deck. These also appeal greatly to young couples, for obvious reasons.

Grand Vista Suites

These were not designed as resort villas but four model homes. The appointments are beautiful and classy, and services available include daily newspaper delivery, nightly bed turndown, free golf cart and bicycle rental, and a refrigerator stocked with staple foods.

Dining Options

In addition to the eateries at the Village Resort, the ones at Pleasure Island and the Marketplace are extremely convenient. Next to the Pro Shop is the **Disney Village Clubhouse Snack Bar**, serving pastries, coffee, sandwiches, hot dogs, snacks, hot and cold beverages, and ice cream.

At the Village Clubhouse is the **Pompano Grill**. Those of you who remember this restaurant from its days as the Lake Buena Vista Club will be surprised to find that the clubby atmosphere has been replaced by an attitude of casual Southern elegance. The cuisine is family-oriented, yet decidedly not fast food. Menu items include prime rib, chicken, filet mignon, New York strip steak, and burgers, while breakfasters can taste fruit, omelets, crepes, waffles, and pancakes. Reservations are accepted, but not required.

Roaming the LBV Golf Course is the **Refreshment Cart**, serving sandwiches, beer, soda, and other snacks. The Club Suites' and Vacation Villas' **Villa Centers** have snack bars that serve sandwiches, soda, beer, and snack fare.

Those who want to take advantage of the kitchen facilities in the villas can buy groceries at the **Gourmet Pantry** in the Marketplace. The store has a good selection of deli meats, vegetables, and candies, as well as staples. The Gourmet Pantry will deliver your groceries and place them in your refrigerator if you request, touch "31" on your in-room telephone or call 827-1100 from outside your villas.

Where to Drink

Those who want a bigger selection of lounges can stroll over to the Marketplace or Pleasure Island. The **Pompano Lounge**, next to the Pompano Grill, serves drinks, appetizers, sandwiches, and pizza from noon until 10 PM.

Shopping

Great shopping is within sight from the Village Resort, as the Disney Village Marketplace and Pleasure Island are only a few minutes walk away. The only shop in the Village Resort proper is **Disney's Village Resort Pro Shop**. Sold here are men's and women's clothing, golf supplies, and sundries. On the lower floor of the Clubhouse.

Recreation

Biking is a big deal here, as there are 8 miles of bike trails here in addition to the quiet and uncongested roadways. Bikes can be rented at the Villa Centers.

Boat rentals, specifically canoes and pedal boats are available at the marina at the Club Suite Recreation Center.

You can fish in the canals that surround the Treehouse Villas, Club Lake, or Buena Vista Lagoon.

Located at both Villa Centers are small gamerooms.

The 18-hole, par-72 **Lake Buena Vista Golf Course** winds through the Village Resort. The course plays from 5,315 to 6,763 yards, and with the new Eagle Pines course, shares the distinction of being the shortest course on WDW turf (Eagle Pines is shorter from the women's tees but longer from the championship). The Lake Buena Vista Club also has a driving range, a restaurant, and two snack bars. Fairways here are narrow, like the Disney Inn's Palm, but the only water hazards here are the canals that transverse the property.

Also located at the Clubhouse is the Village Resort's health club, where equipment includes a Stairmaster, aerobicycle, and Nautilus equipment. Daily and family memberships are available. Check in at the Pro Shop to use the club between 7 AM and 10 PM.

There are 3.4 miles of jogging and fitness trails running throughout the Village Resort. The course has 32 exercise stations scattered throughout. Maps are available at the Reception Center and Recreation Centers.

First-run movies can be seen at the AMC Pleasure Island 10 Theatre on the opposite side of the Island. No cover charge.

Playgrounds are located at the Vacation Villas, Fairway Villas, and Club Suite Recreation Centers, and Disney Village Marketplace.

Great nighttime entertainment is available a short stroll away at **Pleasure Island**. Six clubs plus two restaurants and nine shops make it easy to pass an entire evening here. Admission charge after 7 PM, minors not admitted alone after then.

There are six small swimming pools, open from 7 AM to 10 PM. The pools are located at the Vacation Villas, Club Suite Recreation Center, Conference Center, Vacation Villa Center, Disney's Village Clubhouse, and the Treehouse Villas. Whirlpools are also available at each pool.

Tennis players can use the three lighted courts at the Clubhouse. Racquets can be rented at the Pro Shop.

GETTING DISCOUNTS AT DISNEY HOTELS

You say that you would like to stay inside Walt Disney World, but the cost of the hotels is prohibitive? Well, a myriad of discounts can be had, but only by those who know how to get them.

• **Off-Peak Travel**. Rates during off-peak seasons can be as much as $40 less than during peak seasons.

• **AAA Discounts**. Privately owned hotels inside WDW and out offer discounts of up to 25% to AAA members. HoJo's, Travelodge, and the Dolphin (Sheraton) are just a few of the hotels that offer a discount. In summer 1991, Disney offered AAA members a 15% discount on Disney resort rates and 20% off package deals.

• **Magic Kingdom Club**. Many companies, credit unions, and organizations offer membership in the Magic Kingdom Club as a fringe benefit. Members get up to a 30% discount on hotels plus a small discount on admission media, so ask your employer if it is offered. If it is not, you can get a Magic Kingdom Club Gold Card, which entitles the holder to a 2-year subscription to the Disney News, savings at Disney hotels and attractions, and savings on various cruise lines, Delta Airlines, and National Car Rental. The Gold Card is available for $49, call 800/248-7833 or write Magic Kingdom Club Gold Card, P.O. Box 3850, Anaheim, CA, 92803-3850.

• **Ocala Information Center**. The Disney information center on I-75 offers discounts of up to 43% to visitors who don't already have hotel accommodations. The number of available units depends on season and hotel, but this is a risky way to get discounts during peak seasons, because rooms may not be available. Information: 904/854-7040.

• **Travel Agents**. Travel agents are a good source of information on money-saving deals and packages that may not be otherwise known.

DISNEY VILLAGE HOTEL PLAZA

The seven hotels of the **Disney Village Hotel Plaza**, while neither owned nor operated by the Disney company, share many of the same amenities as the WDW-owned-and-operated establishments. Hotel Plaza guests have free use of the WDW bus system, access to early reservations at EPCOT and Studio restaurants, and priority at golf, tennis, and other recreational facilities, among other things.

As a rule, the establishments here are less expensive and less luxurious than the WDW-owned resorts, and also tend to be more faceless. However, the location of these hostelries — on Hotel Plaza Boulevard between the Marketplace and Crossroads of Lake Buena Vista — is extremely convenient, and some of the area's best privately-owned hotels are located here. Also, Arthur's 27 in the Buena Vista Palace has been awarded numerous awards as one of Florida's best restaurants.

BUENA VISTA PALACE HOTEL

Address: 1900 Hotel Plaza Boulevard (827-2727 or 800/327-2990). *FAX:* 827-6034. *Rates:* Rooms, $130 to $245; Suites, $255 to $435. *At a Glance:* The largest and most luxurious hotel on the Plaza, this establishment boasts one of the state's finest restaurants. *Ratings:* Room Comfort 8; Amenities 7; Eateries 10; Shopping 6; Convenience 7; Decor 7.

The **Buena Vista Palace** is the focal point of the entire Hotel Plaza, and is also the hotel closest to the Marketplace and Pleasure Island. The 27-story tower here is the highest point in the entire Vacation Kingdom.

This hotel has undergone major uplifting over the past few years. In 1989, every guest room was redecorated to the tune of $2 million. And in 1991, the Palace Suites, a 200-suite addition next to the recreation island opened, price tag: $15 million.

When you enter this hotel, you're disappointed — you really expected more from what the hotel's brazen exterior looked like. There's a reason for that. You've entered on the third floor. The ground floor shows the hotel's true size and scope: immense.

Rooms

The rooms are found in a 27-story tower and three smaller towers, while the 200 Palace Suites are located on the recreation island in two five-story structures connected by a seven-story atrium building. Every one of the 1,228 rooms in the Palace and the Palace Suites has its own balcony or patio, and all of the rooms are spacious. The decor consists of combinations of varying shades of tan, and the furniture has a slightly modernistic twang to it. The appointments of the rooms include king beds or two queens, remote controlled color cable TVs, ceiling fans, and two telephones — one in the bathroom and a Mickey Mouse phone in the bedroom. *HINT:* Many rooms in the Palace's 27-story tower have sweeping views of either the Disney Village Marketplace, Pleasure Island, or EPCOT Center.

The rooms adjoining the atrium of the main tower are not advisable for light sleepers, as noise from the nightclub below permeates the room's walls. Request one of the other towers if you are severely partial to quiet.

Suites and Concierge Rooms

There are 45 suites in the main building, plus 200 more at the new Palace Suites building, which is connected to the main building by landscaped walkways. The suites are available with one bedroom or two, and features of the suites include sitting areas with sleeper sofas, dining areas, refrigerators, and coffee-makers. The suites were designed explicitly for families. There are also 78 Crown Level concierge rooms on the eleventh and twelfth floors. Concierge services include continental breakfasts, morning newspaper, and cocktail hour.

Dining Options

Arthur's 27 ranks right up there with Victoria and Albert's as one of the best restaurants in the World. This restaurant will set you back $60 for a six-course meal, $45 for four courses. Drinks are not included in that price, and a la carte items are more expensive ($24 and up for entrees). Here, a wine list ranges from the commonplace to the priceless. This restaurant is most popular on weekends, and there is only one seating nightly, so reservations are a must as soon as you book your room.

The **Courtyard Pastries and Pizza Shop** can satisfy those not in the mood for Arthur's 27 with simple meals and snacks. The **Outback Restaurant** is an Australian-themed eatery with pools, rock structures, and dull wood walls that make this interesting spot resemble a set from Crocodile Dundee. The food is rugged, jumbo lobster and steaks. Broiled lamb, beef, seafood, and veal is also served.

The **Pool Snack Bar** serves the usual selection of fast food and snack fare. A pleasant 24-hour restaurant, the **Watercress Cafe and Bake Shop**, is located on the ground floor of the hotel, next to a picturesque lake. The theme here is a casual Mediterranean one, and the menu is priced and designed for families, and a character breakfast is held here each morning. A la carte items include sandwiches, salads, soups, and pasta, all with an American or Florida flair.

Watering Holes

The **Buena Vista Palace Lobby Lounge** is a pleasant place to sit with your choice of mixed drinks, wines, specialty coffees and teas, and pastries, all to a piano accompaniment. One of the Hotel Plaza's most active nightclubs is the **Laughing Kookaburra "Good Time Bar"**, featuring dancing, 99 different brands of beer, a Happy Hour with free appetizers from 4 PM to 8 PM, and a dance floor. The place is usually packed with young singles, and they have a live band Tuesday through Sunday.

The Palace's **Pool Bar** serves cool beverages, tropical cocktails, and a Florida raw bar. On the 27th floor of the hotel is the **Top of the Palace Lounge**, where the live entertainment and the 800-bottle wine list take a backseat to the enchanting views of the Vacation Kingdom.

Shopping

Palace Fashions sells jewelry and clothing for men and women. **Palace Gifts and Sundries** stocks just that — plus a selection of Disney character merchandise.

Services

There is a beauty salon here for both men and women, run by Niki Bryan.

Recreation

There is a large gameroom located here. The hotel's health spa features whirlpools, saunas, and a good selection of exercise machines. Jogging enthusiasts can avail themselves of the pathways crisscrossing the resort. Located on the hotel's recreation island is a small playground.

Three swimming pools, including a wading pool, are located on the recreation island. Complimentary tennis play is available on four lighted courts.

Babysitting

The Palace has a kids' program, **Kid Stuff**. It is an organized recreational program for children 5 to 17.

GROSVENOR RESORT AT WALT DISNEY WORLD VILLAGE

Address: 1850 Hotel Plaza Boulevard. (828-4444 or 800/624-4109). *FAX:* 828-8120. *Rates:* $99 to $160. *At a Glance:* The best bargain in the Hotel Plaza, this is a pleasant hotel with a slight Bahamas feel and some interesting restaurants. *Ratings:* Room Comfort 7; Amenities 5; Eateries 6; Shopping 5; Convenience 7; Decor 7.

The **Grosvenor Resort** was literally a completely different hotel a few years back, the Americana Dutch Resort. The 1988 refurbishment has seen the addition of 20 rooms, and the redecoration of all the guestrooms, restaurants, public halls, and shops. The $8 million renovations also included the complete change of the hotel's theme — from Dutch to British Colonial.

This is the least expensive of the Hotel Plaza establishments, and has some of the most interesting restaurants and lounges on the block. The cavernous lobby is decorated in a mix of faint teal and rose, and a nice pub sits just off it to welcome back park guests.

Rooms

The rooms, all of which have been recently redecorated, are all nicely laid out. Each guestroom has two double beds or a king-sized sleeper, and cots are available. The rooms have a slight Bahamas angle to their decor, a pleasant blend of pale greens, pinks, and peach. Amenities of the rooms include VCRs, color cable television, bathrooms bigger than the norm, and a small stocked bar and refrigerator.

Dining Options

Baskerville's is a casual restaurant serving continental fare for breakfast, lunch, and dinner. But here, the food takes second billing to the atmosphere, namely, a Sherlock Holmes museum. In the center of the restaurant is a glassed-in model of the parlor of 221B Baker Street. The mock-up contains items such as Mr. Holmes's violin, his tobacco, his newspapers, and his correspondence —pierced with a knife. Very interesting, a must for Holmes aficionados.

In the lobby is **Crumpets**, a small cafe serving continental breakfasts and snack fare. Burgers, salads, and sandwiches are also served. Open 24 hours. The **Murderwatch Mystery Theatre** is a murder mystery dinner featuring an unlimited prime rib dinner and a cast of professional actors. The people who solve the puzzle win prizes to take home. Held every Saturday night at Baskerville's.

Watering Holes

The **Crickets International Cafe** serves drinks and light snack fare. **Moriarty's Pub**, an unpretentious lounge next to the lobby, features darts and live entertainment and is centered on Sherlock Holmes's arch-enemy, whose portrait can be seen hanging on the wall.

Shopping

Grosvenor Disney sells an assortment of goods, including sundries and character merchandise.

Recreation

For recreation, you've got your choice of basketball courts; a small gameroom; handball courts; two tennis courts; volleyball; and horse-shoes. A selection of over 200 movies is available at the guest services desk for use on the in-room VCRs.

A playground is located near the hotel. Racquetball can be played here on two courts. A shuffleboard court is located here, and there are two swimming pools and a hot tub.

GUEST QUARTERS SUITE RESORT

Address: 2305 Hotel Plaza Boulevard (934-1000 or 800/424-2900). *FAX:* 934-1011. *Rates:* $165 to $260. *At a Glance:* The latest addition to the Hotel Plaza, the Guest Quarters is the first all-suite hostel on Disney turf. *Ratings:* Room Comfort 10; Amenities 6; Eateries 6; Shopping 5; Decor 6; Convenience 7. *Check-in:* 4 PM.

This is the latest trend in the hotel industry of late. All-suite hotels are popping up in every city. So, it's only fitting that a suite hotel has appeared on Hotel Plaza Boulevard. This is a stereotypical all-suite hotel, to a certain extent. Like many others, there's an impressive atrium, a lobby restaurant and lounge, and a free breakfast each morning. This hotel is located at the northeastern terminus of Hotel Plaza Boulevard. Located within two blocks of the hotel are two non-Disney shopping/dining/entertainment complexes, Vista Centre and the Crossroads of Lake Buena Vista. I-4 is also very convenient from here.

Suites

The 229 suites here measure about 600 square feet, about 40% bigger than standard rooms in Disney-owned lodgings. Each suite can sleep six persons on two double beds in a bedroom and on a sleeper sofa in the living room. Two-bedroom suites are also available.

The suites' amenities include custom-designed furniture, televisions — remote controlled ones in bedroom and living room plus a smaller one in the bathroom, in-room movies, custom-made furniture, full-length mirrors, vanities, stocked refrigerators, coffee-makers, wet bars, and built-in hair dryers. Microwaves are available in 100 suites.

Dining Options

Located in the midst of a two-story tropical aviary, the **Parrot Patch** is the only full-service restaurant at the Guest Quarters. Diners can choose to take their meals indoors or out, and the complimentary breakfast is served here each morning. The atmosphere is pleasant, but the food is nothing special. Seasonal specialty dishes are also served, as is a breakfast buffet. There is also a children's menu. The **Poolside Bar and Ice Cream Parlor** serves snack food and drinks.

Watering Holes

The soothing **Parrot Perch Lounge** is located in the midst of the lobby atrium. Outside is the **Poolside Bar**, where ice cream, snacks, and drinks are served.

Shopping

The **Guest Quarters Disney Gifts and Sundries Shop** sells a wide range of goods, including character merchandise and sundries.

Recreation

There is a gameroom and a playground by the pool, an exercise room, a swimming pool plus a whirlpool and wading pool, and two tennis courts.

HILTON AT WALT DISNEY WORLD VILLAGE

Address: 1751 Hotel Plaza Boulevard (827-4000 or 800/728-4414). *FAX:* 827-4872. *Rates:* Rooms, $159 to $269; suites, $480 to $650. *At a Glance:* The second-largest of the Hotel Plaza establishments, this hotel has quite a few interesting restaurants and lounges. *Ratings:* Room Comfort 8; Amenities 8; Eateries 6; Shopping 6; Convenience 7; Decor 8.

This 813-room hotel flanks the southern end of Hotel Plaza Boulevard and is directly across the street from the Disney Village Marketplace. **The Hilton** is unique among Walt Disney World properties by virtue of its modernnesses. For example, you step in the elevator and press "6". In a short while, a computerized voice says, "Sixth floor, going up."

The rooms have sophisticated systems that operate the TV, climate control, lights, and call hotel personnel at the touch of a button. This hotel is also quite popular with young couples with children under twelve, because of the Youth Hotel, a supervised children's activity program which allows Mom and Dad to drop the kids off and head over to Pleasure Island for some entertainment.

Rooms

Allow me to affirm what I said above: if you want all the modern conveniences in your hotel room, this is the place to stay. To enter your room, you use a magnetized punchcard to open the door. And when you enter the room, the lights go on automatically. The *piece de resistance* of the rooms here are the telephones, which are integrated with all the controls of the room. With the touch of a button, the phones can adjust heating/ air conditioning, change the TV channel or volume, or call the concierge or other hotel staff.

The decorations here are contemporary, yet casual. The rooms are decked out in light mauves, peaches, and earthy tones. Rooms are brightened up by oversized windows.

HINT: If, when you check in, your room is on one of the lower floors, the clerk can upgrade you to a higher room, if available. The cost of this service is $45.

Suites and Concierge Rooms

A variety of both suites and concierge rooms are available on the ninth and tenth Towers floors. Amenities of the concierge floors include separate check-in and check-out, concierge, private lounge, continental breakfasts each morning, morning newspaper, bathrobes, and afternoon cocktails and hors d'oeuvres.

Dining Options

American Vineyards is a reasonably-priced, excellent American restaurant, offering a full lineup of regional American dishes, such as hickory-smoked Vermont turkey with stuffing and all the fixings, Florida stone crabs, Maine lobster, and quail. Dinner only. Outstanding brunches are also offered during spring, fall, and holiday seasons.

A representative of the **Benihana's — The Japanese Steakhouse** chain is located here, where diners feast on Japanese specialties like shrimp, scallops, lobster tail, Japanese onion soup, fresh vegetables, chicken, and of course, the steak that has made Benihana's famous, all prepared with great pomp and show on a hibachi grill. The **County Fair Restaurant** offers extensive buffets at breakfast, lunch, and dinner, plus a la carte items at dinner. The dinner buffet features unlimited prime rib and BBQ chicken and beers from around the world. The breakfast buffet features various entrees, fruit, and pastries.

The **Pool Snack Bar** offers ice cream, fruit, and other snack food. Hot dogs, burgers, and other snack fare is also available at **Rum Largo Broiler**.

Watering Holes

John T's is a comfortable lobby lounge with nightly entertainment. The **Rum Largo Bar** serves tropical drinks and appetizers in a green-house.

Shopping

Hilton Disney Gifts and Sundries sells character merchandise and necessities. **Hilton Ladies'** and **Hilton Men's Resort Wear** shops sell vacation clothes and jewelry.

Recreation

There is a gameroom located near the Youth Hotel. A health club here features sauna, whirlpool, and exercise equipment. There are two swimming pools here. Tennis players can use the two courts here.

HOTEL ROYAL PLAZA

Address: 1905 Hotel Plaza Boulevard (828-2828 or 800/248-7890). *Rates:* $140 to $190, suites $370 to $750. *At a Glance:* A hotel complex consisted of a 17-story tower and two-story garden wings. *Ratings:* Room Comfort 8; Amenities 7; Eateries 7; Shopping 4; Convenience 7; Decor 6.

This hotel, which just underwent major renovations, is one of the smaller properties in the plaza — only 396 units in its 17-story tower and two-story wings. The renovations modernized every guestroom and public area in the hotel. The atmosphere, casual, yet buzzing with energy, makes this hotel a prime choice among young adults and families with older children and teenagers.

Rooms

Each room is decorated harmoniously in contemporary hues, and each spacious room has a balcony or patio. Amenities of the rooms include safe deposit boxes, color cable televisions, and clock radios.

HINT: If you are counting on getting a lot of uninterrupted sleep, request a room on one of the higher floors or in one of the wings.

Suites

There are twenty, including two celebrity suites. The Barbara Mandrell and the Burt Reynolds each have memorabilia of their namesakes.

Dining Options

Memory Lane is a dinner theater where a four-course meal is served as a prelude to a musical revue. The **Plaza Diner** serves all-American food in a nostalgic Art Deco atmosphere from morning until night. Fare includes daily Blue Plate Specials, pizza, and burgers. Take-out is available.

Watering Holes

The **Giraffe** is the World's only disco, per˘se, and accordingly, is very popular. Visitors dance to Top 40 hits and live entertainment. Hot and cold hors d'oeuvres are served during Happy Hour from 4 PM to 9:30 PM, and the disco is open until 3 AM. The new **Intermissions** lounge features an odd Happy Hour: from midnight until 2:30 AM.

Services

There is a beauty salon located here, as well as a barber shop. There is a one-day film development service on the premises. Video cameras can be rented at **MagiCam**, a kiosk at the hotel.

Recreation

There is a gameroom here. There are men's and women's saunas here. Shuffleboard can be played at the hotel. A heated swimming pool and a hot tub are available here for use. Four lighted tennis courts are available for use.

HOWARD JOHNSON RESORT - WALT DISNEY WORLD VILLAGE

Address: 1805 Hotel Plaza Boulevard (828-8888 or 800/223-9930). FAX: 827-4623. *Rates:* $75 to $165. At a Glance: This is a typical HoJo's establishment and the most uninteresting of the Plaza hotels. *Ratings:* Room Comfort 6; Amenities 3; Eateries 5; Shopping 5; Convenience 7; Decor 6. *Check-in:* 4 PM.

This hotel, while one of the cheapest in the Village, is also the one with the least personality. The guestrooms here are located in a 14-story tower and a 6-story extension. HoJo's, being HoJo's, is a predictable establishment and lacks the originality that can be found in a multitude of other hotels across the area. Most of the public areas are located in the lobby, directly at the center of a 14-story atrium with no charisma whatsoever.

Rooms

The rooms here are decorated adequately (if unmemorably) in light pastel greens and pinks. The rooms in the main building open up onto an inner hallway that overlooks the lobby and each feature a balcony or patio. One advantage for families, rooms here are spacious.

Dining Options

Howard Johnson's. The name says it all. What can I really tell you about HoJo's that is not already common knowledge? American food, twenty-four hours a day. Fried clams? Stellar. Ice cream? This restaurant has a veritable wine cellar of ice creams. The rest of the menu is inexpensive, predictable, and utterly American. Seasonal clown show during dinner hours.

The **Sidewalk Cafe Cart** in the lobby serves continental breakfast and snack food.

Watering Holes

In the atrium lobby is the **Terrace Lounge**, a small spot serving various cocktails and soft drinks.

Shopping

The **Howard Johnson Disney Shop** sells sundries and character merchandise.

Recreation
The exercise room here has Nautilus equipment. There is a small gameroom here. There is a playground located here. Swimming can be done in two medium·pools and a wading pool.

TRAVELODGE HOTEL

Address: 2000 Hotel Plaza Boulevard, Lake Buena Vista, FL 32830 (828-2424 or 800/348-3765). FAX: 828-8933. *Rates:* Rooms, $85 to $95; suites, $179 to $279. *At a Glance:* Formerly the Viscount Hotel, this is a nice establishment that is relaxing, yet zestful. *Ratings:* Room Comfort 6; Amenities 5; Eateries 7; Shopping 4; Convenience 7; Decor 6.

This hotel is undoubtedly one of Travelodge's finest properties. Rooms here are spacious and nicely decorated, while the public areas are aesthetically pleasing and myriad in number.
Many of the restaurants, lounges, and services of the Travelodge are located just off the lobby, which is about as pleasant and relaxing as a lobby can be, with floral printed sofas and chairs, and a virtual overflow of tropical plants. The hotel's theme is that of a Barbados plantation manor house.

Rooms
The rooms here are quite spacious and geared towards families, with two queen-sized beds in each room. The walls, carpeting, and bedcovers are done in light pastels while the furniture is hued a light cream. Each room has a private balcony overlooking the Village, a stocked bar, in-room coffee, hair dryers, remote-control TV with the Disney Channel and pay movies, and morning newspaper.

Suites
Four suites are available.

Dining Options
The **Parakeet Cafe** is a coffeeshop in the lobby, serving homemade pizza, sandwiches, burgers, and salads. This is also the place for afternoon tea. The largest restaurant here is the **Traders Restaurant**, serving a la carte items plus buffets at breakfast and dinner. The menu is moderately priced and the atmosphere is casual. Diners can also eat on an outdoor terrace, weather permitting. Specialties include shrimp, chicken, steak, and ribs.

Watering Holes
Calypso's Pool Bar serves a selection of tropical drinks including

Caribbean coolers. The **Flamingo Cove Lounge** serves a variety of mixed drinks, beer, wine, and cocktails in a comfortable setting. The **Toppers Nite Club** offers entertainment plus a sweeping vista of the Village. From here, the nightly Pleasure Island fireworks and the IllumiNations show can be viewed.

Shopping

Travelodge Disney has a selection of character merchandise and sundries.

Recreation

There is a gameroom here. Children can enjoy the Travelodge's modular playground. There is a swimming pool here as well as a wading pool.

ACCOMMODATIONS OUTSIDE DISNEY WORLD

I've listed below the means for you to procure information on hotels outside of Disney World, as well as the communities in which they are located. I will also describe ways to get discounts and special treatment. Also, the best establishments in each locale will be noted.

LAKE BUENA VISTA

S.R. 535, Apopka-Vineland Road, intersects I-4 at this point, also serving as the entrance to the Disney Village area. Lake Buena Vista probably has had more visitors who don't know that they've been there than any town in the world, because WDW is also included in its confines. Along S.R. 535 are two major shopping/dining/entertainment areas, Vista Centre and Crossroads of Lake Buena Vista. The road also plays host to a multitude of family-style restaurants, souvenir shops, and the like.

The Top Choices
GRAND CYPRESS RESORT

A perfect 10. This is a 1,500-acre complex consisting of a high-rise Hyatt Regency hotel and a cluster of villas, along with 45 holes of golf, 12 tennis courts, and a multitude of fine restaurants. Quite impressive, this resort is unanimously considered the best in the area. Rates at the resort range from $180 to $2000. If you want info on the Grand Cypress, contact them at 239-4700 or 800/835-7377. For information on the Hyatt Regency specifically, call at 239-1234. Write them at 1 North Jacaranda for the Grand Cypress, 1 Grand Cypress Blvd., both Orlando, FL 32836.

MARRIOTT'S ORLANDO WORLD CENTER RESORT

Excellent, a solid 9. One of the largest high-rise resort hotels in Florida, the Marriott's grounds also includes two villa complexes. There are 18 holes of golf, twelve tennis courts, and several restaurants. AAA slapped the World Center with the Four Diamond Award, making it an excellent choice. It is slightly less glamorous than the Hyatt, but likewise, is less overwhelming. Rates start at $199 for rooms and villas alike. Information: call 239-4200 or write 1 World Center Drive, Orlando, FL 32821.

VISTANA RESORT

Nice facilities. Although pricey, the **Vistana** is arguably the nicest villa resort outside WDW. This is a full-fledged tennis resort, with fourteen courts, and is particularly convenient for larger families by virtue of the complimentary breakfast buffet held each morning and its ideal location. Rates run from $225 to $275 and more information can be had by calling the hotel at 239-3100 or 800/877-8787 or by writing at 8800 Vistana Center Drive, P.O. Box 22051, Lake Buena Vista, FL 32830.

Other Good Bets
EMBASSY SUITES RESORT LAKE BUENA VISTA

(8100 Lake Ave., Lake Buena Vista, FL 32830, tel. 239-1144), $125 to $235. Two-room suites with full kitchen, tennis, swimming, exercise room, sauna, free breakfast, game room, and free cocktails, right next to Walt Disney World.

RESIDENCE INN BY MARRIOTT, LAKE BUENA VISTA

(8800 Meadow Creek Dr., Lake Buena Vista, FL 32830, tel. 239-7700), $125 to $236. You can get a spacious, two-bedroom suite for a reasonable rate. Formerly the Hawthorn Suites.

HOLIDAY INN LAKE BUENA VISTA

(13351 S.R. 535, Lake Buena Vista, FL 32830, tel. 239-4500 or 800/ FON-MAXX), $75 to $139. Each room has a mini-kitchen with refrigerator and microwave, and the hotel has three restaurants and a special children's program.

DOUBLETREE CLUB HOTEL

(8688 Palm Parkway, Lake Buena Vista, FL 32830, tel. 239-8500 or 800/228-2846), $79. Spacious rooms, free made-to-order breakfast, and a common area for all hotel guests with a big screen TV and a library.

HOWARD JOHNSON PARK SQUARE INN & SUITES

(8501 Palm Parkway, Lake Buena Vista, FL 32830, tel. 239-6900 or 800/FLORIDA), $75 to $115. Complimentary transportation to Walt Disney World theme parks, roomy suites, restaurant, and lounge.

KISSIMMEE

Kissimmee means "Heaven's Place" in the language of the Caloosa Indians who lived here centuries ago. Back before the advent of automobiles, the small town was known informally as the "cow capital" of the state. Ranching was big business here, and Kissimmee attracted cowboy passers-by with bars that could serve them without their having to dismount. Many of the town's buildings date back to these days.

Today, what most travellers see of Kissimmee is a line of neon, budget chain motels, family-owned inns, t-shirt shops, family restaurants, and gas stations, a line known as U.S. 192. Many of the nicer establishments are set back away from the highway or are on side streets.

The Top Choices
ORANGE LAKE COUNTRY CLUB

Extensive recreation. Golf, tennis, and water sports are featured at this resort, which offers villa accommodations that can sleep eight people. This is an impressive resort 4 miles west of the Walt Disney World main gate. Rates go from $85 to $225 and information is available by calling 846-0000, 239-0000, or 800/877-6522. Or, write at 8505 W. Irlo Bronson Memorial Highway, Kissimmee, FL 34746-8799.

HYATT ORLANDO

Convenient, modern. **The Hyatt** offers 896 rooms and 30 suites in nine, two-story buildings, plus tennis, swimming, and fine dining options aplenty. The 56-acre resort is divided into four clusters of rooms, giving the place a more intimate feel. Call 396-1234 or write them at 6375 W. Irlo Bronson Memorial Highway, Kissimmee, FL 34746.

HOLIDAY INN MAIN GATE EAST

Terrific for families. This is one of the most family-oriented hotels in the entire Orlando metropolis. There is a buffet restaurant and a food court, plus tennis courts, pools, playgrounds, gamerooms, and special children's programs. Each room contains a TV with VCR (movies can be rented in the lobby) and a kitchenette with microwave, refrigerator, and dishwasher. Rooms go for $68 to $108. FYI: 396-4488 or 800/FON-KIDS, write 5678 W. Irlo Bronson Memorial Highway, Kissimmee, FL 34746.

Other Good Bets
HOLIDAY INN MAIN GATE
(7300 W. Irlo Bronson Memorial Highway, Kissimmee, FL 34746, tel. 396-7300 or 800/621-9378), $79 to $109. Three restaurants, children's program, three tennis courts, complimentary shuttle transportation to WDW.

QUALITY SUITES MAINGATE EAST
(5876 W. Irlo Bronson Memorial Highway, Kissimmee, FL 34746, tel. 396-8040 or 800/848-4148), $79 to $199. All-suite hotel located two miles from WDW. One and two bedroom/two bath suites with full kitchens sleep up to ten. Free continental breakfast and manager's reception daily.

RAMADA RESORT MAINGATE EAST AT THE PARKWAY
(2900 Parkway Blvd., Kissimmee, FL 34746, tel. 396-7000 or 800/634-4474), $69 to $105. Extensive resort grounds, newly renovated, 718 rooms, free-form pool w/waterfall and slide, heated pool, tiki bar, deli, playground.

LARSON'S LODGE KISSIMMEE
(2009 W. Vine St., Kissimmee, FL 34741, tel. 846-2713 or 800/624-5905), $35 to $69. Inexpensive rooms, pool, restaurant, lounge, all within easy reach of all attractions.

RESIDENCE INN BY MARRIOTT
(4768 W. Irlo Bronson Memorial Highway, Kissimmee, FL 34746, tel. 396-2056 or 800/468-3027) $135 to $236. Located on Lake Cecile, this consists of spacious penthouse and studio apartments.

WYNFIELD INN MAINGATE
(7491 W. Irlo Bronson Memorial Highway, Kissimmee, FL 34746, tel. 396-2121 or 800/468-8374), $54 to $74. Excellent value. Swimming pool, gameroom, coffee, tea, and fresh fruit served in lobby 24 hours a day.

INTERNATIONAL DRIVE AREA

International Drive runs from the Belz Factory Outlet World shopping center south past Kirkman Road, Sand Lake Drive, and the Beeline Expressway. There are a great many attractions right in the vicinity of the road. These are, from north to south: Asian Dynasty, Universal Studios Florida, Wet'n Wild, Fun'n Wheels, Mardi Gras, Mercado Mediterranean Village, King Henry's Feast, Caruso's Palace, the Orange County Convention / Civic Center, and Sea World. Past Sea World, International Drive becomes EPCOT Center Drive.

North of Sand Lake Drive, the hotels, fast food establishments, and shops are rather chintzy and overdeveloped, a non-stop line of neon and glitz. South of Sand Lake Drive, the road still has quite a bit of natural beauty, and the development is tasteful and appealing. If considering two otherwise-equal hostelries on opposite halves of the road, the southern (Sea World) end is generally the better choice. Besides, it's closer to Sea World and Walt Disney World.

The Top Choices
PEABODY ORLANDO

Astonishing. This is the only sister property to the Peabody in Memphis, Tennessee, and is equally impressive. For rumbling stomachs, visit the hotel's signature restaurant, the elegant Dux, the trattoria Capriccio's, or for light fare and 50's nostalgia, the B-Line Diner. Featured is the daily duck march, as the famous waterfowl waddle out of a private elevator, down a red carpet, and into a fountain, escorted by a tuxedoed duck master. Rates are $180 to $1,300. Call 352-4000 or 800/732-2639, or write 9801 International Drive, Orlando, FL 32819.

TWIN TOWERS HOTEL AND CONVENTION CENTER

Somewhat upscale. This hotel, right outside Universal Studios Florida, was recently given a $100 million dollar make-over and made more appealing to families. The hotel consists of two high-rise buildings and offers a restaurant, deli, lounge, Olympic-sized pool, a health club, and more. Rates are reasonable, $85 to $195, and you can contact the Twin Towers at 351-1000 or write to 5780 Major Blvd., Orlando, FL 32819.

SHERATON WORLD RESORT

Very appealing. This is an immaculate, ten-year-old establishment adjacent to Sea World. There are nineteen 2- and 3-story buildings, three tennis courts, miniature golf, three pools, Max's Deli, the Brasserie Restaurant and Lounge, and two Gazebo Bars. Casual, family-oriented, and away from the hustle and bustle, the hotel is located at the corner of Westwood Blvd. and International Drive. Rates are $70 to $135 double, but substantial discounts are available. Call 352-1100, 800/327-0363, or within Florida, 800/341-4292. The address is 10100 International Drive, Orlando, FL 32821-8095.

Other Good Bets
STOUFFER ORLANDO

(6677 Sea Harbor Drive, Orlando, FL 32821, tel. 351-5555 or 800-

HOTELS-1), $155 to $245. A luxurious, opulent resort hotel across from the entrance to Sea World.

SONESTA VILLA RESORT ORLANDO

(10000 Turkey Lake Road, Orlando, FL 32819, tel. 352-8051), $95 to $180. Spacious villas, lake, tennis, free supervised kids' program a huge plus.

DELTA ORLANDO RESORT

(5715 Major Blvd., Orlando, FL 32819, tel. 351-3340 or 800/877-1133), $120 to $150. Excellent children's program, nicely landscaped grounds, convenient to Universal Studios.

SUMMERFIELD SUITES

(8480 International Drive, Orlando, FL 32819, tel. 352-2400 or 800/833-4353), $139 to $219. Suites with living room, kitchen, and two separate bedrooms. Perfect location, directly across from Mercado, minutes from Sea World and Convention Center.

HOLIDAY INN INTERNATIONAL DRIVE RESORT

(6515 International Drive, Orlando, FL 32819, tel. 351-5727), $69 to $140. A class act, pool, two restaurants, lounge, and the Comedy Zone, one of International Drive's best nightclubs.

ORLANDO MARRIOTT — INTERNATIONAL DRIVE

(8001 Inter-national Drive, Orlando, FL 32819, tel. 351-2420), $99 to $139. A 48-acre resort, its 15 separate buildings give it an intimate feel.

RADISSON INN AND AQUATIC CENTER ON INTERNATIONAL DRIVE

(8444 International Drive, Orlando, FL 32819-9329, tel. 345-0505 or 800/333-3333), $69. Hotel across from Mercado with 70,000 square foot aquatic and fitness center.

Other Hotels

All told, the Orlando metropolis has well over 200 hotels, some of which are chain establishments. Many of the chains represented in Orlando have an 800 number.

These chains and their **1-800** toll-free numbers are listed in the box on the following page:

Best Western	528-1234	Hyatt	233-1234
Budgetel	428-3438	La Quinta	531-5900
Clarion	221-2222	Marriott	228-9290
Comfort Inn	221-2222	Quality Inn	221-2222
Courtyard	321-2211	Radisson	333-3333
Days Inn	325-2525	Ramada	228-2828
Delta	877-1133	Red Roof Inn	843-7663
Doubletree	528-0444	Residence Inn	331-3131
Embassy Suites	362-2779	Rodeway Inn	228-2000
Fairfield Inn	228-2800	Sheraton	325-3535
Guest Quarters	424-2900	Stouffer	468-3571
Hampton Inn	426-7866	Summerfield	223-5652
Hawthorn Suites	527-1133	Super 8	800-8000
Hilton	445-8667	Travelodge	255-3050
Holiday Inn	465-4329	Westin	248-7926
Howard Johnson	652-2000	Wynfield Inn	346-1551

Several groups manage more than one property, yet are local and thus not chains. But these orginizations include **Galaxy** (tel. 856-7190 or 800/634-3119, write 2345 Sand Lake Drive, Suite 200, Orlando, FL 32809), which operates four villa establishments; **Karena** (tel. 800/369-6935), which operates four excellent, moderately priced hotels; **Rushlake Hotels** (tel. 800-638-7829 or 396-7799), which operates three establishments ranging from economy inns to villa resorts, and **Tamar Inns** (tel. 800/999-6327), which runs four inexpensive motels, and **Sabrina**, (tel. 800/722-7462), which operates two **Travelodge Flags** hotels.

MORE DISCOUNTS

There are many ways to acquire discounted rates at hotels. Most of these can be found in Chapter 3, "Discounts, Deals & Bargains," but here they are in slightly different form for your convenience:

• **AAA**. Many chain and independent hotels offer discounts of up to 25% for members of the American Automobile Association. These include Sheraton, Days Inn, Hilton, and Best Western.

• **AARP**. Seniors and retired persons are given discounts at virtually every hotel.

• **Orlando MagiCard**. This thin plastic rectangle entitles you to discounts up to 40% at selected hotels across the area, in addition to slashed prices at restaurants, shops, and attractions. get your MagiCard by calling the Visitors Bureau (363-5800).

• **Newspapers**. The travel section of hometown newspapers may contain an announcement or two advertising low rates at area hotels.

• **Packages**. Each hotel may offer special package deals that provide a discount on lodging, dining, and entertainment.

• **Frequent Traveler Programs**. If you belong to a frequent travel club of a hotel or airline, you may be entitled to room upgrades, free nights, and other perks.

• **Entertainment Books**. These huge volumes, sold by many non-profit orginizations, contain sections of villa accommodations and a hotel directory offering 50% discounts at more than 35 hotels and motels across the area.

8. WHERE TO EAT

Regardless of whether you're the potbellied fortysomething man with the plaid socks and the Goofy hat or the hawkeyed twenty-year-old in the gleaming tennis whites, you must eat to survive. And despite all the time it would free up, the need for sustenance doesn't stop on vacation.

Disney, foreseeing such a possibility, placed thirty eateries in the Magic Kingdom, thirty in EPCOT Center, fourteen at the Studios, and about fifty million carts vending everything from foot-long hot dogs to ices to bread custard. The minor parks, the Marketplace, and the hotels of Walt Disney World are all loaded with restaurants too, and in this chapter, we will discuss every one of them.

Restaurants in Orlando, Kissimmee, and surrounding areas will be discussed in the chapter on dining in Orlando. Dinner theaters and attractions will be examined in Orlando Nightlife. Vacation plans that include meals "at selected WDW restaurants" include all theme park eateries except counter service restaurants and all hotel restaurants except Victoria and Albert's or those in the Swan, Dolphin, and Hotel Plaza. If a full-service restaurant is not included, it is noted in the description.

ABBREVIATIONS

B: Breakfast **L:** Lunch **D:** Dinner **S:** Snacks **Rsrvtns:** Reservations **Booking:** Ease of getting reservations. **Trad:** Traditional **FF:** Fast food **Amer:** Americanized. Reservations are listed, when accepted, as required or suggested. Dress is casual unless otherwise stated. Kids' menus are stated where available.

DINING IN THE MAGIC KINGDOM

Note that alcoholic beverages are not served in the Magic Kingdom.

In Main Street, U.S.A.
TONY'S TOWN SQUARE CAFE
Service: Table-service. *Meals:* B,L,D. *Location:* East side of Town Square.

Cuisine: Italian. *Prices:* Breakfast: $3.50 to $8.75. *Lunch:* $5.75 to $11.95. Dinner: $11.95 to $18.95. *Children:* Special menu, $2.75 to $5.95. *Rsrvtns:* Suggested, call 824-5993.

Everybody remembers that scene from Lady and the Tramp where the two dine on spaghetti and meatballs outside Tony's Restaurant. Well, Tony's has leapt from the silver screen to the Magic Kingdom. The restaurant is elegantly Victorian, with polished brass, many windows, beautiful woodwork, and a terazzo-floored patio overlooking Main Street.

The food is very good here, especially at breakfast. The specialties include at breakfast, egg dishes, waffles, Tony's Italian Toast, cereal, biscuits, and danishes. At lunch, the fare includes salads, sandwiches, and pasta. At dinner, served after 3:30, there's pizza, lasagna, shrimp scampi, tortellini, ravioli, grilled chicken, steak and lobster, and grilled seafood. The kids' menu has chicken sandwiches, peanut butter and jelly, pizza, and spaghetti with meatballs. After your meal, unwind and "wetta you whistle" with a cup of espresso or cappucino and an Italian pastry with spumoni.

Kosher items are available with 24 hours' notice, vegetarian and health foods are served. Healthier choices are available upon request. *HINT:* This is a great spot to watch the SpectroMagic and Surprise Celebration Parades. Arrive early and ask to be seated in the glassed-in area.

MAIN STREET BAKE SHOP
Service: Counter-service. *Meals:* B,S. *Location:* At the Plaza. *Prices:* $1 to $3. *Cuisine:* Baked goods.

This cozy little coffee house offers pastries, cakes, pies, and lots of cookies. The freshly-baked cinnamon rolls are a real treat. Beverages and fresh strawberries (when in season) are also served.

PLAZA ICE CREAM PARLOR
Service: Counter-service. *Meals:* S. *Cuisine:* Ice cream. *Prices:* $1 to $3. *Location:* At the Plaza.

Sealtest ice cream cones are served. For the health-conscious, there's fat-free ice cream.

THE PLAZA RESTAURANT
Service: Table-service. *Meals*: L,D. *Cuisine:* American. *Prices:* $5.75 to $8.50. *Location:* At the Plaza. *Children:* Yes, $2.75 to $2.95.

This Art Nouveau building houses the restaurant that offers the biggest ice cream sundaes in the World. Other frozen treats available are floats and shakes. The entrees here include sandwiches, big seven-ounce hamburgers, turkey burgers, pot pies, fruit and cheese platters, and quiche. The children's menu includes hamburgers, hot dogs, and peanut butter and jelly. Kosher items are available with 24 hours notice. Vegetarian and health food is also served.

REFRESHMENT CORNER

Service: Counter-service. *Meals:* L,D,S. *Cuisine:* Fast food. *Prices:* $1 to $5. *Location:* At the Plaza.

Diners here sit outside and listen to the ragtime pianist on the porch while they munch hot dogs (with or without cheese), brownies, soft drinks, and coffee.

THE CRYSTAL PALACE

Service: Buffeteria. *Meals:* B,L,D,S. *Cuisine:* American. *Prices:* Breakfast: $4.75 to $5.25. Lunch: $5.75 to $9.50. Dinner: $6.50 to $13.50. *Location:* By the Adventureland Bridge. *Children:* Special menu, $3.25 to $5.50.

This restaurant is a beautiful landmark, its Victorian architecture imitating similar structures that once stood in New York and San Francisco's Golden Gate Park. The restaurant is particularly brilliant after dark, when rows of white lights outline the profile of the restaurant. Inside, the tropical atrium helps to create a harmonious transition betweeen Main Street U.S.A. and Adventureland.

The food is good, and the breakfasts are the Kingdom's best. There's scrambled eggs, biscuits, sausage, hot cakes, French toast, bacon, ham, Danish, and cereal. For lunch and dinner, the fare includes prime rib, spit-roasted chicken, baked fresh fish, pasta dishes, salads, and sandwiches. Dixieland jazz entertainment is offered, and there are smoking and non-smoking sections.

MAIN STREET WAGONS

Service: Counter-service. *Meals:* B,L,D,S. *Cuisine:* Fast food. *Prices:* $1 to $5. *Location:* Center Street, off the east side of Main St.

These wagons, located outside Disney & Co. on Center Street (on the east side of Main Street), vend a variety of items, including foot-long hot dogs, chocolate-covered bananas, baked goods, bakery items, fresh fruit, orange and apple juice, fruit punch, and assorted bottled waters.

ORVILLE REDENBACHER GOURMET POPPING CORN
Carts filled with tasty popcorn roam the entire park.

SEALTEST ICE CREAM WAGONS
Ice cream wagons sell some or all of the following: Disney Bars (vanilla ice cream dipped in dark chocolate), Mousketeer Bars (vanilla ice cream with chocolate Mickey ears), slush bars, Cookies 'n Cream sandwiches, sugar-free ice cream bars, and no-fat strawberry yogurt sandwiches. The carts are found throughout the park.

In Adventureland
ADVENTURELAND VERANDA
Service: Counter-service. *Meals:* L,D. *Cuisine:* Oriental FF. *Prices:* $3.35 to $5.20 *Location:* At the entrance to Adventureland. *Children:* Special menu, $2.90 to $2.95.

This is my choice as the **worst** restaurant in Walt Disney World. The lines move slower than at other eateries, the hamburgers are frightening, and the teriyaki steak sandwiches are mediocre at best. Other menu items include marinated pork and noodles, Polynesian chicken sandwiches, and fruit salad. The children's menu includes fried chicken and hot dogs. If you're in the mood for Oriental food, take the monorail to the Polynesian Resort. The only redeeming feature of this restaurant is the section of outdoor tables with a view of Cinderella Castle.

ALOHA ISLE
Service: Counter-service. *Meals:* S. *Cuisine:* Ice cream, fruit. *Prices:* $1 to $3. *Location:* Next to Adventureland Veranda.

This counter offers pineapple spears, juice, and Dole Whip, a soft serve combining vanilla and pineapple ice cream.

SUNSHINE TREE TERRACE
Service: Counter-service. *Meals:* S. *Cuisine:* Ice cream. *Prices:* $1 to $3. *Location:* Next to Tropical Serenade.

The draws here are citrus specialties including a citrus swirl, frozen orange juice concentrate and vanilla frozen yogurt, orange slush, frozen yogurt, and yogurt shakes.

EL PIRATA Y EL PERICO
Service: Counter-service. *Meals:* L,D,S. *Cuisine:* Tex-Mex, FF. *Prices:* $1 to $5. *Location:* Across from Pirates of the Caribbean.

A very good fast food joint offering Disney Handwiches (sort of a bread cone filled with various ingredients, needs only one hand to be eaten), tacos, taco salads, nachos, and hot dogs with toppings like chili and cheese.

THE OASIS

Service: Counter-service. *Meals:* S. *Cuisine:* Snack fare. *Prices:* $1 to $3. *Location:* By the Jungle Cruise.

Snacks and soft drinks are sold from this kiosk outside the Jungle Cruise and Swiss Family Treehouse.

EGG ROLL WAGON

Service: Counter-service. *Meals:* L,D,S. *Cuisine:* Oriental FF. *Prices:* $2 to $4. *Location:* Outside the Adventureland Veranda.

Pork-and-shrimp, pizza, and hot dog egg rolls are sold off this wagon.

In Frontierland
DIAMOND HORSESHOE JAMBOREE

Service: Table-service. *Meals:* L,S. *Cuisine:* Fast food.*Prices:* $1 to $5. *Location:* Next to the Liberty Tree Tavern. *Rsrvtns:* Necessary, make them outside Disneyana Collectibles on Main Street.

This Old West Vaudeville hall hosts a show five times a day. The food is secondary to the entertainment, in the form of a singing and dancing troupe of actors. You don't have to eat anything to view the show, but if hunger strikes, you can get cold sandwiches, potato and corn chips, freshly baked pies, soft drinks, and fruit punch.

MILE LONG BAR AND PECOS BILL CAFE

Service: Counter-service. *Meals:* L,D,S. *Cuisine:* Tex-Mex, FF. *Prices:* $3 to $5. *Location:* Next to Splash Mountain.

These two establishments, side by side, have identical menus. The only difference is the atmosphere: rustic Old West at the Cafe, with a stick-and-twig ceiling, saloon-like at the Mile Long Bar. The Bar has stuffed animal heads on the walls that turn and wink at one another. You guessed it, Audio-Animatronics. There is outdoor seating at the Cafe. The menu at both places includes tacos, nachos, hot dogs, cheeseburgers, and barbecue chicken sandwiches. Lines tend to move much faster at the Mile Long Bar.

AUNT POLLY'S LANDING
Service: Counter-service. *Meals:* L,,S. *Cuisine:* American. *Prices:* $1 to $3.10 *Location:* Tom Sawyer Island.

This is an ideal place for adults to sit and rest while the kids burn energy on the rest of Tom Sawyer Island. The fare is limited to sandwiches served with an apple and a cookie, pies, iced tea, lemonade, and soft drinks.

FRONTIERLAND WAGON
Service: Counter-service. *Meals:* S. *Cuisine:* Fast food. *Prices:* $1 to $3. *Location:* Outside Frontierland Shootin' Arcade.

Churros, Mexican pastries deep-fried and rolled in cinnamon and sugar, are served with pretzels and soft drinks.

WESTWARD HO
Service: Counter-service. *Meals:* S. *Cuisine:* Snacks. *Prices:* $1 to $3. *Location:* At riverfront.

Snacks, frozen yogurt, and soft drinks are served here.

TURKEY LEG WAGON
Service: Counter-service. *Meals:* L,D,S. *Cuisine:* Fast food. *Prices:* $1 to $3. *Location:* At riverfront.
This cart offers beverages and big, filling, juicy smoked turkey legs that are great bets for no-frills, no-fuss meals or snacks. Chicken noodle soup is also available.

In Liberty Square
LIBERTY TREE TAVERN
Service: Table-service. *Meals:* L,D. *Cuisine:* American. *Location:* Next to the Diamond Horseshoe Jamboree. *Prices:* Lunch: $5.95 to $14.95. Dinner: $15.75 to$17.95. *Children:* Special menu, $2.95 to $4.25. *Rsrvtns:* Suggested, make them at the door.

One of the classiest places in the Magic Kingdom, this quaint colonial inn looks like something out of a history book. The atmosphere includes wooden Venitian blinds, oaken floors, and two-tiered chandeliers. It's the kind of place where you can picture secret meetings about the Boston Tea Party taking place.
The food is colonial as well, and quite palatable. There are oysters and New England clam chowder, for starters. Lunch entrees include sand-

wiches, seafood, hamburgers, and prime rib. For dinner, you can have pasta, chicken, lobster, prime rib, and filet mignon. The best of the desserts are red velvet cake and cream cheese mousse. Chicken, cheeseburgers, hot dogs, and ham and cheese sandwiches are offered for kids. Kosher cuisine is available with 24 hours' notice, and vegetarian and health foods are served. Smoking and non-smoking sections are available.

SLEEPY HOLLOW

Service: Counter-service. *Meals:* L,D,S. *Cuisine:* American. *Prices:* $1 to $5. *Location:* By the Plaza.

Here, by the water, you can fill your stomach with hot dogs, Disney Handwiches, and hot and cold beverages. Great chocolate chip cookies and brownies round out the menu. *HINT:* You can watch the SpectroMagic and Surprise Celebration parades from the brick patio outside Sleepy Hollow.

COLUMBIA HARBOUR HOUSE

Service: Counter-service. *Meals:* L,D,S. *Cuisine:* American. *Prices:* $3.55 to $4.95. *Location:* By the Haunted Mansion. *Children:* Special menu, $3.20 to $3.35.

The seating sections of the restaurant offer the atmosphere of a New England dining room and a sailing ship, depending on where you sit. The menu includes clam chowder, a stellar Monte Cristo sandwich (deep-fried and loaded with turkey, ham, and cheese), a fruit plate, fried shrimp and chicken strips (together or separately), salad, and sandwiches. Kids can eat fried chicken or a hot dog. This restaurant's always a good bet.

LIBERTY SQUARE WAGON

Service: Counter-service. *Meals:* S. *Cuisine:* Fast food. *Prices:* $1 to $3. *Location:* By the Hall of Presidents.

Freshly baked potatoes with a variety of toppings, plus beverages.

In Fantasyland

The food here is mediocre and is perpetually crowded. Eat elsewhere.

TROUBADOUR TAVERN

Service: Counter-service. *Meals:* S. *Cuisine:* Snack fare. *Prices:* $1 to $3. *Location:* By Peter Pan's Flight.

Soft drinks and chips are sold here.

PINOCCHIO VILLAGE HAUS

Service: Counter-service. *Meals:* L,D,S. *Cuisine:* Fast food. *Prices:* $3.55 to $4.25. *Location:* Next to It's a Small World.

Overlooking the loading area of It's a Small World, this restaurant serves up hot dogs, burgers, chicken, club sandwiches, and pasta salad. The restaurant is decorated with cuckoo clocks, brick ovens, and murals depicting characters from Carlo Collodi's classic tale of a puppet who comes to life and yearns to become a real boy.

TOURNAMENT TENT

Service: Counter-service. *Meals:* S. *Cuisine:* Snacks. *Prices:* $1 to $3. *Location:* Next to Fantasy Faire.

Soft drinks, milkshakes, and snacks are on the menu at this establishment. Open seasonally.

ENCHANTED GROVE

Service: Counter-service. *Meals:* S. *Cuisine:* Ice cream. *Prices:* $1 to $3. *Location:* By the Mad Tea Party.

Citrus drinks and soft serve are offered here.

KING STEFAN'S BANQUET HALL

Service: Table-service. *Meals:* L,D. *Cuisine:* American. *Location:* Cinderella Castle. *Prices:* Lunch: $7.25 to $11.25. Dinner: $17.50 to $20.75. *Children:* Special menu, $3.75 to $4.25 at lunch, $4.45 to $6.95 at dinner. *Rsrvtns:* Required, can be made at the door.

Suits of armor carrying swords keep watch and waiters and waitresses in 13th century attire serve you. For many children, the chance to eat inside Cinderella Castle is the highlight of an entire vacation. The excitement trebles when the blonde princess herself sweeps in, dressed to the nines. She poses for pictures and greets children, many of whom are tempted to salaam wildly on the ground while chanting "We're not worthy! We're not worthy!" While Cinderella converses with your awestruck children, try not to wonder what she's doing in a restaurant named after Sleeping Beauty's father.

The fare at the Magic Kingdom's most pricey restaurant is a tad disappointing. At lunch, there's prime rib sandwiches, fish sandwiches, chicken, club sandwiches, and for children, cheeseburgers, fish nuggets, or chicken pot pies. At dinner, house specialties include beef, fresh fish, and a fried chicken breast with fettucine, ham, spinach, and cheese. At dinner, kids can eat prime rib, fish nuggets, or a chicken pot pie.

GURGI'S MUNCHIES AND CRUNCHIES

Service: Counter-service. *Meals:* L,D. *Cuisine:* Fast food. *Prices:* $3 to $5. *Location:* Across from 20,000 Leagues Under the Sea.

This is the only place where kids can get a Disney Afternoon box meal, with grilled cheese or chicken nuggets, cookies, and a prize. Selections for grown-ups include hot dogs, hamburgers, sandwiches, chips, and beverages.

THE ROUND TABLE

Service: Counter-service. *Meals:* S. *Cuisine:* Ice cream. *Prices:* $1 to $3. *Location:* Next to Mr. Toad's Wild Ride.

Great in the heat of a summer afternoon, you can get Sealtest ice cream cones, hot fudge sundaes, and root beer floats here.

FANTASYLAND PRETZEL WAGON

Service: Counter-service. *Meals:* S. *Cuisine:* Snacks. *Prices:* $1 to $3. *Location:* By Pinocchio Village Haus.

Soft pretzels and beverages are served.

In Mickey's Starland
SNACK CART

Ice cream, cupcakes, sodas, iced tea, and juices are sold from this cart that travels the land.

In Tomorrowland
TOMORROWLAND TERRACE

Service: Counter-service. *Meals:* L,D,S. *Cuisine:* Fast food. *Prices:* $3.25 to $5.25. *Location:* By the Grand Prix Raceway. *Children:* Special menu, $1.

The offerings at this restaurant include hamburgers, hot dogs, minestrone and chicken noodle soups, barbecued pork loin sandwiches, marinated grilled chicken sandwiches, and fruit salad. This restaurant has little of a wait due to its immense size.

THE LUNCHING PAD

Service: Counter-service. *Meals:* S. *Cuisine:* Health food. *Prices:* $1 to $5. *Location:* By the Space Port.

Natural and healthy foods are on tap here, mainly frozen yogurt sundaes, fresh fruit, snacks, and juices.

THE SPACE BAR
Service: Counter-service. *Meals:* L,D,S. *Cuisine:* Fast food. *Prices:* $1 to $5. *Location:* Under StarJets.

Chips, Disney Handwiches (bread cones with filling), desserts, and soft drinks are offered here, right under the StarJets and WEDway Peoplemover attractions.

THE PLAZA PAVILION
Service: Counter-service. *Meals:* L,D,S *Cuisine:* Italian FF. *Prices:* $2.75 to $4.95. *Location:* Next to the Plaza.

Halfway decent Italian fast food is served up in this spot adjacent to the Hub Waterways. There's a surprisingly good deep dish pizza by the slice, skinless chicken parmesan sandwiches, meatball subs, Italian hoagies, and pasta salad. Ice cream cups and beverages are on hand to finish up the meal.

DINING IN EPCOT CENTER

Reservations are accepted at fourteen restaurants in EPCOT Center, and here's how to get them. Disney Resort guests can reserve up to 2 days in advance by calling 828-4000. Guests staying in the Hotel Plaza can dial 824-8800. If you're staying off site or just didn't get reservations, go to the WorldKey terminals in Earth Station and just take it from there. For information on the WorldKey system, check out the beginning of the EPCOT Center chapter.

In Future World
STARGATE RESTAURANT
Service: Counter-service. *Meals:* B,L,D,S. *Cuisine:* Fast food. *Prices:* $2.70 to $4.95. *Location:* CommuniCore East.

At breakfast, this pleasant eatery dishes up cereal, Danish, fruit cups, blueberry muffins, cheese omelets with Canadian bacon or ham on an English muffin, sausage omelets, and the Stellar Scramble, an omelet loaded with ham, cheese, onions, and green peppers. The Disney characters are on hand from 9 to 10 AM daily.

Lunch and dinner will see the restaurant serving pizza, salad, cheeseburgers, and chicken breast sandwiches. The chicken and burgers here are good and come with fries. A topping bar lets diners put lettuce, tomatoes, onions, pickles, bacon bits, barbecue sauce, and hot cheese on their sandwiches, a definite plus. Guests can choose to eat indoors or on a canopied patio outside.

BEVERAGE BASE
Service: Counter-service. *Meals:* S. *Cuisine:* Snacks. *Prices:* $1 to $3. *Location:* CommuniCore East.

Beverages, frozen yogurt, cones, and sundaes are offered here.

SUNRISE TERRACE RESTAURANT
Service: Counter-service. *Meals:* L,D,S. *Cuisine:* Italian FF. *Prices:* $3.90 to $4.65. *Location:* CommuniCore West. *Children:* Special menu, $2.45 to $3.65.

The menu here includes fried flounder, fried shrimp, fried chicken strips, subs in three varieties (roast beef, turkey and provolone, ham and provolone), pizza, pasta, lasagna, and antipasto.

PURE & SIMPLE
Service: Counter-service. *Meals:* B,L,D,S. *Cuisine:* Health food. *Prices:* $3.25 to $5.50. *Location:* Wonders of Life.

The kitchen in the Wonders of Life pavilion features fresh ingredients and no frying. Menu items include Beta-Carotene Salad (spinach, carrots, greens, tomatoes, and broccoli, topped with a cantaloupe vinaigrette,) hot-and-sour soup, the Sub-Fat-Sub (loaded with tuna bologna, lettuce, tomato, and cheese on a sub roll, 95% fat free), venison chili, turkey and vegetable hot dogs, low fat hot dogs, and bran waffles with fruit toppings. Beverages sold include fruit juices, mineral water, frozen non-fat yogurt, yogurt shakes, and smoothies.

ODYSSEY RESTAURANT
Service: Counter-service. *Meals:* L,D,S. *Cuisine:* Fast food. *Prices:* $4.05 to $4.95. *Location:* By the World of Motion and Mexico. *Children:* Special menu, $3.35.

The menu at this, the largest eatery in Future World, includes hot dogs, hamburgers, and chicken, tuna, and ambrosia salad platters. There is a topping bar for burgers and sandwiches. The fresh pies baked here are a delicious end to any meal. The Disney characters can be found here four times a day, check the entertainment schedule for details.

THE LAND GRILLE ROOM

Service: Table-service. *Meals:* B,L,D. *Cuisine:* American. *Location:* Upper level, The Land Pavilion. *Prices:* Breakfast: $4.25 to $9.95. Lunch: $5.75 to $17.75. Dinner: $11.50 to $24.50. *Children:* Special menu, $2.95 to $5.50. *Rsrvtns:* Suggested.

The Land Grille Room is a revolving restaurant that overlooks the Listen to the Land attraction below. The fare is excellent regional American. The specialties are Navajo lasagna (tortillas, goat's cheese, spiced beef, and guacamole), Key West chicken, prime rib, Oriental chicken breast, beef tenderloin, barbecue pork sandwiches, pizza, club sandwiches, steak sandwiches, Maine lobster, swordfish, stir-fry, lasagna, and charbroiled steaks.

Much of the produce used in the restaurant's dishes come from the expiremental greenhouse below. These ingredients contain up to 30% less fat content then their farm-grown counterparts. The traditional sit-down breakfasts here are among EPCOT's best. This restaurant is often overlooked for dinner, so try it then.

THE FARMER'S MARKET

Service: Food Court. *Meals:* B,L,D,S. *Cuisine:* American. *Prices:* $3.75 to $6.25. *Location:* On the lower level of The Land pavilion.

This pleasant food court would be a good bet for families who can never agree on where to eat. The only problem is during peak seasons, the seating in the center of the pavilion fills up.

At the **Bakery**, the breakfast menu includes Danish, bagels, cinnamon rolls, and muffins. After breakfast, the fare changes to apple pies, cheesecake, chocolate cake, brownies, cookies, date-nut bread, and cheese bread. At the **Beverage House**, there are vanilla, chocolate, and strawberry shakes, chocolate milk, hot chocolate, coffee, tea, sodas, buttermilk, vegetable juice, peach nectar, and other fruit juices. The **Barbecue Store** sells barbecued beef, pork, and chicken breast sandwiches, plus spit-roasted chicken, beans, and cornbread.

The **Cheese Shop** features quiches, fruit and cheese platters, baked macaroni and cheese, fettucine with chicken, vegetable lasagna, and of course, cheese. The **Ice Cream Stand** has cups, cones, and shakes. At **Picnic Fare**, one can nibble on cheeses, sausages, and fresh fruit. At the **Potato Store**, steaming baked potatoes are served up with bacon and cheddar, beef in wine, or sour cream and chive sauces. The **Sandwich Stand** has beef and cheese, seafood, club, grilled chicken breast, and meatball sandwiches, along with Disney Handwiches. From the **Soup and Salad Stand**, you can have fruit salad, chicken salad, pasta salad, and New

England clam chowder.

Beer and wine are sold as well, but they are not permitted outside the building. Soda and French fries are sold at all counters as well.

CORAL REEF RESTAURANT

Service: Table-service. *Meals:* L,D. *Cuisine:* Seafood. *Location:* The Living Seas. *Prices:* Lunch: $8.95 to $22.95. Dinner: $15.25 to $29.95 *Children:* Special menu, $3 to $5. *Rsrvtns:* Suggested.

Here, you sit on terraces overlooking the 5.7 million gallon aquariums of the Living Seas while you dine on seafood dishes. The view is impressive and the food is excellent (executive chef Keith Keogh won the Florida Seafood Chef of the Year award twice), but it is mostly overpriced. The menu includes citrus and red snapper, lobster, Manhattan clam chowder, clams, oysters, shrimp, scallops, seafood fettucine, lobster Bisque, tuna, snapper, and grilled swordfish steak. For "landlubbers", there's New York strip steak and broiled chicken breast. The children's menu includes fried fish, fettucine, fried chicken strips, and grilled hot dogs. The atmosphere is surprisingly ambient, with each table individually lighted by ceiling-mounted spotlights. The decor is oceanic tones and is accented by a six-million-gallon fish tank.

The bottom line on the Coral Reef is this: it's an excellent restaurant, but really overpriced. First of all, you can get the same view for free at the Living Seas ride upstairs. Second, there are other seafood joints in Orlando which are much cheaper and easier to get into, and finally, there are seafood restaurants where you live. Go for something more unusual.

In World Showcase
SAN ANGEL INN RESTAURANTE

Service: Table-service. *Meals:* L,D. *Cuisine:* Trad Mexican. *Location:* Mexico pavilion. *Prices:* Lunch: $7.25 to $13.75. Dinner: $10.25 to $20.95. *Children:* Special menu, $3.75 to $4.95. *Rsrvtns:* Suggested.

This is undeniably the most romantic restaurant in EPCOT Center, as the dining area overlooks the tranquil Rio del Tiempo where the boats from the attraction sail past a volcano, through a jungle, and onwards. The atmosphere is that of a tranquil Mexican village, with the shops of the plaza making a pleasant backdrop.

As far as the food is concerned, the quality, variety, originality, and value of the menu all score a solid A+. For those of you (much like myself) weaned on tacos, burritos, and nachos from Garcia's and Taco Bell, the menu almost comes as a shock. Those items are offered here alongside exotic regional specialties made of pork, sausage, lobster, chicken, red snapper, beef tenderloins, chicken, and shrimp. Up on your college prep Spanish? The names of the specific offerings include carne asada tempiquena, huachinango a la Veracruzana (red snapper poached with wine, onions, tomatoes, and peppers), mole poblano (it's not mole like the rodent, it's mole like the chocolate sauce served over chicken), queso fundido (corn or flour tortillas with cheese and sausage with guacamole), and pollo en pipian (chicken strips served with a pumpkin seed sauce).

For dessert, there's flan, rice pudding, crepes or vanilla ice cream with caramel, each a delectable treat. The beverages served include lemon water, soft drinks, margaritas, and Mexican beer (both Tecata and Dos Equis brands). If you only have one restaurant to experience in EPCOT Center, put this towards the top of your list.

CANTINA DE SAN ANGEL

Service: Counter-service. *Meals:* L,D,S. *Cuisine:* Tex-Mex FF. *Prices:* $3.35 to $4.50. *Location:* On the Promenade across from the Mexico pavilion.

This stand, whose tables offer the single best vantage for IllumiNations and Surprise in the Skies, offers nachos, tacos, burritos, chicken tostadas, ensalada, and churros, a sweet, deep-fried, cinnamon-rolled pastry. Dos Equis and Tecate beers are served with margaritas and soft drinks. *HINT:* To snag a table here for IllumiNations, arrive 45 minutes in advance.

RESTAURANT AKERSHUS

Service: Buffet. *Meals:* L,D. *Cuisine:* Trad. Norwegian koldtbord. *Location:* Norway pavilion. *Prices:* Lunch: $9.95; Dinner: $14.95. *Children:* Buffet, $4.25 at lunch, $6.50 at dinner. *Rsrvtns:* Suggested.

In 1988, when Norway opened up the only buffet restaurant in EPCOT Center, people were squeamish about eating Norwegian food. Anyone who dared could just walk in. But the restaurant was lauded constantly and more people began eating here. Now, reservations are suggested and may soon be required.

The restaurant sits inside the castle Akershus, whose namesake sits on the harbor in Oslo. It's an imressive building and surprisingly intimate inside. The hot and cold buffet (known as koldtbord) includes hearty, traditional fare like salmon, herring, lamb, pork, beef, venison, Norwegian cheeses, vegetables, hard-boiled eggs, salads, breads, meatballs, casseroles, and other seafoods. Additional dishes are offered at the dinner buffet. Norwegian desserts, wines, spirits, Ringnes beer are offered a la carte alongside soft drinks. The desserts include ring cake; veiled maidens, a delectable concoction of tart apples, cream, and bread crumbs; and when in season, cloudberries, delicate fruits native to the Norwegian Mountains. Hostesses are available to answer questions about the menu.

KRINGLA BAKERI OG KAFE

Service: Counter-service. *Meals:* B,L,D,S. *Cuisine:* Norwegian FF. *Prices:* $1.75 to $4.95. *Location:* Norway pavilion.

This pleasant, open-air courtyard features a stand selling desserts called kringles, which are pretzels with raisins, almonds, and a sweet icing; sugar-dusted, jam-topped, heart-shaped waffles called vaflers; kranesake, almond-pastries; school bread filled with custard and coated with icing and coconut. Open-faced sandwiches called smorbords are also sold here. You can get salmon, ham, beef, or turkey on your sandwich and wash it down with a cold Ringnes beer.

LOTUS BLOSSOM CAFE

Service: Counter-service. *Meals:* L,D,S. *Cuisine:* Amer Chinese FF. *Prices:* $2.80 to $5.25. *Location:* China pavilion.

This counter-service, 200-seat eatery offers guests a chance to munch egg rolls, stir-fried beef or chicken, sweet and sour chicken, pork fried rice, and soup. Red bean ice cream, Chinese beer, and soft drinks are served as well.

NINE DRAGONS RESTAURANT

Service: Table-service. *Meals:* L,D. *Cuisine:* Amer Chinese. *Location:* China pavilion. *Prices:* Lunch: $7.95 to $13.50. Dinner: $9.50 to $20.75. *Children:* Special menu, $4.95 to $5.95. *Rsrvtns:* Suggested.

This is one of the newer EPCOT restaurants but unfortunately, it chooses to give diners Americanized versions of their dishes instead of an authentic representation like those found in Morocco and Norway. Other Chinese restaurants in Orlando are less expensive. However, the service is attentive, and if you want to eat overpriced Chinese food, this is as good a place as any. The chefs in charge here come from the world-famous Beijing Hotel, and the cuisine is regional: Szechuan, Cantonese, Kiangche, and Mandarin.

The entrees include Canton beef, boneless braised duck, shrimp ambrosia, sweet and sour pork, lemon chicken, Kang Bao chicken, and beef and jade tree. Stir-fried meats, veggies, spare ribs, dumplings, soups, and pickled cabbage are also available. Chinese teas, beers, and wine are served. Finish a meal with red bean ice cream, pastries, or toffee apples.

BIERGARTEN

Service: Table-service. *Meals:* L,D. *Cuisine:* Trad. German. *Location:* Germany pavilion. *Prices:* Lunch: $7.25 to $9.75. Dinner: $10.75 to $19.75. *Children:* Special menu, $3.25 to $3.95. *Rsrvtns:* Suggested.

This is considered by many to be EPCOT's premier dining experience, between the tasty and authentic German specialties dished up, the relatively low price, and the Oktoberfest entertainment. The restaurant, located at the rear of the St. Georgsplatz, features a half-hour long dinner show with yodelers, dancers, singers, and an oompah band, all clad in lederhosen. The show is performed throughout the evening and diners are encouraged to join in the festivities. Incidentally, the atmosphere of the restaurant recreates Rothenberg's town square circa the 16th century. The menu includes veal shank, sauerbraten, smoked pork loin with red cabbage, grilled bratwurst, spitted chicken, bierwurst, bauernwurst, jaegerwurst, potato salad, winekraut, breaded veal, seafood stew, roast beef loin, and for dessert, German chocolate cake. The children's menu includes roast chicken, meatballs with noodles, and potato pancakes.

Germany is possibly best known for its beer. Here, you can get yourself a 33-ounce stein of Beck's, or if you're in a wining mood, glasses of H. Schmitt Sîhne wines. The dining is communal (eight to a table) and friendly, the atmosphere is rowdy and festive, making this an excellent choice for anyone, especially families and singles.

SOMMERFEST

Service: Counter-service. *Meals:* L,D,S. *Cuisine:* German FF. *Prices:* $1.35 to $3.25. *Location:* Germany pavilion.

This courtyard stand offers soft pretzels, bratwurst sandwiches apple strudel, Black Forest cake, soft drinks, Beck's beer, and H. Schmitt Sîhne wines.

L'ORIGINALE ALFREDO DI ROMA RISTORANTE

Service: Table-service. *Meals:* L,D. *Cuisine:* Italian. *Location:* Italy pavilion. *Prices:* Lunch: $7.95 to $18.95. Dinner: $11.50 to $19.75. *Children:* Special menu, $4.25 to $4.95. *Rsrvtns:* Required.

The most popular World Showcase restaurant, Alfredo's is generally considered one of its safest, if not best, bets. The atmosphere is as festive as the Biergarten, with strolling accordionists and waiters and waitresses who burst into Italian traditional, opera, and classical songs. The scenery is beautiful, decorated with murals that give the impression of real scenery instead of the two-dimensional flats on the walls.

The cuisine is traditional and lesser-known Italian, and excellent. The house specialty is terrific fettucine Alfredo, whose creator, Alfredo DiLelio, the establishment is named for (along with the original in Rome). The rest of the menu is more than 20 entrees deep, with seafood, veal, chicken, and pasta dishes, accented by sauces including house tomato, pesto, and carbonara. This is EPCOT Center's most popular ethnic eatery, and sometimes fails to live up to overinflated expectations (brought about by the booking difficulty). But it is still a worthwhile choice, as most families can find menu items they will enjoy (who doesn't like Italian?), the kids menu is extensive enough to satisfy picky eaters, including lasagna, fettucine, manicotti, and spaghetti with meatballs. Italian wines, beers, and spirits are available. For dessert, there's spumoni, gelati, tortoni, and ricotta cheesecake, served alongside steaming cappucino or espresso.

The only fault to be found with Alfredo's is this: the tables are packed in like sardines and the restaurant is almost always crowded, so dine early or late.

LIBERTY INN

Service: Counter-service. *Meals:* L,D,S. *Cuisine:* Fast food. *Prices:* $2.95 to $5.75. *Location:* American Adventure pavilion.

This is where families with children and others unwilling to try the ethnic cuisines elsewhere can eat good old American fast food. There's hot dogs, hamburgers, chicken breast sandwiches, fried chicken, salads, barbecue beef, roast chicken, baked macaroni and cheese with ham, French fries, and chili. There are also freshly baked cookies, apple pies, and dessert cups.

AMERICAN ADVENTURE WAGONS

Turn-of-the-century carts like those found on Main Street U.S.A. and the Studios are located on the promenade, vending fresh buttery popcorn, foot long hot dogs, and beverages.

TEPPANYAKI DINING ROOMS

Service: Table-service. *Meals:* L,D. *Cuisine:* Amer. Japanese. *Location:* Japan pavilion. *Prices:* Lunch: $13 to $22. Dinner: $17 to $27. *Rsrvtns:* Suggested.

Sadly, these five rooms offer not a chance to sample authentic cuisine like that in Germany, France, and Mexico, but instead, teppan table cooking like in a Benihana's. The chefs chop, toss, juggle, sizzle, and stir-fry chunks of steak, chicken, vegetables, and seafood on the tables. If you want teppan cuisine, your money would be better spent elsewhere. If you want to try authentic cuisine representing the nations, your time would be better spent elsewhere. The seating is communal and guests often take the opportunity to converse with chefs and each other.

TEMPURA KIKU

Service: Table-service. *Meals:* L,D. *Cuisine:* Amer. Japanese. *Prices:* $13 to $19. *Location:* Japan pavilion.

This corner of the Mitsukoshi dining complex serves up tempura, those tasty, battered-and-deep-fried chunks of beef, chicken, seafood, and vegetables. Sushi and sashimi appetizers are also available, along with Kirin beer, sake, plum wine, and Japanese spirits.

YAKITORI HOUSE

Service: Counter-service. *Meals:* L,D,S. *Cuisine:* Japanese FF. *Prices:* $2.50 to $4.95. *Location:* Japan pavilion. *Children:* Special menu, $2.95.

This stand in the quaint Japanese courtyard sells skewered chicken and beef, teriyaki and yakitori dishes (sandwiches or beef and chicken with rice), seafood salad, plus sweets and beverages. It's a good place to pick up a bite to eat in between meals or for a quick, no-fuss meal.

WAFFLE/ICE CART

A best bet for a snack. When it's hot, you can get four kinds of ice slush concoction called kaki-gori. When the mercury dips, the shop changes to sell hot waffles with red bean paste. Soft drinks are available at all times.

RESTAURANT MARRAKESH

Service: Table-service. *Meals:* L,D. *Cuisine:* Trad. Moroccan. *Location:* Morocco pavilion. *Prices:* Lunch: $7.95 to $12.95. Dinner: $9.50 to $18.50. *Children:* Yes, $3.95 to $4.75. *Rsrvtns:* Suggested.

This excellent restaurant provides an exotic taste of Morocca available in few other locations anywhere in the nation. The surroundings are foreign and zestful, as is the food. Entertainment is provided by beautiful belly dancers and a live three-piece Moroccan combo or piped-in music.

The food is served up in tasty, heaping portions and the menu includes cous cous, a filling dish of steamed semolina topped with vegetables, chicken, beef, or lamb, harira soup flavored with saffron, braised or roast lamb, chicken or shrimp brochette, shish kebab, baked grouper, and bastila, layers of filo dough filled with chicken, almonds, saffron, and cinnamon. Sampler platters are also available. The children's menu includes chicken and Kefta brochette (skewer-grilled minced beef).

Mint tea, Moroccan wine and spirits, and desserts are also available. Since the piquant Moroccan cuisine is virtually unknown to most people, this restaurant rarely fills up. So you can sometimes get in without a reservation. Also, Marrakesh is roomy, so kids won't get the claustrophobic feeling found in other World Showcase eateries.

CHEFS DE FRANCE

Service: Table-service. *Meals:* L,D. *Cuisine:* Trad. French. *Location:* France pavilion. *Prices:* Lunch: $11.50 to $13.75. Dinner: $13.95 to $19.95. *Children:* Special menu, $3.95 to $4.25. *Rsrvtns:* Required.

The master chefs here are a renowned trio: Roger Vergä, Paul Bocuse, and Gaston LeNìtre. Bocuse and Vergä each operate three star restaurants, Bocuse's in near Lyon, Vergä's on the Riviera, while LeNìtre operates six Paris bakeries and is generally acknowledged as one of the world's top pastry chefs. The three collaborated on the menu and often make visits to Chefs de France to make changes to it.

The atmosphere is Victorian-era continental, accented with wood paneling, brass light fixtures, etched glass, linen table cloths, and a dilligent staff dressed in formal wear. The dinner menu is traditional French, starting with the appetizers of foie gras, vichysoisse (chilled potato soup), Lyon-style onion soup, leek soup, salmon souffle with tarragon and white butter sauce, and escargot (snails in garlic butter and hazelnuts). The entrees include grouper in lobster sauce, roast duck with wine sauce and prunes, chicken fricasee, veal, beef tenderloin, seafood stew, beef stew, and the house specialties: roast red snapper wrapped in potato with red wine lobster sauce on a bed of braised cabbage, and beef in red burgundy wine with onions and mushrooms.

The menu is considerably lighter (both in fare and cost) at lunchtime, including cheeses, pates, succulent quiches, croissants stuffed with ham and cheese, seafood casserole, prawns, scallops, sautÇed fish, chicken breast, or strip steak, and braised beef.

Be sure to save room for some of the famous LeNotre pastries and a hot mug of cafe filtre, a strong, thick coffee similar to Italian espresso. One of the best bets for dessert is the chocolate cake layered with chocolate mousse. Beer, spirits, and wine from the modest cellar are offered as well. There is a children's menu offering chicken and spaghetti, fish sticks, and ground beef steak. If you intend to get a table at dinner time, it is imperative that you make reservations days in advance (if you're staying inside WDW) or as soon as the park opens. Note that this can be the most expensive restaurant in EPCOT Center.

BISTRO DE PARIS

Service: Table-service. *Meals:* D. Lunch seasonally. *Cuisine:* French provincial. *Location:* France pavilion, second floor. *Prices:* Lunch: $9.50 to $14.50. Dinner: $18.25 to $24.50. *Children:* Yes, $3.75 to $4.25. *Rsrvtns:* Required.

Originally designed to handle the overflow from Chefs de France, this restaurant, located upstairs from "Chefs", has come into its own. The menu (also created by Vergä, Bocuse, and LeNìtre) includes hearty provincial specialties like grilled beef tenderloin with mushrooms, glazed onions, and a green peppercorn sauce, Southern France seafood casserole in garlic sauce and croutons, chicken breast in puff pastry, steamed filet of grouper, braised beef, chicken crepes, grilled lamb, quail, salmon, swordfish, scallops, blue crabs, and sautÇed duck. The children's menu includes fish sticks, chicken breast casserole, or ground beef steak. There is an unassuming wine list, and beer and spirits are also served.

The only other EPCOT restaurant this romantic is the San Angel Inn in the Mexican pavilion. If you have children, you might want to get a babysitter or one of the kids' clubs to take charge of them for the evening you reserve a table, as it is not very suitable for kids. Note that guests sometimes book this restaurant by mistake, thinking that they were reserving a table at Chefs de France. They lose their reservation when they go to the wrong restaurant. Do that and you'll be told "au revoir". Just remember, the Chefs are downstairs, the bistro is on top.

AU PETIT CAFE

Service: Table-service. *Meals:* L,D,S. *Cuisine:* French. *Prices:* $6.95 to $13.75. *Location:* In front of the France pavilion. *Children:* Special menu, $3.75 to $4.75.

This restaurant represents a Parisian tradition, the sidewalk cafe. Snacks and light meals are served, and this restaurant is a delightful place to sit and relax. However, this restaurant is popular and since no reservations are accepted, long lines can and often do develop. The menu is pleasant, with tuna and vegetable salad, baked chicken breast, quiche, ham and cheese croissant, cheese platter, strip steak, sausage, prawns, Alaskan crab, and escargot. The children's menu includes ground beef steak, fish sticks, and a chicken-and-macaroni casserole.

ROSE & CROWN DINING ROOM

Service: Table-service. *Meals:* L,D,S. *Cuisine:* Amer. British. *Location:* On the promenade, across from the United Kingdom pavilion. *Prices:* Lunch: $6.50 to $9.50. Dinner: $8.50 to $18.75. *Children:* Special menu, $2.95 to $6.95. *Rsrvtns:* Suggested.

This promenade restaurant, along with the pub of the same name, is a pleasant place to dine. The view of World Showcase Lagoon is unsurpassed, and the food is consistently good. There's Scotch eggs (hardboiled, stuffed in sausage, chilled, and served with mustard), steak and kidney pie, chicken and leek pie, broiled fish, roast beef with gravy and mashed potatoes, fish and chips, a vegetable and cheese plate, prime rib, roast lamb, mixed grill (broiled pork loin, beef tenderloin, and veal kidney), and meat pies (try not to think about the story of Sweeney Todd as you eat). The children's menu includes meat pies, fish and chips, prime rib, and roast beef on an English muffin.

Afterwards, get on a sugar high with sherry trifle (made of pound cake, whipped cream, custard, strawberries, and sherry) and raspberry fool (raspberry puree and whipped cream. If you're in the mood for a cold one (even though Britons drink their beer at room temperature), you can get it here. You can linger over a mug of English Bass India Pale, Scottish Tennent's, or Irish Harp lager and Guiness Stout.

UNITED KINGDOM WAGONS

These two carts sell huge baked potatoes with cheese, tea, pastries, and soft drinks.

LE CELLIER

Service: Buffeteria. *Meals:* L,D,S. *Cuisine:* Canadian. *Location:* Canada pavilion. *Prices:* Lunch: $5.75 to $14.75. Dinner: $6.75 to $14.95. *Children:* Special menu, $3.25 to $3.50.

Specialties from Canada make up the menu at this stone-walled cafeteria, which actually does resemble the medieval wine cellars for which it is named. It's a good bet for a quick, hot meal, except when the lunch rush inundates the restaurant, when the restaurant loses speed. Menu items include Canadian cheddar cheese soup, sandwiches, cheese and fruit platters, sautÇed poached salmon, prime rib, chicken and meatball stew, huge slabs of delectable QuÇbec pork-and-potato pie called tourtiäre, cold meat and cheese platter, seafood stew over rice, and braised cabbage roll with minced pork. The children's menu includes chicken and meatball stew and fried chicken.

There is also Labatt's beer, Canadian wine, and soft drinks. The desserts include British trifle and maple syrup pie, great for inflicting a killer sugar rush on yourself. The dinner menu is close to that offered at lunch, but includes a few more items.

CANADA WAGON

Snacks including creamy bread custard and soft drinks are sold from this cart.

DINING AT DISNEY-MGM STUDIOS

To make reservations, show up at the door of the desired restaurant, starting at 9 AM. Or, if you're staying on-site, you can make reservations up to two days in advance by dialing 828-4000 (824-8800 from the seven Hotel Plaza establishments).

THE HOLLYWOOD BROWN DERBY

Service: Table-service. *Meals:* L,D. *Cuisine:* American. *Location:* At the end of Hollywood Boulevard. *Prices:* $6.95 to $14.75 for lunch, $12.95 to $21.50 for dinner. *Children:* Yes, $2.50 to $5.50. *Rsrvtns:* Suggested, make them at the door.

1930s Hollywood is represented here, as the original Vine Street establishment has been transplanted to Florida. The Studios' signature restaurant is one of Disney's best reproductions. There's the Wall of Fame, covered with caricatures faithfully remade from the originals. Louella Parsons and Hedda Hopper even hang out here, or at least actresses representing them. The atmosphere is such that you are tempted to just scan the restaurant from stars.

The fare is American, including the house specialty, the Cobb salad, named for the original restaurant's owner, Bob Cobb. The salad is comprised of chopped salad greens, tomato, bacon, turkey, egg, avocado, and blue cheese. Shrimp and lobster varieties of the salad are also available. Other menu items include rotisserie chicken, filet of red snapper, baked grouper, sautÇed veal, mixed grill, sandwiches, gumbo, corned beef and cabbage, stuffed chicken breast, roast chicken, filet mignon, strip steak, and Fettucine Derby with chicken, Parmesan cheese sauce, and red and green peppers.

For the health conscious, vegetarian and fruit-and-cheese platters are available. Wine and beer are also served. The children's menu includes peanut butter and jelly sandwiches with marshmallows, broiled chicken, pasta Parmesan, and fried fish. To make reservations, show up at the door starting at 9 AM. Or, if you're staying on-site, dial 828-4000 (824-8800 if you're staying in Hotel Plaza).

HINT: The bathrooms shared by the Soundstage and Hollywood Brown Derby restaurants are often extremely crowded. The one upstairs at the Catwalk Bar are often deserted.

STARRING ROLLS

Service: Counter-service. *Meals:* B,S. *Cuisine:* Baked goods. *Prices:* $2 to $4. *Location:* At the end of Hollywood Boulevard.

This bake shop, adjacent to the Hollywood Brown Derby, offers great breakfasts and pastries. Starting at 8:30 AM, there are Danishes, rolls, croissants, fruit tarts, and bear claws. After breakfast, there are sinfully delicious cookies, cakes, and pies. Coffee, tea, and assorted soft drinks are also sold. Since this spot opens half an hour before the rest of the park, it's a good pick for a quick, easy breakfast.

50'S PRIME TIME CAFE

Service: Table-service. *Meals:* L,D. *Cuisine:* American. *Location:* South of Echo Lake, on Vine Street. *Prices:* Lunch: $6.50 to $14.95. Dinner: $9.95 to $16.75. *Rsrvtns:* Suggested, make them at the door.

This restaurant, my pick as the best one in the Studios, dishes up nostalgia in heaping platefuls along with good, homey dishes. The atmosphere is enhanced by Fiesta Ware plates, and TV trays straight from a 50's sitcom kitchen. Televisions show clips from classics like Leave It to Beaver. The waitresses insist on being called "Mom", they check for dirty fingernails before dinner, and then announce to the fellow diners when one of the "kids" clears a plate.

The menu consists of tasty, liberal offerings that the June Cleavers of the TV world might have served their families. There's meat loaf with mashed potatoes, broiled chicken, gigantic sandwiches, chicken pot pies, Swiss steak, burgers, shrimp, beef tenderloin, grilled salmon, and salads. On the side, you can have vegetarian chili, nachos, or the French Fry Feast, plain or with chili and cheese.

The entrees are accompanied by ice cream sodas, root beer floats, milkshakes, beer, wine, and spirits. Afterwards, you can try strawberry-rhubarb pie, S'mores, sundaes, and more. To make reservations, show up at the door starting at 9 AM. Or, if you're staying on-site, dial 828-4000 (824-8800 if you're staying at the Hotel Plaza).

MAMA MELROSE'S RISTORANTE ITALIANO

Service: Table-service. *Meals:* L,D. *Cuisine:* Italian-Californian. *Location:* In the New York area, by the Studio Showcase. *Prices:* Lunch: $5 to $15. Dinner: $10 and up. *Rsrvtns:* Suggested, make them at the door.

This new restaurant is described as "where Italy meets California in the heart of the Backlot". That's pretty accurate. The menu includes brick oven pizza with a variety of toppings (including lobster!), chicken marsala, seafood pasta, lasagna, chicken, veal, and steak dishes. To make reservations, show up at the door starting at 9 AM. Or, if you're staying on-site, dial 828-4000 (824-8800 if you're staying at the Hotel Plaza). Beer, wine, and spirits are served as well.

SCI-FI DRIVE-IN DINER

Service: Table-service. *Meals:* L,D. *Cuisine:* American. *Prices:* $8 to $17. *Location:* Behind the Monster Sound building. *Children:* Special menu, $3.50 to $5. *Rsrvtns:* Suggested, make them at the door.

A soundstage between Monster Sound and New York Street now houses a drive-in where it is always nighttime. Diners enter through the ticket lobby and sit in classic automobiles and watch a 45-minute montage of clips and trailers from movies like Attack of the 50-Foot Woman, Invasion of the Saucer People, and other classic "B" science fiction and horror films. The atmosphere is enhanced by waitresses dressed like carhops.

As for the menu, it's secondary to the entertainment. It includes funky-sounding dishes like the "Monster Mash", a turkey Sloppy Joe; "Revenge of the Killer Club Sandwich", with smoked turkey, roast beef, turkey ham, Swiss cheese, and all the trimmings, served on seven-grain bread; "Tossed in Space", a chef's salad; "They Grow Among Us", a fruit platter; "The Red Planet", vegetables with linguine; "Meteoric Meatloaf", made of smoked meat; "20,000 Leafs under the Sea", a salad of greens, marinated vegetables, fruits, scallops, shrimp, and roast garlic dressing.

The children's menu includes the "Junior Red Planet" and "Space Strips" of breaded chicken. Desserts include the "Cheesecake That Ate New York", a banana split called "Twin Terrors", "When Berries Collide", a strawberry shortcake, and "Science Gone Mad", comprised of fruit cobblers. Beer, wine, and soft drinks are also served. To make reservations, show up at the door starting at 9 AM. Or, if you're staying on-site, dial 828-4000 (824-8800 if you're staying at the Hotel Plaza). Beer, wine, and spirits are served as well.

HOLLYWOOD & VINE CAFETERIA

Service: Buffeteria. *Meals:* B,L,D. *Cuisine:* American. *Location:* Next to the 50's Prime Time Cafe. *Prices:* Breakfast: $4.50 to $5.25. Lunch: $5.95 to $10.95. Dinner: $7.50 to $14.75. *Children:* Special menu, $2.75 to $5.50.

This is the Crystal Palace of the Studios, with good, unpretentious American dishes served up in a cafeteria. The atmosphere inside includes 8-foot murals depicting Hollywood landmarks like the original Hyperion

Avenue Disney Studios, Columbia Ranch, the Warner Brothers Studio, and the Cathay Circle Studio. This is the only full-service restaurant in the Studios serving breakfast. The fare early in the day includes pastries, French toast, pancakes, lox and bagels, fruit, cereals, and the Hollywood Scramble: two eggs, bacon or sausage, grits or hash browns and a biscuit.

The lunch menu includes tortellini, baby back ribs, pork chops, spit-roasted chicken, chopped sirloin, fresh seafood, and seafood and chef's salads. The dinner menu includes salads (chicken breast or seafood), prime rib, pork chops, veal shank, and grilled sirloin. The children's menu is one of the most extensive in the World, includes PB&J sandwiches with marshmallows, broiled chicken, tortellini, fresh fish, and pasta. Desserts are available, as are beer and wine.

SOUNDSTAGE RESTAURANT

Service: Food court. *Meals:* L,D,S. *Cuisine:* International. *Prices:* $1.95 to $5.25. *Location:* Next to the Hollywood Brown Derby. *Children:* Special menu, $1.

This cavernous, 560-seat restaurant was recently renovated to resemble the 18th-century village in which the movie *Beauty and the Beast* takes place. The restaurant is sort of a miniature food court, with three stands. One offers deep-dish pizza, pasta, and salad. The second offers meatball subs, chicken salad sandwiches, and the Soundstage Special, loaded with salami, pepperoni, bierschnicken, jarlsberg, and smoked Swiss cheese. The third stand offers clam chowder, chicken broth with tortellini, chef's salad, and chicken salad with vegetables.

All three stands offer soft drinks, PB&J sandwiches, cheesecake, and pie. *HINT:* The bathrooms shared by the Soundstage and Hollywood Brown Derby restaurants are often extremely crowded. The restrooms upstairs at the Catwalk Bar are often all but deserted.

MIN & BILL'S DOCKSIDE DINER

Service: Counter-service. *Meals:* L,D,S. *Cuisine:* Fast food. *Prices:* $3.75 to $5.50. *Location:* On Echo Lake, a landmark.

This diner takes residence on Lake Echo in the "California Crazy" architecture form of a tramp steamer, the S.S. Down the Hatch. Min and Bill serve up Cucamonga Cocktails of marinated shrimp and fresh veggies, San Pedro Pasta, a tri-colored pasta dish with crab legs and shrimp, fruit plates, and submarine sandwiches including tuna salad, turkey, and the Santa Monica Sub, consisting of provolone, salami, and mortadella. Frozen yogurt is also served.

DISNEY-MGM STUDIOS COMMISSARY RESTAURANT

Service: Counter-service. *Meals:* L,D. *Cuisine:* Healthy FF. *Prices:* $4 to $5. *Location:* Next to the Great Movie Ride. *Children:* Yes, $4.

This huge (550-seat) new restaurant offers healthier fast food, churned out from the open kitchen. The menu includes salads, stir-fried vegetable dishes, chicken breast sandwiches, burgers, chicken teriyaki, and vegetarian chili. For children, there's a box lunch consisting of a bologna sandwich, cookies, and a toy.

BACKLOT EXPRESS

Service: Counter-service. *Meals:* L,D,S. *Cuisine:* American. *Prices:* $3.30 to $6.25. *Location:* Next to Star Tours.

Here, up to 600 people can sit and eat hot dogs, hamburgers, charbroiled chicken with salsa and tortillas, chef's salad, fresh fruit, chili, and for dessert, apple pie, and cake. Beer and wine are offered by the glass. The atmosphere is that of a scenic shop for a movie studio. Props are scattered throughout, and the paint shop section features furniture spattered with paint. An outdoor seating area features plants, trees, and potted plants.

STUDIO CATERING CO.

Service: Counter-service. *Meals:* S. *Cuisine:* Snack fare. *Prices:* $1 to $3. *Location:* On the Backstage Studio Tour.

This stand next to the "Honey, I Shrunk the Kids Movie Set Adventure" sells fruit salads, churros, fruit and cheese platters, ice cream sundaes, milkshakes, soda, and beer.

DINOSAUR GERTIE'S ICE CREAM OF EXTINCTION

Service: Counter-service. *Meals:* S. *Cuisine:* Ice cream. *Prices:* $1 to $3. *Location:* A landmark, on Echo Lake.

The huge brontosaurus that looms over Lakeside Circle chews on greens and conceals a stand offering ice cream and yogurt bars, ice cream sandwiches, frozen bananas and soda.

SNACK TRUCKS

Vintage 1929 trucks sell soft drinks, popcorn, ice cream novelties, and delicious foot long hot dogs.

DINING IN THE MARKETPLACE

The flagship restaurants of the Marketplace, the Empress Room, Fisherman's Deck, and Steerman's Quarters, are on the stern-wheeler Empress Lilly, named for Walt Disney's wife. The riverboat, permanently moored along the shores of Buena Vista Lagoon, is realistic, with hog chains, cooling stacks, and the paddlewheel serenely rotating. The steamer is even more beautiful after dark, when tiny lights outline the boat.

Aboard the Empress Lilly
EMPRESS ROOM

Service: Table-service. *Meals:* D. *Cuisine:* Continental. *Prices:* $25 to $50. *Location:* Empress Lilly, Promenade Deck. *Dress:* Elegant, jackets required for men (available at restaurant). *Rsrvtns:* Required, can be made up to 30 days in advance. Call 828-3900.

Mobil only awarded its coveted 4-Star Award to 359 restaurants of 21,000 listed in the nationwide Mobil Travel Guides, and this is one of them. The style of the intimate, charming restaurant is reminiscent of Louis XV, accented with gold leaf, sparkling chandeliers, etched glass, wood paneling, a tuxedo-clad staff, and soothing harp music.

The menu selections are quite ambitious, including roast loin of veal with wild mushroom sausage and dry vermouth sauce; strip steak in a cognac cream sauce with green and pink peppercorns; sautÇed Dover sole with macadamia nut butter and lime; roast pheasant breast; boneless frog legs; Caesar salad; and cream of artichoke soup with seafood. Despite its impeccable service and elegant surroundings, the food preparation can be spotty at times.

The required reservations are accepted 30 days in advance here, and no guests are seated after 9:30. There is a 20% service charge added to the check. Dress is elegant, jackets are required for men and available at the restaurant. Special requests can be accommodated. Beer, wine, and spirits are served. There is no smoking in the Empress Room.

FISHERMAN'S DECK

Service: Table-service. *Meals:* L,D. *Cuisine:* Seafood. *Location:* Empress Lilly, Promenade Deck. *Prices:* Lunch: $5.50 to $15.95. Dinner: $12.95 to$22.95. *Children:* Special menu, $3.25 to $6.50. *Rsrvtns:* Suggested, can be made up to 30 days in advance. Call 828-3900.

Another of the trio of Empress Lilly restaurants, the Fisherman's deck offers good seafood and a beautiful 180⁻ vista over the lagoon. The menu at lunch ranges from salads, sandwiches, hamburgers, chicken pot pie, grilled turkey steak, and sirloin to heavy-duty seafood specialties like fresh fish, stir-fried seafood with pasta, and seafood cräpes. The dinner menu is a bit more civilized and has somewhat more emphasis on seafood than steak and poultry. There's Maine lobster, fresh trout, catfish, shrimp and crab meat or beef, and a limited selection of steak and chicken. The children's menu includes hamburgers, macaroni and cheese, chicken pot pie, catfish fingers, and prime rib.

STEERMAN'S QUARTERS
Service: Table-service. *Meals:* D. *Cuisine:* Steak. *Prices:* $13.75 to $28.00. *Location:* Empress Lilly, Main Deck. *Children:* Special menu, $3.25 to $6.50. *Rsrvtns:* Suggested, can be made up to 30 days in advance. Call 828-3900.

This is the place for beefeaters to go to enjoy filet mignon, Kansas City strip steak, Porterhouse steak, prime rib, New York sirloin and sautÇed veal chop, grilled turkey steak, and fresh fish. One of the biggest surprises of Steerman's Quarters is its unexpected ambiance and elegance. The upholstery is red velvet, the carpets floral, the wallpaper ivory, and the overall atmosphere surprisingly warm and friendly.

BREAKFAST A LA DISNEY
Service: Banquet. *Prices:* Adults $9.95; children 3-11, $6.95, children under 3 free. *Rsrvtns:* Required, can be made up to 30 days in advance. Call 828-3900 or 934-7639.

The Empress Lilly plays host to a character breakfast twice each morning. It features a visit from Mickey and the gang and hearty breakfast fare for the bacon-and-eggs crowd.

Elsewhere in the Village
VILLAGE ICE CREAM PARLOR
Service: Counter-service. *Meals:* S. *Cuisine:* Ice cream. *Prices:* $1 to $3. *Location:* Next to EUROSPAIN, on the trail leading toPleasure Island.

This stand offers milkshakes, hot fudge sundaes, Breyer's ice cream, soft serve, and other frozen treats. Baked goods and soft drinks sold too.

PLUTO'S DOGHOUSE
Service: Counter-service. *Meals:* L,D,S. *Cuisine:* Fast food. *Prices:* $1 to $5. *Location:* By EUROSPAIN.

Here, you can get hot dogs with chili, cheese, and other fixings, corn dogs, pretzels, beer, and soft drinks.

LAKESIDE TERRACE

Service: Counter-service. *Meals:* L,D,S. *Cuisine:* Fast food. *Prices:* $2.50 to $5. *Location:* By the Cristal Arts shop.

Hamburgers, fish sandwiches, chicken sandwiches, hot dogs, fried shrimp, salads, beer, and soft drinks are sold here. Diners can take their food to tables inside or out.

CAP'N JACK'S OYSTER BAR

Service: Table-service. *Meals:* L,D,S. *Cuisine:* Seafood. *Prices:* $4.75 to $9.95. *Location:* On the waterfront. *Children:* Special menu, $3.75.

Margaritaville" is the theme of this popular lounge-turned-restaurant that juts out over the shores of Buena Vista Lagoon. There's more varieties of frozen margaritas than you can sip a straw at, served up in huge goblets. These can get your evening off to an excellent start. The menu deserves equal credit for making Cap'n Jack's more than a night spot. Seafood lovers can enjoy lobster tails, crab claws, oysters, clams on the half shell, shrimp, seafood marinara, crab cakes, and ceviche (marinated raw fish). Children can eat spaghetti and meat sauce. Beer, wine, and soft drinks are served along with the frozen daiquiris.

CHEF MICKEY'S VILLAGE RESTAURANT

Service: Table-service. *Meals:* B,L,D. *Cuisine:* American. *Location:* At the end of the Marketplace farthest from Pleasure Island. *Prices:* Breakfast: $3.50 to $6.95. Lunch: $5.25 to $7.95. Dinner: $8.75 to $17.95. *Children:* Special menu, $2.50 to $6.50. *Rsrvtns:* Suggested, can be made up to 30 days in advance. Call 828-3723.

If you're agreeable to the idea of eating food reportedly prepared by a six-foot tall mouse, you can enjoy an excellent meal here. Here in Mickey's eatery is some of WDW's tastiest family fare. The restaurant is cheery and unassuming, an atmosphere friendly for both children and adults. Mickey Mouse himself is on hand in the dining room during the dinner hours, from 5:30 to 10 each evening. The children's menu even folds into a Mickey hand puppet. Mickey's recipes can even be taken home.

But now for the menu. At breakfast, there's the usual items like bacon, eggs, pancakes, waffles, and pastries. At lunch and dinner, there's meatloaf, sandwiches, burgers, salads, beef stew, fried chicken, fresh

Florida seafood, pork chops, prime rib, steak, broiled chicken, lasagna, shrimp scampi, and seafood casserole. The children's menu includes hamburgers, fried chicken, fish, and prime rib. To complete the meal, try one of the cobblers *ff* they're a house specialty.

MINNIE MIA'S ITALIAN EATERY
Service: Counter-service. *Meals:* L,D,S. *Cuisine:* Italian FF. *Prices:* $2 to $5. *Location:* Next to Team Mickey's.

This new cafe, by the shores of Buena Vista Lagoon, serves up deep dish pizza, veal and chicken Parmesan, baked ziti, lasagna, calzones, and fresh pastas with various sauces. Beer, wine, soft drinks, and take-out service are all available.

GOURMET PANTRY
Service: Counter-service. *Meals:* B,L,D,S. *Cuisine:* International. *Prices:* $1 to $10. *Location:* Near Minnie Mia's.

The Gourmet Pantry features a delicatessen with great sandwiches plus a bakery with delectable croissants and international coffees. Salads and candies are also sold.

DINING ON PLEASURE ISLAND

The restaurants and snack spots on Pleasure Island are listed below. Dining can also be done in each of the clubs, and the fare offered is discussed later. There is no cover charge to enter Pleasure Island before 7 PM, and there is never a cover charge for the Portobello Yacht Club and Fireworks Factory restaurants. To get to them, take the Island bridge closest to the Empress Lilly.

D-ZERTZ
Service: Counter-service. *Meals:* S. *Cuisine:* Baked goods. *Prices:* $1 to $5. *Location:* Next to the Mouse House.

An excellent choice for snacks to sate the sweet tooth in all of us. There's freshly brewed cappucino and espresso, plus pastries and chocolates, plus candy of all sorts.

PORTOBELLO YACHT CLUB
Service: Table-service.   *Meals:* L,D. *Cuisine:* Italian, seafood. *Location:* By the Empress Lilly. *Prices:* Lunch: $6.95 to $9.95. Dinner: $12.95 to $23.95. *Children:* Yes, $3.95 to $5.50.

Run by Levy Restaurants of Chicago, the Portobello Yacht Club supposedly occupies the former home of the Pleasures. The seafood represents Mr. Pleasure's love of the open seas, while the Italian part of the menu indicates his wife Isabella's heritage. This is one of the most pleasant spots to sit and enjoy a leisurely ethnic meal outside of EPCOT Center. The atmosphere features a collection of oceanic memorabilia, like ship models, photos, and pennants. The diners can sit indoors among brass, chrome, and mahogany reminiscent of pleasure yachts of the 19th century or on an outdoor terrace, suggestive of luxury cruise ships.

The menu is a wonderful blend of classical Italian and seafood dishes. The wood-burning oven pizzas are delicious and come with a variety of toppings including a savory four-cheese blend, spaghetti with seafood, long pasta tubes with Italian bacon, plum tomatos, garlic, and basil, other pasta dishes, salads, sandwiches, fresh fish, grilled sausage, chicken, and sirloin steak. Served with the entrees is wonderful, warm, crusty Italian bread with fresh roasted garlic to spread on the bread like butter. Be forewarned, this bread can easily wreck your appetite.

The desserts include crema bruccioto, the Italian equivalent of flan, and cioccolato paradisio, a layer cake with chocolate frosting, toffee, and caramel. The children's menu includes pizza, hot dogs, spaghetti, and hamburgers. There is a full bar, with a good selection of Italian and domestic wine. Take-out is available.

FIREWORKS FACTORY

Service: Table-service. *Meals:* L,D,S. *Cuisine:* American (barbecue). *Location:* By the Empress Lilly. *Prices:* Lunch: $5.50 to $15.95. Dinner: $12.95 to $22.95. *Childen:* Yes, $3.95 to $5.50.

Once upon a time, a certain Mr. Pleasure happened to be inspecting a warehouse storing pyrotechnic equipment. He was, unfortunately, carrying a lit cigar. A spark flew off of his cigar and ignite the fireworks and BOOM! Next thing you know, this barbecue joint sits in the smoldering ashes. And you can bet that this eatery, also run by Levy of Chicago, blows the explosion theme up (pun intended) to ridiculous proportions.

The menu includes baby back ribs, applewood smoked chicken, prime rib, citrus chicken, pork chops, steak, fried or BBQ chicken, and catfish. There's combination platters that are good for those who don't know what they want. There's the Down Home Barbecue Trio, with applewood-smoked pork tenderloin, beef brisket, and a shredded chicken.

The children's menu includes chicken, hamburger, shrimp, or baby back ribs. The dessert menu is stacked and includes a Toll House pie sundae, Key Lime pie, and Edy's Gourmet Ice Cream. Takeout is available. For those in a tippling mood, there are over 40 brands of bottled beer, plus specialty drinks both "Explosive" - read alcoholic - and "Defused", for those who don't want to imbibe. Both are served with a sparkler. There is a smoking section, "but use caution!" Souvenirs are sold here. Hats, T-shirts, and mugs bearing the logo of the restaurant, and even jars of the restaurant's famed barbecue sauce are all available.

MERRIWEATHER'S MARKET
Service: Food court. *Meals:* L,D,S. *Cuisine:* International. *Prices:* $1 to $5. *Location:* By the Mouse House.

Merriweather's Market, the Island's food court, offers four stands each serving food prepared in a different way. One offers chicken, turkey, sausages, burgers, and fish. Another dishes up oysters, ribs, shrimp, and gator. The third has chicken, beef, shrimp, and egg rolls. The last purveys chicken, tuna, and shrimp salad. Beverages are available at each station. Everything is cooked to order, but that means that lines aren't particularly swift.

SWEET SURRENDER
Service: Counter-service. *Meals:* S. *Cuisine:* Ice cream. *Prices:* $1 to $3. *Location:* Across from 8 Trax.

Soft frozen yogurt and ice cream served with a variety of toppings.

HILL STREET DINER
Service: Counter-service. *Meals:* L,D,S. *Cuisine:* American. *Prices:* $3 to $4. *Location:* On Hill Street.

At this unusual new counter-service eatery, you can sit at tables overlooking the water and enjoy cheesesteaks, pizza, or hot ham and cheese.

In the Clubs
The **Neon Armadillo Music Saloon** has fajita bars offering chicken fajitas, chili, nachos, sausages, pickled eggs, and fresh pepperoni. The **Rock & Roll Beach Club's** "Spinners" on the third floor, sells potato straws, pizza, burgers, chicken, and ice cream.

Inside **Mannequins**, carts offer seafood, chicken, steak, and potato chips. The **Adventurer's Club** has some exotic food and drink, ranging from shrimp Trinidad to Lebanese steak tartare.

DINING IN SEA WORLD

The food available at Sea World is measurably better than that available at the Magic Kingdom.

BIMINI BAY CAFE

Service: Table-service. *Meals:* L,D. *Cuisine:* American (Florida). *Price:* $6 to $13. *Location:* By Hawaiian Rhythms. *Children:* Special menu available.

The menu at this, Sea World's classiest eatery, includes Key West conch chowder, fried gator tail, seafood sandwiches, shrimp scampi, fried chicken, crab quiche, salads, and more. A children's menu includes sandwich platters: grilled cheese or turkey with fruit and a drink.

BIMINI BAY KIOSK

Service: Counter-service. *Meals:* L,D,S. *Cuisine:* Fast food. *Price:* $2 to $6. *Location:* Outside Bimini Bay Cafe.

The fare served at this stand, located outside Hawaiian Rhythms and Bimini Bay Cafe, offers buffalo wings, fish fingers, French fries, beer, soda, coffee, and mixed drinks.

CHICKEN & BISCUIT

Service: Counter-service. *Meals:* L,D. *Cuisine:* Fast food. *Price:* $4 to $6. *Location:* Next to Fantasy Theater. *Children:* Special menu.

This huge restaurant flips you the bird, baked, fried, or barbecued. There are two- and three-piece meals with French fries and a biscuit, or for kids, a platter with either one drumstick or two wings, fries, and a cookie.

TREASURE ISLE ICE CREAM SHOP

Service: Counter-service. *Meals:* S. *Cuisine:* Fast food. *Price:* $1.50 to $3. *Location:* Next to Information Center.

A variety of frozen treats and ice cream novelties are offered at this eatery by the main entrance.

MAMA STELLA'S

Service: Counter-service. *Meals:* L,D,S. *Cuisine:* Italian. *Price:* $2 to $6. *Location:* By Penguin Encounter.

The fare in this restaurant is exactly what its appellation suggests: pizza, spaghetti, eggplant Parmesan, sausage sandwiches, antipasto, and other Italian fare. By Pizza 'N Pasta are two snack stops: Frosted Fruit Coolers, and Soft Serve Ice Cream.

SMOKEHOUSE

Service: Counter-service. *Meals:* L,D. *Cuisine:* American (BBQ). *Price:* $5 to $7. *Location:* Next to Sky Tower.

Here, you can fill up on barbecue platters with cole slaw, a roll, and ribs or chicken, picnic-style. Guests dine on umbrella-covered outdoor tables by Atlantis Lagoon.

SPINNAKER CAFE

Service: Counter-service. *Meals:* L,D,S. *Cuisine:* Fast food. *Price:* $2 to $6. *Location:* By the Tropical Reef.

This nautical-themed restaurant offers sandwiches, soups, and salads, but what the Spinnaker is renowned for is desserts: there's cheesecake, strawberries and cream, Key Lime pie, and Black Forest chocolate cake.

WATERFRONT SANDWICH GRILL

Service: Counter-service. *Meals:* L,D. *Cuisine:* Fast food. *Price:* $4 to $6. *Location:* Behind the Smokehouse. *Children:* Special menu, $4.

This lagoon-view restaurant offers hamburgers and sandwich platters, including the Califoria Light, a turkey breast with sprouts and cheese. A children's platter with a turkey sandwich, fruit salad, and a cookie is available. Guests can sit at closely-spaced indoor tables or more spacious outdoor, dockside areas.

You can also find snack stands are located by the Atlantis Theater and Shamu Stadium. These open 45 minutes before each show and serve sandwiches, beer, and sodas. **Burgers 'N Fries** offers hot dogs, hamburgers, salads, fries, and shakes by Pancho's Tacos. **Snack Encounter** offers similar fare by Terrors of the Deep. **Supercone**, by the Fantasy Theater, offers sodas, cookies, and icy sundaes with a variety of toppings, served in a sugar cone. And don't forget **Buccaneer Smokehouse**, **The Deli**, and **Mango Joe's Cafe**, one of the best eateries in the park.

And if you wish to picnic, pull into **Atlantis Plaza**, by theAtlantis Theater. However, this area may be reserved for private company events.

DINING IN UNIVERSAL

STUDIO STARS RESTAURANT

Service: Table-service. *Meals:* L,D. *Cuisine:* American. *Price:* $6.95 to $17.50. *Location:* Production Central, next to "Murder, She Wrote" Mystery Theater. *Children:* Special menu. *Rsrvtns:* Recommended, make them in person.

This restaurant features "stars on break" and an all-American menu including salads, sandwiches, burgers, pasta, roast chicken, and various sirloin steak and fresh seafood dishes. Diners enjoy their meals in either the bustling, skylighted main dining room or in one of two sunrooms. This is Universal's signature restaurant and one of its best.

HARD ROCK CAFE

Service: Table-service. *Meals:* L,D,S. *Cuisine:* American. *Price:* $5.95 to $12.95. *Location:* Expo Center, on the edge of the park. *Children:* Special menu. *Comments:* You don't need to buy a Universal ticket to visit the Hard Rock Cafe, it has a special and separate entrance.

Doubtlessly you've seen one or two or eighty of those chic Hard Rock Cafe t-shirts floating around various torsos and bootleg stands in major cities. Well, this $5 million, guitar-shaped building houses the Orlando branch of the famed Hard Rock Cafe chain, the largest of the self-named "Smithsonians of rock and roll." The restaurant-cum-nightspot features $3.5 million worth of instruments, gold records, clothing, and memorabilia from luminaries ranging from Elvis Presley to the Beatles to the Monkees.

As for the menu, it's strictly American, with sandwiches, salads, hamburgers, rib-eye steak, and barbecued ribs, pork, and chicken. The 400-seat Cafe opened in June 1990 with name recognition second only to Disney, and expected to bring in more than six million visitors a year. Also, a shop in the Cafe offers those Hard Rock Cafe Orlando t-shirts, hats, and keychains without whom adolescence is incomplete. This restaurant is definitely worth a trip in its own right and is designated as NOT TO BE MISSED.

MEL'S DRIVE-IN

Service: Counter-service. *Meals:* L,D,S. *Cuisine:* Fast food. *Price:* $2.60 to $4.75. *Location:* Hollywood, by the "Murder, She Wrote" Mystery Theater.

Straight out of American ˇ Graffiti, this 50's throwback serves a family-style menu with entrees like burgers, hot dogs, chili, and chicken sandwiches. Rock music plays and a sock-hop atmosphere runs rampant.

FINNEGAN'S PUB

Service: Table-service. *Meals:* L,D. *Cuisine:* Irish. *Price:* $5.50 to $14. *Location:* New York, across from Kongfrontation. *Children:* Special menu, $3.95 to $4.95.

Finnegan's Pub is one of the most convincing spots in Universal, portraying accurately a friendly, Big Apple Irish pub. The menu is comprised of simple Irish fare like Cornish pasti, Scotch eggs, sandwiches, corned beef, bangers and mash (sausage and mashed potatoes), Irish stew, fish and chips, beef casserole, Shepherd's pie, Yorkshire beef, and meat and chicken pies. Guiness Stout, Harp Lager, and Bass ale are available to wash down your meal.

This bar and grill features a live and very good dinner show several times nightly, and piped-in Irish music at other times. A children's menu is available, featuring hamburgers, ham and cheese, fried fish, and chicken fingers.

LOUIE'S ITALIAN RESTAURANT

Service: Cafeteria. *Meals:* L,D,S. *Cuisine:* Italian. *Price:* $2.50 to $13.75. *Location:* New York, 5th Avenue at Canal Street.

Louie's is a good place to pick up pizza with a variety of toppings, linguine, spaghetti, tortellini, lasagne, and antipasto. For dessert, try the authentic Italian ices.

INTERNATIONAL FOOD BAZAAR

Service: Food court. *Meals:* L,D,S. *Cuisine:* International. *Price:* $3.25 to $6.75. *Location:* Expo Center, next to Back to the Future.

The International Food Bazaar is the only Expo Center location that has anything to do with a World's Fair expo. Five counters offer different cuisines. The American counter serves fried chicken, barbecue pork sandwiches, hot dogs, and hamburgers. The Chinese counter sells lo mein, sweet and sour chicken, and stir-fried shrimp. The German stand sells bratwurst and knockwurst with potato salad or red cabbage. The Greek stand sells gyros, Greek salad, and spanakopita. Last, but not least is the Italian counter, serving jumbo shells, pizza, and salads. Desserts available include baklava, black bottom pie, Black Forest cake, Italian amaretto mousse, frozen yogurt, and ice cream.

ANIMAL CRACKERS

Service: Counter-service. *Meals:* L,D,S. *Cuisine:* Fast food. *Price:* $2 to $5.50. *Location:* Expo Center, next to E.T. Adventure.

This snack stand sells decent smoked sausage hoagies, beef brochettes, hot dogs, and hamburgers.

BEVERLY HILLS BOULANGERIE

Service: Counter-service. *Meals:* B,L,D,S. *Cuisine:* Baked goods. *Price:* $1 to $6. *Location:* The Front Lot.

Located at the corner of Plaza of the Stars and Rodeo Drive, this is a great place to pick up sweets like eclairs, cookies, pies, croissants, and other pastries. Sandwiches are also served here. Domestic beer, and domestic and imported wines and champagnes are available to wash down that pastry.

CAFE LA BAMBA

Service: Counter-service or buffet. *Meals:* L,D,S. *Cuisine:* Mexican. *Price:* $5 to $8. *Location:* Hollywood, across from Mel's Drive-In. *Children:* Special menu, $4.

There's an unlimited buffet featuring Mexican dishes like tacos, enchiladas, burritos, quesadillas, fajitas, beans, and rice. If you're not up to gorging yourself, an a la carte menu features Tex-Mex and ranchero burger platters with fries or chicken tostada salad. Beverages and desserts like flan, margarita mousse, and churros are also available.

PIER 27

Service: Counter-service. *Meals:* L,D,S. *Cuisine:* American. *Price:* $2 to $3.75. *Location:* San Francisco/Amity, behind Golden Gate Mercantile.

This little restaurant serves clam chowder, hot dogs, barbecued pork sandwiches, and chips.

SCHWAB'S PHARMACY

Service: Counter-service. *Meals:* S. *Cuisine:* Ice cream. *Price:* $1 to $3. *Location:* Hollywood, on the Boulevard.

Lana Turner was discovered here, according to Hollywood legend, but your likely discovery will be some of the best old-fashioned ice cream treats including sodas, shakes, malts, floats, cones, and sundaes.

BOARDWALK SNACKS

Service: Counter-service. *Meals:* L,D,S. *Cuisine:* Fast food. *Price:* $1 to $2.50 *Location:* San Francisco/Amity, on Amity Avenue.

This snack area in Amity Village sells a variety of traditional boardwalk eats, including corn dogs, hot dogs, potato knishes, and cotton candy.

LOMBARD'S LANDING

Service: Table-service. *Meals:* L,D. *Cuisine:* American. *Price:* $8 to $20. *Location:* San Francisco/Amity, Fisherman's Wharf. *Children:* Special menu, $3.50 to $5.

Fisherman's Wharf hosts the "only restaurant in Florida with views of the Pacific and the Atlantic", said restaurant being the casual, classy Lombard's Landing. Here, you can get casual meals like sandwiches, salads, Maryland crab cakes, New York strip steak, grilled chicken, fish and chips, and fettucine, alongside fancy dishes like grilled swordfish and stuffed veal. Children can enjoy comfort foods like hot dogs, hamburgers, chicken tenders, and pasta.

CHEZ ALCATRAZ

Service: Counter-service. *Meals:* L,D,S. *Cuisine:* Seafood. *Price:* $2 to $5. *Location:* San Francisco/Amity, on the water.

This stand sells a variety of traditional and non-traditional seafood items, ranging from clam chowder, shrimp cocktail, crab cocktail, and a crab salad Conewich, a one-handed sandwich a la Disney Handwich.

SAN FRANCISCO PASTRY CO.

Service: Counter-service. *Meals:* B,S. *Cuisine:* Baked goods. *Price:* $1.50 to $2.25. *Location:* San Francisco/Amity, on the Embarcadero.

This is a relatively authentic European cafe except for the fact that you must stand in line to purchase your food. The menu is filled with so many goodies that you may have some trouble making up your mind. But it's hard to not enjoy the mousse, kiwi tarts, or cheesecake dished up up here.

DINING IN THE MINOR PARKS

In Typhoon Lagoon
LEANING PALMS

This eatery near the main entrance sells hamburgers, hot dogs, chef's salads, pizza, ice cream, soda, and beer.

TYPHOON TILLY'S GALLEY AND GROG

If you're near the Shark Reef attraction, this is the more convenient place to pick up burgers, dogs, pizza, ice cream, frozen yogurt, beer, and soda.

In River Country
POP'S PLACE AND WATERIN' HOLE

These two fast food stands each offer burgers, dogs, ice cream, salads, beer, and sodas. However, the food here is so bad that you would probably be better off with a picnic. Waterin' Hole operates during peak seasons only.

On Discovery Island
THE THIRSTY PERCH

This restaurant, located in a peaceful enclave just hidden from the dock, serves sandwiches, hamburgers, hot dogs, ice cream, beer, and soft drinks. You can take your food to the beach and picnic there.

At Bonnet Creek Golf Club
SAND TRAP BAR AND GRILL

The "19th hole" at the new clubhouse features specialty drinks and snacks, appetizers, sandwiches, and milkshakes.

DINING IN THE RESORTS

The Disney resort hotels can be a great place to eat your meals. They're convenient to the parks and offer better fast food and a more extensive selection of sit-down fare. Restaurants there are never as crowded as those the parks.

In the Disney Inn
THE DIAMOND MINE

Here, you can get fajitas, salads, sandwiches, burgers, coffee, and beer.

THE GARDEN GALLERY

Service: Table-service. *Meals:* B,L,D. *Cuisine:* American. *Location:* In the Disney Inn Clubhouse. *Prices:* Breakfast: $5 to $15. Lunch: $5 to $15. Dinner: $15 and up. *Rsrvtns:* Suggested, call 824-1484.

This restaurant is one of WDW's best-kept secrets. The service is leisurely and the food is nothing short of excellent. There's a bountiful buffet at breakfast (you can also order from an a la carte menu); a salad bar, sandwiches, fajitas, apple-stuffed French toast, steak, and seafood for lunch, and a dinner menu including veal, beef, fowl, and a raw bar. For dessert, try an old-fashioned strawberry shortcake or the spectacular, unique french-fried vanilla ice cream served on a peach half with vanilla sauce. After a round on the Palm or Magnolia, this makes a great spot to relive the glory or forget the agony of the links.

Sand Trap Hot dogs, hamburgers, snacks, coffee, soft drinks, juice, and cereal are available at this poolside spot.

In the Contemporary
CONCOURSE GRILLE
Service: Table-service. *Meals:* B,L,D. *Cuisine:* American. *Location:* On the fourth floor, on the Grand Canyon Concourse. *Prices:* Breakfast: $5 to $15. Lunch: $5 to $15. Dinner: $12 to $24.

Breakfast finds the menu here featuring pancakes, eggs, omelets, and fresh fruit. There's barbecue ribs, fajitas, fresh fish, soups, burgers, steaks, sandwiches and salads at lunch and dinner.

CONTEMPORARY CAFE
Service: Buffet. *Meals:* B,D. *Cuisine:* International. *Location:* On the fourth floor, on the Grand Canyon Concourse. *Prices:* $9.95 adults, $6.95 for kids 3 to 9. Dinner: $15.95 adults, $7.95 for kids 3 to 9.

Goofy is the guest of honor at the character breakfast buffet held each morning. Joined with other characters, the Goof mingles with diners who make trips to the buffet and return with usual breakfast fare. The dinner buffet features a salad bar, carved prime rib, pizza, peel-and-eat shrimp, and other international specialties.

DOCK INN
This snack shop by the marina sells submarines, hot dogs, hamburgers, and ice cream. Open seasonally.

FIESTA FUN CENTER SNACK BAR
Located in the mammoth Fiesta Fun Center, this snack bar dishes up light fare all day and all night. So this makes a great place to cure the Midnight Munchies.

OUTER RIM COCKTAIL AND SEAFOOD LOUNGE
Service: Table-service. *Meals:* L,D,S. *Cuisine:* Seafood. *Location:* On the

fourth floor, on the Grand Canyon Concourse. *Prices:* $5 to $15.

Like Cap'n Jack's in the Marketplace, this is a seafood lounge that has gained a popularity as a restaurant. Seafood appetizers and specialty drinks are the highlights of this scenic restaurant overlooking Bay Lake.

TOP OF THE WORLD
Service: Table-service. *Meals:* D, Sunday brunch. *Cuisine:* American and continental. *Location:* On the fifteenth floor. *Prices:* Brunch: $23, ages 12 to 20, $18, kids 3 to 9, Dinner: Adults, $44.50. Kids 3 to 9, $19.50. *Dress:* Elegant, collared shirts for gentlemen and no shorts. *Rsrvtns:* Required, call 824-3611 for brunch, 934-7639 for dinner.

This elegant restaurant, which features spectacular views of the Magic Kingdom area from fifteen stories up, features a dinner show featuring over 40 songs from Broadway musicals performed by a talented cast of singers and dancers (see Orlando Attractions: Nighttime Entertainment). On Sunday, there's a brunch that includes champagne, hot dishes, pastries, fruit, and breakfast fare.

In Fort Wilderness Campground and Resort
BEACH SHACK
This stand at the marina sells chips, sandwiches, ice cream, beer, and soft drinks. Open seasonally.

CROCKETT'S TAVERN
Service: Table-service. *Meals:* D. *Cuisine:* American/Western. Prices: $5 to $15. *Location:* Pioneer Hall.

Located in rustic Pioneer Hall, Crockett's Tavern serves one-of-a-kind appetizers, hand-cut sirloin steaks, Buffalo Burgers, fresh lake trout, ribs, and chicken. The atmosphere is enhanced by wall-to-wall Davy Crockett memorabilia and live entertainment in the form of folk ballads from 6:30 to 11 each evening.

MEADOW SNACK BAR
This seasonal snack bar offers the regular assortment of hot dogs, hamburgers, sandwiches, chips, ice cream, and soft drinks. Located by the Meadow Trading Post.

TRAIL'S END BUFFETERIA
Service: Buffeteria. *Meals:* B,L,D,S. *Cuisine:* American (Southern). *Location:* Pioneer Hall. *Prices:* B: $1 to $5. L: $5 to $15. D: $5 to $15.

This cafeteria, located in pleasantly rustic Pioneer Hall, sells some of the best breakfasts in WDW. Hearty, lumberjack fare like biscuits and gravy, grits, bacon, sausage, eggs, and bread pudding will get your day off to a great start. For lunch and dinner, you can enjoy ribs, chicken, pot pies, catfish, sandwiches, taco salad, fresh fish, raost beer, carved ham, or turkey. There's a seafood buffet on Friday nights and an Italian buffet on Saturdays. Every night from 9 to 11, there's a make-your-own-pizza bar.

Beer and sangria are sold by the glass or by the pitcher. Folk songs are performed nightly.

In the Grand Floridian
1900 PARK FARE
Service: Buffet. *Meals:* B,D. *Cuisine:* American. *Location:* At the Grand Floridian, main building. *Prices:* Breakfast: Adults $13.75, Children 3-11 $8.75. Dinner: Adults $17.75, Children 3-11 $8.75. *Rsrvtns:* Suggested, call 824-2383.

This restaurant is ruled by Big Bertha, the band organ 15 feet overhead here. She can play the bells, cymbals, drums, pipes, and xylophone at once. At breakfast, there's a character buffet featuring Mary Poppins, Pluto, and Winnie the Pooh. The unlimited buffet includes the standard breakfast offerings. The dinner buffet features a visit from the Rescue Rangers, and includes prime rib, salads, fresh fish, stuffed pork loin, spoon bread, pasta, roast lamb, and other oh-so-American fare. The menu changes weekly.

FLAGLER'S
Service: Table-service. *Meals:* D. *Cuisine:* Italian/French. *Prices:* $19 to $32. *Location:* In the Grand Floridian, main building. *Rsrvtns:* Suggested, call 824-2383.

Meals at this restaurant, the Grand Floridian's largest eatery, are mainly splashy Italian dishes with a trace of French influence. Each meal in the restaurant overlooking the marina begins with a complimentary appetizer. The entrees include veal scallopini with a marsala wine sauce, plum tomatos, and mushrooms, artichokes and sauteed shrimp with garlic sauce and pernod, filet of beef with mushrooms, bouillabaisse, and salmon with asparagus. For dessert, try zagliabone, a creamy combination of marsala wine, sugar, and whipped egg yolks poured over fresh berries.

The waiters and waitresses occasionally sing while they bring you your food. A talented guitarist roves the restaurant at the same time.

GASPARILLA GRILL AND GAMES

Chicken, burgers, dogs, and pastries are served 24 hours a day at this snack bar, located close to the pool.

GRAND FLORIDIAN CAFE

Service: Table-service. *Meals:* B,L,D. *Cuisine:* American (Southern). *Location:* In the Grand Floridian, main building. *Prices:* Breakfast and lunch, $5 to $15. Dinner $7 to $20.

This is a good choice for families, by virtue of its convenience to the Magic Kingdom, its low prices, and its consistent food. The fare is pure South, including honey-dipped fried chicken, catfish filet with bell pepper relish, Cajun burgers, prime rib, salads, Caribbean roast pork, grilled chicken, and more. Sandwiches are also offered, including the house specialty, the Grand Floridian Sandwich, comprised of roast turkey, smoked ham, bacon, and beefsteak tomato, topped with cheddar cheese sauce and crispy onions.

NARCOOSEE'S

Service: Table-service. *Meals:* D. *Cuisine:* Steak & seafood. *Location:* In the Grand Floridian, main building. *Prices:* Lunch: $5 to $15. Dinner: $12 to $44. *Rsrvtns:* Suggested, call 824-2383.

·This eccentric, octagonal restaurant features an open-display kitchen and a splendid view of the Magic Kingdom as diversions to diners who feast on dishes including a 36-ounce Maine Lobster, a 38-ounce T-Bone steak for two, swordfish, lamb and veal chops, and grilled chicken. Desserts here are also a lure, including the glutton's specialty, the Seven Seas, Seven Scoops Delight. There's seven scoops of ice cream, custard, berries, whipped cream, and amaretto, served up in a 48-ounce snifter. The best part is, it's free. Except there's one catch. One guest must be able to finish the entire sundae.

There is a full bar here, serving (among other things) the unique Yard of Beer. As in three feet of beer. The restaurant has nightly entertainment and offers take-out.

VICTORIA & ALBERT'S

Service: Table-service. *Meals:* D. *Cuisine:* Continental. *Prices:* $75 per person. *Location:* In the Grand Floridian, main building. *Dress:* Elegant, evening wear for ladies, jackets required for men. *Rsrvtns:* Required, call 824-2383.

This is the most elegant, elite restaurant in the World. The spectacular restaurant dazzles diners with outstanding service, each table having its own maid and butler. The atmosphere is Victorian and ambient, with special touches like a soothing harpist and settings of Italian Sambonet silver, German Schlott-Zweisel crystal, and English Royal Doulton chinaware.

The Ivy Award-winning menu for the seven-course feast changes daily, but always includes beef, fish, poultry, and game selections. The chef will make a special tableside appearance to accommodate special requests. The night ends on a classy note, the presentation of Godiva chocolates, long-stemmed roses, and souvenir hand-written menus. The wine cellar includes over 350 choices from around the world. The dining room is 100% non-smoking.

In the Polynesian
CAPTAIN COOK'S SNACK AND ICE CREAM COMPANY

This snack bar offers fruit salad, continental breakfast, burgers, hot dogs, hamburgers, ice cream sundaes, soda, and beer.

CORAL ISLE CAFE
Service: Table-service. *Meals:* B,L,D. *Cuisine:* American, Polynesian. *Location:* In the Great Ceremonial House, 2nd floor. *Prices:* Breakfast: $5 to $10. Lunch: $5 to $15. Dinner:$8 to $16.

This bustling, tropical-themed coffee shop overlooks the atrium, fountains, and waterfalls of the main lobby below. The breakfast fare includes eggs, cereal, bacon, pancakes, and a banana-stuffed French toast that has an immense following. This morning treat is worth a special trip. At lunch and dinner, there are sandwiches, salads, and Polynesian items like chicken Maori and Luau barbecue ribs.

PAPEETE BAY VERANDAH
Service: Table-service. *Meals:* B,D, Sunday brunch. *Cuisine:* International, Oriental. *Location:* In the Great Ceremonial House, 2nd floor. *Prices:* Brunch: $11.95, adults, $7.95, kids 3-11. Breakfast: $9.95 for adults, $6.95 for kids 3 to 11. Dinner: $10 to $15. *Rsrvtns:* Suggested, call 824-1391.

This restaurant features a sweeping vista over the Seven Seas Lagoon, with the spires of Cinderella Castle regally tall in the distance. The appetizers on the dinner menu include plates of tempura, Hot Rocks, made of shrimp, beef, chicken, and vegetables grilled on lava rocks, and scallops with coconut milk, horseradish, and sour cream. The main courses include chicken pago-pago (served with honeyed sesame sauce and served in a pineapple half), pork tenderloin, mahi-mahi baked in parchment, lobster, steak, and prime rib.

After that main course, you can sample banana tempura, macadamia nut pie with passion fruit ice cream, poached pear in apricot brandy with strawberry cream sauce, or a make-your-own-sundae bar. During the evening, diners are regaled by a combo and several dancers. Exotic mixed drinks, beer, and wine are served.

From Monday to Saturday, there's Minnie's Menehune Breakfast, starring the famous bow-adorned rodent, plus Chip'N'Dale. The unlimited buffet breakfast includes eggs, bacon, sausage, biscuits and gravy, Polynesian bread pudding, and omelets. There's a brunch served on Sunday.

SNACK ISLE

This snack bar, located by the East Pool, offers dogs, burgers, subs, ice cream, frozen yogurt, beer, and soda.

TANGAROA TERRACE

Service: Table-service. *Meals:* B,D. *Cuisine:* Steak & seafood. *Location:* By the Oahu longhouse. *Prices:* $5 to $10.

Banana-stuffed French toast is the house specialty at breakfast, along with dinnertime dishes like prime rib, steak, and fresh seafood.

In the Caribbean Beach
OLD PORT ROYALE

Service: Food court. *Meals:* B,L,D,S. *Cuisine:* Continental. *Location:* Old Port Royale. *Prices:* $5 to $15.

This food court, which is the hub of the Caribbean Beach, features six stands. The **Bridgetown Broiler** serves prime rib, rotisserie chicken, fajitas, and taco salad. **Montego's Market** offers deli sandwiches, soups, and salads. **Oriental Cargo** features a breakfast buffet and egg rolls, spare ribs, lo mein, and soups. At the **Port Royale Hamburger Shop**, burgers, hot dogs, chicken strips, and hot sandwiches can be purchased. The **Royale Pizza and Pasta Shop** features an all-you-can-eat Italian buffet, pizza made-to-order, and a variety of pasta dishes. For those of the sweet-toothed persuasion, the **Cinnamon Bay Bakery** serves to satiate. You can get muffins, croissants, Danish, cookies, cakes, pies, and ice cream sundaes. Pizza can be delivered to guestrooms, and takeout is available at all six counters.

At the Yacht and Beach Club Resorts
ARIEL'S
Service: Table-service. *Meals:* D. *Cuisine:* Seafood. *Prices:* $15 and up. *Location:* Beach Club. *Rsrvtns:* Suggested, call 924-3357.

Ariel's, the classy signature restaurant of the Beach Club, features a 2,500-gallon aquarium filled with some of the most exotic sea creatures you will sea until your entree arrives. Inside the main dining room, there's more fish, suspended from the ceiling in mobiles. For those who would rather watch fish get chopped up and smacked around a pan, the kitchen is open so as to watch the chefs at work. The menu includes Maine lobster, Ariel's Mixed Bag, a sack full of shrimp, scallops, mussels, clams, and fish filet, and Ariel's Strudel, a chicken breast with a basil pastry and cream champagne mushroom sauce. The menu is rounded out by seafood selections from the Northeast, Northwest, and Southeast. A kids' menu, special dietary considerations, and liquor are available.

BEACHES AND CREAM SODA SHOP
Service: Table-service. *Meals:* B,L,D. *Cuisine:* American. *Prices:* Breakfast: $1 to $5. Lunch & Dinner: $5 to $15. *Location:* Common area.

Flash back to the 1950's. Remember the old sock hops? That's the Beaches and Cream for you. The food here is as undeniably American as the kitschy Art Deco atmosphere, reminiscent of the 50's Prime Time Cafe in the Studios. The house specialties are ice cream concoctions served in tall, metal-soled glasses (try the Milky Way Cake Sundae or Fudge Mud Slide), hot dogs, grilled cheese sandwiches, and the Fowl Ball, a burger made with turkey instead of beef.

But for those of you who prefer the more traditional offerings, what could be more archetypical New English than a Fenway Park Burger? This can be ordered in four sizes: single, double, triple, and a grand slam over the Green Monster! And the Red Sox win!!! Sorry, I don't know what's gotten into me.

CAPE MAY CAFE
Service: Table-service or buffet. *Meals:* B,D. *Cuisine:* Seafood. *Prices:* Breakfast: A la carte $5 to $15, buffet $11.95 adults, $6.95 kids. *Location:* Beach Club. Dinner: $15 to $29. *Rsrvtns:* Required for parties of 12 or more. Call 934-3358.

Each morning, this eatery, named for the Jersey Shore resort town, hosts Admiral Goofy and his crew for a character buffet including eggs, bacon, fruit, pastries, and a multitude of other treats. At suppertime each day, there's an old-fashioned New England clambake, on a rockweed steamer which serves as the focal point of the restaurant. Other selections include lobster, clams, mussels, oysters, shrimp, chicken, and a seafood buffet of sumptuous proportions.

HURRICANE HANNAH'S GRILL

This spot, located alongside Stormalong Bay in the common area shared by the two hotels, offers hot dogs, hamburgers, sausages, sandwiches, fries, and ice cream.

PORTSIDE SNACK BAR

Next to the Beach Club's smaller, quiet pool is the Portside, which offers dogs, sandwiches, salads, soft drinks, beer, wine, and cocktails.

SIP AHOY SNACK BAR

The Yacht Club section of the resort has its own pool too, with a tiki bar to boot. Hamburgers, hot dogs, salads, sandwiches, ice cream, sodas, and alcoholic beverages.

YACHT CLUB GALLEY

Service: Table-service or buffet. *Meals:* B,L,D. *Cuisine:* American. *Price:* $5 to $12.

This cool, nautical restaurant is one of the better buys in the World. There are breakfast and dinner buffets, and a la carte menus are available at all three meals. Items available at lunch include salads, soups, and sandwiches, while the dinner menu includes fried clams, prime rib, and catch of the day. Entertainment is provided by the band of roving musicians who perform nightly. Aside from that, the atmosphere is enhanced by an oceanic mural.

YACHTSMAN STEAKHOUSE

Service: Table-service. *Meals:* D. *Cuisine:* Steak. *Price:* $18 to $22. *Rsrvtns:* Suggested, call 934-3356.

This restaurant is modeled after the great American steakhouse. The glassed-in beef aging room and open-display kitchen enhance the atmosphere, described as a "homage to beef". The house butcher chooses the cut of meat and the award-winning master chefs prepare it, all in plain sight. Just name your cut and the chefs will cook your succulent steak over a hardwood grill. The specialties are Porterhouse steak, Chateaubriand, and rack of lamb. Strolling musicians make nightly appearances here.

In the Dolphin
CABANA BAR & GRILL
This poolside snack bar sells burgers, chicken, sandwiches, yogurt, fruit, ice cream, soft drinks, and beer.

CORAL CAFE
Service: Table-service or buffet. *Meals:* B,L,D,S. *Cuisine:* American. *Price:* $6 to $17. *Location:* Dolphin, first floor. *Comments:* Not available in Disney Vacation Plans

This eatery features themed breakfast and dinner buffets, plus elaborate holiday buffets. The character buffet, which stars Winnie the Pooh, is held twice weekly, on Wednesdays and Saturdays, with a regular buffet the other five mornings.

DOLPHIN FOUNTAIN
Service: Table-service. *Meals:* B,L,D,S. *Cuisine:* American. *Prices:* Breakfast: $1 to $5. Lunch & Dinner: $5 to $15. *Location:* Dolphin. *Comments:* Not available with Disney Vacation Plans.

The fare here includes breakfast muffins, cereals, burgers, fries, and hot dogs, but the main attraction is the ice cream. Eclectic frozen delights like sticky bun ice cream. Shakes, sodas, floats, and sundaes are served by energetic young staffers who frequently sing and dance.

HARRY'S SAFARI BAR & GRILLE
Service: Table-service. *Meals:* D. *Cuisine:* Steak and seafood. Price: $16 to $35. *Location:* Dolphin, third floor. *Children:* Special menu. *Rsrvtns:* Suggested, call 934-4000, ext. 6155. *Comments:* Not available with Disney Vacation Plans.

This is one of those eccentric little spots with a great deal of legend surrounding it. Seems that intrepid Harry the barkeep circled the globe and acquired some odd methods of steak, lobster, and seafood preparation.

RISTORANTE CARNEVALE
Service: Table-service. *Meals:* D, Sunday brunch. *Cuisine:* Italian (Tuscan). *Price:* $13 to $24. *Location:* Dolphin. *Children:* Special menu. *Rsrvtns:* Suggested, call 934-4000, ext. 6165. *Comments:* Not available with Disney vacation plans.

The atmosphere here is pure Carnevale, with jugglers, singers, and musicians serenading you while you eat hearty portions of Tuscan food. Fresh pastas, seafood risotto, grilled swordfish, and borchette with sausage, veal, and quail. The Sunday brunch features appearances by Chip & Dale Goofy, and Pluto, plus breakfast fare, casseroles, cräpes, and desserts. There is a full lounge next to the restaurant.

SUM CHOWS
Service: Table-service. *Meals:* D. *Cuisine:* Non-trad Oriental. Price: $15 to $21. *Location:* Dolphin. *Dress:* Elegant. Jackets not required, but appropriate dress requested. *Rsrvtns:* Suggested, call 934-4000, ext. 6150. *Comments:* Not available in Disney Vacation Plans.

You won't fins many of Sum Chows' menu items in your hometown swear-by-it Chinese restaurant. Or, for that matter, in Nine Dragons Restaurant at EPCOT's China pavilion. The food is quirky, but very, very good. The ambitious dinner entrees include wok-sauteed swordfish, Beijing Duck, deep-fried snapper, steamed crab with black bean sauce, and sauteed pheasant with almonds, lime, and honey.

TUBBI CHECKERS BUFFETERIA – Counter-service restaurant featuring a cool 50's decor and fresh, unpretentious food. Open seasonally.

In the Swan
GARDEN GROVE CAFE
Service: Table-service or buffet. *Meals:* B,L,D. *Cuisine:* American. *Price:* $8 to $25. *Location:* Swan, first floor. *Phone:* 934-3000, ex. 1618. *Rsrvtns:* Suggested, call 934-3000, ex. 1618. *Comments:* Not available in Disney Vacation Plans.

This interesting restaurant, situated at the bottom of a five-story greenhouse, offers buffets daily, including a character buffet every Wednesday and Saturday. Fresh fish, sandwiches, salads, and other American fare round out the lunch menu.

PALIO
Service: Table-service. *Meals:* D. *Cuisine:* Italian. *Price:* $9 to $24. *Location:* Swan. *Dress:* Elegant, jackets not required. *Rsrvtns:* Suggested, call 934-1610. *Comments:* Not available in Disney Vacation Plans.

This fine Italian bistro is decorated with bright, vivid banners representing the Italian counties that competed in the races for which the cafe is named. Strolling guitar and accordion players regale guests who dine on specialties including pizza cooked in a wood-fired brick oven, fettucine Alfredo, spaghetti with seafood, veal scallopini, pork tenderloin, braised veal shank, brochette of veal, and wood broiled grouper or Porterhouse steak. Diners are greeted with a welcoming cup of wine, making for a pleasant start to the evening.

SPLASH GRILL

At poolside, continental breakfasts, sandwiches, salads, and drinks both soft and alcoholic are served.

In the Dixie Landings Resort
BOATWRIGHT'S DINING HALL

Service: Table-service. *Meals:* B,D. *Cuisine:* American (Cajun). *Price:* $5 to $15. *Location:* Dixie Landings, Commercial Center. *Rsrvtns:* Accepted, call 934-6000.

In this new restaurant, guests sit inside the semi-constructed hull of a riverboat whose windows look out onto the mighty Sassagoula River. The food includes some American fare like prime rib and steaks, but mainly, Cajun delicacies like dirty rice, seafood Jambalaya, and a broiled catfish dish called Bayou Tech will be served. At breakfast time, the most interesting selection is the Tin Pan Breakfast, a dish of potatoes, crawfish, and a special Creole sauce. Servers will provide insight on the origins of the specific Cajun foods. Take-out service is offered.

COLONEL'S COTTON MILL

Service: Food court. *Meals:* B,L,D,S. *Cuisine:* American (Cajun). *Price:* $5 to $15. *Location:* Dixie Landings, Commercial Center.

The Mill offers Southern hospitality dished up in five specialty shops. The seating area features a working, 35-foot water wheel and cotton press. The Acadian Pizza 'n' Pasta shop offers pizza and pasta with a variety of toppings. You can get fried or roast chicken plus an assortment of burgers at the Bleu Bayou Burgers and Chicken shop. The Cajun Broiler has a buffet consisting of dishes indigenous to Louisiana. The Riverside Market and Deli sells deli items, snack foods, sodas, and picnic supplies. The Southern Trace Bakery offers freshly-baked breads, huge cinnamon buns, and other pastries. Beverages are served at all stands.

In the Port Orleans Resort
BONFAMILLES CAFE

Service: Table-service. *Meals:* B,D. *Cuisine:* American (Creole). *Price:* $5 to $15. *Location:* Port Orleans. *Rsrvtns:* Accepted, call 934-5412.

The French Quarter-themed Bonfamilles Cafe, which derives its name from the Disney movie "The AristoCats", features a casually unique atmosphere enhanced by courtyards, paddle fans, brick, wood, and tile accents. The menu includes steaks, shrimp & crawfish remoulade, BBQ oysters, Mardi Gras Combos, and Bonfamille's Family Salad.

SASSAGOULA FLOATWORKS AND FOOD FACTORY
Service: Food court. *Meals:* B,L,D,S. *Cuisine:* American (Creole). *Price:* $5 to $15. *Location:* Port Orleans.

This food court features four shops in a Mardi Gras theme. Basin Street Burgers and Chicken offers burgers, batter-fried chicken, and deli items. Jacques Beignet's Bakery sells baked goods, homemade ice cream, and soft-serve. The King Creole Broiler sells roasted chicken, Jambalaya, and other Creole dishes. Last, but not least, the Preservation Pizza Company sells pasta and hand-tossed pizza, the latter of the two available for delivery to all guestrooms.

At the Disney Vacation Club Resort
GOOD'S FOOD TO GO
Fast food is served up at poolside.

OLIVIA'S CAFE
Service: Table-service. *Meals:* B,L,D. *Cuisine:* American (Florida). Price: $5 to $15. *Location:* Disney Vacation Club.

This new cafe offers Floridian cuisine like Turtle Krawl, conch fritters, homemade French fries, and Key Lime white chocolate mousse desserts. Herbs from Olivia's own garden are used to season the dishes offered.

In Disney's Village Resort
DISNEY VILLAGE CLUBHOUSE SNACK BAR
In the Clubhouse, this counter-service eatery offers continental breakfasts and coffee, sandwiches, hot dogs, hamburgers, snacks, ice cream, and soft drinks.

POMPANO GRILL
Service: Table-service. *Meals:* B,L,D. *Cuisine:* American (Florida). *Price:* $5 to $15. *Location:* In the Lake Buena Vista Clubhouse. *Children:* Special menu. *Rsrvtns:* Suggested, call 828-3735.

The clubby atmosphere of the former Lake Buena Vista Club has been replaced by a casual Southern flair. The Grill is much more family-oriented now, and is a favorite of those privy to knowledge of WDW eateries. The menu includes fresh fish, Maine lobster, Key West Caesar salad, nachos, prime rib, chicken, and strip steak. There's a buffet at breakfast, and an a la carte menu including cräpes, waffles, omelets, fruits, and pancakes.

REFRESHMENT CART
This cart roams the links searching for hungry duffers.
Villa Centers These snack bars at the Vacation Villas, Treehouse Villas, and Club Suites sell burgers, hot dogs, fries, sandwiches, soda, ice cream, and beer.

In the Hotel Plaza
ARTHUR'S 27
Service: Table-service. *Meals:* D. *Cuisine:* Continental. *Location:* Buena Vista Palace, 27th floor. *Prices:* $24 and up a la carte. Prix fixe dinners, $44 for four courses, $60 for six. *Dress:* Elegant, jackets required for men. *Rsrvtns:* Required, call 827-3450. *Comments:* Not available with Disney Vacation Plans.

This elegant spot boasts an incredible view of all central Florida. An extensive wine list are available. The restaurant's skilled chefs can satisfy any dietary request with advance notice. Entertainment is provided by the Jazz Trio that performs on Friday and Saturday, the two nights that are most popular at the restaurant. AAA calls it a "unique culinary experience," with "artistic presentations impeccably served." And they slapped Arthur's 27 with a Four Diamond Award.

Orlando Magazine's readers named it one of the top three continental restaurants in the metropolis. It was given the Golden Spoon Award as one of the state's top 12 restaurants, four times. Reservations are required and should be made as soon as possible.

COURTYARD PASTRIES AND PIZZA SHOP (Buena Vista Palace)
This snack bar offers fast food above and beyond the usual hot dogs and hamburgers.

THE OUTBACK
Service: Table-service. *Meals:* D. *Cuisine:* Steak and seafood. *Price:* $13 to $25. *Location:* Buena Vista Palace, third floor. *Rsrvtns:* Suggested, call 827-3450. *Comments:* Not available with Disney Vacation Plans.

This comfortable, Australian-themed restaurant offers oversized Black Angus steaks, six-pound lobsters, fresh seafood, ribs, veal, and lamb, grilled to order. A good bet for hearty eaters, the restaurant is accented with rock grottos, fountains, plants, and pools.

POOL SNACK BAR (Buena Vista Palace)
Located on the recreation island, this offers the usual array of burgers and dogs.

WATERCRESS CAFE AND BAKE SHOP
Service: Table-service. *Meals:* B,L,D,S. *Cuisine:* American (Florida). *Price:* $5 to $15. *Location:* Buena Vista Palace, first floor.

This Mediterranean-themed bistro overlooks a lake and features sandwiches, Florida seafood, soups, salads, and pasta. The menu is priced and designed for families, good news for families out there (and you know who you are!). There is a character buffet breakfast held daily, as well as another buffet at dinner time. The pastries here are great.

BASKERVILLE'S
Service: Table-service. *Meals:* B,L,D. *Cuisine:* American. *Location:* Grosvenor Resort. *Prices:* Breakfast $1 to $5, Dinner $10 to $15. *Comments:* Not available with Disney Vacation Plans.

This restaurant surrounds a Sherlock Holmes museum and serves Sherlock's Breakfast, prime rib, fresh grouper, stir-fry vegetables with shrimp, chicken, or beef, and impressive specialty buffets, including an unlimited Prime Rib buffet held nightly for $14.95. A breakfast buffet is available.

CRUMPETS CAFE
Service: Buffeteria. *Meals:* B,L,D,S. *Cuisine:* American. *Price:* $1 to $7. *Location:* Grosvenor Resort, lobby.

Salads, sandwiches, and pastries are available 24 hours.

PARROT PATCH
Service: Table-service or buffet. *Meals:* B,L,D. *Cuisine:* American. *Prices:* Breakfast $1 to $5, $5 to $15 otherwise. *Location:* Guest Quarters Suite Resort. *Children:* Special menu. *Rsrvtns:* Suggested, call 934-1000, ext. 126.

This restaurant, located in the midst of a 2-story aviary, offers a breakfast buffet daily, plus traditional American fare with seasonal specialty dishes.

POOLSIDE BAR AND ICE CREAM PARLOR (Guest Quarters)
Serves snack food, frozen desserts, and beverages.

AMERICAN VINEYARDS
Service: Table-service. *Meals:* D, brunch. *Cuisine:* American regional.
Price: $14 to $24. *Location:* Hilton. *Rsrvtns:* Suggested, call 827-4000,
ext. 4025. *Comments:* Not available with Disney Vacation Plans.

This, the Hilton's top restaurant, features an outstanding menu filled
with regional American dishes like Florida stone crabs, Maine lobster,
quail, hickory-smoked Vermont turkey with dressing and all the fixings,
and Gulf shrimp sauteed in garlic butter sauce. The decor is devoted to,
as the name suggests, the origins of wine.
This makes an especially attractive spot for couples with children to
go out by themselves because a dinner at the restaurant entitles the diners
to 3 hours of complimentary child care, regardless of whether the diner
is a hotel guest. Sumptuous brunches are offered during the spring, fall,
and holiday seasons.

BENIHANA – THE JAPANESE STEAKHOUSE
Service: Table-service. *Meals:* L,D,S. *Cuisine:* Amer. Japanese. *Price:* $13
to $32. *Location:* Hilton. *Children:* Special menu. *Rsrvtns:* Suggested,
call 827-4865. *Comments:* Not available with Disney Vacation Plans.

The 1,000-year old art of cooking steak, shrimp, chicken, and vegetables at a teppan table is practiced here, much to the amazement of the
diners at this branch of the prominent chain. The highlight is the
Benihana Special: tender New York strip steak, cold water lobster tail,
Japanese onion soup, Benihana salad, shrimp appetizer, Hibachi vegetables, rice, tea, and a special fresh pineapple dessert. There is a full bar
and lounge.

COUNTY FAIR RESTAURANT
Service: Buffeteria. *Meals:* B,L,D. *Cuisine:* American. *Price:* $5 to $15.
Location: Hilton. *Comments:* Not available with Disney Vacation Plans.

At this coffee shop, a buffet breakfast is offered. At lunch and dinner,
there's an prime rib and barbecued chicken buffet. The house specialties
on the a la carte menu are burgers, pasta, seafood, and steaks. There is a
selection of international beers and take-out is available.

POOL SNACK BAR (Hilton)
Burgers, sandwiches, fruit, snacks, and ice cream served at poolside.

RUM LARGO BROILER (Hilton)
This eatery offers hot dogs, hamburgers, sandwiches, and other snack fare in a greenhouse atmosphere.

PLAZA DINER
Service: Table-service. *Meals:* B,L,D,S. *Cuisine:* American. *Prices:* $1 to $5 at breakfast, $7 to $15 otherwise. *Location:* Hotel Royal Plaza.

This nostalgic 50's diner offers homestyle American fare like Blue Plate Specials, pizza, and gourmet burgers. In addition, liquor and take-out are offered.

HOWARD JOHNSON RESTAURANt
Service: Table-service. *Meals:* B,L,D. *Cuisine:* American. *Price:* $5 to $12. *Location:* Howard Johnson Resort. *Comments:* Not available with Disney Vacation Plans.

The HoJo's here is like HoJo's everywhere, offering good, predictable American food from early in the morning until late at night. Entertainment at dinnertime is provided seasonally by a clown show. As for the food, you know HoJo. The fried clams and ice cream are the specialties. Take-out is available.

SIDEWALK CAFE CART (Howard Johnson)
This stand in the lobby offers continental breakfasts and snack fare. Parakeet Cafe (Travelodge) This coffeeshop offers burgers, sandwiches, pizza, and salads in the lobby.

TRADERS RESTAURANT
Service: Table-service. *Meals:* B,D. *Cuisine:* International. *Price:* $5 to $15. *Location:* Travelodge. *Children:* Special menu. *Rsrvtns:* Suggested, call 828-2424. *Comments:* Not available with Disney Vacation Plans.

The fare at this restaurant, styled after a Barbados plantation, includes island specialties like Madagascar sirloin steak, Barbados baby back ribs, and Aegean chicken brochette. Liquor and take-out are served.

LOUNGES

There are many bars, nightclubs, and lounges located within the confines of Walt Disney World. Each of the six clubs in Pleasure Island has a bar or two inside it, and EPCOT Center and the Studios have them as well.

In EPCOT Center
LAND GRILLE ROOM
This restaurant also has a small lounge where patrons can sit and imbibe while waiting for a table.

SAN ANGEL INN
In the Mexico pavilion, guests waiting for a table can sit amongst the stars in the plaza and sip cocktails.

MATSU NO MA LOUNGE
This lounge, located in the Mitsukoshi dining complex on the second story of the Japan pavilion, offers exotic drinks, sushi, tempura, and Kabuki beef or chicken. The lounge provides a sparkling view of World Showcase Lagoon and the nightly IllumiNations display.

ROSE & CROWN PUB
Located on the Promenade in front of the United Kingdom pavilion, the Rose & Crown offers snacks like Stilton cheese, fruit platters, miniature chicken-and-leek or steak-and-kidney pies, and Scotch eggs. A variety of brews from the isles is available, including English Bass Ale, Scottish Tennent's Lager, and Irish Guiness Stout and Harp Lager. Also available are English mixed drinks. Note that reservations are not accepted at the Pub, but they are at the adjacent dining room. The Pub also boasts a magnificently panoramic vista of World Showcase Lagoon and the nightly IllumiNations show.

In the Disney-MGM Studios
TUNE IN LOUNGE
Located alongside the 50s Prime Time Cafe, this whimsical lounge features fiercely personal nostalgia, with the furniture and decor of Beaver Cleaver's (and your!) childhood living room. Appetizers and drinks are served.

CATWALK BAR
This bar, situated above the Soundstage Restaurant, features a menu of bar fare including peel-your-own-shrimp and nachos with red bean salsa.

In the Disney Village Marketplace
BATON ROUGE LOUNGE
Located on the Empress Lilly riverboat is this pleasant bistro, which features live entertainment from the Jazz Connection each evening. The menu offers snacks like the delicious Bayou Chips and drinks like

Singapore Slings and Melancholy Babies.

EMPRESS LOUNGE

This lounge is also located on the Empress Lilly, alongside the Empress Room. It shares the posh restaurant's Victorian splendor and features live harp music nightly.

CAP'N JACK'S OYSTER BAR

(See also earlier in this chapter). Cap'n Jack's is a bar, first and foremost, whose popularity has turned it into a restaurant. The Cap'n offers various hot and cold seafood dishes, all in the $5 to $10 range. As for liquid refreshments, the house specialty? Margaritas! And lots of 'em! Beer, wine, and mixed drinks are also served.

VILLAGE LOUNGE

Adjoining Chef Mickey's Village Restaurant, this lounge is pleasant, comfortable, and one of the most relaxing spots in the entire resort.

On Pleasure Island

Each of the six nightclubs has at least one bar within its confines, offering drinks and snack fare. For information on dining in the clubs, see the "Restaurants in Pleasure Island" section earlier in this chapter.

PORTOBELLO YACHT CLUB

There is a small, though lively, bar situated in the restaurant, where guests can nibble light snacks and try some of the Portobello's specialty drinks. No cover charge is required to enter the lounge at any time. Fireworks Factory Like her sister restaurant, the Portobello, the Fireworks Factory has a no-cover bar located on the premises. The pyrotechnic atmosphere is especially favorable for kicking your feet up and relaxing with a drink in hand. You can get your beverage "explosive" or "defused." There is never a cover charge to enter the Fireworks Factory.

In the Resorts
BACK PORCH (Disney Inn)

The Disney Inn's only lounge, this "19th hole" offers specialty drinks and a wide variety of bar snacks including chili, sandwiches, shrimp, and salad.

OUTER RIM SEAFOOD AND COCKTAIL LOUNGE (Contemporary)

(See under RESTAURANTS earlier in this chapter). This lounge serves sandwiches, seafood appetizers, and drinks.

SAND BAR (Contemporary)
This seasonal pool bar offers snacks and drinks.

TOP OF THE WORLD COCKTAIL LOUNGE (Contemporary)
Fifteen stories above the shores of Bay Lake, the Top offers a spectacular view of the Electrical Water Pageant and the Fantasy in the Sky fireworks, when in season. Beer, wine, and liquors are served in the lounge and on two outdoor observation decks. To see the Water Pageant, head for the more easterly (Fort Wilderness side) of the decks.

GARDEN VIEW LOUNGE (Grand Floridian)
This turn-of-the-century lounge offers tea service each afternoon along with a grand view of the pool and courtyard.

MIZNER'S LOUNGE (Grand Floridian)
This quiet, friendly lounge on the second floor of the main building pays homage to the eccentric father of Palm Beach architecture.

NARCOOSEE'S LOUNGE (Grand Floridian)
Alongside the restaurant of the same name, this lounge features an unusual mode of service: Yards of Beer. You can order brew by the mug, the half-yard, and the yard.

SUMMERHOUSE POOL BAR (Grand Floridian)
This bar serves guests at the pool or beach.

BAREFOOT POOL BAR (Polynesian)
Located at the Swimming Pool Lagoon, the Barefoot offers soda, beer, spirits, and mixed drinks like pina coladas, frozen daquiris, and mai tais.

TAMBU LOUNGE (Polynesian)
Next to the Papeete Bay Verandah, this cozy lounge offers Polynesian appetizers and specialty drinks. Modest entertainment nightly.

THE BANANA CABANA (Caribbean Beach)
This bar, set alongside the pool at Old Port Royale, offers beer, mixed drinks, and light snack fare.

CAPTAIN'S HIDEAWAY (Caribbean Beach)
This 200-seat dive in Old Port Royale offers beer, wine, mixed drinks, and snacks.

ALE AND COMPASS (Yacht and Beach Clubs)
The Yacht Club's lobby bar, the Ale and Compass is open late for guests returning from the theme parks and serves beer, wine, and specialty drinks.

CREW CUP LOUNGE (Yacht and Beach Clubs)
Next to the Yachtman's Steakhouse is this pleasant lounge, styled after a New England waterfront tavern.

MARTHA'S VINEYARD LOUNGE (Yacht and Beach Clubs)
Next to Ariel's, this bar specializes in wines, not only from the Massachusetts town that gives it its name, but also from Long Island, Californian, and European wineries.

RIPTIDE LOUNGE (Yacht and Beach Clubs)
Located in the lobby of the Beach Club, the Riptide offers California wines, wine coolers, frozen drinks, beer, and mixed drinks until 1 AM.

CABANA BAR (Dolphin)
This is the Dolphin Hotel's poolside bar.

CARNEVALE BAR (Dolphin)
Next to the Ristorante Carnevale, this lounge features the same entertainment and atmosphere as the restaurant, except you don't have to buy a meal to enjoy it.

COPA BANANA (Dolphin)
This funky bar is the one most in tune with the eclectic theme of the hotel, with tables shaped like pieces of fruit. Beer, wine, spirits, and Caribbean-themed appetizers are served, and there is live music in the evenings.

HARRY'S SAFARI BAR (Dolphin)
Harry the Barkeep has travelled the world, and boy, has he got some tales to tell.

LOBBY LOUNGE (Dolphin)
Sit here, relax with a cool drink in one hand and an appetizer in the other, and watch the people strolling by.

KIMONOS LOUNGE (Swan)
This Japanese lounge offers exotic drinks and sushi in eye-catching Oriental surroundings.

LOBBY COURT LOUNGE (Swan)
The lobby is peppered with sofas where one can drink while listening to a piano and viewing the passing world.

PALIO LOUNGE (Swan)
This lounge adjoins the Italian restaurant of the same name and offers mixed drinks, beer, and wine.

COTTON CO-OP (Dixie Landings)
This pleasant barroom, designed as a cotton exchange, offers hors d'oeuvres, beer, wine, and specialty drinks.

MUDDY RIVERS (Dixie Landings)
This bar, located on Ol' Man Island, serves drinks and snacks during pool hours.

MARDI GROGS (Port Orleans)
Beer, mixed drinks, and snacks are served at poolside.

SCAT CAT'S CLUB (Port Orleans)
Hors d'oeuvres, beer, wine, and liquors are served in this bar, reflecting the French Quarter theme of the hotel.

THE GURGLING SUITCASE (Disney Vacation Club)
Why does a suitcase gurgle? And what would said suitcase be doing next to a hotel swimming pool? It doesn't matter, all that matters is that you can get beer, wine, and mixed drinks here.

POMPANO LOUNGE (Disney's Village Resort)
Located in the Lake Buena Vista Clubhouse, this bar offers beer, wine, mixed drinks, sandwiches, appetizers, and pizza from noon to 10 PM.

In the Hotel Plaza
BUENA VISTA PALACE LOBBY LOUNGE (Buena Vista Palace)
Here, you can get beer, wine, mixed drinks, specialty coffees and teas, and pastries. Piano music is featured.

THE LAUGHING KOOKABURRA "GOOD TIME BAR" (Buena Vista Palace).
Ninety-nine bottles of beer on the wall, and never the same beer twice. The bar's claim to fame is the availability of 99 different brands of brew. There is a happy hour with free hors d'oeuvres from 4 PM to 8 PM each

night, plus dancing and a live band Tuesday through Sunday. One of the most popular bars in the World.

POOL BAR (Buena Vista Palace)
The bar on the recreation island offers beer, mixed drinks, and a Florida raw bar.

TOP OF THE PALACE LOUNGE (Buena Vista Palace)
Not to be confused with the Top of the World Lounge, the Top of the Palace features a wine cellar with over 800 bottles in stock, live entertainment, and a stellar view of the Vacation Kingdom from 27 stories up.

CRICKETS INTERNATIONAL CAFE (Grosvenor)
Drinks and light fare are served throughout the day.

MORIARTY'S (Grosvenor)
Named for Sherlock Holmes's arch-enemy, this bar features darts and drinks in a Sherlockian atmosphere. Be sure to notice the portrait of Moriarty himself on the wall.

PARROT PERCH LOUNGE (Guest Quarters)
In the lobby atrium, kick back with a drink in hand. The atmosphere here is particularly relaxing.

POOLSIDE BAR (Guest Quarters)
Ice cream, snacks, beer, and mixed drinks are served.

AMERICAN VINEYARDS LOUNGE (Hilton)
Adjoining the restaurant of the same name, the American Vineyards Lounge offers beer, mixed drinks, and wine, around which the restaurant is themed.

JOHN T'S (Hilton)
This lobby lounge features nightly entertainment.

RUM LARGO (Hilton)
Here, you can enjoy tropical drinks and appetizers in a greenhouse atmosphere.

GIRAFFE LOUNGE (Hotel Royal Plaza)
This, the only disco in Walt Disney World, is immensely popular with tourists, locals, and Disney employees ("cast members", please). There is dancing to live Top 40 music. There's a happy hour from 4 PM to 9:30 PM,

with complimentary hors d'oeuvres. The disco is open until 3 AM.

INTERMISSIONS LOUNGE (Hotel Royal Plaza)
Happy hour at this lounge is from midnight to 2:30 AM.

TERRACE LOUNGE (Howard Johnson)
This lounge, located in the lobby, serves beer, wine, cocktails, and soft drinks.

CALYPSO'S POOL BAR (Travelodge)
This bar serves tropical drinks, including Caribbean wine coolers.

FLAMINGO COVE (Travelodge)
A variety of mixed drinks and cocktails is served in the tropical setting here.

TOPPERS NIGHT CLUB (Travelodge)
This 18th-floor lounge offers nightly entertainment and a view of the IllumiNations and Pleasure Island pyrotechnics.

DINING IN CHURCH STREET STATION

Church Street Station, located at 124 West Church Street, Orlando (422-2434), a mostly adult entertainment complex, has seven restaurants. They are:

LILI MARLENE'S AVIATOR PUB AND RESTAURANT
(L,D, $15.95 and up) sits in the painstakingly restored frame of the Strand Hotel, offers specialty cuisine, including steaks, seafood, chicken, and pasta. Sunday brunch is also served.

CRACKERS OYSTER BAR
(L,D, $9.75 and up) serves up 50 beers, 40 wines, and a palate-tempting assortment of fish, oysters, shrimp, crab claws, salads, pastas, gumbos, and clam chowder. Steak, chicken, and appetizers are also served.

CHEYENNE BARBEQUE RESTAURANT
(L,D, $12.50 and up) offers beef, pork, and chicken with buttermilk biscuits, bourbon baked beans, and fruit cobblers.

ROSIE O'GRADY'S
Offers deli sandwiches and hot dogs from 11 AM to midnight.

COMMANDER RAGTIME'S MIDWAY GRILL

Commander Ragtime's dishes up burgers, hot dogs, chicken sandwiches, french fries, and onion rings.

THE EXCHANGE FOOD COURT

Features six counter-service eateries: Bain's Deli, Chinese Cafe, Corrado's Pizza, Cuban Cafe, The Greek Place, and Taco Viva.

THE WINE CELLAR

Bills itself to be "central Florida's only true wine cellar," encompasses 700 square feet, 12 feet underground. With over 4,000 varieties of wine representing 500 vineyards, it is one of Florida's best-stocked. Daily tastings are held, and all the wine is available to take home.

DINING IN AND AROUND ORLANDO

Catering to millions of tourists a year, Orlando needs, and has, a plethora of restaurants to accommodate every taste. Listed below is a cross-section of the restaurants in the area, divided by the style of cuisine offered. This section does NOT include restaurants in WDW, Universal, or Sea World. Restaurants described as budget cost under $9 for dinner entrees. Moderate restaurants cost $10–$19. Expensive restaurants cost more than $20 for entrees.

American

B&A BUFFET

Location: 4944 W. Irlo Bronson Mem. Hwy., Kissimmee. *Price:* Budget. *Phone:* 396-1038. *Meals:* B,L,D.

B&A offers one of the more unusual buffets in the area, with a host of American and British items.

BENNIGAN'S

Locations & Phone: 6109 Westwood Blvd., Orlando, 352-5657; 6324 International Dr., Orlando,351-4435; 244 W. S.R. 436, Altamonte Spr., 862-7200; 7630 S. Orange Blossom Tr., Orl., 851-1266; 4250 E. Colonial Drive, Orlando, 896-6516; 1385 N. Semoran Blvd., Casselberry, 677-5600 *Price:* Budget to moderate. *Meals:* B,L,D.

Bennigan's is a combination bar and restaurant that locals enjoy for happy hour festivities and families like for its hearty, chic American menu. Burgers, salads, and sandwiches are featured.

B-LINE DINER
Location: The Peabody Orlando, 9801 I-Drive, Orlando. *Price:* Budget to moderate. *Phone:* 345-4460. *Meals:* B,L,D.

Located in the swank Peabody Hotel, the B-Line offers good ol' American fare in a 1958 atmosphere twenty-four hours a day. Full bar service and take-out are available.

BONANZA
Location: 3615 W. Vine Street, Kissimmee. *Price:* Budget. *Phone:* 932-4464. *Meals:* B,L,D.

Bonanza offers steaks, burgers, sandwiches, and an all-you-can-eat buffet including wings, fresh soups, and salads.

THE BUBBLE ROOM
Location: 1351 S. Orlando Ave., Maitland. *Price:* Moderate. *Phone:* 628-3331. *Meals:* L,D.

The Bubble Room's decor is a wild melange of junk and antiques from the 1930's and 40's. The menu is just as eccentric, with entrees with names like Hit the Deck, the Eddie Fisherman, and the Hedy Lam(b)arr.

DAMON'S
Location: Mercado, 8445 International Drive, Orlando. *Price:* Budget to moderate. *Phone:* 352-5984. *Meals:* L,D.

Damon's offers some of the best barbecue fare in the area, including ribs, steaks, chicken, prime ribs, and Damon's Onion Loaf, a big brick of golden-brown onion rings.

DUFF'S SMORGASBORD
Location: 4118 W. Vine St., Kissimmee. *Price:* Budget. *Phone:* 847-5093. *Meals:* L,D.

One of the many buffet restaurants in the area, Duff's offers lunch and dinner seven days a week.

DUX
Location: The Peabody Orlando, 9801 international Drive, Orlando. *Price:* Expensive. *Dress:* Jacket required. *Phone:* 345-4550. *Meals:* D.

The Peabody's signature restaurant features a selection of American regional cuisine in an elegant setting from 6 to 11 PM, Monday through Saturday.

FARMER'S BUFFET

Location: Midway Factory Outlet Center, U.S. 192, Kiss., and U.S. 192 across from 192 Flea Market. *Price:* Budget. *Phone:* 696-6532, 396-2700. *Meals:* B,L,D.

The Farmer's Buffet offers entrees including BBQ ribs, fried shrimp, roast beef, roast turkey, spaghetti, veal parmesan, and fried chicken.

FRIENDLY'S

Locations and Phone: 8718 International Drive, Orlando, 345-1655; 4753 S. Kirkman Road, Orlando, 295-6843; 3915 W. Vine Street, Kissimmee, 846-4432. *Price:* Budget. *Meals:* B,L,D,S.

Friendly's really does seem friendly, an envoy from home when you lose your luggage, ding your rental car door, and lose your reservation Frozen yogurt, ice cream, sandwiches, soups, and salads are served.

HARD ROCK CAFE - See Chapter 17.

HOOTERS

Locations and Phone: 5300 Kirkman Road, Orlando, 354-5350; 55 W. Church Street, Orlando, 649-4327; 280 W. S.R. 434, Altamonte Springs, 862-8900; 2699 Cassel Creek Rd., Altamte. Spr., 767-8822. *Price:* Budget to moderate. *Meals:* L,D.

Hooters offers tasty chicken wings, oysters, sandwiches, steaks, and ribs, but people seem to overlook the food when talking about Hooters. Everybody always seems to focus on the Hooters girls, waitresses in tank tops and tiny orange shorts. Happy hours are aptly named here, and there's rock music and an under-30 crowd after dark.

JACK'S PLACE

Location: Clarion Plaza, 9700 International Dr., Orlando. *Price:* Moderate to expensive. *Phone:* 352-9700. *Meals:* D.

Jack's Place, named for Jack Rosen, whose caricatures hang on the wall, offers London broil, filet mignon, shrimp, prime rib, cedar plank salmon, pasta, escargots, and other American specialties. For dessert, go for fried ice cream.

JORDAN'S GROVE
Location: 1300 S. Orlando Ave., Maitland. *Price:* Expensive. *Phone:* 628-0020. *Meals:* L,D, Sun brunch.

Jordan's Grove is an elegant little spot north of the city, offering fresh seafood, wild game, red meats, fowl, and pastas served up in American Regional dishes.

JUNGLE JIM'S
Location: Church Street Marketplace, 55 W. Church Street, Orlando, and Crossroads of Lake Buena Vista, S.R. 535 at I-4 exit. *Price:* Budget to moderate. *Phone:* 872-3111, 827-1258. *Meals:* L,D.

"Superpowerful" tropical drinks, specialty sandwiches, salads, and more are offered in a safari atmosphere.

MORRISON'S CAFETERIA
Locations & Phone: 7440 International Drive, Orlando, 351-0051; 420 E. Altamonte Dr., Altamonte Spr., 339-5741; Winter Park Mall, Winter Park, 644-7853; Florida Mall, Orlando, 859-1607; 1840 E. Colonial Drive, Orlando, 896-2091; Osceola Square Mall, Kissimmee, 846-6011. *Price:* Budget. *Meals:* L,D

Morrison's offers 100 simple, freshly-prepared menu selections daily.

PEBBLES
Location: Crossroads of Lake Buena Vista, 12551 S.R. 535, Lake Buena Vista. *Price:* Moderate. *Phone:* 827-1111. *Meals:* L,D.

Pebbles offers a selection of intriguing, health-conscious soups, sandwiches, salads, bagel crust pizzas, and cocktails in a casual, California atmosphere.

PERKINS RESTAURANT
Locations and Phone: 7451 W. Irlo Bronson Memorial Hwy., Kissimmee, 396-0845; 5170 W. Irlo Bronson Memorial Hwy., Kissimmee, 396-8960; 1400 E. Vine Street, Kissimmee, 846-7556; 3419 W. Vine Street, Kissimmee, 847-3577; 6813 Sand Lake Drive, Orlando (at I-Drive); 7000 Kirkman Road, Orlando; 12559 S.R. 535, Lake Buena Vista, 827-1060. *Price:* Budget. *Meals:* B,L,D.

Perkins, a family place open 24 hours, is well-known for their pancakes. Also served: Eggs Benedict, steak, burgers, and sandwiches.

T.G.I. FRIDAY'S

Location: 6424 Carrier Dr., Orlando, and Crossroads of Lake Buena Vista, S.R. 535 and I-4. *Price:* Budget. *Phone:* 345-8822, 827-1020. *Meals:* L,D.

The Great American Bistro, as Friday's is known, serves up tasty American favorites including sandwiches, steaks, burgers, and over 400 different drinks.

TRADEWINDS

Location: Stouffer Orlando Resort, 6677 Sea Harbor Dr., Orlando. *Price:* Moderate. *Phone:* 351-5555. *Meals:* B,L,D.

Tradewinds, an open-air cafe in the luxuriant Stouffer Orlando, offers a pleasant dining experience across the street from Sea World, an excellent choice for a lunch to break up the day at the marine park.

Chinese

CHINA COAST

Location: 7500 International Drive, Orlando. *Price:* Budget. *Phone:* 351-9776. *Meals:* B,L,D.

Breakfast and lunch are offered buffet-style, and dinner is a la carte at this casual restaurant near Wet'n Wild.

FORTUNE COURT

Location: 8607 Palm Parkway, Lake Buena Vista. *Price:* Budget to moderate. *Phone:* 239-2399. *Meals:* L,D.

The Fortune Court is a personal favorite of mine as far as Chinese food in Orlando is concerned, because the restaurant feels much more like a local place you pop into for wonton soup and an egg roll than a tourist-oriented dive less than a mile from Walt Disney World. Traditional Schezuan and Hunan cuisine is featured.

MING COURT

Location: 9188 International Drive, Orlando. *Price:* Moderate. *Phone:* 351-9988. *Meals:* L,D.

Now this is one joint nobody would dare call quaint. It's flashy as Universal and Disney. It's virtually impossible not to see it. The emphasis is on grilled Florida seafood and steak interspersed with regional Chinese cuisine. There's a dim sum bar and live Chinese music nightly.

TREY YUEN
Location: 6800 Visitors Circle, Orlando. *Price:* Budget. *Phone:* 352-6822. *Meals:* L,D.

This restaurant is particularly convenient to Wet'n Wild, Universal, and the northern half of I-Drive.

Continental

ATLANTIS
Location: Stouffer Orlando, 6677 Sea Harbor Dr., Orlando. *Price:* Expensive. *Phone:* 351-5555. *Meals:* D.

Elegant to the max, Atlantis offers stellar seafood and choice continental cuisine. Even better, for families with children, diners receive three hours of complimentary child care at the hotel's kids' club.

CHALET SUZANNE
Location: P.O. Box AC, Lake Wales. *Price:* Expensive. *Phone:* 813/676-6011. *Meals:* D.

Chalet Suzanne is a historic country inn and restaurant dating back to 1931. Its soups have flown on the Apollo 15 and 16 flights, and its eclectic cuisine has won it the Golden Spoon Award as one of Florida's top ten restaurants for twenty-three years running. Other awards it has won include the Mobil Four Star Award, Travel Holiday Fine Dining Award, and an appointment to the National Register of Historic Places. To get there, take I-4 west to Exit 23, U.S. 27. Take 27 south to Route 17A.

CHATHAM'S PLACE
Location: 7575 Dr. Phillips Blvd., Orlando. *Price:* Moderate to expensive. *Phone:* 345-2992. *Meals:* D.

Chatham's Place has an immense following who swear by their continental and American fare. Seafood, chicken, beef, and wild game dishes are featured.

MAISON & JARDIN
Location: 430 S. Wymore Road, Altamonte Springs. *Price:* Expensive. *Phone:* 862-4410. *Meals:* D.

The "Mason Jar," recipient of the Wine Spectator "Best of Award of Excellence" and Mobil Four Star awards, offering 40 wines by the glass and 800 by the bottle. The restaurant and its grounds are both beautiful, and the food is second to none. Dinner, cocktails, and Sunday champagne brunch are served. The restaurant is an excellent choice for a quiet, romantic night out.

French

LE COQ AU VIN
Location: 4800 S. Orange Ave., Orlando. *Price:* Moderate. *Phone:* 851-6980. *Meals:* L,D.

This restaurant features hearty French classics, with the focus on seafood prepared with flair by chef Louis Perotte, who hails from France's west coast and brings with him the cooking styles of the region.

LE CORDON BLEU
Location: 537 W. Fairbanks Ave., Winter Park. *Price:* Moderate to expensive. *Phone:* 647-7575. *Meals:* L,D.

Le Cordon Bleu features a selection of clasic French entrees like Chateaubriand, rack of lamb, stuffed mushrooms, and more. The pastries are decadent and delicious.

Indian

KABOB EXPRESS
Location: 7511 International Drive, Orlando. *Price:* Budget. *Phone:* 363-0336. *Meals:* L,D.

Kabab Express offers Tandoori cuisine and traditional specialties at fast food prices. Entrees, which come with curry rice and salad, include Tandoori chicken, kabab, qorma, and more.

NEW PUNJAB INDIAN RESTAURANT
Location: 7451 International Drive, Orlando. *Price:* Budget to moderate. *Phone:* 352-7887. *Meals:* L,D.

New Punjab offers a taste of Indian specialties with and without vegetables. Take-out is available, and the restaurant is open seven days a week. Call for reservations.

PASSAGE TO INDIA
Locations and Phone: 5532 International Drive, Orlando, 351-3456; 845

Sand Lake Road, Orlando, 856-8362.   *Price:*   Budget.   *Meals:*   L,D.

Passage to India offers authentic Indian cuisine cooked to order, mild to spicy. There's an all-you-can-eat lunch buffet for those who wish to sample the diverse cuisine of India, and beer and wine are served.

Italian

BERGAMO'S
Location: At Mercado, 8445 International Drive, Orlando. *Price:* Moderate. *Phone:* 352-3805. *Meals:* D.

Bergamo's is a classy place located in the Mercado Mediterranean Village shopping center, featuring "a taste of Italy — New York style." Complete with singing waiters. You may find a few surprises on the menu, which includes homemade pasta and traditional dishes, fresh seafood, and certified Angus steaks.

CAPRICCIO
Location: Peabody Orlando, 9801 I-Drive, Orlando. *Price:* Moderate. *Phone:* 345-4450. *Meals:* D.

Cappricio rounds out the trio of stellar restaurants in the Peabody Orlando, offering Northern Italian cuisine in an Italian modern setting, complete with display kitchen and brick pizza oven.

CARMENTE'S PIZZA
Locations and Phone: 7670 International Drive, Orlando, 351-3686; 7720 S. Orange Blossom Trail, Orlando , 855-3510. *Price:* Budget. *Meals:* B,L,D.

Carmente's is very much a traditional small-town pizzeria and Italian restaurant, serving pizza, pasta, chicken and veal parmesan, and other traditional dishes.

CARUSO'S PALACE
Location: 8986 International Drive, Orlando. *Price:*   Moderate to expensive. *Phone:* 363-7110, 363-3540. *Meals:* D.

This is a new, $5 million restaurant living up to its moniker of "palace". The exterior is designed as a tribute to the Italian Renaissance. The layout contains classical Corinthian columns with sculptures, while the interior celebrates Renaissance with ceiling paintings, faux marble columns, and gold leaf accent. Tapestries, wall murals, statues, and roaming musicians round out the atmosphere. As for the menu, it's pranzo completo, meaning that the entree cost determines the price of the five-course meal. Prices for meals start at $18.95, and each dinner includes a soup or salad, pasta dish, entree, and dessert. An early bird special, available from 5 to 6 PM, includes soup or salad, a pasta dish, dessert, and coffee or tea.

CHRISTINI'S
Location: 7600 Dr. Phillips Blvd., Orlando. *Price:* Moderate to expensive. *Phone:* 345-8770. *Meals:* D.

Ivy Award winner Chris Christini has 40 years of experience under his belt, and still personally orchestrates his culinary team as they prepare pasta, chicken, seafood, and veal dishes ranging from the well-interpreted staples like fettucine Alfredo and veal piccata to the unusual, like a four-cheese chicken breast, Maine lobster flambe, and lobster and shrimp Vesuvio. This restaurant was named one of the top three Italian restaurants in the Orlando Magazine Readers' Choice Awards.

DOMINO'S PIZZA
Price: Budget. *Meals:* L,D.

Call 896-3030 for pizza delivery anywhere in the metro Orlando, 396-0550 for Kissimmee delivery.

ENZO'S
Location: 1130 South U.S. 17-92, Longwood. *Price:* Expensive. *Phone:* 834-8972. *Meals:* L,D.

Enzo's was named the top Italian restaurant in Orlando by the Orlando Magazine Readers' Choice Awards, and for good reason. This placid spot, overlooking a beautiful lake, serves up traditional specialties for lunch and dinner Tuesday through Saturday.

FLIPPER'S PIZZA
Locations and Phone: 7480 Republic Drive, Orlando, 351-5643; 6125 Westwood Blvd., Orlando, 345-0113; 2934 Vineland Road, Kissimmee 396-1202 (from Lake Buena Vista), 239-7276. *Price:* Budget. *Meals:* L,D.
Standard pizzas are served here, and can be delivered to your hotel room. Also served are deli subs, salads, beer, wine, and soft drinks.

OLIVE GARDEN
Locations and Phones: * 7653 International Drive, Orlando, 351-1082;

*5021 W. Irlo Bronson Mem. Hwy., Kiss., 396-1680; 55 W. Church Street, in the Market, 648-1098; 1555 Sand Lake Road, Orlando, 851-0344; * 12361 Apopka-Vineland Road, Orlando, 239-6708. *Price:* Budget to moderate. *Meals:* B (starred locations only),L,D.

The Olive Garden is a great choice for lovers of veal and chicken parmesan, as well as for bar pizzas and traditional veal, seafood, and chicken dishes. The bottomless salad and garlic breadsticks are great complements to any meal, as are the sinful desserts, including cannoli, cheesecake, zuppa inglese, zabaglione, and tiramisu. The starred restaurants offer breakfast buffets daily, and all menu items are available for takeout.

PASTA LOVERS TRATTORIA
Location: 12384 Apopka-Vineland Road, Orlando. *Price:* Budget to moderate. *Phone:* 934-8888. *Meals:* L,D.

You don't have to be a rocket scientist to figure out the house specialty at this restaurant, located at the corner of Palm Parkway and S.R. 535. This restaurant is considered one of the better values in the area.

PIZZA HUT
Locations and Phone: 8128 S. Orange Blossom Trail, Orlando, 855-2287; 7060 International Drive, Orlando, 351-0005; 9100 International Drive, Orlando, 345-8833; 8699 Palm Parkway, Lake Buena Vista, 239-0950; 5801 Conroy Road, Orlando, 297-7676; 8555 W. Irlo Bronson Mem. Hwy., Kiss., 239-4456; 14525 Gatorland Drive, 856-4089 *Price:* Budget. *Meals:* L,D.

Pizza Hut offers great pan pizzas, everybody knows that. For dine-in or carry-out, there are six locations scattered throughout the tourist world. For delivery to International Drive, call 354-1582. To Lake Buena Vista, call 239-0205.

PIZZERIA UNO
Locations and Phone: 55 W. Church Street, in the Market, 839-1800; Crossroads of Lake Buena Vista, LBV, 827-1212. *Price:* Budget to moderate. *Meals:* L,D.

Pizzeria Uno offers Chicago-style pan pizzas in an old Windy City atmosphere. The pizzas come in more exotic varieties than those served at Pizza Hut.

VENEZIA RISTORANTE & PIZZERIA
Location: Old Town, 5770 West U.S. 192, Kissimmee. *Price:* Budget. *Phone:* 396-6244. *Meals:* L,D.

This is the place to go in Kissimmee for Italian dishes like pizza, calzones, fettucine Alfredo, and veal parmigiana.

Japanese

KOBE JAPANESE STEAKHOUSE
Locations and Phone: 2901 Parkway Blvd., Kissimmee, 396-8088; 8460 Palm Parkway, Lake Buena Vista, 239-1119; 468 W. Semoran Blvd., Altamonte Spr., 862-2888. *Price:* Budget to moderate. *Meals:* D.

The Kobe, its Vista Centre location easily visible from I-4, offers steak, chicken, lobster, shrimp, and scallops prepared on a Teppanyaki table.

RAN-GETSU
Location: 8400 International Drive, Orlando. *Price:* Moderate. *Phone:* 345-0044. *Meals:* D.

Ran-Getsu uses a garden atmosphere as a backdrop for tasty sushi, sukiyaki, tempura, and other traditional specialties. There's entertainment on weekends.

SHOGUN
Location: International Inn, 6327 I-Drive, Orlando. *Price:* Moderate. *Phone:* 352-1607. *Meals:* D.

Teppan table cooking is featured at this establishment.

Mexican

CASA GALLARDO RESTAURANT & BAR
Location: 8250 International Drive, Orlando. *Price:* Budget. *Phone:* 352-8121. *Meals:* L,D.

Mexican and Southwestern specialties are offered here, and the standouts are the chimichangas, steaks, and fajitas.

JOSE O'DAY'S
Location: In Mercado, 8445 International Drive, Orlando. *Price:* Budget. *Phone:* 363-0613. *Meals:* L,D.

This is a cool, casual restaurant specializing in authentic Mexican and Tex-Mex specialties.

Steak and Seafood

ATLANTIC BAY SEAFOOD GRILL

Location: 2901 Parkway Blvd., Kissimmee. *Price:* Moderate. *Phone:* 396-7736. *Meals:* B,L,D.

Atlantic Bay, located between the Hyatt Orlando and Arabian Nights, offers live Maine lobster, seven varieties of fresh fish daily, oysters on the half shell, prime rib, steak, pasta, and poultry.

BLACK ANGUS RESTAURANT

Location: 2001 W. Vine Street, Kissimmee. *Price:* Budget. *Phone:* 846-7117. *Meals:* B,L,D.

Black Angus sells certified Black Angus steaks, all-you-can-eat dinner specials, breakfast buffets, and salad and fruit bars. The breakfasts here are bounteous and low-cost.

BROWN DERBY

Location: 6115 Westwood Boulevard, Orlando. *Price:* Budget to Moderate. *Phone:* 352-4644. *Meals:* L,D.

At the corner of Westwood and I-Drive, the Girves Brown Derby offers a varied selection of steaks and seafood.

THE BUTCHER SHOP

Location: In Mercado, 8445 International Drive, Orlando. *Price:* Moderate. *Phone:* 363-9727. *Meals:* D.

The Butcher Shop is one of Mercado's classiest options, serving steaks from 14-ounce filets to 28-ounce T-Bones. Also served are prime rib, fresh fish, and chicken, cooked to perfection over hardwood grills. If you wish, you can take your raw cut of beef to the pit in the center of the restaurant and cook it to your own taste.

CAPTAIN NEMO'S

Location: 5469 W. Irlo Bronson Mem. Hwy., Kissimmee. *Price:* Budget to Moderate. *Phone:* 396-6911, 239-7729. *Meals:* B,L,D.

Nemo's offers a selection of steak and seafood dishes, plus happy hour, satellite sports, and homestyle breakfasts.

CATTLEMAN'S STEAKHOUSE

Location: 298 Vineland Road, Kissimmee. *Price:* Moderate. *Phone:* 397-1888. *Meals:* L,D.

Conveniently located at the corner of U.S. 192 and S.R. 535, the Cattleman's offers a selection of charbroiled, corn-fed beef, including a 32-ounce Porterhouse steak.

CHARLIE'S LOBSTER HOUSE

Location: In Mercado, 8445 International Drive, Orlando. *Price:* Moderate. *Phone:* 352-6929. *Meals:* L,D.

Charlie's brags the "best crab cakes in town," and who's to argue? Other fruits of the Florida and New England waters include chowders and biusques, clams, oysters, steaners, mussels, lobster, shrimp, scallops, crab legs, broiled fish, steaks, and more.

GILLIGAN'S

Locations and Phone: Hwy. 192, 4 1/2 mi. east of I-4. 396-1212; Hwy. 192 at Florida's Turnpike, 932-3002. *Price:* Budget to Moderate. *Meals:* L,D.

Gilligan's offers a variety of steak and seafood entrees, plus an all-you-can-eat seafood buffet with fried shrimp, broiled sole, fried grouper, seafood pasta primavera, New England clam chowder, and more.

HEMINGWAY'S

Location: Grand Cypress Resort, 1 Grand Cypress Blvd., Orlando. *Price:* Expensive. *Phone:* 239-1234, ext. 6238. *Meals:* L,D.

The upscale Hemingway's overlooks the Hyatt Regency's elaborate swimming pool from atop a rocky bluff, and the Key West atmosphere plays host to seafood, game, and steaks.

JONATHAN'S STEAK & SEAFOOD GROTTO

Location: 5600 International Drive, Orlando. *Price:* Moderate to Expensive. *Phone:* 351-7001. *Meals:* L,D.

Jonathan's has just as much atmosphere as any of the World Showcase restaurants, with light music, an 18-foot, 3-tiered waterfall, koi lagoon, and tropical plants throughout. The restaurant serves dishes like filet mignon, stuffed shrimp, chicken breast marsala, and more.

KEY W. KOOL'S
Location: 7725 W. Irlo Bronson Mem. Hwy., Kissimmee. *Price:* Budget to Moderate. *Phone:* 396-1166, 239-7166. *Meals:* B,L,D.

A hat-adorned penguin mugs at Kool's, a steak-seafood-and-cocktail joint west of Walt Disney World's main gate.

THE OCEAN GRILL
Location: 6432 International Drive, Orlando. Price: Moderate. *Phone:* 352-9993. *Meals:* L,D.

The fare at this friendly spot on International Drive (by Wet'n Wild) includes soups, salads, pasta, shrimp, steak, and seafood prepared in a range of styles from Southern to Chesapeake to New English to Pacific. If you enjoy lobster, and lots of it, the restaurant offers fresh, in fact, live, Maine lobster ranging from one to four pounds.

PALM STEAKHOUSE
Locations and Phone: 8460 Palm Parkway, Kissimmee, 239-7256; Crossroads of Lake Buena Vista, LBV, 862-7256. *Price:* Moderate. *Meals:* L,D.

The Palm offers prime, aged, lean, mequite-grilled cuts of beef.

PONDEROSA
Locations and Phone: 7598 W. Irlo Bronson Mem. Hwy., Kiss., 396-7721; 6362 International Drive, Orlando, 352-9343; 8510 International Drive, Orlando, 354-1477; 5771 W. Irlo Bronson Mem. Hwy., Kiss., 397-2477. *Price:* Budget. *Meals:* B,L,D.

Ponderosa offers up seteaks and the All-You-Can-Eat Grand Buffet.

RED LOBSTER
Locations and Phone: 7502 S. Orange Blossom Trail, Orlando, 851-3230; 5936 International Drive, Orlando, 351-9313; 4010 W. Vine Street, Kissimmee, 846-3513; 800 E. Altamonte Dr., Altamonte Spr., 834-0054; 9892 International Drive, Orlando, 345-0018; 12557 S.R. 535, Lake Buena Vista , 827-1045; 5690 W. Irlo Bronson Mem. Hwy., Kiss., 396-6997. *Price:* Budget to Moderate. *Meals*: L,D.

This popular chain offers steak, chicken, pasta, and seafood entrees.

SHEFFIELD'S
Location: 4725 S. Orange Blossom Trail, Orlando. *Price:* Moderate to

Expensive. *Phone:* 851-8760. *Meals:* D.

Sheffield's is an elegant spot set away from the tourist areas of the city. Entrees include choice and prime USDA beef, fresh catch, fresh sea scallops, Alaskan king crab legs, and shrimp and lobster tail, and all come with relish bowl, soup or salad, freshly baked Bavarian bread, fresh vegetables, and choice of potato.

SIZZLER

Locations and Phone: 9142 International Drive, Orlando,351-5369; 2195 Apopka-Vineland Road, Orlando, 345-0018 ; 7602 W. Irlo Bronson Mem. Hwy., Kiss., 397-0097; 4006 W. Vine Street, Kissimmee 846-2900. *Price:* Budget to moderate. *Meals:* L,D.

Sizzler offers steaks, salads, chicken, fish, and the famed Buffet Court.

WESTERN STEER FAMILY STEAKHOUSE
Location: 6315 International Drive, Orlando. *Price:* Budget. *Phone:* 352-9993. *Meals:* B,L,D.

This hearty eaters' haven offers all-you-care-to-eat buffets at all three meals, plus steaks and seafood.

Thai

SIAM ORCHID
Location: 7575 Republic Drive, Orlando. *Price:* Moderate. *Phone:* 351-0821. *Meals:* L,D.

The Siam Orchid, regarded by some as the most exotic restaurant in the International Drive area, offers curry, stir fry, seafood, and other authentic Thai cuisine.

Fast Food

Listed below are the locations of some representatives of national and regional fast-food chains. All are budget.

ARBY'S
8586 S. Orange Blossom Trail, Orlando; 219 W. Vine Street, Kissimmee; 5015 W. Irlo Bronson Mem. Hwy., Kissimmee; 7011 International Drive, Orlando.

BURGER KING
7667 International Drive, Orlando; 800 W. Vine Street, Kissimmee; 12491 Apopka-Vineland Road, Orlando; 800 W. Irlo Bronson Mem. Hwy., Kissimmee; 5760 W. Irlo Bronson Mem. Hwy., Kissimmee; 1920 E. Irlo Bronson Mem. Hwy., Kissimmee; 5515 International Drive, Orlando Dairy Queen Brazier; 6301 International Drive, Orlando.

KENTUCKY FRIED CHICKEN
9879 International Drive, Orlando; 6217 International Drive, Orlando; 5680 W. Irlo Bronson Mem. Hwy., Kissimmee; 1907 W. Vine Street, Kissimmee; 1924 W. Irlo Bronson Mem. Hwy., Kissimmee.

MCDONALD'S
6875 Sand Lake Drive, Orlando; 4706 W. Irlo Bronson Mem. Hwy., Kissimmee; 5725 W. Irlo Bronson Mem. Hwy., Kissimmee; 2110 E. Irlo Bronson Mem. Hwy., Kissimmee; 719 W. Vine Street, Kissimmee; 7627 Space Coast Parkway, Kissimmee; 8530 W. Irlo Bronson Mem. Hwy., Kissimmee ; 12549 S.R. 535, at Crossroads of Lake Buena Vista, LBV; 5400 S. Kirkman Road, Orlando; 9814 International Drive, Orlando.

POPEYE'S FAMOUS FRIED CHICKEN AND BISCUITS
6725 Sand Lake Road, Orlando; 324 W. Vine Street, Kissimmee; 12399 Apopka-Vineland Road, Lake Buena Vista

TACO BELL
12555 S.R. 535, at Crossroads of Lake Buena Vista, LBV; 1550 W. Vine Street, Kissimmee; 4951 W. Irlo Bronson Mem. Hwy., Kissimmee; 9891 International Drive, Orlando.

WENDY'S OLD FASHIONED HAMBURGERS
915 W. Vine Street, Kissimmee; 6320 International Drive, Orlando.

9. SPORTS & RECREATION

In the first part of this chapter you'll find the more popular sports and activities available in WDW, followed by the many possibilities in the greater Orlando area.

IN DISNEY WORLD

Walt Disney World's 43 square miles include five golf courses, numerous tennis courts, boating, swimming, and health clubs. You can ride a horse just as easily as you can ride Star Tours, and you can play baseball, basketball, skee ball, and almost anything else imaginable.

BASEBALL AND SOFTBALL – Diamonds, located in Fort Wilderness, are only open to WDW Resort guests. Bring your own equipment.

BASKETBALL – Basketball courts can be found throughout the camping loops of Fort Wilderness, but are open to resort guests only.

BIKING – Riding a bike is a good way to get around Fort Wilderness or Disney's Village Resort. There are paths and not-too-busy roads in both places. You may bring your own bike or rent one at the Bike Barn at Fort Wilderness or any of the Village Resort's Villa Centers. The cost is $4 an hour or $9 a day for regular bikes, $6 an hour or $10 a day for tandems. Included in some vacation plans. Call 824-2742.

BOATING – Walt Disney World has the world's fifth largest navy and the single largest pleasure boat fleet in the nation. Boating can be done at many locations in the World, and on a variety of craft, ranging from sailboats to speedboats to canoes. Boat rental is included in the cost of some vacation packages. You've got the following options:

Canoes – Canoes can be rented for traveling down the placid canals of Fort Wilderness. Cost is $4 per hour, $9 per day. Available at the Bike Barn.

Outrigger Canoes – Available at the Polynesian Resort's marina, six people can ride and paddle each of these Hawaiian contraptions through Seven Seas Lagoon. Cost is $12 an hour.

Pedal Boats – These are available at the marinas of the Contemporary, Grand Floridian, Polynesian, and Fort Wilderness Resorts for use on Seven Seas Lagoon and Bay Lake; at the Caribbean Beach Resort's marina on Barefoot Bay; at the Yacht and Beach Club Resorts' Bayside Marina; the waterways of Port Orleans and Dixie Landings; and the Dolphin and Swan's Crescent Lake. The cost is $5.50 a half hour or $8 an hour.

Pontoon Boats – These large, motorized, canopied boats cost $35 an hour and are good for families and other large groups. Available at the Contemporary, Fort Wilderness, Grand Floridian, and Polynesian Resorts.

Rowboats – Found at the Yacht and Beach Club marina for $5 a half hour.

Sailboats – Available at the Marketplace and all resort marinas except those at the Village Resort. The cost varies from $10 to $15, dependent on the type of boat: Sunfish, Capris, and Hobie Cat 14s and 16s are all available.

Toobies – Large innertubes with motors are available at the Port Orleans, Dixie Landings, and Caribbean Beach Resorts.

Waterskiing – Boats with driver and equipment can be rented for $65 an hour at any of the marinas on Seven Seas Lagoon or Bay Lake. Call the Contemporary's marina (824-1000) two or three days in advance for reservations.

Water Sprites – Small, two-man speedboats can be found cruising virtually all of the waterways in the World. They are available at all of the marinas for $11 a half hour. The little craft are very popular in the early afternoon, so plan accordingly.

FISHING – You can fish on a guided trip, complete with gear, driver/ guide, and refreshments. The trips depart from Fort Wilderness's marina every day at 8 AM, noon, and 4 PM. A two-hour excursion costs $110 for up to five fishing persons. Each additional hour costs $25.

Or, if you prefer going solo, check out the canals in Fort Wilderness and Disney's Village Resort, particularly in the Village, next to the

Treehouse Villas. No license is required, and those of you who are staying at accommodations with a kitchen can keep what you catch. Rods and reels are available for rent at Fort Wilderness's Bike Barn, and gear is for sale at the Trading Posts in the Fort. Included in some vacation plans. For reservations for the guided trips, call 824-2757.

GOLF

With the addition of the Bonnet Creek Golf Club, there are now 99 holes of golf inside the Walt Disney World complex. There are 45 holes at the Disney Inn, 18 at Disney's Village Resort, and 36 at Bonnet Creek. The golf here is so spectacular that it is an annual stop on the PGA Tour.

Recently, Walt Disney World was recognized as one of the top golf meeting resorts in the United States and was presented with a 1991 ACE Award honoring outstanding golf meeting resorts in a competition sponsored by *Successful Meetings* magazine. Resorts were rated on difficulty of their golf courses, quality of golf professional staffs, meeting facilities, accessibility, and hospitality. Only 100 resorts nationwide were nominated for the award.

The Disney Inn – This hamlet just west of the Grand Floridian Resort houses the original WDW links. The **Magnolia** offers 18 holes at distances ranging from 6,642 to 7,150 yards and the **Palm**, rated one of the nation's top 100 courses by Golf Digest Magazine, has 18 holes measuring 5,398 to 6,957 yards. Both are par-72 layouts, both designed by Joe Lee. The Palm differs from the Magnolia in that the fairways at the former are shorter, narrower, and wooded, and the Palm has nine water hazards. There are driving ranges at both courses.

New to Walt Disney World is the **Executive Course**, a nine-hole, 45-acre course designed specifically for the beginner. The course sits on a part of the resort that once held the Wee Links, a six-hole course designed for children. But the idea was scrapped and what now sits there is a par-36, 2,913-yard layout. There are water hazards and bunkers here, and the cost for 18 holes here is substantially lower than at the other courses. This is a walking course only.

After a round of golf, duffers can relax at the airy Garden Gallery for a snack or a meal or at the Back Porch for a drink. Also, refreshment carts travel the courses, offering sandwiches, snacks, beer, and soda.

Disney's Village Resort – Tucked away between the quiet villa retreat and the shores of Buena Vista Lagoon is the 18-hole **Lake Buena Vista** course. Also designed by Joe Lee, the par-72 links range in distance from 5,315 to 6,829 yards. This is a particularly pretty course as it winds through the Fairway and Treehouse Villas, the Vacation Club Resort, and scrubby forests and streams. At the Clubhouse, you can find the Pompano Grill, a pleasant restaurant featuring Florida specialties, a snack bar, the

Pompano Lounge, a swimming pool, three tennis courts, and a driving range. If you get the munchies while on the course, look for refreshment carts patrolling the links.

Bonnet Creek Golf Club – In January 1992, this pair of courses, located next to Fort Wilderness at the northeast corner of the World, opened with great fanfare. **Osprey Ridge** was designed by Tom Fazio and is a rather unusual course. Start with the natural terrain that surrounds the links. "Some of the factors that have us excited about the project are the vegetation, the water areas, and the wetlands which will become part of the background and framing for the holes," Fazio said. The par-72 Osprey Ridge will range from 5,305 yards from the forward tees, 7,150 from the pro tees. The men's yardage is 6,705.

Environmentally conscious duffers will be glad to know that the circulating 18-hole design of the course uses the existing land patterns to their fullest while preserving all of the adjacent wetlands and other natural areas. Other things that make the Ridge unique are its paths, winding through remote areas and the use of high ridges and mounding, with some tees, greens, and viewing areas 20 to 25 feet above grade. The ridge that gives the course its name has quite a bearing on play. Head pro Eric Fredricksen explains, "The ridge comes into play a variety of ways. You'll tee off of it on No. 3, you'll hit to a green on the side of it on No. 12, you'll shoot to a green on top of it at No. 16."

Eagle Pines, designed by Pete Dye, is another 18-hole, par-72 affair. But this one differs quite a bit from Osprey Ridge. First of all, the course is laid out with a low profile, to be at the same level as or lower than the surrounding land. Second, the yardage is substantially shorter: 5,134 from the women's tees, 6,029 from the men's, and 6,842 from the professional tees. Also, in an interesting touch, the areas outside the fairways are not rough, but pine straw. The low, dished fairways are surrounded with tall, spindly pines, giving it a secluded feel. Note that this is a traditional course in the sense that golfers can return to the clubhouse after the out nine. Head pro Fredricksen on Eagle Pines: "Play will be very fast and enjoyable. The ball will sit up on the pine straw, it'll be a little more forgiving. Not easy, but a fun and challenging course."

After clubbing the dimpled white sphere to oblivion for a few hours, rest and unwind at the clubhouse's Sand Trap Bar and Grille. Reubens, barbecue pork, burgers, and other sandwiches are served. There's also a full bar serving beer, wine, cocktails, soft drinks, snacks, and even ice cream shakes. Also, carts vending snacks, snadwiches, and drinks wind through both courses. The nearby Tournament Room can accommodate up to 150 guests for meetings, breakfasts, lunches, or dinners. To reach the Bonnet Creek Country Club, call your hotel's Guest Services desk in advance to get directions or arrange for private van transportation.

Golf Instruction

The Walt Disney World Golf Studio uses professionals to help duffers to use the skills they already possess to improve their golf game. The hour-and-a-half classes have a low student-teacher ratio and the cost includes video recording and an critiquing of your performance on audio tape for you to bring home. Playing nine holes along with the resident pro will set you back $85. You can purchase your video tape for $15. The Studio is offered three times a day, six days a week. Golf instruction is included in some vacation packages. Individual lessons are also available at the Disney Inn and the Village Clubhouse for $25 per half hour with an assistant, $45 with head pro Eric Fredricksen at the Disney Inn or Rina Ritson at the Village. See below for phone number. Included in some vacation packages.

WDW/Oldsmobile Golf Classic

Each October, the PGA pulls into Lake Buena Vista to hold the annual Pro-Am Tournament on the three older courses. In 1971, 1972, and 1973, the winner was Jack Nicklaus. Now, you can play alongside the pros. Joining the Classic Club will set you back $4,500, and it includes greens fees at all the WDW courses for a year, admission to WDW for six people during the tourney, twelve one-day passes to be used during other times of the year, a week's hotel accommodations, golf alongside three pros for three of the four days of the tourney, and a gift package that changes from year to year.

On Monday of the week of the tournament, there is a reception during which each amateur draws for the pros he or she will play along with. While the pros compete for cash, the amateurs are going for trophies and plaques. The actual golfing is done on Wednesday, Thursday, and Friday. Friday, an awards dinner is held, and on Saturday, a pool party. *HINT:* If you are planning to golf on your WDW vacation and are not a member of the Classic Club, AVOID the week of the tournament.

There are 396 spots open to amateurs during the tournament, they are doled out on a first-come, first-served basis, and former players are given first dibs.

If you want to play in a tournament but don't have the kind of scratch needed to join the Classic Club, call the Tournament Coordinator at 824-2275. There may be a local tournament going on during your stay, and there is a chance that the coordinator could squeeze you in. This is also the number to call to arrange tournaments, at no cost besides the regular cart and greens fees.

Practical Information

Balls: Buckets of balls for use on the driving range go for $4 apiece and are included in some vacation plans. **Carts:** Included in the greens fees. Not allowed at the Executive Course. **Club rental:** Titleist DTR clubs are available for $20. Included in some vacation plans. **Fees:** Greens fees are $75 at the Palm, Magnolia, and Lake Buena Vista courses, $35 for "twilight" tee times after 3 PM; $85 at Eagle Pines and Osprey Ridge, twilight rates $45. Executive Course: adults, $20 for 9 holes, $25 for 18, juniors 17 and under, $10 for 9 holes, $15 for 18. Included in some vacation plans.

Instruction: For the Studio, reserve by calling 824-2250 any time in advance. For private lessons at the Disney Inn, dial 824-2270. For private lessons at the Village, call 828-3741. Included in some vacation plans. Lockers: Available at the three clubhouses. **Reservations:** Strongly suggested. WDW Resort guests and Hotel Plaza guests with confirmed reservations can reserve a tee time up to 30 days in advance. Day guests and those staying off-site may reserve seven days in advance. Call 824-2270. **Shoe Rental:** Available for $6. Included in some vacation plans. **Tournaments:** Can be arranged at no cost beyond regular cart and greens fees. Call the Tournament Coordinator (tel. 824-2275).

HEALTH CLUBS

All of the clubs listed below with the exception of Body By Jake and the Swan Fitness Center are included in some vacation packages.

A branch of the national chain of **Body By Jake** health clubs exists at the **Dolphin Hotel**. Founded by cable TV fitness guru Jake Steinfeld, the facilities include Polaris exercise equipment, aerobics, free weights, and personal trainers. Hours are 8 AM to 10 PM and the cost is determined by the equipment and classes you choose.

At the **Disney Inn**, the **Magic Mirror** has equipment including free weights and an exercise bike. The hours are 8:30 AM to 6 PM, the cost is $4 per visit or $10 for an entire stay. The **Olympiad Health Club** is located on the third floor of the **Contemporary Resort** and offers Nautilus machines, private whirlpools, sauna, and more. The cost is $5 for exercise equipment, an additional $5 for use of the whirlpools. The hours are 9 AM to 6 PM, Monday through Saturday. The club is closed on Sundays. Call 824-3410 for reservations or information. Located in the common area between the Yacht and Beach Club Resorts, the **Ship Shape Health Club** offers exercise machines, aerobics classes, steamroom, sauna, spa, and massage. The cost is $4 per visit or $10 for an entire stay and the club is open from 6:30 AM to 9:30 PM.

St. John's Health Spa, located at the **Grand Floridian Beach Resort**, is open to hotel guests only. The facilities include exercise machines, aerobics classes, a steamroom, nutrition and exercise counselors, massage rooms, lockers, and Nautilus equipment. The cost is $5 per visit or

$10 for an entire stay. The **Swan Fitness Center** is a smaller club featuring exercise equipment, sauna, and whirlpool. The **Village Clubhouse** houses a health club with a stairmaster, aerobycicle, and Nautilus weight equipment. The facility is open from 7 AM to 10 PM daily. Daily and family memberships are available. Call 828-3741 for information. Check in at the Pro Shop.

HIKING

There are some pleasant trails on which to hike. There's the **Wilderness Swamp Trail**, the **Marshmallow Marsh Trail**, and more, in **Fort Wilderness**. Contact Guest Services for information.

HORSEBACK RIDING

Trail rides depart from the middle of **Fort Wilderness** every day at 9, 10:30, noon, and 2 PM daily. The horses are gentle and the ride is relaxing and slow. The cost is $13 per person. Children under 9 are not allowed to ride, but pony rides can be arranged at the petting farm at Fort Wilderness. For reservations and information, call 824-2803 or 934-7639 up to five days in advance.

JOGGING

Even though it is only feasible during the winter or early mornings and late afternoons, jogging in WDW can be done. There are paths crisscrossing the **Village Resort**; a 1.4-mile path around the **Caribbean Beach Resort**; pathways through the **Port Orleans** and **Dixie Landings Resorts**; and the **Fort Wilderness Exercise Trail**. The latter, a 2.3-mile jogging trail peppered with stations where one can do sit-ups, push-ups, pull-ups, and other exercises on special apparatus. The stations, most of which are in the shade, clearly explain each exercise. For maps detailing the trails in the resorts and the best route to the Fort Wilderness, call Guest Services.

SWIMMING

If day visitors or guests staying off-site wish to swim in Walt Disney World, they must purchase a ticket to either River Country or Typhoon Lagoon. However, if you are staying on site, you can make use of the aquatic facilities of the World.

You wouldn't expect to find beaches in the middle of Florida, but here they are. There are strands of powdery white sand at the **Contemporary, Polynesian, Grand Floridian, Fort Wilderness, Caribbean Beach, Yacht and Beach Club, Swan,** and **Dolphin Resorts**. The most notable of these is the long, placid **Fort Wilderness beach**, on lovely **Bay Lake**.

Swimming pools are more abundant. And WDW has plenty, if you consider 49 pools plenty. There's 1 at each of the following: **Grand Floridian, Swan, Port Orleans, Disney Vacation Club, Guest Quarters, Royal Plaza, Travelodge, River Country,** and **Typhoon Lagoon**; 2 at each of the following: the **Disney Inn,** the **Contemporary** (which includes an excellent lap pool), **Fort Wilderness,** the **Polynesian** (which includes the themed Swimming Pool Lagoon), the **Dolphin,** the **Grosvenor,** the **Hilton,** and the **Howard Johnson**; 3 at each of the following: the **Yacht and Beach Club Resorts** (including spectacular Stormalong Bay) and **Buena Vista Palace**; and 6 at each of the following: the **Caribbean Beach** (which includes a themed pool at Old Port Royale), **Dixie Landings** (which includes Ol' Man Island), and **Disney Village Resort**. Most of the places have wading pools and whirlpools as well.

TENNIS

All told, there are a whopping 40 tennis courts in Walt Disney World: 1 at **Disney's Vacation Club,** 2 at the **Disney Inn, Fort Wilderness,** the **Grand Floridian,** the **Yacht & Beach Club Resorts,** the **Grosvenor,** the **Guest Quarters,** and the **Hilton,** 3 at **Disney's Village Resort,** 4 at the **Buena Vista Palace** and the **Hotel Royal Plaza,** 6 at the **Contemporary,** and 8 shared by the **Dolphin** and **Swan Hotels**. All of the surfaces are hard except at the Grand Floridian, which boasts clay courts.

Instruction

The **Contemporary Resort** holds clinics upon request and include a video camera to check out and analyze your playing style, hopefully, finding ways to improve it. The cost is $35. Also, you can have a private lesson with one of the staff professionals, certified by the United States Tennis Association, for $20 a half hour or $37 an hour or with Walt Disney World's head pro for $25 a half hour or $45 an hour. The facilities at the Contemporary include three backboards and an automatic ball machine, the latter going for $10 a half hour. This is included in some vacation packages.

Youth Tennis Camp

The **Contemporary Resort** offers two separate tennis camps, one for children 4 to 8, the other one, for kids 7 to 16. The younger children play with lower nets, smaller racquets, and foam balls for a week of daily 45-minute lessons. The cost is $50. The older children play regulation tennis with regulation equipment for a week for $125, including all court time. This is included in some vacation plans.

Beat The Pro

For $30, you can go up against the head pro at the **Contemporary**

Resort. If you win, you get your money back.

Practical Information
    Balls: New balls can be bought for $4.25 a can, or used ones rented for $3 for a bucket. **Fees:** The courts at the Contemporary go for $10 an hour, $25 for an entire stay, those at the Floridian cost $12 an hour. There is no charge for any of the other courts. Unlimited use is included in some vacation plans. **Hours:** The tennis courts are open from 8 AM to 10 PM. All are lighted for play after dark. Lockers: Available at all tennis court areas. No charge. **Pairing service:** "Tennis Anyone" will find you a playing partner if you need one. Call the Contemporary Pro Shop at 824-3578. **Racquet rental:** Available for $4 an hour.

    Reservations: Accepted up to 24 hours in advance at the Contemporary (tel. 824-3578), Disney Inn (tel. 824-1469), Grand Floridian (tel. 824-2438), the Village Resort Clubhouse (tel. 828-3741), the Swan and Dolphin (tel. 934-6000), and the Yacht & Beach Club Resorts (tel. 934-3256). **Time restrictions:** During the busiest seasons, you may only spend two hours on a court on any given morning, afternoon, or evening. for a total of six hours of court time a day. This is only sporadically enforced. **Tournaments:** Can be arranged for a fee of $40 an hour, call the Contemporary's Pro Shop (tel. 824-3578).

VOLLEYBALL

    Courts can be found scattered throughout Fort Wilderness, plus on the beaches at the Contemporary Resort and the Yacht and Beach Club Resorts. Equipment is provided.

ADDITIONAL ACTIVITIES IN DISNEY WORLD

    Arcades – Video gamerooms are located throughout the World. There's the Penny Arcade on Main Street, U.S.A. (see MAGIC KING-DOM), with old and new coin-operated machines. But outside the parks, the biggest of the bunch is the Fiesta Fun Center on the first floor of the Contemporary Resort.

    Open 24 hours a day, the complex includes computerized games old and new, pinball machines, a movie theater, and a snack bar. Smaller gamerooms are located elsewhere: 2 each at the Disney Inn, Fort Wilderness, and Disney's Village Resorts; and 1 each at the rest of the WDW Resorts and Hotel Plaza establishments.

    Campfire Program – At Fort Wilderness, WDW guests (no day guests, sorry) are treated to a free campfire program, complete with Disney movies, singalongs, and appearances by Chip 'n' Dale.

Croquet – There's a regulation croquet court at the Beach Club. Equipment is available for loan at no charge, just see the people at the Ship Shape Health Club.

Electric Water Pageant – This is a dazzling display of a fusion of light and water as a 1,000-foot procession of illuminated creatures that appear to be swimming. Usually, the floating parade can be viewed from the Polynesian at 9 PM, from the Grand Floridian at 9:20, from Fort Wilderness at 9:45 PM, 10:05 from the Contemporary, and 10:20 from the Magic Kingdom when it's open late.

Handball – There is a handball court at the Grosvenor Resort.

Hayrides – Another one of those neat Fort Wilderness amenities, guests can board a hay wagon for a ride from Pioneer Hall to Bay Lake and back. The round-trip takes an hour and costs $4 per person ($3 for kids 3 to 12). Kids under 12 must be accompanied by an adult.

Horseshoes – A round of horseshoes on the agenda? Horseshoe-tossing facilities are scattered throughout Fort Wilderness.

Marshmallow Marsch Excursion – Held during the summer only, guests take a canoe down a crystalline Fort Wilderness canal, followed by a short walk to a hamlet in the woods where a marshmallow roast is held. From this spot, you can also watch the Elecric Water Pageant floating by. The cost is $6, $5 for kids 3 to 12.

Movies – There's a movie theater at the Fiesta Fun Center in the Contemporary, showing Disney classics three times an evening. Also, the campfire program at Fort Wilderness (see above) includes a Disney film. If you'd prefer something more adult or a first-run film, there's the AMC Pleasure Island 10 (827-1300) cinemaplex adjacent to the Pleasure Island nighttime entertainment complex. Note that you do not have to buy a Pleasure Island ticket to enter the movie theater.

Shuffleboard – There are shuffleboard courts at the Grosvenor Resort.

OUTSIDE DISNEY WORLD

AERIAL TOURS

Several companies operate tours of Orlando area attractions by helicopter, blimp, or hot-air balloon. While costly, these tours offer a once-in-a-lifetime vista of the earth below. All tours fly by reservation only.

AIRSHIP SHAMU

Location: Kissimmee Municipal Airport, 301 Dyer Blvd, Kissimmee. *Phone:* 870-SHAMU. *Admission:* $89 for adults, $79 for seniors, $69.00 for juniors 12 to 17 years, and $29 for kids ages ages 3 to 11. Kids under 3 are free.

What is Airship Shamu? It is, quite simply, the largest passenger airship in the world. The blimp flight really is something to brag about. It's a spectacular way to see Orlando, and is safe and smooth. The plush cabin can accommodate nine people, each of whom is treated to a magnificent vista of the city through huge windows. Limited edition flight certificates are awarded by the captain and crew to commemorate the event. Special backstage tours are available, as are refreshments and babysitting.

BALLOONS BY TERRY

Location: 3529 Edgewater Drive, Orlando, FL 32804. *Phone:* 422-3529. *Admission:* $150 single to $920 for 8 people, less 10% cash discount.

Climb aboard Tequila Sunrise, a 7-story high hot air balloon, for a stunning, almost-silent journey over orange groves, pine trees, and lakes. Most flights begin at sunrise, when the wind is the calmest. Balloons by Terry will give you a wake-up call one hour before sunrise and meet you at the balloon boutique fifteen minutes before takeoff. Flights last one hour, and the chase crew greets you with wine and cheese.

CHAMPAGNE BALLOON FLIGHTS

Location: 129 W. Church Street, Orlando, FL 32801. *Phone:* 841-UPUP. *Admission:* $140 per person.

Rosie O'Grady's Flying Circus and Col. Joe Kittinger's crew of professional pilots operate a bunch of hot air balloons. The flight includes coffee and orange juice, transportation to and from the launch site, a post-flight champagne brunch in Lili Marlene's, a souvenir gift packet and champagne glass, a photograph of your flight, and free admission to Church Street Station.

FALCON HELICOPTER TOURS

Location: 8990 International Drive, Orlando, and at the Hyatt Orlando, 6375 W. Irlo Bronson Mem. Hwy., Kissimmee. *Phone:* I-Drive: 352-1753. Kissimmee 396-7222. *Admission:* See below.

One of the most fascinating ways to tour Orlando and Walt Disney World is from above. Helicopter tours offer fantastic photo/video opportunities. Falcon operates two heliports offering a total of six tours in Bell Jet choppers with pilot narration. Reservations are suggested. All tours require a minimum of two adult fares and child fares apply to kids under 11 traveling with two adults.

The *International Drive* heliport, located next to Caruso's Palace, offers these tours. The Wet'n Wild/Sea World Spectacular ($35 adult/ $20 child) takes you over the length of International Drive, including Wet'n Wild, Mercado Mediterranean Village, the Convention Center, the Peabody Hotel, and Sea World. The Disney Delight ($60/$30) carries you over Sea World, the Magic Kingdom, EPCOT Center, the Butler Chain of Lakes, and Lake Buena Vista.

The *Kissimmee* heliport, on the grounds of the Hyatt Orlando, offers the following: the EPCOT ($35/$20) tour, taking you over EPCOT Center and the Disney's Caribbean Beach Resort. The Lake Buena Vista ($35/$20) tour includes Disney Village Marketplace, Pleasure Island, Typhoon Lagoon. Those two tours can be combined for $45/$35. The Kissimmee Disney Delight tour ($60/$30) includes Disney's Village Resort, Disney Village Hotel Plaza, Disney Village Marketplace, Pleasure Island, Typhoon Lagoon, the Magic Kingdom, and EPCOT Center.

Both heliports offer the Grand Tour ($98/$50), which lives up to its name. You will fly over Universal Studios, Sea World, Wet'n Wild, Mercado, Bay Hill, the Magic Kingdom, EPCOT Center, the Disney-MGM Studios, Disney's Caribbean Beach and Village Resorts, Typhoon Lagoon, Pleasure Island, and the Disney Village Marketplace.

HELICOPTERS, INC.

Location: 6805 Visitor Circle, Orlando, FL 32819. *Phone:* 354-5203. *Admission:* See below.

This sightseeing tour company operates McDonnell Douglas 500E 5-blade helicopters from its heliport across from Wet'n Wild. Their tours include the First Timers ($20), in which you fly 7 miles from the heliport past Wet'n Wild to Universal Studios and back. The Universal/Sea World/Wet'n Wild tour ($35) carries you the length of International Drive. The "Ultimate Ride" ($60) will fly you over Universal Studios, the Magic Kingdom, Discovery Island, Fort Wilderness, amd Sea World. The Magic Excursion ($95) gives you an aerial view of Universal Studios, the Magic Kingdom, the Disney-MGM Studios, EPCOT Center, Typhoon Lagoon, Pleasure Island, Disney Village, Sea World, and Wet'n Wild.

Children are half price with two adult fares, and two adult fares are required as a minimum. To get to the jetport, take exit 30A from I-4

(Republic Drive). Go south one block, to International Drive, and turn right. Visitor Circle is one block on your right.

ORANGE BLOSSOM BALLOONS
Location: P.O. Box 22908, Lake Buena Vista, FL. *Phone:* 239-7677. *Admission:* $150 per adult, $100 for children 5 to 12. $280 per couple, family rate $500 for up to four adults.

Each morning, before sunup, Orange Blossom Balloons' customers set off on a hour-long flight over Walt Disney World. After the flight, you can enjoy an unlimited breakfast buffet at the Sonesta Villa Resort. Guests meet at Fort Liberty (5260 W. U.S. 192) in Kissimmee.

RISE & FLOAT BALLOON TOURS
Location: 5767 Major Boulevard, Orlando. *Phone:* 352-8191. *Admission:* $250 per couple or $135 per person for 1-hour cruise, $325 per couple for a 1 1/2-hour cruise For Lovers Only.

Rise & Float offers two different balloon tours, one of them the Champagne Balloon Excursion, the other one the For Lovers Only cruise, with champagne, fruit, cheese, crackers, and pastries. Both tours require reservations and depart from the Mystery Fun House.

MINIATURE GOLF
If it seems like a strange transition, going from blimp tours to putt-putt, it probably is. But I just had to mention one of the things that made my first Orlando vacations so memorable. Corny as it sounds, it was miniature golf.

Pirate's Cove (8601 International Drive, Orlando, FL 32819, tel. 352-7378; Crossroads Shopping Center, Lake Buena Vista, FL, tel. 827-1242; and 2845 Florida Plaza Blvd., Kissimmee, FL 32741, tel. 396-7484) is truly a work of art. The three, 36-hole complexes feature lushly landscaped holes, some of them intricate works that take up an entire hillside, flanked by waterfalls, streams, bridges, boulders, caves, and dungeons, all to carry out the pirate theme. Music is piped in, and signs along the holes tell the stories of Blackbeard and Captain Kidd. Hole-in-one prizes are given daily, and snacks and beverages are sold.

The Orlando and Lake Buena Vista courses are open from 9 AM to 11 PM, and greens fees for 18 holes are $6 to $6.50 adults, $5 to $5.50 for kids, depending on which course they play; $10 per person for 36 holes, and $12 per person for an all day pass. The Kissimmee course is open from 9 AM to midnight and greens fees are $5 for adults, $4 for children.

In particular, the International Drive location is absolutely spectacular and rated as not to be missed. The International Drive course to be the most fastidiously manicured, and has more atmosphere. Why? It might have something to do with the fact that it looks out to the mission-style Mercado Mediterranean Village. With the combination of the miniature golf and the shopping village, one could easily spend an entire evening on that one block.

Other miniature golf courses in the area are **Pirate's Island** (4330 W. U.S. 192, Kissimmee, FL 34746, tel. 396-4660), another pirate-themed course; **Congo River Golf & Exploration Co.** (6312 International Drive, Orlando, FL 32819 tel. 352-0042; 4777 W. U.S. 192, Kissimmee, FL 34746, tel. 396-6900), two courses based on the Stanley and Livingstone expeditions; **River Adventure Golf** (4535 W. U.S. 192, Kissimmee, FL 34746 tel. 396-4666), and **Bonanza Golf** (7771 W. U.S. 192, Kissimmee, FL 34746, tel. 396-7536).

A step above miniature golf is pitch-and-putt golf: **Million Dollar Mulligan** (2850 Florida Plaza Blvd., Kissimmee, FL 34746, tel. 425-5505) offers 9 holes of pitch and putt plus a unique hole-in-one contest.

SPECTATOR SPORTS

Baseball, Spring Training – Twelve teams hold their spring training each year in central Florida.

Here are the teams and their stadiums, towns, and phone numbers:

SPRING TRAINING ESSENTIALS			
Balt. Orioles	Huggins-Stengel Fld	St.Pete	813/892-5971
Chi. White Sox	Ed Smith Complex	Sarasota	813/366-8451
Cinc. Reds	Plant City Stadium	PlantCity	813/752-1878
Cleve. Indians	Chain O'Lakes Park	WinterHvn	813/291-5803
Det. Tigers	Marchant Stadium	Lakeland	813/682-1401
Fla. Marlins	Cocoa Expo Spts	Ctr Cocoa	unavailable
Hous. Astros	Osceola Cty Stadium	Kissimmee	407/933-6500
KC Royals	Baseball City Cmplx	Davenport	813/424-7211
Phil. Phils	Jack Russell Stad	Clearwatr	813/441-9941
Pitt. Pirates	Pirate City	Bradenton	813/747-3031
St.L. Cardinals	Busch Complex	St.Pete	813/894-5000
Tor. Blue Jays	Dunedin Stadium	Dunedin	813/733-9302

Regular Season, Majors – In 1993, Florida received the expansion **Florida Marlins** (305/779-7070), who play in Miami's Joe Robbie Stadium, about 225 miles southeast of Orlando via Florida's Turnpike.

Regular Season, Minors – Central Florida hosts several minor league baseball teams, including the **Orlando Cubs** (Chicago-N, AA), who play at Tinker Field (849-6346), the **Osceola Astros** (Houston, A) at Osceola

County Stadium in Kissimmee, (933-2500), **Baseball City Royals** (Kansas City, A) at Baseball City Stadium in Haines City (839-3900), **Clearwater Phillies** (Philadelphia, A) at Jack Russell Stadium (813/441-8638), the **Daytona Cubs** (Chicago-N, A) at Jackie Robinson Stadium (904/257-3172), the **St. Petersburg Cardinals** (St. Louis, A) at Al Lang Stadium (813/822-3384), and the **Sarasota White Sox** at Ed Smith Stadium (813/954-7699).

Basketball– Orlando's hottest ticket since 1989 has been that of the **Orlando Magic**, and with the recent addition of superstar Shaquille O'Neal, their home, the new Orlando Arena (839-3900 or 896-2442), has been affectionately called the "Love Shaq". The Magic are a recent expansion team, so their record over their first few years has been less than spectacular, but nevertheless, they sell out every home game, and they have steadily improved each of the last three seasons. It is virtually impossible to get tickets on the day of game. Tickets cost $10 to $45, and should be purchased as far in advance as possible. And if you go, and if the game gets out of hand, you can feast your eyes on the Magic Girls or the antics of the mascot: Stuff, the Magic Dragon.

Football – There's an arena football team here: the **Orlando Predators**. You can watch them play in the O-rena (648-4444) for $8.50 to $19.50 per ticket. The NFL's **Tampa Bay Buccaneers** play in Tampa Stadium (813/870-2700), an hour and a half from Orlando. But bigger than the Bucs is the college football Citrus Bowl game, played in the downtown Citrus Bowl on January 1 of each year. The game is nationally televised and involves two of the top NCAA teams in the nation. The game always sells out, so tickets must be purchased in advance.

Golf – Orlando hosts several major PGA tournaments. They are the **Nestle Invitational**, formerly the Bay Hill Classic, held at Arnold Palmer's Bay Hill Country Club less than a mile from the junction of Sand Lake Road and International Drive. The tournament, which takes place every March, solicits some of the top names in the sport. Daily and tourney-long tickets are available, call 351-2800.

The golf tournament that draws the most and best pros, however, is the **Walt Disney World Oldsmobile Classic**, played every October on the Palm, Magnolia, and Lake Buena Vista courses. For more information on this event, see pages 10 and 351.

Hockey – The **Tampa Bay Lightning**, playing at Tampa's Mack Center, is Florida's first NHL franchise, and the first Southern team since the Atlanta Flames left for Calgary. For ticket and schedule information, call

813/229-2658. The **Florida Panthers** are slated to begin play in the southern part of the state in October 1993.

Soccer – In 1994, the city of Orlando will host four to seven **World Cup games.** The event has people states away planning visits and ticket purchase. For information, call 246-0012.

Tennis – The tournament of note, held at Heathrow Tennis Club in Lake Mary, is the $425,000 **Prudential-Bache Securities Classic.** Ticket prices vary for the different matches, but for semifinal and final matches, you might want to get your tickets early, as the tournament is immensely popular among local tennis buffs.

WATER PARKS
Orlando is home to seven great water parks, mostly outside Disney World – a great way to cool off on a hot summer day!

ADVENTURE ISLAND
Location: 3000 E. Busch Blvd., Tampa.   **Phone:** 351-3931, 813/988-5171, 813/987-5660.   *Hours:* Open continuously from end of March to beginning of September. Open weekends in September and October; 10 AM to 5 PM and 9:30 AM to 6 PM in the spring and fall, 9 AM to 8 PM in June, July, and August. *Admission:* $14.95. Kids under 3 free.

Adventure Island is adjacent to Busch Gardens and is owned by the same parent company, Busch Entertainment Corporation. The 22-acre park features a great number and variety of slides and attractions, including the new **Fabian's Funport**, an all-new and expanded children's water play area, the **Water Moccasin**, three twisting tubes, the **Caribbean Corkscrew**, a high-speed adventure down twin braided translucent tubes, the **Calypso Coaster**, a 450-foot snaking chute, the **Tampa Typhoon**, a 7-story freefall slide, the adjacent **Gulfscream**, a speed slide that pales next to the Typhoon, the **Everglides**, toboggan slides, the **Barratuba**, an inner tube slide, **Runaway Rapids**, a 300-foot slide down a jungle mountain, **Rambling Bayou**, a lazy stream that carries you through the whole park, **Endless Surf**, where you can be battered by four-foot waves, and **Paradise Lagoon**, where you can unwind and overcome the hydrophobia that hit you when you went down the Typhoon.
Also at Adventure Island is an arcade, a gift shop, three volleyball nets, several stretches of beach, and two snack bars, the **Surfside** and **Gulfscream Cafes**. From Orlando, take I-4 west, exit to North I-75., take I-75 to exit 54 (Fowler Ave.), and follow signs to Busch Gardens. It's about an hour and a quarter drive.

BUCCANEER BAY

Location: At Weeki Wachee Spring, 6131 Commercial Way, Brooksville.
Phone: 363-0900, 904/596-2062, 800/236-0297 (FL), 800/678-9335.
Hours: Open from the beginning of April through mid-September.
Spring and fall, from 10 AM to 5 PM. Summer, from 10 AM to 6 PM.
Admission: $6.95 for adults, $5.95 for kids 3 to 11. Kids under 3 admitted free.

Tucked alongside Weeki Wachee Spring on Florida's left coast is a very special place. **Buccaneer Bay** is the only water park I know of with the action centered around a natural river. The Weeki Wachee River plays host to rides like **Pirate's Revenge**, the only river flume in the state, the spiraling **Thunderbolt**, **River Slides**, or **Lazy River tube ride**. To get there, take I-4 east to Colonial Drive (S.R. 50) west. Take it to U.S. 19 and turn right. Go about 1 mile, the park will be on the right.

RIVER COUNTRY – See Chapter 13.

TYPHOON LAGOON – See Chapter 13.

WATER MANIA

Location: 6073 W. Irlo Bronson Mem. Hwy., Kissimmee. *Phone:* 396-2626, 800/527-3092. *Hours:* Open from March 1 to the end of November. Hours vary. Summer, opens at 9:30. Spring and fall, opens at 10. Closes at 8:30 PM in summer, 5 PM in spring and fall. *Admission:* $17.95 adults, $15.95 kids 3 to 12, kids under 3 admitted free. Seniors 20% off.

Water Mania is one of the two area water parks that predates WDW's River Country, and is the more convenient of the two to WDW. Located on U.S. 192, just east of I-4, the 38-acre park has rides including the winding, 400-foot **Anaconda raft ride**, the **Banana Peel**, a two-person plunge down a water-filled chute, the **Looney Flumes**, three twisting slides, **Whitecaps**, a wave pool, **Wipe Out**, which pits you on a boogie board and one-on-one against large waves, **The Screamer**, with a 7-story drop, **Cruisin' Creek**, a placid, winding inner-tube ride, **Riptide**, a whitewater adventure, and last but not least, **Aqua Xpress** and the **Rain Forest**, aquatic playgrounds for the small folk.

If you prefer your fun without water, there's a miniature golf course, volleyball nets, a beach, and a wooded picnic area. A snack bar and gift shop are also available. One disappointment about Water Mania, it lacks any of the natural beauty or lush landscaping that make Adventure Island, Typhoon Lagoon, River Country, and Buccaneer Bay so special. But on the other hand, Water Mania is often less crowded than headliner parks like Typhoon Lagoon and Wet'n Wild. Take exit 25A off I-4.

WET'N WILD
Location: 6200 International Drive, Orlando. *Phone:* 351-WILD, 800/ 992-WILD. *Hours:* Open from 2/10 to 1/3. Hours vary. During summer, 9 AM to 11 PM. Shorter hours during spring, fall, and winter. *Admission:* $19.95 adults, $17.95 kids 3 to 12, kids under 3 admitted free. 2-day and annual passes are available, see below.

Wet'n Wild was the best-attended water park in the country in 1991, according to Amusement Business magazine, and for good reason. The 25-acre park has the best assortment of water rides in the area. For family togetherness, ride the new **Bubba Tub**, a 6-story, triple-dip slide in a tube big enough for the whole family; the **Black Hole**, an ominous-looking spaceship concealing a two-person raft adventure down a 500-foot, pitch-black tube for 30 seconds of simulated space reentry; **Der Stuka**, a 6-story, 250-foot speed slide; the **Blue Niagra**, a twisting, 300-foot slide that starts six stories over the park; the **Mach 5**, a set of five twisting flumes totalling 2,500 feet; the **Hydra Maniac**, a translucent tube slide with a 360° loop; **Raging Rapids**, a whitewater tubing adventure; **Lazy River**, a gently flowing stream; **Surf Lagoon**, a 17,000 square foot pool with four-foot waves; the **Knee Ski**, in which you ride a cable-towed kneeboard around a half-mile course at speeds up to 15 mph; **Bubble Up**, a wet vinyl mountain for kids to climb and slide down into three feet of water; **The Wild One**, in which you ride tubes towed by a motorboat (additional charge); and the **Kid's Park**, containing miniature versions of all the big rides, for children 48" and under.

During the summer, nighttimes are special in Wet'n Wild. **The Beach Club** features live entertainment, karaoke, and dancing to videos. This event draws a large crowd of locals, mainly in their teen years. In addition to single-day tickets, two day passes ($29.90 adults/$26.90 kids) and annual passes ($59.95 adults/kids) are available. Snack bars and a gift shop are located on the premises. To get to Wet'n Wild, take exit 30A (Kirkman Road south) to International Drive and turn right. Or, take exit 29, turn east on Sand Lake Drive, go one block, and turn left onto I-Drive.

WILD WATERS
Location: 5656 E. Silver Springs Blvd., Silver Springs. *Phone:* 363-0900, 904/206-2121, 800/243-0297 (FL). *Hours:* Open April to September. Spring and fall, 10 AM to 5 PM. Summer, 10 AM to 7 PM. *Admission:* $9.95 adult, $8.95 child 3-11, $7.95 senior citizen; children under 3 admitted free.

Wild Waters, located adjacent to Silver Springs, has a wave pool, eight flumes, Water Bonanza child's play area, 9-hole miniature golf course, volleyball, snack bar, and gift shop. Take I-4 to Florida's Turnpike north. Take the Turnpike north to I-75 north. I-75 north to exit 69, U.S. 40 east.

10. THE MAGIC KINGDOM

INTRODUCTION

Most people think that Walt Disney World is composed of **The Magic Kingdom**® and nothing else. Well, WDW encompasses 28,000 acres of Florida land, of which the Kingdom takes up only 98. Still, this is the most recognizable part of the Vacation Kingdom and the foremost drawing card for many families.

Many children prefer the Magic Kingdom to the other parks, and visiting this park first may pose a problem. Younger kids who visit the MK first expect the same thing from EPCOT and the Studios and tend to dislike the somewhat cerebral theme of the other parks. This problem can be alleviated by visiting EPCOT first , then MGM, and the MK. The Magic Kingdom is best described by the dedication, by Roy O. Disney, on October 25, 1971:

Walt Disney World is a tribute to the philosophy and life of Walter Elias Disney and to the talents, the dedication, and the loyalty of the entire Disney orginization that made Walt Disney's dream come true. May Walt Disney World bring joy and inspiration and new knowledge to all who come to this happy place... a Magic Kingdom where the young-at-heart of all ages can laugh and play and learn – together.

GETTING AROUND – To get to the Magic Kingdom from:

Polynesian Resort, Grand Floridian Resort: Take the monorail or the motor launch.

TTC: Take the monorail or the ferry.

Contemporary Resort and EPCOT Center: Take the monorail, a transfer is required from EPCOT.

Disney Inn: Take the green-flagged bus.

Fort Wilderness, River Country, Discovery Island: Take the green-flagged motor launch.

Disney-MGM Studios Theme Park: Take the blue-and-white-flagged bus marked MK.

Typhoon Lagoon, Pleasure Island, and Disney Village Marketplace: Take the red-flagged bus to the TTC and switch to the monorail or ferry.

Disney Village Hotel Plaza: Take the red-and-white-flagged bus marked MK.

EPCOT Resorts: Take the purple-and-gold-flagged bus marked MK.

Disney's Village Resort: Take the green-and-gold-flagged bus marked MK.

Port Orleans, Dixie Landings, and Vacation Club Resorts: Take the pink-and-green-flagged bus marked MK.

Caribbean Beach Resort: Take the orange-and-white-flagged bus marked MK.

All off-site hotels, via I-4: Take the exit for U.S. 192 West – Magic Kingdom and keep your eyes peeled for signs. You can't miss it, but if you begin to pass concentrations of motels, restaurants, and kitschy souvenir shops, you just did the impossible. Feel free to laugh at yourself.

PARKING – The Magic Kingdom's parking lot can accommodate 12,156 vehicles. The cost is $4, free for resort guests (remember your ID!) and there is no cost for leaving and returning or switching parks on the same day (retain your receipt!). But the three most important points regarding WDW parking are: 1. Write down where you park! 2. Write down where you park! 3. Write down where you park!

The parking sections are named after Disney characters, and each row is numbered. Write it down! That one point can not be stressed enough! Note that the handicapped can park in a special lot adjacent to the TTC.

FERRY OR MONORAIL?

The debate rages on! Should day visitors take the monorail or the ferry? Let's line them up:

	Ferry		Monorail
Transit time:	6 1/2 minutes		3 1/2 to 5 minutes
Handicapped:	Fine		Steep waiting ramp
Capacity:	1 ferry	=	3 monorail trains

OVERALL: The monorail is more crowded in the morning, the ferry is more popular during the afternoon. Peak seasons will see the ferry as the better choice, while during off seasons the monorail is the best option unless you catch a ferry about to board.

Here are a few of the rules and facts that apply to all three major parks:

ADMISSION – Walt Disney World passports and tickets are available at the TTC, the park's main entrance, and at most hotels' guest services desks. All admission media includes unlimited use of all rides, shows, and experiences in the park(s).

• A **one-day ticket** allows admission to ONE of the major theme parks (Magic Kingdom, EPCOT Center, or the Disney-MGM Studios). Adult $34; Child $27.

• A **Four-Day Super Pass** allows admission to the Magic Kingdom, EPCOT Center, and the Disney-MGM Studios Theme Park for four days. Adult $118; Child $92.

• A **Five-Day Plus Super Duper Pass** allows five days admission to the MK, EC, and Studios, plus admission to River Country, Discovery Island, Pleasure Island, and Typhoon Lagoon, valid up to seven days from the pass's first use. Adult $162; Child $138.

• A **4-Season Salute Passport** allows unlimited admissions to the MK, EC, and MGM for 144 days over the course of the year. Adult $95; Child $85.

• A **One-Year World Passport** allows unlimited admissions to the MK, EC, and MGM for one calendar year from the date of purchase. • Adult $190; Child $165.

• **One-year Passport Renewal.** Adult $169; Child $144.

The prices above do not include 6% sales tax. The multi-day passports include unlimited use of the WDW transportation system, but a one-day ticket only allows use of the monorail or ferry.

Tickets and passports are available at all Disney Stores, or by mail. Send a check or money order for the exact amount plus $2 for handling to Walt Disney World, P.O. Box 10030; Lake Buena Vista, FL, 32830-0030; Attn: Ticket Mail Order. Admission media is said to be nontransferable, but there is nothing on the multi-day passes to identify you. No photo, no signature, nothing. Hmm . . .

HINT: Tickets for all attractions can be purchased at the Visitor Information Center at Mercado Mediterranean Village, saving valuable time. Also, many hotels offer tickets and passports through their guest services desks.

MONEY – **For tickets:** Cash, travelers' checks, personal checks, MasterCard, Visa, and American Express are accepted. Personal checks must be imprinted with your name and address, and must be accompanied by a major credit card and driver's license. WDW resort guests may use their ID and charge the tickets to their rooms.

For sit-down restaurants and merchandise: Cash, travelers' checks, American Express, MasterCard, and Visa are accepted. Disney resort IDs are also accepted at EPCOT and the Studios. **For fast food:** Counter service establishments only accept cash and travelers' checks. Branches of the Sun Bank is located on Main Street, U.S.A. (MK) and the Entrance Plaza (EC), each offering an array of banking services. There is an automated teller machine at the entrance of the Studios, as well. Disney Dollars are available in one, five, and ten-dollar denominations and are redeemable for U.S. dollars at any time. They encourage guests to spend money that they wouldn't otherwise, because few people consider them "real money" and spend it accordingly.

DRESS CODE – Shirts and shoes must be worn, as a rule. However, this rule is broken as often as it is obeyed during the summer.

REFURBISHMENT AND INTERRUPTION OF ATTRACTIONS – Since WDW stays open 365 days a year, attractions may be closed from time to time for upkeep. This, known as "rehab", can be heartbreaking if you had your mind set on riding Jungle or seeing the Treehouse but you're told, "sorry, it's closed" (it happened to me – twice!). The pain can be dulled somewhat by calling 824-4321 in advance and finding out before you get there what will be closed. Also, continually running attractions such as World of Motion and Peter Pan's Flight are stopped momentarily to board physically challenged guests. Out of courtesy, the reason for stoppage is not announced.

PACKAGE PICKUP – Whether you buy a $5 ceramic Mickey or a $5,000 piece of jewelry, you don't have to lug it around the whole park. Send it to Package Pickup. They forward your purchases to the main entrance of the park. In the Magic Kingdom, it's at Guest Services, at EPCOT, it's at the Entrance Plaza, at the Studios, it's at the Entrance Plaza. Note that the human traffic at Package Pickup is at its worst between 5 and 6 PM and then again in the half-hour before closing.

VITAL STATISTICS

Location: Walt Disney World, P.O. Box 10,040, Lake Buena Vista, FL 32830-0040. Phone: 824-4321. *Hours:* Vary. Gates open at 8:30 AM, attractions at 9 AM. *Admission:* $34 for adults, $27 for kids. See above. Parking: $4. *Time to see:* A minimum of a day and a half during quiet seasons, two days during the busier times of the year. *When to See:* From least to most crowded, Friday, Sunday, Saturday, Thursday, Wednesday, Tuesday, and Monday. *Don't Miss:* Space Mountain, Splash Mountain, Big Thunder Mountain, Country Bear Vacation Hoedown, Diamond Horseshoe Revue, Pirates of the Caribbean, Jungle Cruise, Haunted Mansion, It's a Small World, Spectro*Magic.

PRACTICAL INFORMATION – **Alcoholic Beverages:** Forbidden in the Magic Kingdom. **Baby Services:** Changing and nursing facilities are located next to the Crystal Palace Restaurant on Main Street, U.S.A. **Baby Strollers:** Can be rented for $6 a day at the Stroller Shop, on the right side of the entrance plaza. *HINT:* Strollers may not be taken into attractions. Sometimes, when you are in an attraction, your stroller mightbe ripped off. You won't have to pay for it, just take your receipt back to the stroller shop, and they'll replace it. Or, to lock the barn before the horses escape, tie any personal object (make sure it's something that you won't miss if it is stolen) to the stroller. This will prevent all but the most audacious from taking the stroller.

Banking: There is a branch of the Sun Bank, a Floridian chain, located on Main Street (see below). **Cameras:** The Kodak Camera Center on Main Street has a full array of cameras for rent, film, videotapes, and two-hour development (see below). **Cigarettes:** For sale at Main Street Bookstore, Elephant Tales, Trading Post, Royal Candy Shoppe, Heritage House, and Mickey's Mart. **First Aid:** Next to the Crystal Palace is the First Aid Center. **Foreign Language Assistance:** Maps and assistance are available at Guest Relations. **Guided Tours:** Available for $3.50 in addition to admission. Visit City Hall for details. **Hearing-impaired Guests:** A Telecommunications Device for the Deaf (TDD) is available at City Hall.

Information: City Hall is the place to go for info on the day's entertainment schedule. **Kennel:** Pets are not allowed in WDW Resorts or attractions. There is, however, an air-conditioned kennel next to the TTC. Reservations are not needed. **Lockers:** Available for $.25 or $.50, at the TTC and under the Main Street Railroad Station. **Lost and Found:** Claim or report missing items at City Hall on Main Street. **Lost Children:** Report to Baby Services or City Hall. **Smoking, eating, and drinking:** For the enjoyment of other guests, smoking, eating, and drinking are not allowed in any attractions. **Transportation:** Information is available at the TTC. **Visually-impaired guests:** Complimentary tape cassettes and players are available at City Hall. A deposit is required, though. **Wheelchair Guests:** Wheelchair rental is available at the Stroller Shop. Disabled Guests Guidebooks are available at City Hall.

MAIN STREET, U.S.A.

At the foot of **Main Street** is the entrance to the park and about 99.9% of Magic Kingdom visitors stroll up the street, laden with shops and eateries, all from the turn of the century. Speculation has led us to believe that Main Street in Disneyland was directly based on Marceline, Missouri, Walt Disney's hometown.

The street has a certain air of Victorian splendor to it, and there are many necessaries located here. There's a bank, the City Hall Information Center, first aid and baby centers, and Guest Relations.

Overall Tips

Attractions - The attractions on Main Street are not among the most popular in the World, but many are still worth your time. If you're not going to watch the afternoon parade, stay away from Main Street between 2:30 and 3:30. The best bet for visiting Main Street is to arrive before opening time, when the entire concourse can be experienced at a leisurely pace while waiting for the other "lands" to open.

Dining - While the Magic Kingdom is not noted for its food (actually, it's more of an ignominy), Main Street has several of the parks better dining options. Also, they are among the few in the park that offers full breakfasts. The best bets are Tony's Town Square Cafe, the Plaza Restaurant, the Crystal Palace, and the Main Street Wagons.

Shopping - The best selection of souvenirs of all sorts in the park can be found lining the Street. However, for souvenirs like stuffed animals, toys, key-chains, and the like, you'd be better off visiting Mickey's Character Shop at the Marketplace. However, shops of note are the Harmony Barber Shop, House of Magic, Main Street Confectionery, and Crystal Arts. Stop by before 2:30, after which the parade will trap anyone on the Street, followed by a mass exodus of the park, which continues on until about 5 PM.

Attractions
WALT DISNEY WORLD RAILROAD
Rating: 5 1/2. A great way to associate yourself with the park's sights. *Location:* The first thing you see when you enter the park. *Duration of Ride:* 19 minutes, round trip. **Best Time to Go:** Before 11 AM.

The **Walt Disney World Railroad** offers visitors a great way to get from point A to point B without tiring out. The four locomotives, the Lilly Belle, Roy O. Disney, Walter E. Disney, and the Roger Broggie, were all built in Philadelphia between 1916 and 1928, and were once hauling freight cars filled with jute, sugar and hemp across Yucatan jungles.

Disneyland visitors will be disappointed to know that the WDW Railroad lacks the Grand Canyon Diorama and Primeval World sections that the Disneyland Railroad has. As for the stations: the Main Street U.S.A. is closest to Town Square and the entrance; the Frontierland station is closest to Liberty Square and Adventureland; and the Mickey's Starland station, wedged in between Fantasyland and Tomorrowland. The circuit tour is about 1.5 miles long and is great for people who want to sit down and enjoy a breeze while getting somewhere. Trains arrive at each station every five to seven minutes.

HINT: Lines are often shortest at Main Street.

THE WALT DISNEY STORY

Rating: 5. Walt Disney deserved homage like this. *Location:* On the east side of Town Square, adjacent to the railroad. *Duration of Show:* 23 minutes. *Best Time to Go:* Between 11 AM and 2 PM.

No matter if you remember Walt Disney or if he was from before your time, you will enjoy seeing the **Walt Disney Story**, a monument to the man who brought us Mickey, Minnie, Donald, and the rest of the gang. The yellow Victorian houses a museum featuring Disney memorabilia and a theatre presentation.

Some of the exhibits in the Walt Disney Story's pre-show area include cels from Snow White, some of Disney's awards (including the Oscar won by that picture), letters from dignitaries including Harry Truman, Dwight Eisenhower, Winston Churchill, and Leopold Stokowski, among others; movie posters, photos of the Mousketeers, and Zorro's cape. Disney devotees could spend all day looking at the memorabilia, but when the doors open, the film begins. The film details Disney's rise to glory from his youth in Marceline, Missouri to the conception of the Walt Disney World Resort. Disney himself narrates some of the action, which includes never-before-seen film footage. Overall, an interesting homage to the man behind the magic.

MAIN STREET CINEMA

Rating: 5. Pleasant, a great way to get out of the searing afternoon heat. *Location:* At the middle of Main Street, east side. *Duration of Show:* Continuous presentation. *Best Time to Go:* Anytime except the half-hour on either side of the parade time. *Comments:* Most pleasant between noon and 2:30when the heat is at its worst and other attractions are packed.

This attraction, by virtue of its inconspicuous location and its image, is never crowded. Here, kids and adults alike revel in six separate films being shown at once. Five of them are silent, but the sixth, the theater's piece de resistance, was the first cartoon with sound. This particular movie, **Steamboat Willie**, introduced to the world a mouse named Mickey, who met another mouse called Minnie, and the rest, as they say, is history.

PENNY ARCADE

Rating: 4 1/2. Beguiling, though not necessarily unforgettable. *Location:* At the north end of Main Street. *Best Time to Go:* If you arrive before the park opens, or before 2:30. *Comments:* Kids will insist on a trip here.

Disneyland patrons are intrigued (or disheartened) by the presence of several ordinary arcades in the park. WDW has an arcade as well, though this one actually relates to the land it is situated in. Anyone with a penchant for video games will be fascinated by the Victorian era machines located here. The cost ranges from one to twenty-five cents. There are Minute-o-scopes (circa 1900), viewing devices operated by turning them by hand; and Cali-o-scopes, their newer siblings, the PianOrchestra player-piano, and the usual array of pinball and video game machines. Worth at least a look.

MAIN STREET VEHICLES
Rating: 5 1/2. A delightful way to travel up MainStreet. *Location:* Town Square. *Duration of Ride:* Varies. *Best Time to Go:* Anytime. *Comments:* If you ever wanted to see (or ride) an old-fangled vehicle, now's your chance!

Enjoy a breezy ride up Main Street in a horse-drawn trolley, a refitted and modernized horseless carraige, jitney, an open-sided double-decker omnibus, or a bright red fire engine. Not worth the wait if the line is long. *HINT:* If you wish to see the Percherons and Belgian horses who pull the carraiges at home, visit the Horse Barn at Fort Wilderness.

Shopping
On the West Side of Main Street
EMPORIUM – This is the Magic Kingdom's largest gift shop, and located on Town Square in an easily discernible location, lures many a visitor to its realm. Due to its size and proximity to the lockers (beneath the station), this is a good place to pick up stuffed animals, toys, t-shirts, sweatshirts, towels, handbags, hats, and Mousketeer ears, many adorned with Mickey, Minnie, or the WDW logo. Also, the store sells gifts, books, film, records, and sundry items. Very crowded in the late afternoon.

NEWSSTAND – Sold here are mementos, toys, stuffed characters, ceramic figurines, compact discs, books, video and audio cassettes, film, and sundries, but (IRONY!!) no newspapers. If you're in the Magic Kingdom and have a yearning for the Sentinel or USA Today, you'll have to take the monorail to any of the on-line hotels. The selection of the forementioned items is limited, but offers a good amount of things that you may have forgotten to purchase elsewhere.

HARMONY BARBER SHOP – Here, you can get an old-fashioned shave or haircut. Appointments are necessary and available by calling 824-6550, The trims come with musical accompaniment courtesy of the Dapper

Dans, the Kingdom's own barbershop quartet. Also, nostalgic items like moustache cups and shaving gadgets are available for purchase.

DISNEY CLOTHIERS – If it's meant to be worn, and if it bears any likeness of Mickey, Minnie, and the WDW logo, it can be purchased here. Possibly the nicest souvenirs for Disney film buffs are the black satin jackets and golf shirts depicting Fantasia's Sorcerer's Apprentice, portrayed by the one and only Mouse. Fashions for men, women, and children are sold here.

HINT: The ties sold here are fascinating – Mickey is not obviously present at first glance. However, close examination of the cravats will reveal the city's celebrated mouse hiding behind that paisley pattern...

HOUSE OF MAGIC – Demonstrations of necromancy here, like disappearing cards, water pouring from empty jugs, coins passing through paper, and other tricks make the clientele long to purchase a starter Blackstone kit, or other tricks, gimmicks, gifts, gags, books, and joke items. And Disney intends to satisfy that craving.

MAIN STREET BOOK STORE – Here, items purveyed include books (many of which feature Disney art), magazines, stationary, writing utensils, paper plates, napkins, wrapping paper, and greeting cards.

On the East Side of Main Street
DISNEYANA COLLECTIBLES – This small market offers a selection of rare and new Disney memorabilia, including limited edition plates, cels, and animation art. Two features distinguishing this from the many other WDW outlets may make this a mandatory stop.

First of all, the necessary reservations for the Diamond Horseshoe Jamboree can only be made here (and on a first-come, first-serve, same-day basis). Secondly, when the weather turns foul, this is where the Disney characters seek refuge.

THE CHAPEAU – Hats are the house specialty here, and they have all sorts. Visors, straw hats, top hats, derbies, and of course, those Mouseketeer ears. If you want your ears, and you want 'em monogrammed, drop in here. Costume party ahead? Whether you want to be Zorro or a Southern Belle, the Chapeau people can usually help you out.

KODAK CAMERA CENTER – Cameras and photographic paraphernalia are available for sale or rental here, including 35mm cameras plus film, repairs (only minor ones), and camcorders.

CAMERA RENTAL RATES		
	Per Day	Deposit
Disc Cameras:	Free	$50
35mm Cameras:	$5	$145
Camcorders:	$40	$400

The refundable deposit can be charged to MasterCard, American Express, and Visa cards. Also available is two-hour express photo processing. Just drop off your film at the drop-off center and pick them up here before you leave.

MAIN STREET CONFECTIONERY – The sweet tooth in everyone urges a visit to this elysium of chocolates, pastilles, jelly beans, nougats, mints, marshmallow crisps, and peanut brittle — the house specialty. A good place to get that sugar rush.

UPTOWN JEWELERS – Here, a myriad of trinkets and baubles are available for purchase, ranging from ceramic Mickeys and Donalds for a few bucks to watches and jewels for a few thousand. Of interest are 14-karat gold and sterling silver charms featuring that mouse guy, Tinkerbell, the WDW logo, and Cinderella Castle. Timepieces are also stocked here, including Mickey Mouse watches and those that play the theme to "It's a Small World."

DISNEY & CO. – This quaint Victorian shop sells a variety of Disney T-shirts, sweats, hats, stuffed animals, pens, bags, and other souvenir items, albeit a smaller selection than the Emporium.

MAIN STREET MARKET HOUSE – This authentic turn-of-the-century general store sells snack and sundry items like pickles, honey, teas of all sorts, and tobacco products. The souvenir matchbooks given out with each purchase make a nice touch.

THE SHADOW BOX – The staff here is skilled at cutting black paper into the profiles of customers while they wait. Framed, the silhouettes cost only $4, a relative bargain here.

CRYSTAL ARTS – This shop sells a variety of cut-glass bowls and vases, plates and glasses, all created by a glass-blower here. Engraving is also available, and either the glass-blower or the engraver can always be seen working his magic.

Services

SUN BANK – Credit card cash advances with Visa or Mastercard from $50 to the credit limit, foreign currency exchange, cash and sell travellers' checks, cash personal checks (up to $1,000 with AmEx), and arrange wire transfers. On Town Square, next to City Hall.

MAGIC KINGDOM BABY CENTER AND FIRST AID – At the north end of the Street, the Baby Center offers changing and nursing facilities, as well as a place to prepare formula or purchase essentials like bottles, diapers, and baby food. First aid is located in the same building as the Baby Center.

STROLLER SHOP – Adjacent to the entrance, this offers rental strollers and wheelchairs. However, the price tag is $6 for a stroller. Bring your own if at all possible.

CITY HALL INFORMATION CENTER – City Hall offers information on the day's entertainment, Magic Kingdom guidebooks, lost-and-found facilities, and transportation info. On the left side of Town Square. *HINT:* The characters tend to hang out next to this building.

GUEST RELATIONS – Window Information and ticket upgrades are available here.

DISNEY VACATION CLUB INFORMATION CENTER – Details on WDW's timeshare can be found next to Tony's.

LOCKERS – Souvenirs and stuff can be stored in the lockers directly underneath the Main Street Railroad Station.

ADVENTURELAND

The first bridge on the left from the Hub leads here, the home of tropical vegetation and the World's best adventure rides. The landscape resembles that of a rain forest more than a one-time Florida swamp. The architecture is particularly faithful to the theme, as every building looks like it could have come out of *Indiana Jones* or *Romancing the Stone.* Imported items are the major bill of fare at the shops here, featuring the products of Africa, India, the Caribbean, Honk Kong, and Bangkok. Many rate this as their favorite land.

Overall Tips
Attractions – This land has some of Disney's best creations, and

inevitably long lines. The queues at the Swiss Family Treehouse and Jungle Cruise are notoriously slow, however, the Pirates of the Caribbean waiting area is more like a show in itself! Best bet: get Adventureland out of the way early in the morning or late in the afternoon.

Dining – Adventureland's only restaurants are fast food eateries, and some are things you'll want to avoid. However, Aloha Isle is a good bet for a cool snack.

Shopping – There is a large concentration of shops at Caribbean Plaza, at the exit from "Pirates". The shops there and at Adventureland Bazaar hold a great deal of interesting goods, including many imports from Asia and Africa.

Attractions
SWISS FAMILY TREEHOUSE
Rating: 7. Lets your imagination run wild! *Location:* Next to the Hub. *Duration of Tour:* Varies, but usually 10-15 minutes. *Best Time to Go:* Before 11:30 AM. *Comments:* Stairs! Lots of lots of stairs! If you can't handle the climbing, you may want to skip this one.

A spectacular re-creation of the Robinsons' lost paradise. It has everything the marooned family could want in treetop living. Patchwork quilts, mahogany furniture, candles stuck in abalone shells, and a system of running water in each room. Pulleys carry buckets full of water from below and pour them into pipes of hollowed-out wood and carry it into, oh, never mind. It's just one of those things you have to see to understand.

Some people think that the Treehouse is boring. Some even consider it a labor to climb the many steps. Granted, it may be a challenge, but the Robinson domicile at the top is worth it! Also, enjoyment of the exhibit is increased greatly by visitation in the morning, when you aren't likely to be tired out by hiking up a lot of steps. If you can't get there early (this attraction crowds up fast!), visit around 5:30.

JUNGLE CRUISE
Rating: 9. Disney's pride and joy, one of the best attractions in the park. Don't miss it. *Location:* Next to the Swiss Family Treehouse. *Duration of Ride:* 10 minutes. *Best Time to Go:* Early morning or late afternoon. *Comments:* Another attraction that gets crowded fast. Most enjoyable during the day.

For those souls who dream about going on a safari, this is your chance. You can visit the African veldt, a southeast Asian jungle, the Amazon rain forest, and the Nile valley, all without leaving central Florida.

Audio-Animatronics (Disney's sophisticated robotic system) animals representing their habitats are found along every step of the journey. The populace of the Jungle includes a family of bathing elephants, hippos, lions, and cannibals, also of interest is a section of the cruise that plunges cruisers into a dark Cambodian temple, home to a ferocious white tiger! And if you were wondering, the tropical vegetation is real and not robotic — and is kept warm in the winter by 100 heaters hidden in the rocks.

Best of all, the boats, bearing great alliterative names like Amazon Annie, Nile Nellie, and Senegal Sal, are not on a track but are piloted by real people, and the Jungle, inspired by the film The African Lion, is the only ride in the Magic Kingdom to be narrated by a human. The pun-heavy prattle covers topics like previous guests who didn't make it, the headhunters, and the rest of the sights. The scenes are about as genuine as you can get, and some kids are squeamish at first, but most soon sit back and enjoy the ride. Some of it is gruesome and odd, but it is all fun.

"TROPICAL SERENADE" (ENCHANTED TIKI BIRDS)

Rating: 4 1/2. Cheesy and repetitive, not Disney's best work. *Location:* Across from Jungle Cruise and next to the Adventureland Bazaar. *Duration of Show:* 15 minutes. *Best Time to Go:* Mid-afternoon.

The best thing about this attraction, created for the 1964-5 World's Fair in New York, is the respite its air-conditioned theater offers guests during the muggy afternoon hours. The show, better known as the **Enchanted Tiki Birds**, features what were the first Audio-Animatronics figures ever made. That explains why they seem wooden and cheap.

The show is hosted by four birds — Jose, Michael, Fritz, and Pierre, and features the same music over and over and over again. The Tiki Tiki Tiki Tiki Room song (seems more like the Tiki Tiki Tiki Tiki Tiki Tiki Tiki Tiki Tiki Tiki Tiki Tiki Room) is cute the first time around, but the repetition prompts some families to sneak out mid-show. A major problem of this show is its coherence, or lack thereof. The primitive robots, by their sheer number, make it hard to follow, even somewhat disconcerting. Visit this if you have two days at the Magic Kingdom. Walt Disney Imagineering (WED) is considering adding a comical slant to the show.

PIRATES OF THE CARIBBEAN

Rating: 10. Unbelievable! DO NOT MISS IT!!! *Location:* At the far end of Adventureland. *Duration of Ride:* 7 1/2 minutes. *Best Time to Go:* In the morning or late afternoon. *Comments:* This ride is tame, except for a steep flume-like drop.

As you walk through the queueing area, you immediately feel like you should be wearing an eyepatch and a pegleg. At the entrance, a parrot wearing a hat and patch sits, singing "Yo Ho," the first of many of this attraction's citizens to croon that tune. Then, you walk through stucco-walled rooms to a dark, dank, humid passageway through pirate dungeons. One cell has two prisoners hunched over a checkerboard. As you approach the loading area, you pass a cannon, a stack of cannonballs nearby. You may hear sentries yelling, "Sound the alarm" as you board your craft and set sail. The only sound is the water, for a while, then the lonely cry of a seagull, whose only companionship is a skeleton, posthumously defending his treasure on a desert island. The ship then sails right in the crossfire of the pirates and the law-abiding citizens. Cannons fire, sending up spouts of water as the ship sails on.

The pirates are coming! The pirates are coming! The pirates- oh, never mind, they're already here and they've taken over the town. A woman looks out of her window to survey the situation, but is quickly "discouraged" by bullets that shatter the flowerpots on either side of the windowsill.

Pirates pillage, pirates burn. One mildly sexist scene portrays the auction of village wenches, another pictures a lustful pirate chasing a young lass. As the scenes progress, the tide turns. The buccaneers drink and share their potables with, among other things, a couple of pigs. They can be seen getting chased with broomsticks by their women, and eventually, fighting over their treasure. These Audio-Animatronic figures are remarkable for their individuality, personality, and immaculate detail (One buc even has wiry hair on his legs). Especially uncanny are the movements and noises (attitudes?) of the chickens, dogs, and pigs found throughout the attraction.

There's one steep drop — a pitch-black plunge down a chute to the accompaniment of a roaring waterfall. But it's over before you know it. And the horrible sights are animated by the omnipresent choruses of "Yo Ho, Yo Ho, a pirate's life for me." This song is something of a pirate standard, seemingly used in every pirate movie in the history of film.

One of the best things about this attraction is the speed of the lines. Despite the popularity of this attraction, their is rarely a wait over half an hour, and then only during peak seasons. If you only have the chance to experience a few rides, put this at the top of your list.

Shopping
<u>At the Adventureland Bazaar</u>

ZANZIBAR SHELL COMPANY – Here's the place to find goods imported from exotic ports of call like Hong Kong, Beijing, and Singapore. Elephant Tales - Forgot your khakis? Need a new pith helmet? A variety of safari garments for both men and women is available here, plus jewelry, accessories, and stuffed animals.

TRADERS OF TIMBUKTU – Traders sells a variety of African imports, including striking ethnic jewelry (including that made of sharks' teeth), wood carvings, and khakis. Apparel is also available.

TIKI TROPICS SHOP – Jewelry, shoes, shorts, and T-shirts are sold here. Island Supply Surf gear is sold here, including T-shirts, shorts, bathing suits, jewelry, and surfboard wax.

Shops at Caribbean Plaza

HOUSE OF TREASURE – Here, kids can find their fantasy with pirate hats, swords, eye patches, toy rifles, and other memorabilia. HINT: If you are flying back home, pack any toy guns, knives, and swords in your luggage. Otherwise, you might encounter trouble from airport security.

THE GOLDEN GALLEON – Blackbeard's crew ne'er saw so much gold as is in this small shop. The treasure here is all nautical in its motif, ranging from model ships to ships' wheels, brass schooners, and racing yachts, plus fashions with maritime themes.

PLAZA DEL SOL CARIBE – This emporium sells candy, clothes, silk flowers, gift items, pinatas, pottery, and straw bags.

LAFFITE'S PORTRAIT DECK – Kids love to dress up as pirate lads and lasses, then pose with chests of treasure. Souvenir 8x10 photos of your child as a buccaneer make for lasting memories.

LA PRINCESA DE CRISTAL – Pretty much the same wares are sold here and in the Crystal Arts shop on Main Street, albeit in a completely different atmosphere. Glass blowing, cutting, and engraving are the skills practiced here. If you have more than one day to spend at the MK, it is enjoyable to spend a few minutes watching the master craftsmen at work.

CROW'S NEST – Cameras, film, and accessories are available here. This is also a drop-off point for the Photo Express service.

FRONTIERLAND

Out of the jungle and into the Old West, Frontierland is like some great old Western "B" movie come to life, with cacti, red concrete paths, sandstone mountains, rickety wooden structures, and a distinctively rugged feel throughout. Buildings have unpainted barn sides, stone, or clapboard, and all have a weathered look.

Overall Tips
Attractions – Four of WDW's best experiences are located here: Big Thunder Mountain Railroad, Diamond Horseshoe Revue, Country Bear Vacation Hoedown, and Splash Mountain. It is recommended to tour Frontierland early in the morning.

Dining – Eating and entertainment can be combined at the Diamond Horseshoe. All of the Frontierland eateries are decent, and the churros and turkey legs sold by wagons are worth note. However, there is no full-service restaurant on the Western front.

Shopping – A good place to go if you got a hankerin' fer Western goods, cowboy hats, leather, toy guns, and other Southwestern and Indian crafts.

Attractions
BIG THUNDER MOUNTAIN RAILROAD
Rating: 10. Another not-to-be-missed attraction, this is a wild ride through through a beautifully themed mountain. *Location:* A landmark in itself, it can be seen from most of the park. *Duration of Ride:* 3 1/2 minutes. *Best Time to Go:* Early morning or early evening. *Comments:* Children must be 3' 4" to ride. People in line may switch off at the ride. Kids 7 and under must be accompanied by an adult.

The lines wind up a path, through what appears to be a gold-mining operation. As you enter the main building, you overlook some hot springs and the railroad below. Occasionally, a geyser erupts. Then, you make your way down the ramp and to the boarding area. Those under the height requirements or those who just chickened out can get off here. But the rest of us board mine trains for a journey through the Gold Rush Days.

The trains set off, entering a cave filled with cool mists, shrieking bats, and falling rocks. As you ascend, notice the rumble as rocks shimmy and slowly fall towards you. Waterfalls and phosphorescent pools also can be seen. As you exit the dark cave, the trains slowly gain speed and zoom down the hill!

The scenery is excellent, especially the flooded-out town of Tumbleweed, in which a man sits, wearing his pajamas and a puzzled look as a Professor Cumulus Isobar's rainmaking machine sputters and pops, the flood beneath him, as he lays in a bathtub. All told, more than 20 Audio-Animatronics goats, people, chickens, and donkeys populate this section of the Old West. The trains careen around, dodging dinosaur remains and whipping by the Gold Dust Saloon (where a party still rages on), and eventually back to the loading platform.

Overall, the ride itself is tame as roller coasters go (there are no loop-de-loops, steep drops, or terribly sharp curves like in the Python or the Great American Scream Machine), as any thrill ride zealot will tell you, but this is an adventure. Where as the forementioned rides just zoom about the air with no real purpose, Big Thunder takes riders on a quest through a mining town, complete with about $300,000 worth of mining equipment — the real Mccoy. Even if you loathe roller coasters, give this one a whirl. It's so tame that it barely qualifies as a roller coaster, and it's so striking that it would be a crime to miss it.

Some statistics of note: Big Thunder took 15 years of planning and two more to build it, contains 650 tons of steel, 4,675 tons of cement, and 16,000 gallons of paint, and at a height of 197 feet, it is Florida's third highest peak. *HINT:* Try riding the Railroad after dark. The experience is completely different from (and somewhat more convincing than) a daytime tour.

TOM SAWYER ISLAND

Rating: 5. Relaxing, but you could forgive yourself for skipping this if you don't have any kids with you. *Location:* A landmark, can be seen from almost anywhere in Frontierland or Liberty Square. The raft docks, are next to Big Thunder Mountain and Splash Mountain. *Best Time to Go:* Anytime. Most enjoyable early in the day or mid-afternoon. *Comments:* Attraction closes at dusk.

Kids love this attraction, where they take a raft across the Rivers of America to an island loaded with caves to explore, bridges that lead to Fort Sam Clements, and there, a dozen or so air guns that they can fire at nearby mountains, passing steam ships, or the occasional tourist.

This attraction, which may seem boring to adults if toured early in the day, makes for a good out-of-the-way retreat for the heat of the afternoon. While the kids are off burning blood sugar like water, the grown-ups can relax at Aunt Polly's with a sandwich and a cool glass of lemonade. There are maps posted for those who manage to get lost. In busy seasons, a second raft landing may be brought into use.

COUNTRY BEAR VACATION HOEDOWN

Rating: 9. A Disney classic, good rhythmic fun. Don't miss it! **Location:** In the center of Frontierland. *Duration of Show:* 15 minutes. *Best Time to Go:* Before 11:30 AM or after 5 PM. *Comments:* The show changes twice annually — at Christmas and again in the summer.

Everybody seems to love the Country Bear Vacation Hoedown (formerly the Jamboree), which would account for the fact that this show almost always has a substantial wait. Also, Grizzly Hall, the theater in which the Hoedown plays, is smaller than adequate to accommodate the crowds who flock here.

Here, da bearsss perform like never before — in a musical revue filled with fun. Led by Henry, the master of ceremonies, they kick up a storm. One bear has a knack for impersonating Elvis Presley, while three other bruins, Bubbles, Beluah, and Bunny, harmonize "Wish They All Could Be California Bears". Other performers include the heartthrob Teddi Barra, who sings in the rain a la Gene Kelly (complete with raincoat and galoshes), a country-western band known as the Bear Rugs: Zeb, Zeke, Ted, Fred, and Tennessee, Liver Lips McGrowl, Wendell, Gomer the pianist, Trixie the Tampa Temptation (a torch-song crooner), Melvin the Moosehead, and Big Al, who is nothing short of a cult hero at WDW. His face can be seen on postcards, T-shirts, and other memorabilia — one of only a handful of Audio-Animatronics characters to have a following.

FRONTIERLAND SHOOTIN' ARCADE

Rating: 4 1/2. Not worth it if you only have one day to spend at the Kingdom. *Location:* Near the passageway to Adventureland. *Best Time to Go:* Any time. *Comments:* Costs 25¢ per play.

At this attraction, you can be the Lone Ranger, Clint Eastwood, or your favorite Western hero as you pick up a Hawkins 54-caliber buffalo rifle (modernized: they shoot infrared beams now) and can blow away any or all of almost a hundred targets each one procuring a different reaction. Digital sound effects add to the realism of this arcade.

DIAMOND HORSESHOE JAMBOREE

Rating: 10. Great fun for any and all. Don't miss it! *Location:* At the border with Liberty Square. *Duration of Show:* 30 minutes. *Best Time to Go:* Whenever your reservations are for. *Comments:* That's right, reservations. If you don't have 'em, you can't get in. Book your time at the Disneyana Collectibles shop on Main Street.

This show has rapidly become a Disney favorite, although seeing it is a real pain in the butt. First, you must go to Disneyana Collectibles on Main Street, make the necessary arrangements, then show up about thirty minutes before showtime to be admitted to the theater, fifteen minutes for food orders to be taken and filled, then finally, the show.

The show, composed in the same style as the Hoop-Dee-Doo Revue, features a troupe of live actors and actresses who sing, dance, and joke their way through the wholly entertaining show. The cast is energetic and brims with youthful exuberance, and overall, the show rarely fails to amuse. *HINT:* If you want to avoid wasting time but still want to see the Diamond Horseshoe (ha!), arrive before the rest of the park opens, go to Disneyana, and make your reservations before 9 AM. If you want, you can combine the show and lunch by choosing the 12:15 seating.

About lunch: a small selection of sandwiches, soft drinks, freshly baked pies, and snacks is available before the show.

SPLASH MOUNTAIN

Rating: 10. Unforgettable! Don't miss it! *Location:* A landmark, next to Big Thunder Mountain. *Duration of Ride:* 10 minutes. *Best Time to Go:* As soon as the park opens. *Comments:* Kids must be 3' 6" tall to ride, kids under 7 must be accompanied by an adult. The last drop is not nearly as bad as it looks.

When this opened up, it became the fastest ride in Walt Disney World — outrunning the Humunga Cowabunga and Space Mountain by a good ten miles an hour. It's also been the most highly touted of all the MK expansion projects, and that, coupled with its Anaheim predecessor's popularity, should make the latest Disney mountain adventure by far the resort's busiest ride.

In Splash Mountain, guests board log flumes and are set off on a ten-minute adventure chronicling Br'er Rabbit's wily escape from Br'er Fox and Br'er Bear. Riders are diverted by some of Song of the South's (Splash Mountain's origin) Oscar-winning music, including "Everybody's Got a Laughing Place" and "Zip-A-Dee-Doo-Dah", that ever-popular Disney anthem. Over 100 Audio-Animatronic animals populate Splash Mountain to tell the tale of those wacky briar patch animals. The flume ride itself is about half a mile long, travelling through bayous and over waterfalls, culminating in a 52-foot, 45-degree drop off Chickapin Hill, reaching a top speed of about 40 MPH. The logs then hit the water with a huge splash and seemingly sink into the lake.

Compared to the California version, this Splash Mountain is described as the "new and improved model," with more emphasis on the highly themed show areas and a slower pace through the mountain, making it easier to follow the story.

HINT: You will get wet. No matter where in the log you sit, you will step off Splash Mountain dripping, soaked, saturated, and otherwise, wet. If the idea doesn't really appeal to you, you can fashion yourself a rain poncho out of a garbage bag, or buy one from the Emporium on Main Street.If you are REALLY intent on riding Splash Mountain without crowds, it is imperative that you arrive at the MK before official opening time. Walk up Main Street and turn left at the Crystal Palace Restaurant. In front of the Palace is the bridge leading to Adventureland. It is NOT the bridge at the Hub. Get as close as possible to the barrier rope. When the rope is dropped, walk quickly or run to the passageway just across from the Swiss Family Treehouse. There will be phones and restrooms there. Go through this passageway and turn left. You should have a clear view of Splash Mountain across the waterfront. Run for it!

WALT DISNEY WORLD RAILROAD – This station, situated as a transition area between Splash Mountain and Big Thunder Mountain, was recently rebuilt, having been shut down to allow for the construction of Splash Mountain. See the entry for the Railroad under MAIN STREET U.S.A. earlier in this chapter.

Shopping
FRONTIERLAND TRADING POST – This shop sells a variety of souvenirs with a Western theme. You can get provisions like venison chili, buffalo, and boar meat, or cowboy can't-live-without's like six-shooters, rifles, and toy horses, or Indian sundries like peace pipes and tom-toms. Also, clothes from the frontier are available, like ten-gallon hats, moccasins, brass belt buckles, sheriff's badges, and Western jewelry.

TRICORNERED HAT SHOP – Indian headdresses, ten-gallon hats, and a variety of other headgear are sold here alongside leather goods.

FRONTIER WOOD CARVING – This is the spot to get personalized wooden gifts.

PRARIE OUTPOST AND SUPPLY – Here, one can procure various Southwestern gift items, art, and apparel.

BIG AL'S – Big Al, the bruin with a cult-like following, has his own shop, where harmonicas, toy guns, coonskin caps, rock candy, and big lollipops can be found, along with the big bear's image on almost everything.

LIBERTY SQUARE

Here, you are transported from the Gold Rush-era West to the Colonies around 1776. The buildings are clapboard and brick, with weathervanes and gingerbread moldings.

One of Liberty Square's foremost pieces of work was crafted by Mother Nature: it's the Liberty Tree, a 130-year-old live oak. It was found at the property's southern fringe and was transported to its present location twenty years ago. Thirteen lanterns hang on the tree, one for each of the original colonies.

Overall Tips
Attractions – The attractions here include a boat ride, a tour of a haunted mansion, and a show featuring every single U.S. President. Like Main Street, if you opt to experience any of the land's adventures at parade time, don't expect to be able to get to the hub. However, you can get through to Fantasyland.

Dining – If you care to sit down and relax in a full-service restaurant, the Liberty Tree Tavern may be your cup of Boston Tea Party. It serves good food and is often overlooked at lunch. If faster fare appeals to you more, the Columbia Harbour House offers the best light fare in the park.

Shopping - Colonial-era antiques are the main bill of fare here.

Attractions
THE HALL OF PRESIDENTS
Rating: 7 1/2. Very moving. *Location:* Between the Columbia Harbour House and the Liberty Tree Tavern. *Duration of Show:* 23 minutes. *Best Time to Go:* Anytime. *Comments:* Many kids are not mature enough to appreciate the show.

The two attractions in WDW that focus on the U.S. (this and the American Adventure at EPCOT) make you proud to be an American. I know, it's trite and cliche, but it's true. This attraction traces its origins back to Great˅Moments˅with˅Mr. Lincoln, one of the Disney-designed pavilions at the 1964-65 World's Fair in Flushing, New York. The attraction of the same name can be found today on Main Street U.S.A. in Anaheim's Disneyland.

The first portion of the show is a 70mm film about the magnitude of the Constitution throughout history. Then, an Audio-Animatronics Abraham Lincoln delivers a speech preceded by a roll call. All the presidents are here, from George Washington to Bill Clinton, who was installed just after his inauguration. The detail is almost frightening, as the chief executive officers fidget, nod, and whisper. Each president is dressed in the costume of his period, from his hairstyle to his shoes to the fabric of his pants. Even their personal effects were painstakingly re-searched and recreated, like Washington's chair and FDR's leg brace. This is the epitome of the trademark Disney attention to detail. Major changes to this attraction are under consideration by Imagineering.

HINT: If you arrive at the theater a few minutes early, you can get a look at the historical artifacts on display — they include flags, muskets, and portraits from as far back as the revolution.

If you are a history buff or just someone who feels especially proud of his red, white, and blue heritage, you will particularly appreciate this show. However, if you only have limited time and have seen the American

Adventure, you can skip it, although not without a few pangs of guilt. However, small (and some not-so-small!) kids find the show boring, so if that's a major consideration, you can skip it. And don't worry if there's a substantial line here: it turns over 700 people every 25 minutes.

LIBERTY SQUARE RIVERBOAT

Rating: 5 1/2. Scenic, but not special. *Location:* On the bank closest to the Hall of Presidents. *Duration of Ride:* 16 minutes. *Best Time to Go:* Anytime. *Comments:* If you're the type who's prone to seasickness, don't worry — the boat travels on a rail.

This is a steamboat ride down the half-mile Rivers of America, aboard the *Richard F. Irvine*, named for a key WDW Imagineer. It is a real steamboat in all aspects except one: it travels around Tom Sawyer Island on a guide rail. From the boat, you will pass Tom Sawyer Island and Fort Sam Clemens, Big Thunder and Splash Mountains, and props that enhance the Wild West theme. It's a relaxing way to beat the heat on a sticky afternoon.

MIKE FINK KEELBOATS

Rating: 5 1/2. Very similar to the Riverboat. *Location:* On the bank closest to the Columbia Harbour House. *Duration of Ride:* 9 1/2 minutes. *Best Time to Go:* Morning or late afternoon. *Comments:* Closes at dusk.

This attraction is a boat journey that goes along the same path as the Liberty Square Riverboat. The only major differences are the loading speed (considerably slower than the Riverboat) and the fact that the top decks of the two ships, the Berthe´Mae and the Gullywhumper, are exposed to the elements. Incidentally, the Keelboats are named for the riverboat captain who lived from 1770 to 1823. I knew you were wondering.

THE HAUNTED MANSION

Rating: 9. Great Disney entertainment! Don't miss it! *Location:* By the entrance to Fantasyland. *Duration of Ride:* 7 minutes. *Best Time to Go:* Anytime.

This attraction is one of my favorites for several reasons: the awesome special effects, the eerie sets in which the special effects are rigged, and the legend that surrounds the Mansion. One of the best things about the Haunted Mansion is the way that you experience something new every single time you ride it. Like the movies The *Naked Gun* and *Airplane*, there's a lot of details in the margins that you probably won't notice the first time, or even the second. Another thing that makes the ride so appealing is the fact that you can experience it as often as you like – the lines move like greased lightning.

HINT: As you are in the queue outside the Mansion, notice the tombstones and their epitaphs. They're good for yucks.

First, you are led into a portrait hall (known in inside circles as the Stretching Room) by cast members dressed as morticians. They grumble instructions, never smiling and never meeting your eyes. Then comes the classic spiel about how there are no windows and no doors, while either the floor sinks or the ceiling rises (they won't tell me!) and you are loaded into your "doom buggies". A gleefully evil voice tells you how to behave to coax the spirits into sight, and sure enough, your car is lurching forward between tableaus of dancing ghosts and organ players who look less than human.

One of the nicest touches in this ride is located at the very end, and it's more fun as a surprise, but let it suffice to say that any warnings about hitchhikers should be heeded.

Shopping

UMBRELLA CART – If it starts raining as you find yourself between Cinderella Castle and the Hall of Presidents, this is the place to pick up personalized umbrella.

OLDE WORLD ANTIQUES – Who comes to Disney World to buy antique furniture? I don't personally know anyone who does, but if you are one of those people, you can pick up furniture and decorative items crafted from mahogany, pine, oak, brass, pewter, and copper.

This isn't exactly The Price Club, so don't expect to get a steal on a particular item. Some even poke into four digits. All of the antiques, though, are in good shape. If the idea of buying family heirlooms at WDW doesn't appeal to you, take heart. The shop also deals clothing, perfume, and accessories.

SILVERSMITH – This market sells jewelry and housewares are sterling silver or silver-plated. Incidentally, the name "J. Tremain" listed as the shop's proprietor comes from Johnny Tremain, a silversmith's apprentice who joined the Boston Tea Party and the basis for the 1957 Disney movie of the same name.

HERITAGE HOUSE – Here, you can purchase parchment replicas of historical documents. Pewter items are also available, plus a good assortment of other housewares.

ICHABOD'S LANDING – This shop, found on the return path from the Haunted Mansion, is geared towards guests just coming back from that major attraction. Gags items are sold as well, but a better selection can be had at Main Street's House of Magic.

THE YANKEE TRADER – Cookware makes up the majority of the items for sale here, ranging from the mundane (cookie cutters, spatulas, and egg-timers) to the wild (souffle dishes and escargot holders). There are also cookbooks, including collections of recipes from days long gone. Also, in the "Jelly's Last Jam" department, Smucker's sells all of its varieties here. How many are there? Take a guess. Got it? Good. Now triple it.

SILHOUETTE CART – Profiles are for sale here, created while you wait.

THE COURTYARD – Topiaries, wind chimes, flowers, and garden merchandise are sold here.

FANTASYLAND

This is where dreams come true and fairy tales are personified. This is truly the heart and soul of WDW. This is where Disney's classic films, Peter Pan, Alice in Wonderland, 20,000 Leagues Under the Sea, Cinderella, Dumbo, Snow White, and The Wind in the Willows come to life. Sleeping Beauty's father is also here (in Cinderella's Castle! What's the deal with that, hmm?). This is many children's favorite land, although there are only two or three memorable attractions here. The buildings in which the adventures here are housed resemble an Alpine village, complete with a Swiss-made air gondola.

Planned for Fantasyland is a ride based on the Disney smash movie The Little Mermaid, which will be the first new attraction in the land since 20,000 Leagues Under the Sea (1971).

Overall Tips

Attractions – Most of the attractions here appeal to younger children more than any other land. If you have children under the age of ten, KEEP A CLOSE EYE ON THEM HERE, for all the rides here can captivate a child into "better-dealing" his parents for Dumbo or Snow White.

Dining – The only table-service restaurant in the land, King Stefan's Banquet Hall, offers a chance to check out Cinderella Castle and meet the lady herself. Other than that, it might be a good idea to avoid Fantasyland food.

Shopping – Most of the shops here sell character merchandise and are worth only a cursory glance, but the King's Gallery, in Cinderella Castle, is an exception.

CINDERELLA CASTLE AND THE HUB

The Castle is the symbol of all Walt Disney World, but it comes as a surprise to many visitors that they can not freely tour Cinderella Castle and that there is no ride or show in it. Still, it is arguably the most beautiful building in the whole World, and one of the most-photographed in the real world (as in the Earth!). The gold, grey, and blue spires of the castle reach 189 feet over Main Street (100 feet higher than Sleeping Beauty Castle in Disneyland) and serve as the final bridge between the melancholy burden of reality and quixotic fantasy.

Some trivia and history for you. How many stones were used to build Cinderella Castle? The same number that you had for lunch today. Zero. What do you mean, you ate stone for lunch? The architecture of the castle was borrowed from French palaces around the end of the 1100s, but with flavors of Mad King Ludwig of Bavaria's mansion and the castle from the Disney film.

Cinderella Castle is also, for lack of a better term, the brain of the Magic Kingdom. It is here that the nerve center of the park is located, both above ground and below it. If you were to travel up past King Stefan's Banquet Hall on the second floor, there are broadcast rooms, security centers (guardhouses, if you will), and an apartment meant for but never occupied by the Disneys. Below ground Disney employees change out of their "real people" outfits (yes! they are real people, not Audio-Animatronics) and into a Mickey suit or khakis and a pith helmet. They then travel through underground corridors to their designated "land" and inconspicuously melt into the scenery.

What makes the castle Cinderella's besides the name? Certainly not the restaurant inside. King Stefan was Sleeping Beauty's father, not Cinderella's. However, there is a series of five mosaic murals depicting the familiar tale. The panels, measuring 150 square feet apiece, were designed brilliantly by artist Dorothea Redmond and constructed by master craftsman Hanns-Joachim Scharff. They contain over one million tiny bits of Italian glass in 500 colors, plus bits of real silver and 14-karat gold.

There are also coats of arms here. They belong to prominent families in WDW history. The hostess of King Stefan's has a book telling whose is whose on the walls. An interesting note: many of the families represented on the walls of the Castle can also be found inscribed on the windows on the second story of Main Street.

The Hub is a small island at the dead center of the park. From here, you can directly reach every land but Frontierland and Mickey's Starland. As you enter the Hub from Main Street U.S.A. in the south, going clockwise: the first path leads to Adventureland and Frontierland, the second to Liberty Square and Frontierland, the third to Fantasyland via Cinderella Castle, the fourth to Fantasyland and Tomorrowland.

Attractions
MAD TEA PARTY

Rating: 4 1/2. Strictly Coney Park, not the kind of ride Disney excels at. *Location:* On the border with Tomorrowland. *Duration of Ride:* 1 1/2 minutes. *Best Time to Go:* Anytime in the morning or evening. *Comments:* May induce motion sickness.

Here, you sit in oversized teacups that circle around each other on a sheltered platform. The ride is loosely based on the scene in Alice In Wonderland where the Mad Hatter holds his un-birthday party. If you take away the teacup decorations and the central teapot with the mouse inside this is just a larger version of the Tilt-A-Whirl, a common ride found at every amusement park and carnival in the country. However, it is a fun ride and definitely one worth experiencing if there's not much of a line. You say you like spinning around and projectile vomiting? Me too! Well, here's how to twist your way into a nauseous seventh heaven. See the wheel in the center of the cup? Spin it. But hold onto the booook.....

20,000 LEAGUES UNDER THE SEA

Rating: 5 1/2. One of WDW's most overrated rides. *Location:* A landmark, the lagoon at the northern fringe of the park. *Duration of Ride:* 8 1/2 minutes. *Best Time to Go:* Before 9:30 or after dark. *Comments:* Better experienced at night.

Here, you get to make like the savings and loan industry and go under (rim shot). No, seriously, you get to live the life of one of Captain Nemo's crew aboard one of nine submarines that transverse the lagoon amidst some of the park's poorer special effects. The subs are narrow, almost claustrophobic, humid, and dimly lit. Passengers sit and look through portholes across the sub.

What they see is underwhelming. There are fake coral reefs, fake fish (not Audio-Animatronics, just fake), a sunken city, a polar ice cap, fake vegetation. Pretty much the only thing in the lagoon that's real is the 11.5 million gallons of water. However, the ride is aesthetically pleasing after dark, and the submarines are cool to look at, with the spikes and the eyeball-like windows. Overall, younger kids like it, while many people over the age of thirteen will find it lame. Still, it's Fantasyland's most popular ride and lines are perpetually long, and worse, the lines are unprotected from the elements. If you're planning on visiting the Living Seas pavilion at EPCOT Center or Sea World, you might want to skip this one, as this ersatz undersea voyage isn't even better than the real thing.

MR. TOAD'S WILD RIDE

Rating: 3. One of the few true duds in the Magic Kingdom. *Location:* Across from the Mad Tea Party. *Duration of Ride:* A little over 2 minutes. *Best Time to Go:* Before 11 AM, after 5 PM, or never. *Comments:* There are two almost identical rides in the building, and if both are running, waits are halved.

Mr. Toad disappoints. The ride is short, uneventful, and definitely a notch or two below the Disney reputation of quality. The first time I queued up for this ride, I waited forty-five minutes. My family finally got on the ride. I blinked, and the next thing I knew, they were unloading us. I am exaggerating, of course, but not by much. There are black lights (the kind that makes your socks glow purple) and two-dimensional cutouts illustrating your journey on the Road to Nowhere in Particular, the same road that was traveled by Mr. J. Thaddeus Toad in a stolen car, for which he traded the deed to his mansion in the book Wind in the Willows and the Disney movie adaptation *The Adventures of Ichabod and Mr. Toad.*

You go through a fireplace, under a falling suit of armor, through haystacks, into coops of chickens, and nearly into a speeding locomotive. But since this is Disney World, Nobody is seriously injured by any of these obstacles. But you may never get on the Ride to Nowhere in Particular again.

SNOW WHITE'S ADVENTURES

Rating: 5. Good. For teens, it's a good remedy for "It's a Small World". *Location:* By the carousel. *Duration of Ride:* 2 1/2 minutes. *Best Time to Go:* Before 11 AM, after 6 PM.

This ride is good, but not one of Disney's best. Although it is in the same genre of ride as Mr. Toad, Snow White is much better, by virtue of more realistic effects and thicker tension. Tell the kids beforehand that they will not see Snow White in the ride, as it is told from her first-person point of view. At the end of the ride, watch out for falling rocks. And I mean it! Major show changes are under consideration by Walt Disney Imagineering.

"MAGIC JOURNEYS"

Rating: 7 1/2. Very good, but very, very weird! *Location:* By the carousel. *Duration of Show:* 18 minutes. *Best Time to Go:* Anytime after noon.

This 3D film follows a group of children and their imagination, and plays like an acid trip. But oddness aside, it's a great movie. Originally seen at EPCOT Center and exported here upon the arrival of Captain EO, Magic Journeys is a visual feast with barely a sliver of plot. But it's still great fun, there's rarely a line, and in the heat of the day, twenty minutes in an air-conditioned theater can revitalize anyone.

As you enter the theater, attendants hand you pairs of purple-rimmed 3D glasses and lead you into the pre-show area, where you watch Working for Peanuts, a classic 1953 short featuring Chip 'n' Dale and a certain neurotic, hyperactive duck. This was the first-ever three-dimensional cartoon.

After the cartoon, you begin your magic journey, through some of the most incredible 3D footage ever. A circus, apple blossoms, a kite, lightning, bats, and balloons bombard you. The film is so realistic that audiences regularly react to different items, like shying away from the lightning or reaching out to touch a kite. The music is lazy and flowing, and it is an all-around pleasant experience.

DUMBO, THE FLYING ELEPHANT

Rating: 4. Undistinguished, but great fun for everyone who's ever longed to ride a flying elephant. *Location:* At the center of Fantasyland. *Duration of Ride:* 1 1/2 minutes. *Best Time to Go:* Before 10 AM or after 5 PM.

Young kids absolutely love this ride, while anyone over thirteen is likely to find it dull and childish. As if the idea of cruising above the Magic Kingdom in an aerodynamic grey elephant wasn't attractive enough, there are buttons inside each elephant that raise or lower them. Cool!

Little kids will insist on riding this, but its lines are probably the slowest-moving in all WDW. Go early in the morning. In fact, if you arrive before 10 AM, you might even be able to let the kids ride it twice. However, if there are no young children in your party, skip it.

CINDERELLA'S GOLDEN CARROUSEL

Rating: 6. Beautiful. *Location:* Center of Fantasyland. *Duration of Ride:* 2 minutes. *Best Time to Go:* Anytime in the morning or evening.

This is one of those attractions, like the Swiss Family Treehouse, that places the emphasis not on action but on beauty and attention to detail. Probably the most picturesque merry-go-round you will ever see, the Carrousel is an authentic item, built in Philadelphia in 1917. Originally dubbed "Liberty", it had 72 horses and several stationary chariots on a 60-foot platform. "Liberty" was discovered at Olympic Park in Maplewood, New Jersey. Refurbishments replaced the chariots with fiberglass horses, and the mechanics were completely modernized. Each of the 90 white horses is different, each with personality-lending details. Also, eighteen separate scenes, each six square feet, were hand-painted by Disney artists. The horses glide effortlessly around with accompaniment from a band organ that plays classic tunes from Disney movies. This ride is especially breathtaking at night.

IT'S A SMALL WORLD
Rating: 8 1/2. Happy, cheerful, colorful, and innocent. Don't miss it. *Location:* On the west side of Fantasyland. *Duration of Ride:* 11 minutes. *Best Time to Go:* In the afternoon.

Saccharine overload! It really is a Small World after all, according to the cutesy, if not sappy, lyrics to the theme song that plays all through the boat ride. You board pastel-hued boats and set sail through rooms filled with Audio-Animatronics dolls representing almost every culture group in the world. There are also nursery rhyme characters.

You can find can-can dancers, Tower of London guards, leprechauns, Dutch kids with wooden clogs on their feet, Thai dancers (remember the King and I?), snake charmers, kite flyers, hula-dancing Polynesians, Don Quixote lookalikes, and countless others. The costumes are particularly faithful, and the overall effect is glowing and alive with warmth. This ride is particularly relaxing, and the oft-times mammoth lines move quickly, so there's rarely much of a wait. Also, "Small World", as it is commonly called, offers a great video taping opportunity.

Oh, did I neglect the music? It's a Small World, the ride's theme song, is possibly one of the most-recognized Disney songs ever. It was composed by Richard and Robert Sherman, the brother team who brought us Mary Poppins and other Oscar-winning music. Ride it, but be prepared: you WILL hum the song afterward. It's state law.

PETER PAN'S FLIGHT
Rating: 9. Fantasyland's best ride. *Location:* At the border with Liberty Square. *Duration of Ride:* 3 minutes. *Best Time to Go:* Morning or evening.

The legend of Peter Pan is one of a rare breed, one that has been shown as a full-length animated feature, a live action film, and a stage musical. Riders here view Pan from the perspective of the cartoon. You board a replica of Captain Hook's pirate ship, suspended from above, and sail off through Peter's cries of "Here we go!" as the Darling children fly with him to Neverland.

The flight over London is breathtaking, as the Thames, Big Ben, and

Parliament pass underneath. Other highlights are the sword fight between Pan and Captain Hook and the finale: the crocodile holding Hook between his jaws. All of the characters are here, including the Darlings, Mr. Smee, Tinkerbell, and Tiger Lily. WDW's most underrated attraction.

SKYWAY
Rating: 5 1/2. Relaxing, great view. *Location:* At the border with Liberty Square. *Duration of Ride:* 5 minutes one way. *Best Time to Go:* In the morning or during special events. *Comments:* The ride is not a round trip: it's one way only.

You follow winding forest trails to the **Skyway** station, where you board small cars for an aerial ride across this land, Mickey's Starland, and Tomorrowland. The view is magnificent, and it offers an opportunity to relax in a crowdless, outdoor atmosphere. Among the more memorable of the sights are Cinderella's Golden Carrousel and the "20,000 Leagues" lagoon.

The ride conserves a little bit of energy that would otherwise be spent walking, but if there is any line, it is just as fast to go on foot. But other than as a method of transit, it makes for dazzling, sweeping vistas. Note that the Fantasyland station is usually the more crowded of the two. Note that if you intend to ride to Tomorrowland and back, you will have to disembark and get in another line.

Shopping
THE MAD HATTER – This shop, located just outside Magic Journeys, sells Mouseketeer ears, hats, and ready-to-wear clothing.

TINKERBELL TOY SHOP – Peter Pan's sidekick hosts this boutique, jam packed with Disney memorabilia including wind-up toys, stuffed animals, games, clothing, and Madame Alexander dolls. This is also where you can replace a stolen stroller or wheelchair.

THE KING'S GALLERY – One of only two ways that you can check out the Castle (the other being King Stefan's Banquet Hall), this is the only Fantasyland shop worth devoting substantial amounts of time to, as it offers an exceptional selection of unique gifts and medieval souvenirs. Included are all sorts of European clocks, tapestries, suits of armor, decorative boxes, swords, beer steins, chess sets, and handcrafted jewelry. A visit this magical shop is a must unless you are pressed for time.

MICKEY'S CHRISTMAS CAROL – Who can forget Mickey Mouse's heart-wrenching Bob Cratchitt and Scrooge McDuck's miserly Ebenezer

Scrooge in the annual Disney TV special? Well, there aren't any spirits here (supposedly!), but instead, the Magic Kingdom's year-round Christmas shop, selling ornaments, stockings, and such. You can't help but feel merry as you walk around this store.

THE ARISTOCATS – Fantasyland's foremost Disney souvenir shop, selling the usual selection of T-shirts, stuffed animals, keychains, china figurines, and so on and so forth.

ROYAL CANDY SHOPPE – In addition to a small selection of Disney memorabilia, this shop sells sundries, film, and candy.

KODAK KIOSK – This booth, which also serves as a drop-off point for two-hour Photo Express service, offers film and information.

NEMO'S NICHE – Another booth, just outside "Leagues", has film, stuffed animals, and information.

MICKEY'S STARLAND

In 1988, a three-acre section of the Grand Prix Raceway was reformed into an attraction commemorating the Mouse's 60th birthday. The architecture of this town, Duckburg, is cartoonish: the only buildings constructed to scale are Mickey's House and Hollywood Theatre. Everything is like a 3D cartoon cell, from Daisy Duck's Millinery to Scrooge McDuck's Bank. On the whole, this is a fun place for kids of all ages.

There are several minor outdoor play areas, Mickey's Treehouse and Minnie's Dollhouse, with slides, tunnels, swings, and ladders. However, there is no shade for weary parents. There is also the "Mousekamaze," a topiary maze for kids to wander in.

Overall Tips
Attractions – The only ride here isn't technically here: it's the WDW Railroad. There really aren't substantial lines for that or the stage show.
Dining – A cart patrols the land with ice cream and drinks.
Shopping – Mickey stuff is sold off a cart.

Attractions
WALT DISNEY WORLD RAILROAD – This station was created in 1988, along with then-known-as Mickey's Birthdayland. See the entry for the Railroad under MAIN STREET U.S.A. earlier in the chapter.

MICKEY'S HOUSE AND STARLAND SHOW and MICKEY'S HOLLY-WOOD THEATER

Rating: 7. A lot of zip-a-dee-doo-dah fun. *Location:* Next to the railroad. *Duration of Show:* 14 minutes. *Best Time to Go:* In the afternoon.

Walk through Mickey's **Mouse House**, full of Disney memorabilia and Mickey's personal effects, and into a tent in the backyard (doesn't everybody have a tent in their backyards?) where cartoons featuring (guess who!) Mickey are shown. After watching them for a while, you are escorted into the main theater where a character show is presented.

The show features afternoon heroes like Darkwing Duck of the show of the same name, Scrooge McDuck and Launchpad McQuack of DuckTales, Louie and Baloo of TaleSpin, and Chip and Dale of Chip'n'Dale Rescue Rangers in a madcap mystery that involves a plane crash and an explosion. Typical family fun. The show ends in an audience sing-along.

After the show, you are escorted into another tent, called **Mickey Mouse Club Funland**, which has interactive video stations that can put you on TV, a hallway filled with boxes that make different noises when opened, much like at the Loony Bin at the Disney-MGM Studios. More in the category of "Stuff They Took from the Studios," **Mickey's Walk of Fame**, based on its Hollywood namesake, has stars with the characters' names. When you step on the star, you hear his or her voice. By and large, though, this attraction is for kids. And though classified as a separate attraction, here we lump **Mickey's Hollywood Theater** together with the **Starland Show**. This is a tent that you enter to find Mickey's dressing room and the chance to pose for pictures and get autographs.

His dressing room is filled with Mouse stuff, like his Sorcerer's Apprentice hat from Fantasia. Groups of about four families each are escorted into the room, where the Mouse waits. Each group spends about five minutes with Mickey.

HINT: There are two little-known ways for meeting Mickey herewith as little of a wait in line as possible. The first technique, if executed properly, gives you a thirty-foot head start over your fellow audience persons. In the waiting area for the show, get as close to the door farthest left as possible, then when they open the doors, proceed to the next set of doors, again at the farthest left. Then you will be let into the theater. Enter a row of seats and move all the way to the end. As soon as the show ends, go out the door to your immediate left, exit the post-show area, and go outside. The Theater will be on your right. The second way: after the show, mill around Duckburg, check out the petting farm, or buy a snack, in any case, kill about fifteen minutes. Then, get in line for the Theater. Most of your group will have dissipated, and the next show will not have let out yet.

GRANDMA DUCK'S FARM

Rating: 5. Cute. *Location:* Across from Mickey's Hollywood Theatre. *Best Time to Go:* Anytime. *Comments:* Surprise! The animals are real!

In this modest petting farm, kids and grownups can mingle with chicks, pigs, ducks, sheep, goats, and Minnie Moo, a cow with Mickey's face pictured across her left side.

Shopping
MERCHANDISE CART - Mickey Mouse memorabilia and gifts.

TOMORROWLAND

Actually, this is kind of a misnomer as it stands right now. This was the vision of tomorrow, back in the 1960s, and except for Space Mountain, all of the attractions are dated. The bleak concrete and steel architecture is more nostalgic than futuristic.

It is for this reason that the current **Tomorrowland** has been scrapped. It will be completely revamped by 1996. Space Mountain will stay, but older attractions like Mission to Mars will be replaced. "American Journeys" will be replaced by a new Circle-Vision 360 film paying tribute to Western civilizations, combining the movie and Audio-Animatronics figures that will disappear into the film at key moments, blurring the line between fantasy and reality, coming in 1994. Then, in 1996, Tomorrowland becomes an intergalactic spaceport for arriving aliens.

The featured attractions will be Alien Encounter, a thrill ride that will put guests in a teleportation experiment gone wrong, pitting them against a terrifying alien, and Plectu's Galactic Revue, featuring a band of musical Audio-Animatronics aliens.

Overall Tips

Attractions - When Splash Mountain opened, it replaced Space Mountain as the biggest draw in the park. So crowds there will be a little thinner. However, most of the other attractions rarely have long lines, so they are best visited during the hot, crowded part of the day.

Dining - Surprisingly, some of the best fast food restaurants in the Magic Kingdom are here. The Plaza Pavilion is the best of the bunch, the Tomorrowland Terrace is good and quick, same with the Space Bar. The Lunching Pad is one of the few MK eateries with a full, healthy menu.

Shopping - Only The Space Port has anything beyond the usual WDW souvenirs, but Mickey's Star Traders has a great selection of character merchandise and park mementos.

Attractions
MISSION TO MARS
Rating: 2 1/2. Obsolete, dull. *Location:* At the entrance to Tomorrowland. *Duration of Show:* 12 minutes. *Best Time to Go:* From 11:00 to 4:30. *Comments:* The digital clock outside the theater tells the amount of time before the start of the next show.

This current attraction is an absolute flop. The pre-show features an Audio-Animatronics flight engineer who gives a discourse on your upcoming "mission." After that, guests are loaded into a round room. The seats shake, the room rumbles, and you are on Mars. There is grainy old footage of the Mariner Nine landing, and a feeble description of Mars, most of the information in which can be traced to in a sixth-grade science textbook. This ride is marked for death in the revamping of Tomorrowland.

"AMERICAN JOURNEYS"
Rating: 8 1/2. One of the best films anywhere in the World. *Location:* At the entrance of Tomorrowland. *Duration of Show:* 20 minutes. *Best Time to Go:* Between 11:00 and 4:30. *Comments:* The audience must stand during the show.

"American Journeys" was the first of a new type of film, the CircleVision 360. The production of a CV360 film uses a 700-pound rig with nine cameras mounted to face a circle of mirrors. Nine projectors show the film, while fifteen speakers make for unforgettable stereo sound.

The stops on this grand tour of the nation include locations from all 50 states. It took four years to complete, and is fast-paced, entertaining, and stirring. The realism is enough to make some guests motion-sick during the flight sequences.

And even better, this theater can accommodate 3100 people an hour, the single highest capacity in the MK. So most of the time, you will get into the show. The down side about these movies in general is that the audience must stand for the duration of the show. There is no place for tired kids to sit, and many kids find the CircleVision movies boring. Unfortunately, the tombstone for "American Journeys" is being prepared for when Tomorrowland is revamped.

DREAMFLIGHT
Rating: 5. Mildly enjoyable. *Location:* In front of StarJets. *Duration of Ride:* 6 minutes. *Best Time to Go:* Anytime.

This tame ride starts off sluggish, with various sets consisting of two-dimensional cartoon-like people, planes, and inanimate objects. The special effects are childish and a less-than-wonderful ride is seemingly promised. However, film footage giving the illusion of flight is impressive and the film of aerial stunts always gets oohs and aahs (this section was filmed in the Northwest specifically for the attraction). The finale features pretty sets of Paris and Tokyo. This ride, formerly known as "If You Had Wings," almost never has lines, so you can ride it whenever you like.

WEDWAY PEOPLEMOVER

Rating: 6. Relaxing, a change of pace. *Location:* Below StarJets. *Duration of Ride:* 10 minutes. *Best Time to Go:* Anytime.

The **PeopleMover** track can be seen winding all throughout Tomorrowland, but if you wish to ride, you have to go to the boarding area, near StarJets. The ride is a scenic overview of Tomorrowland, passing each of the attractions. There is a pleasant-sounding computer narration, and the 10 mile per hour ride is good for getting acquainted with the layout of Tomorrowland, checking out the crowds at Space Mountain, and getting a view of the actual ride, the rockets zooming through the blackness. Environmentalists take heart! This ride produces very little noise and is propelled by a electromagnets, uses limited power, and does not pollute.

STARJETS

Rating: 3 1/2. Boring, not worthwhile. *Location:* A landmark. *Duration of Ride:* 1 1/2 minutes. *Best Time to Go:* Before 11 AM or after 5 PM. *Frightening?* Only to those afraid of heights.

This is a midway ride primarily for those kids between Dumbo and Space Mountain. Small aircraft circle a model rocket connected by large metal arms, and the height of your vehicle's flight can be altered. The shuttles rotate eleven times a minute for a top speed of 26 MPH, rising up to 80 feet.

It's too tame for most people over twelve and is more time-consuming than most other attractions, because you have to go up an elevator, then get in line for a minute-and-a-half journey. Skip this one or ride it during the morning, evening, or special events.

CAROUSEL OF PROGRESS

Rating: 6. A delightful way to spend a few air-conditioned minutes. *Location:* At the southeast corner of Tomorrowland. *Duration of Show:* 18 minutes. *Best Time to Go:* Between 11:30 and 4:30.

This is a happy show depicting the advancement of technology throughout the twentieth century, although since it only goes up to the advent of computers, so it's less tomorrow than yesterday.

The show stars a typical family going from generation to generation. The Audio-Animatronics folks here tell how we evolved from ice cubes and fans to air conditioning, from radio to television, and so on and so forth. This show is worth seeing, especially in the hot hours when other attractions are filled. Unfortunately, the Carousel of Progress show will be retired and the building converted into a new space-themed adventure.

SKYWAY

For a full description of the Skyway, see the "Fantasyland" section of this chapter. Note that lines are usually shorter here.

SPACE MOUNTAIN

Rating: 10. One of the Magic Kingdom's premier attractions. Don't miss it! *Location:* A landmark. *Duration of Ride:* Almost 3 minutes. *Best Time to Go:* As soon as the park opens or in closing hour, or between 6 and 7 PM. *Comments:* Children must be 3'8" tall to ride, those under seven must be accompanied by an adult. Not recommended for expectant mothers, those with heart, back, or neck problems, or those prone to motion sickness. *Frightening:* A ride much wilder than Big Thunder Mountain, and in the dark to boot, frightens many.

Space Mountain is a psychological thrill ride. While the thrill in conventional roller coasters lies in the actual twists, turns, drops, and loops, Space Mountain tries to terrify by sending you off through passageways of flashing lights, strobes, and strange sounds, and eventually into a cavernous place where the only thing you can see is the dark shape of a head in front of you. Not to say that the ride isn't savage, it is; just ask anyone who ate a good, hearty breakfast just before boarding. Roller coaster enthusiasts are likely to find the ride, only measuring 28 miles an hour at its fastest, tamer than the special effects, and this roller coaster can't be described as diabolical like some others, though those not weaned on the Great American Scream Machine and the Cyclone may disagree with me on that point.

The tension begins to mount in the queueing area, where on either side of the passageway, bent-plastic windows give a strange perspective into space, with stars aplenty. When you get to the boarding area, look up and you will see shooting stars, created by a light shining off a disco ball, and meteors, reportedly projections of chocolate chip cookies. As the shuttles take off, you hear screams in the distance. And you begin to wonder if this was such a great idea. If you wimp out in line, just ask the Disney personnel to show you to the "ride bypass" (more commonly known as the chickens' exit) and they will do so.

If you choose to remain (and good for you), put any loose articles in a safe place unless you want to see it under the track. You will eventually be loaded onto a shuttle, six rows. Unlike most roller coasters, only one person sits in each row. That way, there's nobody to lean on when the butterflies hit. But you start climbing up the track, with flashing signs on the side of the track tell you how many seconds to liftoff. But once you do, hold on!

HINT: Like Splash Mountain, there will always be people who are Space Mountain groupies who line up at the central Hub thirty minutes before park opening to wait for the rope to drop so they can make for the large white dome to be the first one on the ride. Well, I've got a secret for you. There's a way to beat them there! They're all lining up at the Hub, so you go up past the Plaza Restaurant and stop under the arch reading *The Plaza Pavilion Terrace Dining.* Here, you'll be cool, comfortable, ready, and 100 yards closer to Space Mountain than your counterparts at the Hub. Feel free to laugh at them. Now, as soon as the Disney employee takes down the barrier rope, walk, jog, or disregard his instructions discouraging running, as fast as you can to Space Mountain.

HINT: Let's say there's a family, Mom, Dad, and little Joey. Mom and Dad are both dead set on riding Space Mountain. But alas, little Joey is not tall enough to ride. So what can you do? Get in line twice? You don't have to! Just get in line, and tell the first attendant that you see that you want to switch off. He will radio to a second attendant and tell him to expect you. When you reach the second attendant, one parent will go on ahead while the other waits with the kid(s). After the first parent gets off the ride, another attendant will lead him/her up a staircase to the boarding area. There, the parents swap custody of little Joey, the second one rides, and the first parent and Joey go to the unloading area and meet again. Happy happy joy joy! This technique can also be used on Big Thunder Mountain and Splash Mountain, both in Frontierland.

After you get off your shuttle, slightly nauseated and giddy from the ride, or, if you chickened out (and boy, did you miss out!) you step on a moving sidewalk that carries guests past scenes with Audio-Animatronics people who talk about discovering a new planet in RYCA 1: Dream of a New World. There's also video cameras and televisions that guests appear on as they pass by, making faces at the cameras. These systems retail for $70 to $80 grand each. Don't break them!

GRAND PRIX RACEWAY

Rating: 5. Not worth the wait. *Location:* A landmark, next to Space Mountain. *Duration of Ride:* About 4 minutes. *Best Time to Go:* Morning or evening. *Comments:* Children must be 4'4" tall to ride alone.

What a **Grand Prix Raceway** has to do with the future, I can't seem to figure out. But in any case, this ride is perpetually crowded. Kids really love it, but unfortunately, those under 4'4" can't ride because they can't steer and reach the pedals at once. The first time I went on this ride, I was just over the height limit and I kept on smacking the steel guide rail, again and again (I still haven't heard the end of it). Adults find this one boring, teenagers could take it or leave it. The track makes for a rather dull ride, as the cars' top speed is a gut-wrenching 7 miles an hour and you can't bump the car in front. Skip it if there's a line.

HINT: If your kid is too small to drive, get in the car together. Let your child sit on your lap and steer while you work the pedals. This gives the illusion of driving to your kids.

Shopping

MICKEY'S STAR TRADERS - This large shop, located near the Grand Prix Raceway, offers a very good selection of stuffed animals, clothes, collectibles, film, and sunscreen.

SKYWAY STATION SHOP – Next to the Tomorrowland station and across from Space Mountain, this sells selected Magic Kingdom memorabilia.

THE SPACE PORT – This is the only shop in Tomorrowland selling something other than character merchandise and park mementos, instead, kitschy futuristic gifts, toys, games, fashions, jewelry, and the like. Strollers and wheelchairs can be replaced here.

SPACE PLACE – Situated in the booth next to StarJets are clothing, gifts, snacks, and hats.

FILM & GLOW KIOSK – Film and camera merchandise all day long, plus glow-in-the-dark merchandise after dark. Also, this is a Photo Express drop-off point.

ENTERTAINMENT IN THE MAGIC KINGDOM

There is always some sort of live entertainment going on around the MK, and here is a basic outline of entertainment during a typical week. All of the entertainment below is subject to change or cancellation.

ALL-AMERICAN COLLEGE MARCHING BAND – College students from around the country perform throughout the park during weekday afternoons and early evenings. The program occurs during the summer.

BANJO KINGS – A band plays 20's songs on banjos and washboards.

CHARACTERS – Next to City Hall, a character waits in Tour Guide Gardens for kids to pose with in pictures and to give autographs to. It's someone different every day. Daily, from 9 AM to 2:30 PM and from 3:30 PM to 7:15 PM. In case of inclement weather, the daily character will be high and dry at Disneyana Collectibles. Many characters can be found loitering around Mickey's Starland and Fantasyland at various times every day. Mickey's Hollywood Theater offers an opportunity to meet the big cheese in person. See MICKEY'S STARLAND for more information.

COKE CORNER PIANIST – There's a ragtime piano player outside the Refreshment Corner restaurant who performs throughout each day.

THE DAPPER DANS – This barbershop quartet can usually be found either at the Harmony Barber Shop or up and down Main Street, on foot or a four-seater bike. The flawless harmonies emanating from the men in straw hats and striped vests are enjoyable, and they enhance the reality of Main Street's Victorian atmosphere. For info on the Harmony Barber Shop, see MAIN STREET U.S.A. at the beginning of the chapter. They perform various times throughout the day.

DIAMOND HORSESHOE JAMBOREE – This is a dance hall show in Frontierland during the afternoon. Reservations are required, go to the Disneyana Collectibles store on Main Street. For a detailed description of the Jamboree, see the FRONTIERLAND section earlier in this chapter.

DISNEYMANIA – Some of the newest Disney characters join up with the old favorites and the Kids of the Kingdom in a musical show at the Castle Forecourt Stage. Performed at various times during each day.

DISNEY WORLD IS YOUR WORLD – Disney characters and the Kids of the Kingdom present a musical celebration of Walt Disney World, twice a day, two days a week at the Tomorrowland Theater.

FLAG RETREAT – Each day at ten minutes after five o'clock, a small color guard, accompanied by the WDW Marching Band, takes down the American flag that flies in Town Square. A flock of homing pigeons is then released. They fly to their home, behind the castle, in about twenty seconds.

FRONTIERLAND – Shootouts are staged here. If you happen to be around when one does go down, I hope you brought your Kevlar.

J.P. AND THE SILVER STARS – Hey, mon, thees ees the place for listening to an authentic Caribbean steel drum band. At Caribbean Plaza, performances run several times a day five days a week.

JUNGLE BOOK – A show featuring the stars of Disney's classic film is in the planning stages.

MICKEY'S STARLAND SHOW – This live show features Mickey and the cast of the Disney Afternoon. Performed every half hour between 10:30 AM and 2:30 PM, and then again between 4 PM and 5:30 PM.

ONE MAN'S DREAM – This show, which has been running in Tokyo Disneyland for five years now, pays homage to 65 years of musical highlights from favorite Disney films like Peter Pan, Snow White, the Jungle Book, and Lady and the Tramp.

"SPECTROMAGIC" – Returning guests are probably looking at the entertainment schedule and wondering, "Where's the Main Street Electrical Parade?" Well, folks, it's off blinking and bleeping in Euro Disneyland. That's right, ladies and gentlemen, it was unplugged and exported. But don't fret. Disney has instead given the Florida Magic Kingdom a brand new evening parade: SpectroMagic.

If you like electro-luminescence, prismatic holography, fiberoptics, thermoplastics, liquid nitrogen, xenon flashlights, and mirror balls (and don't lie, we know who you are), you will love this parade. If you like Mickey Mouse, Donald Duck, the Little Mermaid, and Cinderella, you will love this parade. One way to describe this parade is to say that the Imagineers behind it have been snorting pixie dust again. SpectroMagic features lights so brilliant that you may see thousands of tiny beams glancing through the air, threads of light that create strands of hair, thousands of inch-thick glowing dragonfly wings, and wild patterns of chaser lights. And that's just the beginning!

Mickey Mouse is the master of this parade, accompanied by SpectroMen. Roger Rabbit conducts an orchestra, Chernabog, the demon from Fantasia, spreads his wings to an incredible 38 feet, and Cinderella rides in her 150 foot-long coach and carrousel. The dazzling array of colors disappears as Practical Pig touches his paintbrush to it, making all the lights a brilliant white, then touches it again, restoring the color. And it's all done to the accompaniment of a 72,000 watt symphonic orchestra.

During the summer and holiday seasons, SpectroMagic takes place twice a night, at 9 and 11 PM, with fireworks at 10 PM. During the off-season, it is performed at 6:30 nightly Friday through Tuesday, and on

SpectroMagic Saturdays, the park is open until 11 PM, and the parades and fireworks happen as they do during the summer. The nine o'clock parade is always more crowded than the 11 PM rendition. Absolutely ot to be missed. See PARADE VIEWING below.

"SURPRISE CELEBRATION" PARADE – This happening, specially created for the 20th Anniversary Celebration (or maybe rehashed Party Gras balloons, you be the judge!), features Roger Rabbit as a court jester, plus Mickey, Minnie, and the rest of the gang in the form of four-story balloons. The parade celebrates WDW's 20th by saluting parties around the world, like Mardi Gras, Carnival del Rio, Chinese New Year, and a Venetian festival. Live people, over 100 of them parade down the street as jesters, acrobats, dancers, stilt walkers, courtiers, and revelers. See PARADE VIEWING below.

TINKER BELL'S FLIGHT and **"FANTASY IN THE SKY" FIRE- WORKS** – Tinker Bell flies from Cinderella's Castle to trigger a spectacular four-minute fireworks display. 150 shells are set off, a rate of one every two seconds. Performed at 10 PM during peak seasons and the summer. *HINT:* Everyone assumes that the best vantage point for Fantasy in the Sky is right at Cinderella Castle. Not so. Since the fireworks are unleashed from behind 20,000 Leagues Under the Sea, excellent views can be had from the cafe tables in Fantasyland.

WALT DISNEY WORLD MARCHING BAND CONCERTS – This band performs at Town Square twice six mornings a week, and on occasion at Fantasy Faire.

HOLIDAYS – There are special events in the Magic Kingdom for Easter, Christmas, New Year's Eve, and the 4th of July. For more information on holiday doings, see SPECIAL EVENTS in Chapter 2.

PARADE VIEWING – Most people who decide to watch a parade, either the Surprise Celebration Parade or SpectroMagic, choose spots on Main Street U.S.A. or the central Hub, totally clogging those areas. True, some of the best vantage points are along this section of the parade route (the ones from the train platform are magnificent), but they must be grabbed as much as forty-five minutes early.

In Liberty Square and Frontierland are many excellent vantage points that are often overlooked:

• At **Sleepy Hollow**, in Liberty Square close to the Hub, you can arrive ten to twenty minutes early, buy some refreshments, and take a table by the rail.

- Any spot on the pathway between **Sleepy Hollow** and the **Castle** on the Liberty Square side of the moat.
- The covered walkway between **Liberty Tree Tavern** and the **Diamond Horseshoe Saloon**.
- The raised platform in front of the **Frontierland** facade.
- The central hub, between the **Adventureland** and **Liberty Square bridges**.
- **Waterfront** at the Rivers of America.

SPECIAL GUESTS – Occasionally, guests of particular interest to special groups appear at the park. For example, the last week I was there, Egidio Guerra, the master sculptor of Capodimonte porcelain flowers, appeared at Uptown Jewelers on Main Street.

MAGIC KINGDOM MISCELLANY

Ride These Early
ADVENTURELAND: Jungle Cruise
FRONTIERLAND: Splash Mountain, Big Thunder Mountain Railroad
FANTASYLAND: Dumbo, the Flying Elephant, Cinderella's Golden Carrousel, Mad Tea Party
TOMORROWLAND: Space Mountain, Star Jets, Grand Prix Raceway

All of these rides are either immensely popular rides that are quick-loaders but are inundated with tourists anyway, like the three mountains (Splash, Space, Big Thunder) or on the other extreme, slow-loading, midway type rides. The rest are somewhere in between.

Scary? And Why?
FRIGHTENING RIDE, INTENSE EFFECTS: Space Mountain.
FRIGHTENING RIDE: Splash Mountain.
VISUALLY INTENSE: Big Thunder Mountain, Pirates of the Caribbean, Jungle Cruise, Haunted Mansion, Mr. Toad's Wild Ride, Snow White's Adventures, Magic Journeys.

Memorable Shopping
MAIN STREET, U.S.A.: Harmony Barber Shop, Disneyana Collectibles, Uptown Jewelers, Crystal Arts
ADVENTURELAND: Zanzibar Shell Company, Traders of Timbuktu, The Golden Galleon, La Princesa de Cristal
FRONTIERLAND: Frontier Trading Post
LIBERTY SQUARE: Olde World Antiques, Heritage House, The Yankee Trader

FANTASYLAND: The King's Gallery, Mickey's Christmas Carol
TOMORROWLAND: The Space Port

Beat the Heat!
There are several attractions where you can get out of the heat for a while and relax. There's the WDW Railroad (it's not air conditioned, but it makes a nice breeze), plus:
MAIN STREET U.S.A.: The Walt Disney Story
ADVENTURELAND: Tropical Serenade
FRONTIERLAND: Country Bear Vacation Hoedown, Diamond Horseshoe Jamboree
LIBERTY SQUARE: The Hall of Presidents, Liberty Square, Riverboat
FANTASYLAND: "Magic Journeys"
MICKEY'S STARLAND: Mickey's Starland Show
TOMORROWLAND: Mission to Mars, "American Journeys" Carousel of Progress

Outta my WAY, I Gotta GO!
Just my way of telling you where the least crowded rest rooms in the Magic Kingdom can be found:
• Behind the Enchanted Grove (Fantasyland).
• The passageway between Frontierland and Adventureland.
• At Baby Services
• At any table-service restaurant.

11. EPCOT CENTER

INTRODUCTION

On October 1, 1982, EPCOT Center opened on 260 acres of land between the Magic Kingdom and the Disney Village. EPCOT is comprised of two sections, Future World and World Showcase.

The former features pavilions paying tribute to various aspects of modern civilization and the earth, for example, there are attractions focusing on agriculture, the seas, communication, imagination, transportation, energy, and medical science.

The latter consists of eleven pavilions representing the cultures of different nations around the world. The architecture, merchandise, food, and even the cast members are faithful to the nation.

Planning for EPCOT (short for **Experimental Prototype Community of Tomorrow**) began as early as 1964. Walt Disney described the concept:

EPCOT will take its cue from the new ideas and new technologies that are now emerging from the creative centers of American industry. It will never be completed, but will always be introducing and testing and demonstrating new materials and systems. And EPCOT will be a showcase to the world for the ingenuity and imagination of American free enterprise.

Through all of the planning, Walt's original idea of a living, working community changed to that of a sort of a world's fair, and eighteen years, and 14,000 workers later, EPCOT Center opened.

GETTING AROUND – To get to EPCOT Center from:

Magic Kingdom, Polynesian Resort, Contemporary Resort, Grand Floridian Resort: Take the monorail to the TTC and switch to the EPCOT Center line.

TTC: Take the monorail or the red-flagged bus.

Disney Inn: Take the green-flagged bus to the TTC and switch to the monorail.

Fort Wilderness: Take the blue-flagged bus to the TTC and switch to the monorail.

Disney-MGM Studios Theme Park: Take the water taxi to any

EPCOT Resort and from there, take a tram or walk to the International Gateway.

Typhoon Lagoon, Pleasure Island: Take the red-flagged bus.

Disney Village Marketplace: Take the green-and-gold-flagged bus marked EC/V or the red-flagged bus.

EPCOT Resorts: Walk or take the tram to the International Gateway.

Disney's Village Resort: Take the green-and-gold-flagged bus marked EC/V.

Port Orleans, Dixie Landings, and Vacation Club Resorts: Take the pink-and-green-flagged bus marked EC.

Caribbean Beach Resort: Take the orange-and-white-flagged bus marked EC.

Hotel Plaza: Take the red-and-white-flagged bus marked EC.

Off-site Lake Buena Vista hotels: Take 535 to International Drive. Go towards I-4. It will change to EPCOT Center Drive. Take the jughandle to parking lot.

Off-site Kissimmee hotels: Take U.S. 192 to World Drive (maingate). Take World Drive to EPCOT Center Drive. Take the jughandle to the parking lot.

Off-site International Drive hotels: Take International Drive south, it will turn into EPCOT Center Drive. Take the jughandle to the parking lot.

Off-site hotels via I-4: Take I-4 to exit (EPCOT Center). Take the jughandle to the parking area.

PARKING – The EPCOT Center parking lot can accommodate 11,391 vehicles. The cost is $4, free for resort guests (remember your ID!) and there is no cost for leaving and returning or switching parks on the same day. Be sure to keep your receipt. Also, it is VITAL that you write down where you park!

The parking sections are named after themes of the Future World attractions. Write the section down! This can not be stressed enough. Note that the handicapped can park in a special lot next to the entrance plaza.

ADMISSION, MONEY, REFURBISHMENT AND INTERRUPTION OF ATTRACTIONS, PACKAGE PICKUP & DRESS CODE – See Chapter 10.

VITAL STATISTICS

Location: Walt Disney World, P.O. Box 10,040, Lake Buena Vista, FL 32830-0040. *Phone:* 824-4321. *Hours:* Vary. Gates open at 8:30 AM, attractions at 9 AM. *Admission:* $34 for adults, $27 for kids. See pp. 211-212. *Parking:* $4. *Time to see:* A minimum of one day. *When to See:* From least to most crowded, Friday, Sunday, Saturday, Thursday, Wednesday, Tuesday, and Monday. *Don't Miss:* Spaceship Earth, Universe of Energy, Horizons, World of Motion, Body Wars, Cranium Command, Journey into Imagination, Mexico pavilion, Wonders of China, The American Adventure, Impressions de France, O Canada!.

PRACTICAL INFORMATION – Alcoholic Beverages: Allowed, sold at most table-service establishments. **Baby Services:** Changing and nursing facilities are located at the Odyssey Complex. **Baby Strollers:** Can be rented for $6 a day at the Stroller Shop, on the left side (as you enter) of Spaceship Earth. **Banking:** There is a branch of the Sun Bank, a Floridian chain, located at the Entrance Plaza (see below). **Cameras:** The Camera Center, presented by Kodak, has a full array of cameras for rent, plus film, videotapes, and two-hour development (see below). **Cigarettes:** Available at most shops throughout the park. Special blends of tobacco are available at some World Showcase shops. **Dress Code:** Shirts and shoes must be worn, as a rule. However, this rule is broken as often as it is obeyed during the summer.

First Aid: Located at the Odyssey Complex. **Foreign Language Assistance:** Personal translator units, available at Earth Station, translate some theater presentations into Spanish, French, or German. WorldKey Information Satellites also provide information in Spanish. Maps and assistance are available at Earth Station. **Guided Tours:** Available for $3.50 in addition to admission. Visit Earth Station for details. **Hearing-impaired Guests:** Written descriptions for most attractions are available at Earth Station. A Telecommunications Device for the Deaf (TDD) is available at Earth Station.

Information: Earth Station offers all sorts of info, plus entertainment schedules. Also, the WorldKey Information System, developed by Bell and Disney, has up to 40 minutes of information about EPCOT, with maps, pictures, and recountings of the various pavilions. Stick with the system for a minute and you will eventually see a prompt asking if you want to speak to an attendant. If you choose to connect with a WorldKey attendant, they can answer your questions, find lost children, or make restaurant reservations, all via video cameras, touch-sensitive screens, and intercoms. There are twenty-nine consoles spread throughout EPCOT at four sites: Earth Station, World Showcase Plaza, the causeway between World Showcase and Future World, and in front of the Germany pavilion.

Kennel: Pets are not allowed in WDW Resorts or attractions. However, there is an air-conditioned kennel by the east (left, as you face it from outside the gates) side of the Entrance Plaza. Reservations are not needed. **Lockers:** Available for $.25 or $.50, these are located on the west (right, as you face it from outside the gates) side of the Entrance Plaza, at Bus Services, and at the International Gateway. **Lost Children:** Report to Baby Services or Earth Station. **Reservations:** Accepted at fourteen restaurants in Future World and World Showcase. May be made at any WorldKey terminal, or, for WDW resort and Hotel Plaza guests, up to two days in advance by calling 828-4000 (828-8800 for Hotel Plaza guests). Reservations can also be made in person. **Smoking, eating, and drinking:** Not allowed in any attractions. **Visually-impaired guests:** Complimentary tape cassettes and portable tape recorders are available at Earth Station. A deposit is required, though.

Wheelchair guests: Wheelchair and motorized three-wheeled convenience vehicle rentals are available in limited quantities at Stroller & Wheelchair Rental at Spaceship Earth. The standard kind of wheelchair is available for rent at the International Gateway. Disabled Guests Guidebooks are available at Earth Station.

FUTURE WORLD

This section of EPCOT Center features themes of humanity's achievements in various areas of technology, and offers a somewhat academic view of the world as it was, is, and might be. Many people confuse Future World and Tomorrowland. Tomorrowland, in the Magic Kingdom, is whimsical and amusing, but not intended to be taken seriously as a vision of the future. Future World is. Also, the latter is less science-fiction and more real-future in its architecture. There's less of that bleak, cold feel that runs rampant in the streets of Tomorrowland.

Future World is lined up for major expansion, including the addition of a Space pavilion in which flight simulators and special effects will send guests into orbit via a thrill ride a la Body Wars. Also slated to open in 1994 is a new 3D musical movie from George Lucas and the Walt Disney Studios.

Overall Tips

Attractions – Future World is most crowded during the morning and least crowded from about 2:30 on. The Wonders of Life pavilion is the newest and is almost always crowded, and Journey into Imagination is very popular also.

Dining – The two full-service restaurants here (the Land Grille Room and Coral Reef) are very good, but very popular and hard to book. The

fast food quality is stellar here as compared to the Magic Kingdom's eateries; the Odyssey Restaurant and Farmer's Market are good choices.
Shopping – Future World shopping has little more to offer than Disney and EPCOT memorabilia plus future-themed gifts, toys, novelties, and the like.

ENTRANCE PLAZA

HINT: Lines to enter the park are often shortest at the manned admission gate farthest to the left.

Shopping
GIFT STOP – On the right side of the entrance plaza, this small stop offers guest mementos and convenience items.

Services
SUNBANK, N.A. – Credit card cash advances, foreign exchanges, and traveler's check services are available from 9 AM to 4 PM.

LOST & FOUND/PACKAGE PICKUP – This building, adjoining the Gift Stop, is where found articles and cumbersome packages are forwarded to.

PETCARE KENNEL – Pets may not be brought into EPCOT Center, but can be boarded for $4 per day, per pet, and may not be boarded overnight here. Restrooms and phones are located here.

SPACESHIP EARTH

This is the recognized symbol of EPCOT, much like Cinderella's Castle is in the MK. Measuring 180 feet in height and 164 feet in diameter, this geosphere is visible from either coast on a clear day. It is kept aloft by six huge pylons sunk 100 feet into the ground. Here you'll find two shops, one of the park's top rides, and Earth Station, the city hall of tomorrow, which also serves as the home base for the WorldKey system.

Attraction
SPACESHIP EARTH
Rating: 10. It's EPCOT's crowning achievement, so don't miss it. *Location:* A landmark, at the park's entrance. *Duration of Ride:* 16 minutes. *Best Time to Go:* Before 9:15 AM or after 5 PM. *Comments:* Guests move forward in a dark, enclosed area in slow-moving cars up a steep incline, and ride backward for the slow return.

Here, you board small cars ("time machines") and venture deep into the bowels of the **Spaceship Earth** geodesic sphere. Journalist **Walter Cronkite** narrates as you begin your ascent through a black tunnel. Lightning flashes at the end of the tunnel and fans blow air in your face to give the illusion of speed. Finally, you arrive at the Cro-Magnon age, 40,000 years ago. Eerie holographic projections of cavemen and wooly mammoths melt and metamorphose as if blown by a breeze. The displays are dark and black-lighted, and a strange soundtrack presents a foreboding atmosphere. Scenes then show the advent of communication, from Egyptian hieroglyphics (real!) and a pharaoh dictating a letter (taken from an actual letter from an Egyptian ruler), to cave drawings to ancient peoples chewing the fat as they imprint symbols on stone tablets, to the Phoenician merchants who introduced the written alphabet in the ninth century before Christ.

Traveling on through the ages, you see a performance of Oedipus Rex, witness the fall of Rome (during which you will smell smoldering wood through the rubble — it's not your imagination, it's a Disney effect called "smellitzer" that shoots aromas at you at appropriate times), where you may notice the graffiti on the walls... identical to that in real Pompeii. There's Audio-Animatronic monks and scholars trying to hand-copy precious documents and scriptures, one of whom has fallen asleep and can be heard snoring and seen breathing. A working Gutenberg press sits in one scene, its operator thoughtfully examining a page of a replicated Bible from California's Huntington Library. Particularly impressive is the robotic Michaelangelo who lays on a scaffold, putting the finishing touches on the awesome Sistine Chapel ceiling.

From there, we zoom into the information age. A man stands by a rumbling printing press, his hands and clothing slathered with ink. Then, to the finished product: a pile of newspapers, and a newsboy holding one up and crying "Extra, extra, New York's daily." There's a radio studio, and then a movie marquee. Past that, several movies are played on the screens. Some of the radio broadcasts include The Lone Ranger and the Max Schmeling-Joe Louis rematch in 1938, and a commentary by Walter Winchell. The TV segments include Ozzie and Harriet, the 1964 NFL championship game, and the Ed Sullivan show. There are then displays showing computers in the home and office, and an AT&T phone system.

But most stirring of all is the finale at the top of the Spaceship, a huge dome filled with tiny stars and one small blue-green sphere swathed in clouds. The effect is produced by a "star ball," created by Disney when the Imagineers discovered that the dome was too large for traditional planetarium equipment. This is arguably the best attraction in Future World, and everyody seems to love it. Thus, it is almost always crowded. But the lines move quickly and see it you must, so go early or late.

Shopping

GATEWAY GIFTS – Located on the west side of Spaceship Earth, this shop offers a variety of souvenirs and sundries, mainly t-shirts, mugs, toys, games, books, ceramic figurines, suntan lotion, Pepto-Bismol, tissues, and so on and so forth. There are restrooms and phones located alongside this shop.

CAMERA CENTER – Kodak film, video tape, camcorder and camera rental, and two-hour film processing are offered here. Minor camera servicing and photography tips are also available. Located next to the camera center on the east side of Spaceship Earth, are restrooms and phones.

Services

EARTH STATION – This is the nerve center of EPCOT, at the exit from the Spaceship Earth ride, or accessible via a separate entrance on the south side of the building. Inside, there are WorldKey terminals, where meal reservations and information can be procured. Screens above the action show a basic overview of all Future World has to offer. There are also live hosts and hostesses to answer your questions. They have lists of lost children who may be at the Baby Services building at any given time. Additionally, personal checks for up to $25 may be cashed here with proper identification.

STROLLER & WHEELCHAIR RENTAL – Wheelchairs and a limited supply of motorized vehicles are available for rent, as are strollers. Sundries, guest convenience items, and EPCOT Center mementos are sold here.

COMMUNICORE

CommuniCore (short for Community Core) is right at the heart of Future World, at the "core" of this futuristic "community". It is divided into two halves, east and west, each of which are subsequently split into smaller sections. Trying to find your way around is difficult if you don't have a park map or a sixth sense for direction.

Everything here is fun to try out, and most of the exhibits are hands-on, so this is a pleasant place to spend a few minutes. However, a quick breeze-through won't benefit you much, as a little time and mental effort is required for many of the exhibits.

Note that crowds in Future World flock here during thunderstorms.

CommuniCoreEast

Attractions

"BACKSTAGE MAGIC"

Rating: 5 1/2. Enjoyable. *Location:* The section closest to the Universe of Energy. *Duration of Show:* 20 minutes. *Best Time to Go:* Anytime. *Comments:* Translation to Spanish, French, or German available.

A computer operator named Julie and her animated sidekick I/O present a lively, saccharine-loaded show27 about computers, explaining thoroughly the role of computers in the day-to-day operations of the Vacation Kingdom, from how they keep track of thousands of hotel reservations annually to the controlling of the 700 Audio-Animatronics characters at EPCOT Center. Everything at EPCOT is computer-controlled, from the firing of the fireworks in the IllumiNations show to the cooking of hot dogs at the Liberty Inn.

ELECTRONIC FORUM

Rating: 5. Interesting but not compelling. *Location:* The part of CommuniCore East closest to World Showcase. *Duration of Show:* Varies. *EPCOT Poll:* varies. *Person of the Century Poll:* not applicable. *Best Time to Go:* Anytime.

Until the end of 1999, computer terminals in one section of CommuniCore East will let guests pick the person who they feel has made the most significant contribution during the century. There are representatives from politics, sports, entertainment, humanitarianism, and more. There are 89 nominees (including Walt Disney, of course) to choose from, or, guests can add their own.

Also, in the EPCOT Poll, sessions going on from 11 AM to 7 PM in the Future Choice Theater, a moderator first presents an issue to the audience. It could be a purely trivial issue, or a question of vital importance, for example, the use of nuclear energy. The moderator's speech on the issue is often accompanied by related video clips. The audience then votes by way of pushbutton panels on the seats. The results are broken down by age groups and gender also.

Outside the forum are booths where guests can catch up on news in their hometown, or get sports and weather reports, all received by the two satellite dishes outside the attraction. This way, any time spent waiting is bearable.

EPCOT COMPUTER CENTRAL

Rating: 6. Fun, different. *Location:* The section of the building closest to the Universe of Energy. *Best Time to Go:* Anytime.

Here, you can play with a bunch of computers with touch-sensitive screens. There are five main areas of Computer Central. The first, **SMRT-1**, is a robot who resembles a small purple spaceman. SMRT-1 communicates to guests via telephone lines and quizzes guests with ridiculous and easy questions, laughing heartily when a guest screws up an answer.

The **Compute-A-Coaster** is the cream of the crop here, where you use touch-sensitive screens to build a roller coaster. You can use all the standard tools of the trade: the loops, the drops, the climbs, the curves, all of it. The computer then puts you on the coaster for a strikingly realistic ride through your creation.

You will be surprised at how much the **Great America Census Quiz** computers can tell you about the populace of the country. The categories that questions are drawn from include The Fifty States, School Days, On the Farm, Communication Line, Home Sweet Home, and the Population Clock. Interesting! **The Get Set Jet Game** pits your hand-eye reflexes against the clock. Here, you must load the greatest possible amount of passengers and cargo onto a plane and complete the safety and maintenance checklist, all within 60 seconds. **The Flag Game** shows how computers can be used in manufacturing by letting guests construct American flags by touching the part of the flag on the screen and then the place on the uncompleted flag where it should go.

Exhibit
ENERGY EXCHANGE – Here, programs illustrate the use of various types of energy in the future. There are videotapes dealing with hydroelectric, geothermal, and wind energy, and displays on energy efficiency, conservation, and the outlook for the energy situation. Exhibits delve into coal and oil exploration and mining, and guests get the chance to stack the energy they create on a stationary bike up against the potential energy of a gallon of gasoline. Also, guests get the chance to turn a crank to illuminate a light bulb. A computer monitor tells how long it would take them to produce a dollar's worth of electricity.

Services
TRAVELPORT – A few booths in this section of CommuniCore, in the part of the building nearest the Wonders of Life pavilion, offer a chance to preview your next vacation. These "vacation stations," as they are known, have touch-sensitive screens that allow you to choose to view film from locales as varied as the French Riviera and California. Prompts offer a chance to view lodging, dining, shopping, and sightseeing choices.

The TravelPort also offers financial services to American Express cardholders. If the clips of the vacation spots whet your appetite for travel, visit the American Express Travel Service office. They can make the arrangements for you, in addition to selling you traveler's checks and insurance.

Shopping

CENTORIUM – The **Centorium**, located next to the rest rooms, offers EPCOT Center's best selection of park mementos and character merchandise. There's the usual watches, hats, pencils, stuffed animals, figurines, bumper stickers and books, plus one character whose sole domain is EPCOT Center, Figment. Figment is the googly-eyed baby dragon found at Journey Into Imagination. He is represented here with plush figures, ranging from little tiny baby Figments to straight-out-of-Jurassic Park monster Figments that every self-respecting rich little kid has. There's also Figment combs, hats (similar to the hats with the Goofy ears), patches, magnets, keychains, and a set of plastic figurines, all Figment in poses from Imagination.

Aside from Disney souvenirs, there's also some unusual jewelry, like earrings or charms with three-dimensional holograms on them, plus watches, toys, and models. The coolest store in Future World. *HINT:* Be sure to notice the space ship suspended in midair in the Centorium, as it contains some of Disney World's most memorable characters.

CommuniCore West

Exhibits

FUTURECOM – This exhibit follows up the narrative given in nearby Spaceship Earth with displays of cutting-edge communications technologies in action. One exhibit extols the virtues of teleconferencing, another lets guests see themselves on television. Yet another lets guests find out what's going on in their home states via touch-sensitive TV screens.

Other major areas of FutureCom are as follows: **The Phraser**, my favorite FutureCom exhibit, consists of a screen with several different-looking characters on it. You choose one of the characters, and type in "Hello, Jay, you bum." And then you hear a slightly monotone voice from the computer say, "Hello, Jay, you bum." However, since it converts the written letters to spoken sounds using standard English pronunciation, if you type in "Bonjour, monsieur, qui dit a moi ce soir?," you're begging for trouble. Another set of computers takes a photo of your face. And if you ever wondered what you'd look like with a moustache? Put one on! A clown nose? Put one on? You can get a nose job raise your cheekbones, or just mutilate the picture of someone you love. Usually good for a laugh.

The Network Control game demonstrates how network controllers at telephone companies manage the millions of long-distance calls that travel its lines daily. Lastly, **Chip Cruiser** puts you at the controls of a laser beam with which you must defend a microchip from its mortal enemies:

dust, water, and static electricity.

EXPO ROBOTICS – Here, you can get a free portrait of yourself. This in itself would be unmemorable, except the artist happens to be a robot. This exhibit, one of EPCOT's newest, also features a show in which five robots perform delicate operations with spinning tops. This is CommuniCore's most fast-paced and exciting component, so see it when you have a chance.

Services
EPCOT OUTREACH – If you have a question that's been bothering you all day, take it here. Attendants armed with computers can answer any sort of question you might have about EPCOT Center. The information, found in encyclopedias, periodicals, and wire services, is all accessible through the computer system. If the personnel can't answer your question, they can call the Disney Archives in beautiful downtown Burbank, California. Whether your inquiry is purely trivial or vital, they can usually help you out.

TEACHER'S CENTER – Here, educators can preview films, videos, multimedia kits, educational software, and other educational media. Also, they can receive complimentary lesson plans, geared to all age groups, on all Future World themes.

Shopping
FUTURE WORLD KIOSK – This booth sells guest convenience items and mementos.

KODAK IMAGE MAGIC SYSTEM – Here, photo technicians can take a snapshot of you and superimpose it on photos of EPCOT Center landmarks. Ever wanted to climb on top of Spaceship Earth?

UNIVERSE OF ENERGY

NOTE: The entire pavilion is devoted to this one ride.
Rating: 9. Striking, brilliant, not to be missed. *Location:* A landmark, next to Wonders of Life and CommuniCore East. *Duration of Show:* 26 1/2 minutes. *Best Time to Go:* Before 10:30 or after 4:30. *Frightening:* The dinosaurs scare some younger kids.

There are four distinct segments to this ride-cum-show, the first being an eccentric, eight-minute pre-show. In it, vivid images of falling water, fire, burning coal, piles of logs, all illustrating today's energy sources. But the renown here lies not in the film but the screen on which it is projected. As its creator, Czech filmmaker Emil Radok, calls it, this "kinetic mosaic" is made up of 100 triangular panels that rotate on computer-given cues. Then, guests enter a seemingly normal theater with a capacity of nearly 580 and slide into bench seats. They then view a short (4´-minute) animated film about the creation of the fossil fuels we use today. As for the film's characters, we're not talking Dumbo and Bambi here, folks. We're talking dinosaurs. The screen measures an incomprehensible 35 feet by 155 feet and presents an eerie atmosphere teeming with volcanos, extinct plants, and bizarre insects. At the end of the film, the theater splits into six, ninety-six-passenger cars and one by one, they enter the prehistoric terrain explored in the previous film.

The cars slowly enter a world where the air is rich with sulfur and the sky flashes with lightning. The profile of a brontosaur is visible in the distance. Fog fills the warm, dank air and lava bubbles next to the cars. The lava is so realistic that few guests are convinced when informed that its main ingredient is hair gel. Audio-Animatronic dinosaurs battle on a rocky ledge, a mighty allosaurus against the armored stegosaurus. There are 250 prehistoric-looking trees, all manmade, and various other creatures of the era, from millipedes to pteranodons. An elasmosaurus sticks his head out of a lagoon. The dinosaurs here are frighteningly realistic, some of Disney's best Audio-Animatronic characters.

The theater cars, which move on a rail only one eighth of an inch thick, then move into another theater, the EPCOT Energy Information Center, where a 12 1/2minute film is shown on a 210-foot screen that wraps around an incredible 220°. This film explores the energy sources of today and tomorrow.. The is 65mm footage is memorable, especially the finale, which lets you witness a takeoff of a Space Shuttle from Kennedy Space Center, film so extraordinary that NASA wanted a copy.

This is one of Future World's most popular attractions, for good reason. I don't recommend seeing this in the morning. It gets crowded in a hurry (by 10:30), and there are other attractions that are best experienced in that time period because they're crowded the whole day. However, crowds here seem to disappear at about 4:30, so try it then.

WONDERS OF LIFE

EPCOT Center's newest pavilion, this $100 million dome houses ten attractions and exhibits related to health and the human body, all presented in a smoke-free environment. This pavilion also includes the park's only thrill ride, plus one of its most entertaining multimedia productions. Outside the pavilion, be sure to notice the 72-foot tall DNA molecule.

Attractions
"BODY WARS"
Rating: 9 1/2. Spectacular ride and effects! *Location:* As you enter the pavilion, it's on the far side of the dome. *Duration of Ride:* 5 minutes. *Best Time to Go:* As soon as the park opens. *Comments:* Guests with heart, back, or neck conditions as well as expectant mothers and those prone to motion sickness pass up this ride. *Frightening:* Visually and physically, this is as intense as any ride in WDW.

Get ready for the ride of someone else's life! Here, you are set in one of four 40-passenger flight simulators and "miniaturized" in order to be injected into a patient, where you pick up the intrepid Dr. Lair who has been examining a splinter imbedded just under the skin. A normal day in the office for anyone, right?

But something is bound to go awry, as is the Disney thrill-ride tradition, and the ship piloted by actor Tim Mathison almost reaches Dr. Lair, played by Elizabeth Shue, when whoosh, these white blood cells scream onto the scene like bats out of hell, and next thing you know, you're chasing after her in a wild ride through the circulatory system. Along the way, a contaminant in this particular human's body (that contaminant being you) is assaulted by white blood cells, is pumped throughout the body, and into the heart, where it runs out of energy. The technicians sitting safely outside this guy's body can be heard screaming over the intercom "You're out of power! We can't beam you out of there if you have no power," and you're either terrified or overjoyed at this, when your pilot and the doctor come up with an idea. You ride the bloodstream up to the brain, where the electrical impulses allow them to beam you out and return you to normal.

This is a very rough ride, so be sure to buckle your seat belt when they instruct you to do so, even though the cars only travel a few feet in any direction, and it is known for its ability to cause motion sickness. In fact, they sometimes have to shut down one of the cars to remove, ahem, a souvenir left by the last motion-sick rider. If you start feeling queasy, close your eyes. Much of the thrill is visual, so if you take out one sense, it'll feel better. But if you get off the ride and feel like you're gonna chunder, there are restrooms just outside the attraction.

CRANIUM COMMAND
Rating: 9. Funny, entertaining, don't miss it. *Location:* As you enter the pavilion, it's on the far side of the dome. *Duration of Show:* 20 minutes. *Best Time to Go:* Before 11 AM or after 3 PM.

Okay, troopers, don your battle helmets! Batten the hatches! You are about to join an Audio-Animatronic Cranium Commando named Buzzy, who has a tough job ahead of him in order to earn his stripes. He has to pilot a twelve-year-old boy through his daily routine. Gasp! A cartoon character named General Knowledge barks out the assignment to Buzzy in the witty pre-show. Buzzy balks at the idea, but changes his mind when threatened of being put "inside the head of a chicken." Note that if you miss the preshow, you'll have a harder time understanding the rest of the presentation. If you arrive as the preshow is ending, it'd probably be a better idea to wait for the next show.

Two hundred guests at a time are led into the semi-circular theater where the main presentation takes place. Buzzy sits in a contraption that allows him to oversee various organs of the body, all of whom are depicted by actors. The left brain is represented by Charles Grodin, the right brain is portrayed by Jon Lovitz, formerly of Saturday Night Live, the stomach is played by George Wendt (*Cheers'* Norm Peterson), the heart is pumped up by SNL regulars Kevin Nealon and Dana Carvey as Hans and Franz, and Bob Golthwait is a hyperactive adrenal gland.

Anyhow, this unlikely team wakes up inside the head of this 12-year-old, goes to school without eating his breakfast, fights off bullies, impresses a beautiful female classmate, and does all the other things that twelve-year-old boys do. It is easy to get into the story and relate to Buzzy's charge, but if you've forgotten what it was like to be twelve, you may be less enchanted.

"THE MAKING OF ME"

Rating: 6. An excellent film. *Location:* At the center of the pavilion. *Duration of Show:* 14 minutes. *Best Time to Go:* After 4:30 PM. *Comments:* Since this deals with the sensitive subjects of human reproduction and birth, parents may want to use discretion when deciding whether their family should view it. *Frightening:* No, but this is graphic at times.

Glenn Gordon Caron directed this funny film starring Martin Short as a man who ponders his conception, and not being one to leave us hanging, travels back in time to watch his parents date, fall in love, marry, and eventually decide to have him. There is actual footage of a developing fetus and yes, the birth. The sexual information necessary to a production like this is handled tastefully, and although it is considered controversial for a company like Disney, most guests take it in stride.

This quality film is shown in a tiny room which only seats 100 people at a time, not nearly the number of fans it draws, so unless you can visit after 4:30 PM, you're likely to hit a long line.

"GOOFY ABOUT HEALTH"

Rating: 5 1/2. Pleasant. *Location:* In the center of the pavilion. *Duration of Show:* 10 minutes. *Best Time to Go:* Anytime. *Comments:* Guests can come and go as they please.

Who'da thunk it? Your pal and mine, Goofy, smokes. He also drinks, doesn't sleep regularly, doesn't eat right, never exercises, and lives a stressful life. But on this seven-screen production, Goofy changes his ways and becomes a healthy guy. This production, which plays continuously in a 100-seat theater, mixes long-lost Goofy cartoons and newly-made footage to illustrate the road to good health.

ANACOMICAL PLAYERS

Rating: 6. Enjoyable. *Location:* In the center of the pavilion. *Duration of Show:* Varies, usually about 15 minutes. *Best Time to Go:* Anytime. *Comments:* Guests can come and go as they please.

The show here features live improv actors and audience participation in a 100-seat theater in the center of the pavilion. The humor is corny, but it's always there and always fun. Consult the EPCOT Entertainment Program, Earth Station, or the WorldKey system for scheduled performance times, usually six or seven times every day.

Exhibits

MET LIFESTYLE REVUE – Here, touch-sensitive screens let you type in statistics about your health habits, and the computer tells you how you're doing and how you could improve your life, reduce your stress level, and live longer. That's always fun.

COACH'S CORNER – If you play tennis, golf, or baseball, you'll want to stop by. You'll be put into a cage where you take a swing with a club, racquet, or bat, and a well-known professional athlete tells you (via videocameras, tapes, and Disney cast members who urge you to "say hi to Gary Carter") what's wrong with your swing. Should you listen? I think that Gary Carter, Chris Evert, and Nancy Lopez know what they're doing. So just sit there and listen to what they have to say. The instant replay of your swing in slow motion is also pretty cool.

FRONTIERS OF MEDICINE – The only 100% serious exhibit here, Frontiers of Medicine, located near the exit from Body Wars, lets guests check out cutting-edge technology and educational, scientific exhibits. These are changed on a somewhat regular basis.

SENSORY FUNHOUSE – Lots of hands-on exhibits dealing with one of the five senses and the tricks they can play on your mind. While you're here, check out the 50-foot mobile swinging in the air. You may have trouble getting kids to leave this exhibit.

WONDERCYCLES – These are stationary bikes with a computer screen that tells you your speed, how far you've traveled, and how many calories you've burned. On this same screen, travel footage is played as you pedal. You can choose from an everyday town, the Rose Parade, or Disneyland. *NOTE:* If you've just ridden Body Wars, you might consider giving your stomach a few minutes off before jostling it again on a bike.

HORIZONS

NOTE: The entire pavilion is devoted to one attraction. *Rating:* 9 1/2. Whimsical and interesting, not to be missed. *Location:* Between Wonders of Life and World of Motion. *Duration of Ride:* 15 minutes. *Best Time to Go:* Before 10:30 or after 3:30.

This sleeper hit of Future World revolves around our ancestors' perceptions of the future, followed by a look at the "real" future, narrated by a 21st century Audio-Animatronic couple. The four-passenger vehicles depart from the FuturePort for a look at this couple and their life. But first, a segment called Looking Back at Tomorrow. In this section of the ride, you are shown visionaries' images of the future. There's Jules Verne floating with a dog and a chicken in a bullet-shaped spaceship, 1950 Paris as artist Albert Robida saw it in the 19th century with blimps providing mass transit, and the depression-era dream of 1990 America, with robotic butlers, barbers, and tan-o-matic machines.

Following that sequence is one of the most dramatic parts of the journey: a hemispheric screen 80 feet in diameter on which plays filmed scenes that give the impression of flight. Shown are a city, a micro-processor, a DNA molecule (so realistic that it fools your senses into thinking that you're spiraling into a double helix), and more.

You then travel to the couple's home, Nova City, a metropolis of the future where holographic phones bring new meaning to the phrase "reach out and touch someone" and trains suspended by magnets encourage transportation. One of their daughters lives in the next stop, Mesa Verde, a desert-turned-farmland ("Send a city kid to college for seven years and what happens? The city kid becomes a farmer!") where computers and robots help produce citrus fruits (the air smells of them) and sleek jets take them to market. You see the daughter in the control station as a thunderstorm approaches.

Sea Castle is the next stop, a floating city in the Pacific Ocean where kids prepare for a dive. Mining and kelp-farming operations are headquartered. It's then off to Alpha Centauri, a city in space to which the Audio-Animatronic husband contemplates relocating. The exercise programs in this display are particularly interesting and look like the Wondercycles at the Wonders of Life pavilion. This also serves as the backdrop for one of WDW's most dramatic pieces of instrumental music, entitled, simply, Space.

Then, the couple's beeper goes off, telling them that the time for their grandson's birthday party has come, and the whole family attends, in person or via those holographic phones. At this point, guests are allowed to choose the medium in which they'll complete the last 30 seconds of their journey. The choices are a high-speed flight over a desert, a rocketing space flight, or a submarine voyage. There are four voting panels in each car, and if you have a son aged between eight and thirteen, watch out or they'll change your selection to match their own. Majority rules.

This is arguably the most underrated attraction in Future World, and the large crowds it draws are usually absorbed easily. The only instance when lines are longer than 15 minutes would be when the nearby Universe of Energy pavilion lets out close to 600 people.

WORLD OF MOTION

This wheel-shaped pavilion features a ride chronicling the advent and development of transportation. The attraction here is rarely crowded despite its immense popularity, and there is never any wait at the Transcenter at the ride's end, making this a good pavilion to visit during the hot, crowded period of the day.

Attraction
WORLD OF MOTION
Rating: 10. These are EPCOT's best Audio- Animatronic figures. *Location:* A landmark, next to the Odyssey. *Duration of Ride:* 14 1/2 minutes. *Best Time to Go:* Before noon or after 4 PM.

With the use of 22 scenes featuring over 150 Audio-Animatronics, this endearing ride traces the history of transportation from walking to flying and beyond. In the first scene, a group of cave dwellers have discovered the painful hazards of travel on foot. Then, along comes the wheel, in its present form after several unsuccessful attempts. Following the wheel, there are scenes illustrating other forms of transportation. There are tributes to the bicycle and the Sunday drive, to air shows, and to classic automobiles of the latter part of the century.

But the triumph of special effects here are the speed rooms resembling the OmniSphere screens at Horizons. These speed rooms give the impression of motion with an almost-dizzying realism. There are scenes on whitewater rapids, submarine voyages, bobsledding, and others, followed by animated abstracts with wild sound effects. In the ride's finale, the cars pass a mirror where they take on the holographic appearance of futuristic cars (oddly, they resemble today's minivans). Guests are then droppped off at the Transcenter.

Many of the vehicles are authentic, for example, the Western wagons are 150 years old and all of the cars are real, too. The other exhibits are clever, almost perfect mockups. The best settings are the train robbery and the city scenes, which explore the downside of increased mobility. This ride is deserted until 10 AM and then again after 4 PM. Try to ride then.

Exhibit
TRANSCENTER – The World of Motion ride spills out here, but the **GM Transcenter** is accessible by a separate entrance as well. There are numerous exhibits dealing with the future of automotive transportation.

The exhibits include Aero 2000, an experimental four-seat subcompact; the Aero Test Center, a replica of a GM wind tunnel in Warren, Michigan; Bird and the Robot, featuring a cigar-smoking toucan (resembling Groucho Marx) who was originally constructed for Tropical Serenade in Tokyo Disneyland and an assembly-line robot who together illustrate the use of machines in construction; Concept 2000, another aerodynamic masterpiece; the Lean Machine, a tiny bullet-shaped car that gets 200 miles to the gallon; and the Water Engine, a film about engine construction in the future. This exhibit is entertaining and there is never a wait if you enter through the rear gate. See this one late in the day or on your second day at EPCOT if you have one.

ODYSSEY COMPLEX

This pavilion consists of the park's most attractive fast-food restaurant, the Odyssey Restaurant, and three services, listed below. The complex is accessible by three bridges: one from the World of Motion pavilion, one by World Showcase Plaza, and one by World Showcase's Mexico pavilion.

Services
First Aid – If you need this kind of help, it's comforting to know that there are Registered Nurses staffing this establishment.

Baby Services – Open from one hour before the park opens to two hours after it closes, the Baby Services amenities include nursing and changing facilities, and a place where you can buy formula, baby food, and diapers.

Lost Children – Located alongside Baby Services, this is where young people who've been lost are taken by Disney staff who find them. Since it's rather unlikely that your kids could find their way there on their own, tell them that if they are separated from you, they should go to anyone with a Disney name tag. If you're all the way to Spaceship Earth or the Japan pavilion before you discover the loss of your charge, go to a phone and call 560-7928 or report it to Earth Station or any WorldKey terminal.

JOURNEY INTO IMAGINATION

Outside this pavilion are waterfalls and fountains that defy logic – one waterfall shoots water up and over a cliff face instead of the other way around. A fountain shoots blobs of water at regular intervals, most kids can't help but smack the blobs. My personal favorite is the **Leap Frog Fountain**, which winds across a landscaped courtyard, shooting streams of water from one planter to the next to the next, even over paths (and often guests' heads as well!). One of my favorite WDW photos is of my youngest brother catching the one-inch stream in the face!

The pavilion itself is impressive, with the pair of mirrored-glass pyramids serving as a backdrop for the monorail and the crystal-like structures by the **Upside Down Waterfall**.

JOURNEY INTO IMAGINATION

Rating: 8 1/2. Warm, happy, not to be missed. *Location:* As you enter the pavilion, it'll be on your right. *Duration of Show:* 13 minutes. *Best Time to Go:* Before 10:30 or in the evening. *Frightening:* Surprisingly, some small children are afraid of Figment, the little dragon who hosts the attraction.

As the trains carrying guests wind their way into the bowels of the pavilion, you hear a joyful, melodic tune emanating from the distance. You arrive to see that the song has been coming from the Dreamfinder, a cheerful man with a red beard and a purple suit. The first time you see him, he is piloting a blimp-like contraption across the sky to pick up ideas, dreams, "anything that sparks the imagination." He's telling us about imagination and figments and decides to introduce his favorite.

This figment, appropriately named Figment, is part steer, part dragon, all full of a certain boyish charm and exuberance to him and together, the Dreamfinder and his dragon search the universe. They take the ideas to be stored in the Dreamport and then, basically run through all aspects of life in which imagination is present. Writing, music, theatre, dance, movies, art, and ambition are all explored.

The picks of the crop are the video screen in which a green Figment cavorts around gleefully and the round room with multiple screens depicting Figment lifting weights, in space, climbing mountains, and the like. I find "Journey" pleasant, relaxing, fanciful, well worth seeing, and many others share this appraisal. However, scores of others find it boring, dull, even a waste of time. I recommend that you try it for yourself.

MAGIC EYE THEATER: CAPTAIN EO

Rating: 8. Really a blast! *Location:* Just to the left (east side) of the pavilion. *Duration of Show:* 17 minutes. *Best Time to Go:* In the morning or evening. *Frightening:* The special effects and high volume may be too intense for small children.

This 3D film, directed by Francis Ford Coppola of *Godfather* fame, stars Michael Jackson (in the title role), Anjelica Huston, and Dick Shaw and is an absolute favorite of many teenagers and preteens. It is one of the most awesome three-dimensional films anywhere, with more action and special effects than Magic Journeys in the Magic Kingdom, plus a more excitement than Muppet*Vision 4D in the Studios. Incidentally, the film was produced by George Lucas, the same person who brought us *Star Wars* and *Indiana Jones*.

You are first led into a small room where an 8-minute preshow uses photographs to illustrate the history of photography in everyday life. There is, of course, a hummable theme song to it, Making Memories. The somewhat vacuous story follows Jackson as outer space's **Captain EO** and his crew, consisting of Geex, Fuzzball, and Hooter, the latter being an owl who flies over the audience at one point in the show, prompting the guests to reach out at him. The crew's mission is to attempt to change the dark, depressing planet ruled by the Supreme Leader (Anjelica Huston) into a cheerful place with the use of song and dance.

Jackson sings two original songs here: "We Are Here to Change the World" and "Another Part of Me" and is accompanied by a troupe of dancers who impeccably carry out the impressive choreography. The film is filled with stereo surround sound, loud rock music, awesome special effects, and pure adrenaline. All told, it's a lot of fun and well worth seeing. And if you intend to see it without having to deal with crowds, visit after 5 PM.

Exhibit
THE IMAGE WORKS – This "creative playground of the future" allows

kids from one to one hundred to test their imagination at displays that will amaze, amuse, and entertain. To visit the **Image Works**, follow the signs once you get off the Journey into Imagination ride or bypass the line to ride and take the door on the left side of the pavilion (by Captain EO) and walk up the stairs to the exhibit. The exhibit is never really crowded, so visit any time of day.

Individual offerings in the Image Works include **Bubble Music**, where you make some odd electronic melodies by propelling bubbles into a colored screen; the **Electronic Philharmonic**, which lets you conduct an orchestra by raising and lowering your hands over colored discs; the **Light Writer**, which produces dazzling geometric effects with lasers; the **Magic Palette**, where you can use light pens to draw a sketch or color in images of Figment, Dreamfinder, or the pavilion; the **Rainbow Corridor**, which you walk through, accompanied by a rainbow of neon lights; the **Sensor Maze**, which reacts to guests' presence by emitting lights and sounds; **Stepping Tones**, where patches of color light on the floor produce musical chords from various sources when stepped upon, ranging from a men's chorus to a harp; plus kaleidoscopes and pin screens. Then there's my personal favorite, **Dreamfinder's School of Drama**.

This is a stellar attraction where groups of volunteers are "cast" in a short film, either a western, a sci-fi, or a fantasy using blue-screens and the ChromaKey system. The volunteers stand in front of a camera and listen to spoken instructions from the Dreamfinder. They just jump up and down, clap, or whatever, and they appear on the monitors overhead in a saloon, spaceship, or castle. Really cool.

THE LAND

This pavilion, covering six acres and containing two stories, is shaped like a greenhouse and contains a real greenhouse with actual cultivation going on inside it. The Land Grille Restaurant, a full-service eatery, is often overlooked for lunch, but the Farmer's Market below, being an attractive food court with several separate stands, is not. However, it's one of the best places in EPCOT for families of finicky eaters to go. The attractions, though, are often thronged with crowds at mealtimes.

Attractions
HARVEST THEATER: SYMBIOSIS
Rating: 7 1/2. Informative, definitely worthwhile. *Location:* On the entry/exit level of the pavilion. *Duration of Show:* 18 1/2 minutes. *Best Time to Go:* Anytime. *Comments:* Translation to Spanish, French, and German available.

This is a stirring 70mm Panavision movie detailing man's relationships to the earth. The production was filmed in over thirty countries from around the world. There is some doomsaying, stories about the pollution of lakes and streams, but there are also accounts of the reclamation of Lake Constance and the Thames and Willamette Rivers and forest management policies in the Pacific Northwest, Sweden, and Germany's Black Forest.

Despite the excellent quality of this film, there is rarely a line. It is possible that people are scared off by its erudite title, or maybe the theater is merely overlooked by guests on their way to the major attractions downstairs. For this reason, you can see this film at any time.

KITCHEN KABARET

Rating: 7. Corny and lively. *Location:* On the lower level of the pavilion. *Duration of Show:* 13 minutes. *Best Time to Go:* Before 11 AM or after 3 PM. *Comments:* Translation to Spanish, French, and German available.

This is an Audio-Animatronics show starring Bonnie Appetit and a fridge full of food. The show has four acts, each focusing in on one of the major food groups. The more memorable cast members are the Cereal Sisters (Connie Corn, Rennie Rice, and Mairzy Oats), a trio who celebrates the Boogie Woogie Bak'ry Boy ("the bread with a sound!"); Hamm and Eggz, a comedy team, Mr. Broccoli, a punk-rocker; and Mr. Mayonnaise, the drummer of the Kitchen Krackpots.

This show features the great Disney light-hearted humor, found elsewhere in the Magic Kingdom's Country Bear Vacation Hoedown. Immensely popular, this attraction is best avoided during lunchtime, as it is located right next to the Farmer's Market, the only food court in Future World.

LISTEN TO THE LAND

Rating: 7. Relaxing, informative. *Location:* On the lower level of the pavilion. *Duration of Ride:* 12 minutes. *Best Time to Go:* Before 11 AM or after 3 PM.

The only ride in EPCOT Center narrated by a real live person, the boats of **Listen to the Land** first pass through Audio-Animatronics scenes of the African veldt, the American prairie as it used to be, and a turn-of-the-century farm. Then, the boats proceed into greenhouses. As opposed to the "biomes" explored in the first segment of the ride, the plants are real here. Many different modern systems of agriculture are demonstrated here.

For example, there are plants thriving in a desert atmosphere, feeding off of drip irrigation that provides the exact amount of nutrients and water needed. Other vegetables are suspended in a drum that revolves, reproducing the effects of gravity. This is a technique that could be employed in outer space in the future. Other plants are hung from the ceiling and are conveyed through sprays that provide the necessary nutrition. There are also hydroponics, the one method of farming whose name really sticks in your mind. At the end of the ride is a fish farm that breeds a great assortment of seafood. Many of the products of the greenhouse are served in restaurants in Future World.

This attraction is one of Future World's most popular attractions, and is thronged with guests most of the time. However, an early-morning or evening visit may allow you to walk right on. Avoid it during mealtimes, though, when the entire pavilion is teeming with people.

Services

HARVEST TOUR – If you are intrigued by the agricultural technology presented in the Listen to the Land boat ride, sign up for the **Harvest Tour**, a 45-minute walking tour of the greenhouse. They depart every half-hour from 9:30 to 4:30, cover in great detail the same topics as the boat ride, and allow guests to ask questions. Reserve your spot next to Broccoli & Co. on the lower level of the pavilion.

Shopping

BROCCOLI & CO. – This shop, next to the Kitchen Kabaret, sells placemats, refrigerator magnets, books, topiaries, hydroponic plants, and mementos featuring Mr. Broccoli of the Kitchen Kabaret.

THE LIVING SEAS

This $100 million pavilion, the second addition to Future World, features a restaurant and a multi-faceted attraction/exhibit. Outside, be sure to notice the striking designs on the exterior walls and the waves that crash behind the "**Living Seas**" sign outside every few seconds.

THE LIVING SEAS

Rating: 4 1/2. An excellent concept flawed in execution. *Location:* A landmark. *Duration of Ride:* 3 minutes. *Best Time to Go:* After 3 PM. *Comments:* Guests who choose to remain in their wheelchairs bypass a short Seacab ride between the Hydrolators and Seabase Alpha.

Whoever had the idea it was to create an attraction with lots of live marine mammals, fish, and crustaceans should be commended. However, most people consider the Living Seas a disappointment because the ride portion of the attraction is over almost as soon as it has begun. The first parts of the attraction, serving as an introduction to the rest of it, are a 2 1/2-minute multi-media presentation and a 7-minute film that laud the pioneers of undersea research and describe the oceans as a resource. These are too academic to be thoroughly enjoyed.

Guests then board "hydrolators," elevators that simulate a plunge of many fathoms while in truth, descending about 2 inches. The illusion is created by the vibrating of the 20-passenger hydrolators and the bubbles that are pumped through the water screens outside their windows.

Finally, you reach the **Caribbean Coral Reef Ride** and board gondolas for an all-too-short ride between sections of the 5.7 million gallon tank. This section of the tank simulates the Caribbean, and some of the 5,000 specimens include bass, barracudas, sharks, dolphins, sea lions, diamond rays. An interesting note: the navy here includes divers in JIM suits, two one-man submarines, and two robotic submersibles. The divers can talk to guests about their operations by wireless radios.

The ride ends at **Sea Base Alpha**. This is the major portion of the attraction, so it's a shame that many visitors exit the pavilion here and miss the exhibits. The six stations include JIM suits that guests can try on, a module dedicated to the study of aquatic mammals, another featuring a show in which Jason, an Audio-Animatronic submersible (named for the sub which helped Dr. Robert Ballard find the sunken Titanic) explains the history of robotics in deep-sea exploration, one detailing the oceanic food chain, and more.

Shopping
LIVING SEAS SHOP – Here, at Sea Base Alpha, a small selection of guest convenience items, gifts, and mementos from the Living Seas.

WORLD SHOWCASE

The other half of EPCOT Center is a celebration of the cultures and people of the world community. The architecture, culture, history, and people of eleven nations are featured. However, since there are very few attractions, adults and older children are more likely to appreciate World Showcase, while younger children may find it boring.

World Showcase, on the whole, is least crowded in the morning, when the majority of guests are checking out the pavilions at Future World. Entertainment, in the form of guest artisans, native musicians, dancers, and actors is often featured at all eleven pavilions.

World Showcase is slated for expansion. A Switzerland pavilion is in the planning stages, while the long-awaited Russia pavilion will debut in late 1994 or early 1995, featuring "**The Bells of Change**," a film exploring

Russia's volatile history, and a ride based on the folk tale "Ivan and the Magic Pike." A ride similar to Disneyland's Matterhorn Mountain Bobsled is also planned. It will either appear towering over the Switzerland pavilion or behind Japan, in which case it will be called Mount Fuji.

Overall Tips

Attractions – The only attraction in World Showcase that draws large lines is the Maelstrom in Norway. The others can all be experienced with little of a wait. World Showcase is least crowded during the morning.

Dining – All of the national pavilions have at least one restaurant faithful to the country. Many demand reservations, but some others do not. The best are Le Cellier in Canada, Au Petit Cafe in France, and the Cantina de San Angel in Mexico.

Shopping – Browsing the World Showcase shops is always fun. The most interesting of the shops are Mitsokushi in Japan, Norway's The Puffin's Roost, and China's Yong Feng Shangdian.

Transportation

The "Friendship" boats crisscross World Showcase Lagoon at regular intervals, from two docks on either sides of Showcase Plaza, with their destinations Germany and Morocco. Double-decker buses circle the lagoon, stopping outside Canada, France, Italy, and Mexico. Both suspend operation during events on or around the lagoon.

Shopping in Showcase Plaza

DISNEY TRADERS – Located on the left side of Showcase Plaza, this is the place for Disney character souvenirs, decorative gifts, and clothing representing the nations of World Showcase. Sundry items are also available.

PORT OF ENTRY – Across from Disney Traders, this shop offers film, guest convenience items, and one-of-a-kind gifts from countries all around the world, including several not in World Showcase.

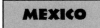

MEXICO

This pavilion is housed inside a pyramid whose Meso-American likenesses date back to the third century A.D. As you walk inside, it immediately becomes dusk. The air is filled with the excitement of a Mexican mercado (marketplace) and the romance of the San Angel Inn. The inside is beautiful on a grand scale and amazing in its intricate detail. Although it is not an attraction, I consider the inside of the pavilion not to be missed, even if you have no intention of riding El Rio del Tiempo.

Attraction
EL RIO DEL TIEMPO
Rating: 7. Excellent, well-tailored blend of film and Audio-Animatronics.
Location: In the back of the pavilion. *Duration of Ride:* 7 minutes.
Best Time to Go: Before 11 AM or after 6 PM.

This is a slow, pleasant boat ride suggestive of It's a Small World in the Magic Kingdom. As you embark, you pass the San Angel Inn and a glowing volcano for a journey through the past and present of Mexico. There are artifacts and scenes representing the Mayan, Aztec, and Toltec peoples, meshed with video screens which give the attraction a more serious feel. There are dolls of children at play, these the ones reminiscent of Small World.

The monitors also depict Mexico today, with cliff divers, speed boats, flying dancers, and a shopping mercado. The finale of the ride is a breathtaking fireworks display created by fiberoptics.

Exhibit
ART OF MEXICO – This exhibit, subtitled "Reign of Glory," is a celebration of pre-Colombian art including vases, masks, and sculpture. Note that if a line for El Rio extends outside the pyramid and you only want to see the art, it is acceptable to bypass the line and just go in.

Shopping
PLAZA DE LOS AMIGOS – Just inside the pavilion (past the art collection), this is an excellent place to pick up baskets, clothing, papier mache, and pre-Colombian artifacts. Paper flowers, wooden trays and bowls, and pinatas are available here.

ARTESANIAS MEXICANAS – Ceramics and gifts of a different type are sold here, including onyx ashtrays, plaques, chess sets, and bookends.

LA FAMILIA FASHIONS – Ready-to-wear fashions, jewelry, and accessories for women and children are featured here.

EL RANCHITO DEL NORTE – Gift items and souvenirs from Northern Mexico are purveyed at this shop, alongside World Showcase Lagoon. You can also watch artists create rings here.

NORWAY

World Showcase's newest pavilion is one of its best, featuring an adventure boat ride similar to Pirates of the Caribbean, one of the World's most exciting restaurants, and a vivid blend of architectural styles. The Restaurant Akershus is named for the Norwegian castle of the same name, built in Oslo's harbor in the 1300s and still standing today, a wood-stave church mimicking the Gol church built around the year 1250. Incidentally, when Viking kings adopted Christianity and spread it throughout Scandinavia, the presence of churches of this type was confined to Norway. Very few still exist.

Outside the Maelstrom is a lovely courtyard surrounded by more traditional buildings. On the lagoon sits the Norseman, a 50-foot ship duplicating a thousand-year-old Viking ship. This was given to the pavilion by a Norwegian maritime group.

Being new and containing what is generally considered World Showcase's most exciting ride, this pavilion gets a lot of attention and is often mobbed after 11 AM.

Attraction
MAELSTROM
Rating: 6 1/2. Exciting, promising, but too short. *Location:* In the rear of the courtyard. *Duration of Ride:* 4 1/2 minutes. *Duration of Show:* 5 minutes. *Best Time to Go:* Before 11 AM or after 6 PM. *Comments:* Short wait to enter theater after disembarking boats. *Frightening:* A three-headed troll and a steep, backwards drop frighten some kids.

Maelstrom puts you on a 16-passenger boat with a dragon's head carved onto it for a journey through the mythology and the reality of Norse culture. After passing a 10th century Viking village, you meet up with a three-headed troll who obviously got up on the wrong side of the bed. The troll puts a spell on you and you speed towards a waterfall that looks like you will be dumped into the courtyard below, but at the last moment, the boat reverses direction and accelerates down a chute into the wind-swept North Sea. You pass a drilling platform and get out of your boat in a recreation of a harbor village.

Here, you wait to be admitted to a theater that shows a short but powerful presentation on how the sea affects Norwegian life. This film is shown through the perspective of a young boy visiting a museum.

Exhibits
"TO THE ENDS OF THE EARTH" – This is an impressive display of 20th century artifacts from two polar expeditions.

TRAVEL INFORMATION – If the pavilion's sights, sounds, smells, and tastes whet your palate for a sojourn in the Land of the Midnight Sun, representatives of the Norwegian Tourism Board will be more than happy to provide you with necessary information.

Shopping
THE PUFFIN'S ROOST – The only shop in the pavilion stocks all sorts of imports, including clothing, jewelry, pewter candlesticks and table-ware, glassware, blankets, wood carvings, decorative gifts, candy, and toys like the famous and popular-once-more trolls and Playmobil sets.

CHINA

As aesthetically pleasing as any of the other pavilions, **China** features a half-sized replica of Beijing's Temple of Heaven, a pond, and a courtyard suitable for resting up with a red bean ice cream or a Chinese beer while others in your party shop. The premier cinematic exhibit in EPCOT Center can be viewed in the Temple of Heaven, called Wonders of China; this CircleVision 360 film is described below.

Attraction
WONDERS OF CHINA
Rating: 9 1/2. Exciting, breathtaking scenes. Not to be missed. *Location:* In the Temple of Heaven. *Duration of Show:* 19 minutes. *Best Time to Go:* Any time of the day. *Comments:* The theater has no seats.

After the original World Premiere CircleVision, American Journeys, the Disney film-sters hauled their 700-pound, 9-camera contraption to the People's Republic of China. Ports of call on this whirlwind journey include the Forbidden City of Beijing, the vast plains of Mongolia, the 2,400-year-old Great Wall, Shanghai, European in its look, Ghangzhou, a developing economic center, and many others. The film is dramatic and well-done, worth a visit. To see without a crowd, see this before noon or after six.

HINT: If you want to see Wonders of China and then the Maelstrom, assume a position on the far left of the theater (as you face the attendants' podium) and dart for it as soon as the doors open. You'll have a leg up on the rest of the folks in the audience who have the same intentions.

Exhibit
HOUSE OF WHISPERING WILLOWS – This is a display of art and artifacts native to China, changed periodically, usually every six months, but at latest the featured exhibit was Artistry In Time, a collection of magnificent timepieces from the eighteenth century. On loan from the People's Republic of China.

Shopping

YONG FENG SHANGDIAN – Otherwise known as "Bountiful Harvest" to you and me, this huge emporium sells all sorts of Chinese memorabilia, including silken robes, prints, paper umbrellas and fans, purses, glassware, and as you climb up the price ladder, dolls, jewelry, figurines, rugs, porcelain masks, carved chests, and antique tables and chairs. For the younger set, toys include nunchuks, ninja swords, and toy snakes. The selection of Chinese goods is better than that found anywhere else.

GERMANY

Of of the five World Showcase pavilions that have no formal attractions, **Germany** is the most festive. The village, its architecture an amalgam of several sources, including towns on the Rhine, in Bavaria, and the north of the nation, with some influence from Frankfurt and Rothenberg.

The centerpiece on the plaza, St. Georgsplatz, is the Biergarten, an Olde World tavern where authentic German fare and authentic German entertainment are presented. The merry atmosphere is helped by communal seating and huge steins of beer. There is a half-hour-long dinner show performed several times a night. Street entertainment is also offered. *HINT:* There are several WorldKey terminals outside the pavilion.

Shopping

SUSSIGKEITEN – If you are planning to blow your diet, this is as good a place as any. H. Bahlsen chocolates, tons of cookies of all sorts: chocolate, butter, and a spicy cookie crisp called Lebkuchen, a traditional Christmas treat, nuts, almond biscuits, caramels, and that everlasting standby, the Gummi Bears imported from the Black Forest area.

WEINKELLER – The translation of this shop's title is evident as soon as you walk in: wine cellar. Most of the 250 varieties of H. Schmitt Sîhne wine sold here are of the white variety. Prices range from the humble to the humbling, and tastings are held daily. In addition to the grape, beer steins, wine glasses, goblets, decanters, and assorted cheeses are available.

GLAS UND PORZELLAN – Art is the featured attraction here, with Goebel giftware, ceramic figurines including those of M.I. Hummel, plus renderings on paper. Of particular interest is an informative display of how the figuines are manufactured, including the ceramics at each stage of production. Wheelchairs and strollers can be replaced here.

DIE WEINACHTS ECKE – This shop celebrates Christmas 365 days a year, with nutcrackers and other traditional German gifts and ornaments made by companies from all over Germany. Replacement batteries for WDW rental video cameras are also available.

VOLKSKUNST – The main objects in this small shop are clocks of all sorts, chiefly cuckoo clocks, plus beer steins and a variety of gift items, scarves, nutcrackers, and incense burners in the guise of small wooden dolls. Ceramics are also sold here.

DER BUCHERWURM – English-printed books on Germany, ashtrays, spoons, and vases adorned with the images of German cities, sundries, film, and hand-painted Faberge eggs, created by a master egg-painter are offered here.

DER TEDDYBAR – Toys and more toys! The fanciful creations here are all traditional playthings to German youth, including building blocks, LGB-brand miniature trains, a spectacular collection of dolls, and stuffed animals, including teddy bears.

KUNSTARBEIT EN KRISTALL – Glassware is featured here.

GERMANY CART – Close to the Lagoon, this offers t-shirts, pins, souvenirs, novelties, and film.

ITALY

Italy, like its next-door neighbor in World Showcase, Germany, is a festive pavilion featuring fine dining, shopping, and street entertainment. A campanile atop the detailed replica of the Doge Palace towers over the pavilion, along with pedestals on which St. Mark the Evangelist and his lion companion stand, as in the square named for the apostle in Venice. In the Lagoon, there are peppermint-striped poles to which gondolas are tethered, and around the piazza, a fountain and cheery landscaping liven up the atmosphere.

Shopping
DELIZIE ITALIANE – If you didn't stop at Sussigkeiten or Patisserie Boulangerie and your kids are sore at you for it, a visit here will smooth out any rough edges between you. Luscious Perugina chocolates, cookies, and candy are sold here.

LA GEMMA ELEGANTE – The jewelry sold here ranges from the inexpensive to the exorbitant, and includes gold and silver chains, Venetian-glass beads, pendants, earrings, and mosaics.

IL BEL CRISTALLO – This pretty shop purveys Capodimonte ceramic flowers and figurines, Venetian glass objets d'art like paperweights, lead crystal bowls and candlesticks, alabaster figurines, and inlaid wood music boxes.
Italy Cart Visit this cart if you have a sudden urge to buy T-shirts, magnets, souvenirs, and novelties of the pavilion.

THE AMERICAN ADVENTURE

When a dinner party is held, the host sits at the head of the table. In this World Showcase, it is only fitting that **America** serve as the centerpiece. With a facade comprised of 110,000 bricks, the pavilion's main building houses a fast food restaurant, a shop, and the title attraction.

Attraction
THE AMERICAN ADVENTURE
Rating: 10. Arguably EPCOT's best attraction. Not to be missed. *Location:* The centerpiece of the pavilion. *Duration of Show:* 29 minutes. *Best Time to Go:* Before noon and after 3:30 PM. *Comments:* Translation to French, Spanish, and German available.

American history is celebrated here, in a moving presentation hosted by Samuel Langhorne Clemens (Mark Twain) and Benjamin Franklin. As you rise on the escalator to the theater, you pass under forty-four flags that had flown over what is now the United States. When you enter the theater, check out the statues representing the spirits of America.

The show then begins with the Pilgrims' arrival at Plymouth Rock. It then progresses to view the soul of the country at various points in its history. In one scene, a Ben Franklin robot walks up a flight of stairs to visit the author of the Declaration of Independence, Thomas Jefferson. All over, the realism is incredible. Mark Twain smokes a cigar. Audio-Animatronic figures of Nez Perce Chief Joseph and Susan B. Anthony repeat the words of the originals. The voices of the robot Will Rogers and Franklin Delano Roosevelt are their own, the price of gas in the Depression scene is an accurate eighteen cents.

The sets are as impressive as the cast, including a nearly life-size replica of Independence Hall in Philadelphia, Philly's Centennial Exposition, and a roadside gas station during the Depression, where one man strums a banjo, humming "Brother, Can You Spare Me a Dime?" while another bemoans the cost of gasoline. Their antique radio plays a speech from FDR. Incidentally, this last scene was inspired by a photo in Life magazine.

The musical accompaniment, provided by the Philadelphia Symphony Orchestra, is among the best in the World, and the finale, "Golden Dream," is absolutely breathtaking, presented along with video clips of among other people and events, the moon landing of the Eagle, John F. Kennedy's inaugural speech and Dr. Martin Luther King's "I have a dream" speech. This moving, stately conclusion often brings people to tears.

According to the Disney public relations department, this attraction has been revised over one thousand times during its lifetime and is extremely popular and thus, quite crowded between noon and 3:30 PM, so plan to witness the production outside those hours. Even during peak hours, the huge capacity of the theater effectively manages crowds. And even when there is a wait, it is bearable thanks to the entertainment provided by the carillon and the Voices of Liberty chorus. Not to be missed.

Exhibit
"PATCHWORK QUILTS: A FOLK ART TRADITION" – Quilts from the turn of the century are on display here.

Shopping
HERITAGE MANOR GIFTS – Hand-crafted goods and pre-1940s Americana items including glassware, food, toys, porcelain, and items of wood and cloth. Replicas of historic documents like the Constitution and the Declaration of Independence are available. This shop also serves as a drop-off point for two-hour photo processing.

AMERICAN ADVENTURE CARTS – Souvenirs from the American Adventure pavilion such as shirts, magnets, pins, and some sundries.

KODAK KIOSK – Camera accessories, film, and two-hour photo processing service are available.

JAPAN

A five-story, blue-roofed pagoda, modeled after an eighth-century building in the Horyuji Temple in Nara, majestically overlooks the rest of **Japan**, easily distinguished from the other World Showcase countries by the torii gate at the edge of the Lagoon. The bright red torii was designed like the one at the Itsukushima Shrine in Hiroshima Bay.

Perhaps the most beautiful and soothing part of the pavilion is the lovely garden, with streams and waterfalls, boulders, evergreens, and a small pond filled with koi, Japanese goldfish. At the present time, the only attractions in Japan are the architecture and landscaping. However, there is talk of adding a Mount Fuji thrill ride based on Disneyland's Matterhorn Mountain.

Exhibit
BIJUTU-KAN GALLERY – "Echos Through Time" is on exhibit here, featuring traditional and contemporary Japanese art forms. The exhibits are changed periodically.

Shopping
MITSUKOSHI DEPARTMENT STORE – This branch of the 300-year-old "Japanese Sears" is the largest shop in EPCOT Center, offering traditional Japanese items, including a vast selection of dolls whose prices range from $3.50 to $3,500, kits for cultivating bonsai trees, bowls and vases for flowers, china, kimonos, T-shirts, porcelain, wind chimes, jewelry, stationery, and snack items.

MITSUKOSHI KIOSK – Mementos, toys, and gifts are available in a more limited selection than at the department store.

MOROCCO

You can almost hear Peabo Bryson singing "A Whole New World" as you enter the courtyard of a replicated Arabian village. If you look carefully at any of the pieces that make up the 9 tons of tile, you would notice a flaw or imperfection with every single piece. This was done purposely by the Moroccan artists imported to EPCOT to construct the pavilion because the Koran, the Islamic holy book, says that only Allah may create perfection. This touch adds to the authenticity and the apparent age of the pavilion, including the Koutoubia Minaret, the landscaped Medina, and the Bab Boujouloud gate, all imitations of the real articles.

Exhibits
GALLERY OF ARTS AND HISTORY – An ever-changing collection of Moroccan art, artifacts, and costume is on display on the left side of the courtyard, in the building closest to the lagoon.

FEZ HOUSE – This is an early example of Moroccan architecture.

TRAVEL INFORMATION – The Moroccan National Tourist Office hosts this information outlet, with a Royal Air Maroc desk for booking a flight, literature on the country, and a continuously-playing slide show on Moroccan peoples and landscapes.

Shopping
CASABLANCA CARPETS – Wall hangings, prayer rugs, throw pillows, and Berber and Rabat carpets. And no, Aladdin, they do not fly.

JEWELS OF THE SAHARA – Sold here is an assortment of hand-crafted Berber jewelry of silver and gold with glass, amber, and beads.

FASHIONS FROM FES – Contemporary women's clothing, accessories,

MARKETPLACE IN THE MEDINA – Wicker, leather, and straw objects are offered here, mainly baskets, handbags, wallets, and lampshades.

TANGIER TRADERS – Contemporary fashions, leather purses, and accessories like fezzes, woven belts, leather sandals, and traditional Moroccan clothing.

THE BRASS BAZAAR – Pottery is sold alongside with pitchers, planters, vases, trays, and serving sets of brass and copper.
MEDINA ARTS – A selection of crafts from all over Morocco plus jewelry, sweatshirts, blouses, and film.

BERBER OASIS – Located in a tent by the Lagoon, this shop sells baskets, leather, brass, jewelry, and curios.

FRANCE

From Morocco's rugged mystique, we then progress to the charm of **France**. This interpretation of the country features narrow street, quaint sidewalk cafes, fountains, and shopping boutiques. The architecture is turn-of-the-century Paris and is towered over by a replica of the Eiffel Tower, which, ironically, is visible from everywhere in World Showcase except the France pavilion.

There is a small enclave by the river connecting the International Gateway to the EPCOT Resorts, this enclave housing a beautiful, small park inspired by A Sunday Afternoon on the Island of La Grande Jatte, Georges Seurat's famed painting. The park is relaxing and peaceful, but if exciting and breathtaking is more your cup of tea, try the gorgeous film playing at the Palais du Cinema theater towards the rear of the pavilion.

Attraction
IMPRESSIONS DE FRANCE
Rating: 8 1/2. Excellent, not to be missed. *Location:* The rear of the pavilion. *Duration of Show:* 18 minutes. *Best Time to Go:* Before 11 AM and after 7 PM. *Comments:* Translation to French, Spanish, and German available.

Many people lump **Impressions de France** together with the two CircleVision 360 films. There are some similarities, like the travelog presentation with superb musical accompaniment, but the differences are major: while the CV360 films cover all 360 degrees, the huge screen on which Impressions de France is shown covers only 200 degrees. Because viewers need not stand to see a full circle, the Disney people installed seats in the theater, a godsend for families who've been trekking around the world and praying for a chance to sit.

The film is absolutely stunning, featuring picturesque footage from Versailles, the Eiffel Tower, Mont St. Michel, Cannes, the Alps, and 43 other locations. A highlight, for sure, is the beautiful music, played by the London Philharmonic Orchestra and composed in the classic style by Frenchmen who lived in the late 1800s and early 1900s, including Jacques Offenbach, Charles-Camille Saint-Saâns, Claude Debussy, and Erik Satie. To view this production without much of a wait, visit in the morning or evening.

Shopping
PLUME ET PALETTE – French art, including elegant prints of country-side scenes, oil paintings, sparkling crystal creations, Limoges porcelain miniatures, tapestries, and china boxes.

LA MODE FRANCAIS – This shop sells French fashions and accessories.

GUERLAIN BOUTIQUE – Perfumes and cosmetics are sold here.

LA SIGNATURE – French apparel, fragrances, and bath products are offered in this intimate, tasteful shop.

LA MAISON DU VIN – French wine of all sorts is sold here, with prices ranging from a few bucks a bottle upwards to $300 for a rare vintage. Wine tastings are held here. There is a nominal fee, but you get to keep the glass. Wine accessories are also sold here.

GALERIE DES HALLES – The largest shop in France, this market offers cookies, chocolate, souvenirs, books, toys, and ready-to-wear items.

ART FEST – Portraits are inked out here.

FRANCE CART – Vastly overpriced T-shirts, flags, sweatshirts, magnets, and other knick-knacks. Film and sundries are also sold here.

INTERNATIONAL GATEWAY

This is EPCOT's second entrance, designed for guests coming from the EPCOT Resorts and the Disney-MGM Studios Theme Park. The World Traveler shop here is one of the best bets for EPCOT mementos.

Shopping
SHOWCASE GIFTS – This small shop sells convenience items, sundries, film, and EPCOT Center mementos and also houses the package pickup.

WORLD TRAVELER – A good selection of EPCOT Center mementos, character merchandise, and Disney ready-to-wear, plus sundries, film, cameras, camcorder rental. A drop-off point for two hour photo processing.

STROLLER AND WHEELCHAIR RENTAL – Convenience items, film, keepsakes, and sundries.

UNITED KINGDOM

You can picture Chevy Chase saying "Hey look, kids, Big Ben, Parliament!" (as in National Lampoon's *European Vacation* movie) as you wander the streets of a quaint British town here in Florida. There are no attractions per se in the UK pavilion, but a walk through the shops here is a most pleasant way to spend a few minutes, or hours. The entertainment is provided here by the Old Globe Players, an improvisational street theater troupe.

Shopping
THE TEA CADDY – Every dog must have his every day, every Brit must have his tea, and if you want to pick up some R. Twining and Co. tea bags or loose leaves, both mundane and exotic, this is an excellent place. Hard candies, biscuits, shortbread, teapots, and accessories are also available. Incidentally, the design of this shop resembles very much the architecture of Stratford-upon-Avon, Shakespeare's birthplace.

THE MAGIC OF WALES – The items presented in this small shop all hail from the corner of the United Kingdom known as Wales. The Welsh handicrafts, gifts, and mementos include jewelry, pottery, slate, and other hand-crafted items.

THE QUEEN'S TABLE – Royal Doulton china, figurines, crystal, and statuettes, ranging from five dollars to five digits. A very pretty shop.

PRINGLE OF SCOTLAND – Socks, scarves, hats, and ties are all sold here with various plaids on them, if you're the kind of guy who'd feel uncomfortable in a "skirt", plus lots of woolens, sweaters and golf clothes.

LORDS AND LADIES – Gift items like tobacco, bath products, fragrances, pipes, plaques, mugs, chess sets, coins, stamps, and record albums are sold in this shop.

THE TOY SOLDIER – British kids play, too! And here, you can check out the tools that they use to have a good time. There are wooden boats, toys, games, coloring books, books, stuffed animals, and a vast variety of dolls. U.K. Cart A cart on the Promenade selling souvenirs.

CANADA

Canada's landscape features the Victorian Gardens, an attractive little park based on the Butchart Gardens in British Columbia, a replicated Quebec hotel, towering elegantly over the pavilion, a stream, waterfall, and a small Rocky Mountain. The pavilion represents French Canada, the Canadian Rockies, the gardens of the city, and other areas.

Attraction
O CANADA!
Rating: 8 1/2. Well done, not to be missed. *Location:* At the very back of the pavilion. *Duration of Show:* 18 minutes. *Best Time to Go:* After 3:30 PM. *Comments:* Translation to French, Spanish, and German available. The theater has no seats.

Believe it or not, the theater housing the CircleVision 360 is inside a mountain. But the attraction is not the theater but the splendid film, dramatic and awesome at points. All of Canada's famed landmarks are featured, plus some not-so-famous hamlets where wilderness is still king. There is also footage of the Royal Canadian Mounted Police (better known as Mounties), pristine woodlands, a rodeo, the Calgary Stampede, and Montreal with all its Old World charm. This film is very well done, but since it is right at the center of the park, seeing it without a crowd can be difficult unless you check it out in the late afternoon or early evening.

Shopping
NORTHWEST MERCANTILE – Canada's largest shop sells stereotypical items like lumberjack shirts, maple syrp, and sheepskin. There are also real Native American artifacts alongside kitschy items like toy tomahawks, fur vests, moccasins, and headdresses. Other items sold here include toys, clothes, gifts, and crafts. Film can be dropped off here for two-hour processing.

LA BOUTIQUE DES PROVINCES – Hand-crafted item, figurines, jewelry, fashions, accessories, dolls, and gift items from French Canada are offered here.

WOOD CART – Souvenirs of Canada are sold at the edge of the lagoon.

ENTERTAINMENT IN EPCOT CENTER

In EPCOT Center, especially World Showcase, live entertainment is king. At the various "countries" expect either live and native entertainment or piped-in music.

ALFREDO'S RESTAURANt – Strolling musicians and singing waiters entertain nightly at World Showcase's most popular restaurant.

ANACOMICAL PLAYERS – An improvisational acting troupe produces funny, lively sketches about health and life six times a day every day. Inside the Wonders of Life pavilion.

CALEDONIA BAGPIPES (Canada) – A band consisting of two pipers and a drummer entertains while illustrating Canada's rich British heritage. They perform seven times a day, five days a week.

CHARACTERS – The Disney characters were once painfully missing from all of EPCOT Center, as their presence was seen as incompatible with the EPCOT theme. Now, they are here en force. They can be found wandering Future World, but in a higher concentration in World Showcase, in which they wear costumes representing the nations in which they appear.
The characters can also be found in the Stargate Restaurant between 9 and 10 AM, and in a show at the Odyssey Restaurant performed four times throughout the day. To see the whole gang at once, try Showcase Plaza at 1:05 and 4:55 daily for the Character Carnivale.

COMMEDIA DI BOLOGNA (Italy) – A troupe of actors invitest the audience to help recreate folk tales in this commedia dell'arte. The fifteen-minute shows are held in the Italy courtyard six or eight times each day.

COURTYARD ENTERTAINMENT (Morocco) – The unique sounds of Moroccan music are heard in the courtyard at selected times of the day five days a week.

COURTYARD TRIO (Germany) – This group brings the spirit of "gemutlitchkeit" (coziness) to the courtyard seven times daily.

DREAMFINDER – The red-bearded host of the Journey into Imagination pavilion wanders outside with his faithful dragon, Figment, throughout each weekday. He delights by saying things like "Have you ever seen a baby dragon before? You're from New Jersey?!? That's why." and "You with the video camera (which happened to be me), give the camcorder to your mother and pose in this picture. Kiss Figment. He's a girl, you know." And when I did, he informed my mother to keep the camera rolling so she could use it to blackmail me later in life. He's funny and well worth seeing if you have the chance.

EPCOT CENTER WORLD DANCERS AND WORLD DANCERS BAND – A show highlighting dances from all around the world goes up in front of the footlights of the America Gardens Theater by the Shore four times a day, five days a week.

FANTASY DREAMMAKER (Japan) – A man named Nasaji Teresawa performs his 2,400-year-old craft: molding bits of rice toffee into swans, unicorns, and other creatures... blindfolded!

FUTURE CORPS – A marching band plays contemporary music in the traditional style of a drum and bugle corps.

FUTURE WORLD BRASS – This group of brass and percussion musicians plays a wide variety of songs, including many Disney classics. Performed outside CommuniCore East.
Genroku Hanamai (Japan) – This ensemble presents classical music and dance outside the pagoda.

I CANTANAPOLI (Italy) – An Italian soprano and accordionist fill the courtyard with song.

ILLUMINATIONS – This not to be missed show could easily be the highlight of any EPCOT Center visit. This show, presented at closing time nightly, features fireworks, dancing fountains, lasers, fiber optics, and lights, all woven together with classical music. Music from each nation plays as white lights outline the pavilion. Lasers shine high overhead, fireworks explode, and messages trail across the globe in the center of the lagoon. The experience is unforgettable and serves as the exclamation point to a day at EPCOT. There are some superb, often overlooked points from which viewing IllumiNations and other lagoon events is convenient and hassle-free. See Lagoon Viewing Tips below.

MAPLE LEAF BRASS (Canada) – This show is described as "comic musicians performing some well known songs in a not so well known way." Performed seven times a day on weekends.

MARIACHI COBRE (Mexico) – The traditional sounds of mariachi music is performed on the pavilion steps or inside the pavilion at Plaza de los Amigos.

MARIMBA MAYALANDIA (Mexico) – Marimba music is performed in the Plaza de los Amigos and the Cantina de San Angel.

NORDAVIND (Norway) – Traditional songs of Norway are performed outside the Restaurant Akershus.

OKTOBERFEST MUSIKANTEN (Germany) – Inside the Biergarten Restaurant, experience a rollicking fest atmosphere with a dinner show, complete with sing-alongs, yodelers, dancers, and musicians.

OLDE GLOBE PLAYERS (United Kingdom) – See a troupe of actors present comedy with special guest stars from the audience.

RESTAURANT MARRAKESH (Morocco) – Belly dancers and musicians perform throughout the day.

SOLID BRASS – A wacky quintet performs classical music all around the Promenade over the course of the day three days a week.
Strolling Accompanist (Germany) – Traditional polkas and waltzes are played in the courtyard and Biergarten throughout each day.

SUE & PETER BARBOUR (United Kingdom) – This couple brings fun to the streets outside the Rose & Crown Pub in the form of stilt-dancing puppeteers or a Pearlie King and Queen.

SURPRISE IN THE SKIES – This is a new afternoon show created to correspond with the 20th anniversary and features paraplanes piloted by characters, boats, hang gliders, and aqua kites. For the finale, 4´ story balloons of Mickey, Minnie, Donald, Goofy, Chip, Dale, and the rest of the gang begin to rise from the eleven pavilions. See Lagoon Viewing Tips below.

TRIO BAL MUSETTE (France) – A group strolls the courtyard playing songs like "Alouette", "Fräre Jacques" and "Sur le Pont d'Avignon" along with some you may not be familiar with.

VALHALLA (Norway) – Valhalla features the spirit of Scandinavia and brings it to life with traditional song and dance.

VOICES OF LIBERTY (American Adventure) – This is a near-perfect choir whose lovely melodies can be heard inside the rotunda of the pavilion.

YUEN CHEN CHIN (China) – Native Chinese song, dance, magic, and solo flute are all performed under the Great Arch.

LAGOON VIEWING TIPS

The absolute best viewing spots for IllumiNations and Surprise in the Skies are at Showcase Plaza, as anyone could tell you. But these spots are often snatched way ahead of time. There are other, more comfortable spots which are often overlooked.

These include:
• If you arrive about 45 to 60 minutes beforehand, grab a table on the lakeside terrace of the Cantina de San Angel outside the Mexican pavilion. You can buy a churro and a margarita to tide you over until the show begins.
• There is a small park between the International Gateway and the United Kingdom pavilion, adjacent to the Rose and Crown dining complex. The park has benches, a perfect view, and virtually no crowds.
• The Promenade between China and Germany offers an excellent view.
• The outdoor terrace at the Rose & Crown Pub in the United Kingdom. Again, you can relax with a drink and a snack... and be seated.
• Italy's gondola landing often goes all but unnoticed.
• The boat dock outside of Germany is another good spot.
• If you can, get a lagoon-view table at the Mitsukoshi Dining Rooms and you will be able to see the program in spite of the torii gate at the water's edge.
• The bridge connecting the U.K., France, and the International Gateway hides a small island with an excellent, though slightly obstructed, view of the proceedings.

Special Guests

Past guest performers at EPCOT Center have included "The President's Own" United States Marine Band and the United States Air Force Presidential Honor Guard Drill Team, ring carvers from Mexico, a Hummel figurine painter and an egg-painter from Germany, a sculptor from Italy, brass artisans and carpet makers from Morocco. Special guests are listed in the weekly entertainment program.

EPCOT CENTER MISCELLANY

Experience These Early
- **FUTURE WORLD:** Spaceship Earth, Body Wars, Captain
- **EO WORLD SHOWCASE:** Maelstrom All of these rides and shows are among the most popular at EPCOT Center and are accordingly thronged with people.

Scary? And Why?
- **FRIGHTENING RIDE, VISUALLY INTENSE:** Body Wars
- **VISUALLY INTENSE:** Universe of Energy, Captain EO, Maelstrom

Memorable Shopping
While all of the World Showcase shops are interesting, here is the EPCOT pick of the crop:
- **FUTURE WORLD:** Centorium, Broccoli & Co.
- **WORLD SHOWCASE:** The Puffin's Roost (Norway), Yong Feng Shangdian (China), Mitsukoshi Dept. Store (Japan), Galerie des Halles (France), World Traveler (Int'l. Gateway), Northwest Mercantile (Canada)

Beat the Heat!
Every attraction at EPCOT Center is indoors and air conditioned except the Maelstrom, so this category is mutated to Where to Wait Out a Storm.
- **FUTURE WORLD:** Communicore, Wonders of Life, TransCenter (World of Motion), Image Works (Journey into Imagination), Seabase Alpha (The Living Seas)
- **WORLD SHOWCASE:** Mexico, Japan, and China pavilions.

Outta my WAY, I gotta GO!
The least crowded bathrooms in EPCOT are as follows:
- On either side of the Entrance Plaza
- Inside our outside the Odyssey Restaurant
- At the International Gateway.

12. DISNEY-MGM STUDIOS THEME PARK

INTRODUCTION

In May 1989, the **Disney-MGM Studios Theme Park** opened to great fanfare and was immensely popular, not only among tourists, but also with the locals. Crowds thronged the place during normally quiet seasons and the park often reached capacity by noon. As a result, Disney decided to double the size of the park created to commemorate the "Hollywood that never was and always will be," a 1930s Hollywood facade with real production facilities, an animation studio, and a whole array of other attractions.

The expansion includes auditions for the Disney Channel, in which guests will compete against each other for bragging rights and for those with outstanding performance talents, professional roles in future productions.

The major addition will be **Sunset Boulevard**, featuring more dining and shopping plus attractions like **Roger Rabbit's Hollywood**, an area centered around the Toontown Depot. It will include shops, the Terminal Bar and Grill, the "Toontown Trolley," an animated flight simulator adventure (with Roger Rabbit will be at the helm), and Baby Herman's Runaway Baby Buggy Ride, which sounds like a cross between Mr. Toad's Wild Ride and Tummy Trouble, an animated short starring Baby Herman and Roger Rabbit.

Also, **Mickey's Movieland** will be a replica of the original Hyperion Avenue Disney Studios with hands-on equipment inside. Also planned are a ride based on Dick Tracy and the Twilight Zone Tower of Terror, a thrill ride in which Disney will "make use of Twilight Zone properties, take guests into the fifth dimension, and climax in a free fall from the 13th floor of an abandoned hotel." Look for the first of these to begin operation in 1994.

A spectacular nighttime show is being planned for the waterway connecting EPCOT and the Studios. Entitled **Noah's Ark**, the production will feature original music composed by Andrew Lloyd Weber. There is also talk about adding an attraction saluting Broadway.

GETTING AROUND – To get to the Studios from:

The Magic Kingdom: Take the blue-and-white-flagged bus marked MK.

EPCOT Center: Take the blue-and-white-flagged bus marked EC. Or, take the International Gateway exit, walk to the Beach Club Resort, and catch a motor launch. Be prepared to show the attendant your multi-day passport.

TTC: Take the black-and-gold-flagged bus marked STW to the Polynesian and walk to the TTC.

Typhoon Lagoon: Take one of the four buses to the Marketplace and switch to the green-and-gold-flagged bus marked STV.

Disney Village Marketplace, Pleasure Island, or Village Resort: Take the green-and-gold-flagged bus marked STV.

Discovery Island, Contemporary Resort, Fort Wilderness, or Pleasure Island: Take the black-and-gold-flagged bus marked STE. From Discovery Island, take the blue- or green-flagged launch to Ft. Wilderness and switch to the bus.

Polynesian Resort, Grand Floridian Beach Resort, Disney Inn, or Pleasure Island: Take the black-and-gold-flagged bus marked STW.

EPCOT Resorts: Take the water taxi.

Port Orleans, Dixie Landings, and Vacation Club Resorts: Take the pink-and-green-flagged bus marked ST.

Hotel Plaza: Take the red-and-white-flagged bus marked ST.

Caribbean Beach Resort: Take the orange-and-white-flagged bus marked ST.

Off-site hotels: Take I-4 to exit 26A and follow the signs.

PARKING – The Studios lot was recently expanded. The cost is $4, free for resort guests who choose to drive (be sure to remember your I.D.) and there is no cost for leaving and returning on the same day. Keep your reciept and WRITE DOWN which section you parked in.

ADMISSION, MONEY, REFURBISHMENT AND INTERRUPTION OF ATTRACTIONS, PACKAGE PICKUP, and **DRESS CODE** – See these sections starting on page 210.

VITAL STATISTICS

Location: Walt Disney World, P.O. Box 10,040, Lake Buena Vista, FL 32830-0040. *Phone:* 824-4321. *Hours:* Vary. Attractions open at 9 AM. *Admission:* $34 for adults, $27 for kids. See pg. 115. *Parking:* $4. *Time to see:* Eight hours. *When to see:* From least to most crowded, Sunday, Friday, Saturday, Monday, Thursday, Tuesday, Wednesday. *Don't Miss:* Great Movie Ride, Star Tours, The Magic of Disney Animation, Jim Henson's Muppet*Vision 4D, Backstage Studio Tour, Inside the Magic.

PRACTICAL INFORMATION – Alcoholic Beverages: Allowed, sold at most table-service establishments and a few lounges. **Baby Services:** Changing and nursing facilities are located at Main Entrance Guest Services Building. Diapers, food, formula, and other items are available for purchase. **Baby Strollers:** Can be rented for $6 a day in Oscar's Super Service inside the Main Entrance. **Banking:** There is an automated teller machine next to the Production Information Window at the Main Entrance. **Cameras:** The Darkroom, presented by Kodak, has a full array of cameras for rent, film, videotapes, and two-hour development (see below). **Cigarettes:** Available at most shops throughout the park. **Dress Code:** Shirts and shoes must be worn, as a rule. However, this rule is broken as often as it is obeyed during the summer.

First Aid: Located outside the Guest Services building. **Foreign Language Assistance:** Foreign language maps and assistance are available at Guest Services. **Hearing-impaired Guests:** A Telecommunications Device for the Deaf (TDD) is available at Guest Services. **Information:** To get facts about attractions, shows, and dining, visit the Guest Information Board at the end of Hollywood Boulevard at Sunset Plaza. For an entertainment schedule, visit Guest Services or most shops. **Kennel:** Pets are not allowed in WDW Resorts or attractions. There is, however, an air-conditioned kennel outside the left side of the Entrance Plaza. Reservations are not needed. **Lockers:** Available for 25¢ or 50¢, these are located next to Oscar's Super Service on the right side of the Entrance Plaza. **Lost Children:** Report to Guest Services or call 560-4654.

Reservations: Accepted at four restaurants in the park. May be made at the door or, for WDW resort and Hotel Plaza guests, up to two days in advance by calling 828-4000 (824-8800 for Hotel Plaza guests). **Smoking, eating, and drinking:** For the enjoyment of other guests, smoking, eating, and drinking are not allowed in any attractions. **Visually-impaired guests:** Complimentary tape cassettes and portable tape recorders are available at Guest Services. A deposit is required, though. **Wheelchair guests:** Wheelchair rentals are available in limited quantities at Oscar's Super Service. Disabled Guests Guidebooks are available at Guest Services.

Attractions
THE GREAT MOVIE RIDE
Rating: 9 1/2. Not to be missed. *Location:* At the Chinese Theater at the end of Hollywood Boulevard. *Duration of Ride:* 19 minutes. *Best Time to Go:* Before 10 AM or after 5 PM. *Frightening:* Some segments are visually intense.

As you enter a full-scale replica of **Grauman's Chinese Theater**, you wend your way past props from classic films, like the ruby slippers from the *Wizard of Oz*. As you near the trams, you watch trailers from classic MGM films on a huge screen. Finally, you reach the boarding area, behind it, a painted backdrop with spotlights and a sign reading **"Hollywoodland"** underneath a sunset. You get into cars piloted by real live men and women and head off past the corner of Hollywood and Vine and under a marquee promising "A spectacular journey into the movies! A cast of thousands! A sweeping spectacle of thrills! Chills! Romance!"

Musicals are the first genre of movie explored, as sixty of Disney's less sophisticated Audio-Animatronics women dance atop a revolving cake (from the Busby Berkeley musical *Footlight Parade*). Then, you go to a rainy night where Gene Kelly croons "Singin' in the Rain." Kelly inspected his Audio-Animatronic likeness before it was shipped to Florida. Then to a Disney flick, *Mary Poppins*, where Julie Andrews floats, singing "Chim Chim Cher-ee" while Dick Van Dyke dances on a rooftop.

Ya then progress to a back alley where a coupla gangsters ("businessmen, please") prepare for an ambush but then decide "Nah, they're just a bunch of rubberneckin' tourists." But a shootout occurs and you are forced to detour into the **Wild West**. There, John Wayne sits on a horse, brandishing a rifle while he talks to the audience. A little later, a bank heist goes down and the robber's Audio-Animatronic accomplice fires at the crowd. The bank blows up, and the flames can be felt as you ride by. Overhead, hay begins to smolder.

Now, there are two different things that happen in the gangster/western scene. In the bank heist or the shootout, your driver-emcee-actor stops the car and goes in to investigate. But then, a robber or gangster runs out, brandishing a tommygun or a rifle and commandeers the vehicle. She/he leaves the driver and takes off with you as hostages. You then head into the **spaceship Nostromo** (of *Alien* fame), where Sigourney Weaver's Ripley stands with weapon in hand, sweating and leaning against the wall of a corridor, then... gross, what is that? It's one of the title creatures, dripping with pus and lunging at you from the side. Another one swings at you overhead.

You pass under and reach Harrison Ford and John Rhys-Davies lifting up the ark from *Raiders of the Lost Ark*. Snakes! Why do they have to be snakes? You will then reach an Egyptian scene with a huge gem on an idol. Greed gets the better of your "host" and the criminal runs up to grab the gem, not hearing a belated warning about a curse. The crook reaches the gem, grabs it and smoke begins to envelop him/her. The smoke clears and the crook is gone. A monk throws off his robe, revealing your original driver, yelling a cheery "Remember me?"

Tarzan swings on a vine, Cheetah and Jane sit below, a reassuring sign. You leave the jungle but you're not out of the jungle yet. Where are you? **Casablanca**. The plane's engine sputters, the propellors whirl, and Rick bids Ilsa farewell. Then, it's off to a happy place. You hear Munchkins sing "Ding dong, the witch is dead," and the subject of the song's sister pops out of a puff of smoke, threatening your driver. You leave the frightened Munchkins and follow the yellow brick road ("Why didn't I think of that?" the driver says after asking the Munchkins for directions), where you see Dorothy, Toto, the Tin Man, Scarecrow, and Cowardly Lion gaping at the Emerald City.

The finale of the ride is an impressive montage of 90 Academy Award-winning films squeezed into three minutes. This tribute was created by Oscar-winner Chuck Workman. As you exit, the driver yells after you to remember them "when Oscar time comes around!" Not to be missed. Ride this in the first hour after opening or in the evening if you wish to avoid crowds. If the line extends outside the theater, you will have a twenty-five minute wait or more.

BEAUTY AND THE BEAST

Rating: 7 1/2. As Broadwayesque as the movie. *Location:* At the Theater of the Stars. *Duration of Show:* About 25 minutes. *Best Time to Go:* Anytime.

This new live show relives the romance between Belle and the Beast, along with the rest of the characters from the movie, Lumiere, Chip, Mrs. Potts, and the rest. The music from the film is featured. *HINT:* If you or your kids want to meet any of the characters, you can do so at the Soundstage Restaurant, which has been renovated to bear the look of the 18th century village in which the film takes place.

SUPERSTAR TELEVISION

Rating: 8. Funny, worthwhile. *Location:* Lakeside Circle. *Duration of Show:* 30 minutes. *Best Time to Go:* After 10 AM.

Guests are chosen at random to appear in well-known television programs and special events. It's fun , especially in the 1,000-seat theater, where the live actors' footage is merged with classic clips from the shows and shown on eight monitors. If you want to be picked to be in the production, arrive 15 minutes before showtime, stand near the director, volunteer vocally, and dress bizarrely. The TV programs represented include: the Today show, I Love Lucy, General Hospital, Gilligan's Island, the Ed Sullivan Show, Cheers, a baseball game at Shea Stadium, the Golden Girls, the Tonight Show with Johnny Carson; Late Night with David Letterman, and last, but "soitanly" not least, the Three Stooges.

MONSTER SOUND

Rating: 7. Entertaining and informative. *Location:* Lakeside Circle.
Duration of Show: 12 minutes. *Best Time to Go:* Before 10 AM.

This is another funny show that utilizes audience participation. The
project at hand is not a TV show, but a brief comedy/mystery starring
Chevy Chase and **Martin Short**. The former plays an insurance salesman
visiting Short, who plays a would-be murderer. Several Foley artists are
selected from the audience at random and are instructed in the use of the
objects that create thunder, rain, wind, breaking glass, and all the other
cool effects. They show you the film twice, once as it was produced and
the second time, with the effects added by the amateurs. It's very, very
funny unless the Foley artists are very, very good.

Before you enter, you are treated to a pre-show with **David Letterman**,
who reads off the Top Ten Good Things About Sound and warns you that
"if you break anything, security guards in mouse suits will beat you
senseless." As you leave the theater, you pass the Soundsations, which are
darkened, soundproof booths in which you don headphones and listen to
stereo sound that gives the impression of really being there. Also, the
SoundWorks are like the Image Works at EPCOT only with sound
replacing imagination as the featured attraction. Crowds are usually a
problem here, so if you want to avoid a long wait, visit before 10 AM.

INDIANA JONES EPIC STUNT SPECTACULAR!

Rating: 7 1/2. Spectacular action sequences, but dry narrative. *Location:*
Lakeside Circle, by the dinosaur. *Duration of Show:* 22 minutes. *Best Time
to Go:* After 10 AM. *Frightening:* Visually intense at points.

This show demonstrates how fights, explosions, and other movie
magic are safely performed. The show opens with a Harrison Ford
lookalike in the scene from *Raiders of the Lost Ark* where Indy gently
replaces a golden idol with a bag of sand, then is chased down an incline
by a huge, 12-foot high stone ball and is seemingly run over. But no, the
director yells "cut" and the stuntman pops up. The production crew
explains how movie stunts are done and then proceeds to make a fiery
demonstration thereof. The two other scenes are the Cairo marketplace
where Indy is ambushed by sword-wielding acrobats, and then to a scene
with an attempted escape with a Nazi plane, the runaway truck, and the
explosive finale. There are machine gun battles and a climax of unbelievable magnitude.

In case you were wondering, everything is real. You will realize that
after the first explosion when heat hits your face. The stuntmen have been
hurt on more than one occasion, but the production usually goes off

without a hitch. The one and only flaw of this production is the slow pace of the narration between the action sequences. A retooled script could breathe new life into the show.

At the beginning of the show, ten extras are selected from the audience to perform in the show, but don't worry, there is absolutely no danger for nine of the extras. The tenth is used to demonstrate how to "take a punch." But don't worry, this one's a plant. You'll know which one he is because of the comments about his wardrobe. Look on your entertainment schedule or on the board outside the attraction for showtimes, plan on arriving 30 minutes beforehand and you will have little or no wait. If before the house is opened, the line extends to the dinosaur at the shore, you probably will not be seated in the next show.

STAR TOURS

Rating: 10. Absolutely spectacular! Not to be missed. *Location:* Next to New York Street. *Duration of Ride:* 7 minutes. *Best Time to Go:* As soon as the park opens. *Comments:* Expectant mothers, those with back, neck, or heart conditions and those prone to motion sickness are advised against riding. Children under 3 can't ride, children under 7 can not ride without a parent. *Frightening:* Visually and physically intense.

A model Ewok village and an Imperial Walker tower over front of Disney's most breathtaking work, a sensational flight simulator adventure called **Star Tours**. The ride is based on the Star Wars trilogy and was created by Disney and George Lucas. As you enter the queueing area, you pass dozens of Audio-Animatronics droids, including C3P0 and R2D2, who now work for an intergalactic travel agency. The displays on either side of the queue are fascinating and make long waits in line somewhat bearable. Threepio, Artoo, and the other robots converse while they, among other things, prepare the Starspeeders for takeoff.

You enter the **Starspeeder** and buckle up. Then, you meet your pilot, a rookie robot played by Pee-Wee Herman. Your trip gets off to a bumpy start almost immediately as you make a wrong turn and almost smash the ship before you even take off. But you eventually get your bearing and fly straight to the Moon of Endor. But unfortunately, you wind up taking a detour through an asteroid field and into a comet. As you smash through the wall of the comet, you are out in open space, just you, the pilot, and an Imperial TIE fighter! The tie fighter fires on you and you somehow wind up in the tractor beam of the Death Star. But a Rebel pilot steers you out of the tractor beam and leads you on an attack on the Death Star. After one more near miss, your Starspeeder docks and you get off saying with a huge grin on your face, "Let's do it again!" as you exchange high-fives.

This is by far the most popular ride in the Disney-MGM Studios and is crowded from the second the park opens. If you are not at the gate by 9:00, expect a sizable wait. As soon as they drop the gates, head towards the Chinese Theater. Turn left after you pass Mickey's of Hollywood (on your left) and run along the perimeter of the park, past the Indiana Jones Epic Stunt Spectacular! and the Backlot Express restaurant. If you only had one ride to experience in Walt Disney World, this is it. Not to be missed.

JIM HENSON'S MUPPET*VISION 4D

Rating: 10. Hilarious, not to be missed. *Location:* In the New York area. Look for the balloon overhead. *Duration of Show:* 17 minutes. *Best Time to Go:* In the morning or after 3 PM.

This wild insanity of an attraction goes WAY beyond 3D, as the film is supplemented by the presence of Audio-Animatronic figures, live characters, and dazzling, live special effects like bubbles raining down on the audience or a gentle spray of water when Fozzie Bear shoots water from a corsage, plus a theater that actually changes as the show goes on. The plot of the story is thin, but done in spectacular fashion.

After an explanation of the technology behind **Muppet*Vision** from Dr. Honeydew (with the perpetual abuse of his assistant, Beaker), the Muppets attempt to mount a musical production, but run into the usual Muppet mishaps, prompting Bean Bunny to run away with Waldo, the computer-generated "spirit of 3D." The Muppets roam the theater looking for him. Bean pops up in the upper balcony and there is a happy, albeit destructive ending at the hands of the Swedish Chef, who happens to be working the projector as well as a cannon.

At the beginning of the film, Kermit assures the audience that at no time will they "be resorting to cheap 3D tricks." The words barely get out of his mouth. At the end of the show, the two famous critics, Waldorf and Stadler, who are sitting in one of the balconies, ask if they should get up and go to the bathroom before the next show. The answer: "We can't! We're bolted to the seats!"

The pre-show is equally amusing, held in a warehouse filled with crates to be delivered to the Muppets. The Muppets cavort about three television screens overhead, preparing for the show. Disney prepared for the large crowds who frequent the theater by making it large enough to accommodate them. The only time when you may experience a wait of more than twenty minutes is immediately after the nearby Indiana Jones Epic Stunt Spectacular! discharges an audience.

HONEY, I SHRUNK THE KIDS MOVIE SET ADVENTURE

Rating: 6 1/2. Original, great for young kids. *Location:* Next to New

York Street. *Best Time to Go:* Before 10:30 AM or after dusk.

This is a playground based on the motion picture *Honey, I Shrunk the Kids*. There are 20-foot tall blades of grass, rolls of film to play in, huge bugs, enormous Legos, and a garden hose that drips on unsuspecting passers-by. It's fun, but nonessential, and worth skipping if there are no children in your party.

JIM HENSON'S MUPPETS ON LOCATION

Rating: 5 1/2. Great for Muppet fans. *Location:* New York Street. *Best Time to Go:* Anytime. *Comments:* Check Entertainment Schedule for show times.

The Muppets take five from the filming of their latest musical epic, "The Days of Swine and Roses," and sign autographs, pose for pictures, and generally mug about to the wild rhythms of Dr. Teeth and the Electric Mayhem Band.

VOYAGE OF THE LITTLE MERMAID

Rating: 7. Similar to the movie. *Location:* Just inside the Studio Arch. *Duration of Show:* About 15 minutes. *Best Time to Go:* Anytime.

This new show features songs from the movie, puppets, live actors, and Audio-Animatronic characters, including a 12-foot high Ursula singing "Poor Unfortunate Soul." Ariel and Sebastian sing other songs from the movie. Special effects are also featured, like wind, rain, bubbles, and a black-light scene.

THE STUDIO SHOWCASE

Rating: 6. Informative, reflective. *Location:* The New York Street area. *Best Time to Go:* Anytime.

Here, on permanent display are set pieces, costumes, and props worn, handled, and used by today's biggest stars in today's biggest motion pictures.

"DINOSAURS" LIVE

Rating: 4 1/2. Not worth a special trip. *Location:* In front of the Chinese Theater at the end of Hollywood Boulevard. *Duration of Show:* About 15 minutes. *Comments:* Performed at 1 PM daily.

The Sinclairs, stars of the ABC-TV show "Dinosaurs," arrive on a rolling stage for "a special on-location shoot." Earl, Fran, Robbie, Charlene,

Grandma Ethyl, and Baby Sinclair all appear for the daily festivities. The show also features accompaniment from the Hollywood Brass.

TEENAGE MUTANT NINJA TURTLES·

Rating: 5. Kids love it, adults are indifferent. *Location:* New York Street. *Duration of Show:* 5 minutes. *Best Time to Go:* Anytime. *Comments:* Performed six times daily.

The world's only singing, dancing, pizza-eating, teen-aged, mutated, amphibian ninjas star in a show at the Backlot. They perform their theme song, dance around, then mingle with kids in the audience, sign autographs, and pose for pictures. Check the entertainment schedule for performance times. There are hokey two-dimensional cutouts of the Turtles nearby where photos can be taken, and of course, carts vending Turtle figures, t-shirts, and memorabilia.

BACKSTAGE STUDIO TOUR

Rating: 9. Informative, fast-paced, not to be missed. *Location:* Inside the Studio Arch. *Duration of Tour:* 30 minutes. *Best Time to Go:* Anytime. *Frightening:* The Catastrophe Canyon sequence is somewhat intense.

You board a shuttle and venture inside the production of movies. After passing the Bungalows, where production facilities for several projects, including the New Mickey Mouse Club, are contained, you reach your first destination: Costuming, where skilled designers create the clothes worn by the stars. The costumes on display include those worn by Bob Hoskins in "Who Framed Roger Rabbit?," Julia Roberts in "Pretty Woman," Warren Beatty and Madonna in "Dick Tracy", and Michael Jackson in "Captain EO." Next to Costuming is the Scenic Shop, where sets needed for the various productions are designed and constructed.

Then, the tram passes the topiary, camera, prop, and lighting department, where the pieces are stored until needed. You then ride past famous homes, including those of the Golden Girls and Vern from the film "Ernest Saves Christmas", and other houses with a real "lived-in" look. But as you turn around and view the "homes" from behind, you realize that they can't be lived in, they're only facades. As soon as you're out of camera view, the house's exterior vanishes. You pass the Boneyard, where vehicles used in films like the ship from "Flight of the Navigator" and the trolley from "Who Framed Roger Rabbit?" are stored.

Then, it's off to Catastrophe Canyon. The guide warns you at the beginning of the tour, "Those of you on the right side of the cars are going to get a little wet, those of you on the left are going to get soaked." This is the place he meant. You enter an oil drilling operation, only to be hit by rain, earthquakes, fires, explosions, and flash floods (sounds like California!) and then suddenly, it's over, just as quickly as it began. You've survived. As you pass around behind Catastrophe Canyon, you see the inner workings of it. Impressive.

Your last port of call is New York Street, where a technique called forced perspective turn two blocks of two-dimensional "buildings" into a cityscape. You depart the trams here. You may continue with the second part of the tour, Inside the Magic, eat, drink, shop, go to the bathroom, or just save the second half for later. Check the Entertainment Schedule so you won't miss the last departure.

INSIDE THE MAGIC: SPECIAL EFFECTS AND PRODUCTION TOUR
Rating: 9. Not to be missed. *Location:* By New York Street. *Duration of Tour:* 60 minutes. *Best Time to Go:* Anytime.

The second segment of the tour, this part done on foot, begins at the **Water Effects Tank**, where blue screens, simulated strafing attacks and depth charges, explosions, and other effects combine to turn one person from the audience into a certain Captain Duck and star in a short film. You then enter the prop room, where props on display include the chessboard from Star Wars, the gold-plated Johnny Five from Short Circuit 2, and a few of the characters from Captain EO.

Then it's into the **Special Effects Workshop and Shooting Stage**, where technicians and children from the audience combine to show how models, blue screens, and editing create a scene. The demonstration recreates the scene from *Honey, I Shrunk the Kids* where two kids fly on a giant bee. The three Soundstages, on which filming may be done at any time, are the next stop. You overlook from a sound-proof chamber high above, so filming can continue uninterrupted. Note that no photography or videotaping is allowed in the soundstages (for legal reasons).

It's then on to the **Audio department**, where technicians complete the job after the photography is complete. Then, at **Post-Production**, C3PO, R2D2, and George Lucas help to explain what happens in editing. The final stop is the **Walt Disney Theater**, where sneak previews of films from Disney, Touchstone, and Hollywood Pictures are shown. Note that if you take the tram tour and the walking tour subsequently, you will end up where you began.

THE MAGIC OF DISNEY ANIMATION
Rating: 10. Whimsical, fun, not to be missed. *Location:* Next to the Backstage Studio Tour. *Duration of Tour:* 36 minutes. *Best Time to Go:* Before 11 AM or after 5 PM.

This is a self-guided, walking tour that begins in the pre-show area, where 13 of the Oscars won by the Disney animators and cels from classic films are all on display. You enter a theater for "**Back to Neverland,**" an uproarious film starring Robin Williams and Walter Cronkite, an unlikely pair if ever there was one. Williams becomes a cartoon character, one of the Lost Boys from Peter Pan, and plays it to the limits. At one point, he turns himself into a variety of objects, including Mickey Mouse ("I can even be a corporate symbol!"), and gets stern admonitions from Cronkite throughout. By the way, this 8-minute film was difficult to complete because Cronkite kept on cracking up.

Then, you follow Williams and Cronkite through the **Animation Department** for a step by step explanation of the animation process. Animators are at work here from 9 AM until 5 or 6 PM, so try to visit between these hours. The various chapters in the story are displayed on overhead monitors. You can linger as long as you like in this part of the tour to watch the animators at work. The tour finishes up at the **Disney Classics Theater**, where a montage of clips from animated films from Snow White to Beauty and the Beast are shown. After that, you are released into the **Animation Gallery**, where limited-edition cells, lithographs, and animation art can be purchased.

Shopping

OSCAR'S CLASSIC CAR SOUVENIRS – The main items sold at this "gas station" are automotive memorabilia like key chains, models, and mugs. The **1947 Buick** is authentic (and not for sale), and the gas tanks bear the name Mohave Oil Co., the same moniker found at Catastrophe Canyon. Lockers, wheelchair and stroller rental, infant products, and postage stamps are available at Oscar's Super Service, adjacent to the shop.

MOVIELAND MEMORABILIA – A kiosk on the left side of the Entrance Plaza selling souvenirs like toys, hats, books, key chains, sunglasses, film, and sundry items.

SID CAHUENGA'S ONE-OF-A-KIND – Sid and his wife Rose have a house filled with antiques and curios. Autographed photos, movie posters, and movie magazines, and other collectibles are sold here.

CROSSROADS OF THE WORLD – Mickey stands watch on top of his kiosk, right in the middle of Hollywood Boulevard, sells sundries, film, sunglasses, and raingear. Information is also available here.

THE DARKROOM – Film, videotapes, and cameras for sale; cameras and camcorders available for rent. Two-hour photo processing is available.

COVER STORY – Here, you can get your mug on the front cover of magazines like Sports Illustrated, Time, Life, Cosmopolitan, and more. Costumes and accessories are provided.

CELEBRITY 5 & 10 – This replicated five-and-dime Hollywood-themed ready-to-wear, magnets, jackets, teddy bears, and movie-themed items, including a director's clapboard.

SWEET SUCCESS – "Starry-eyed hopefuls come here for a special taste of Sweet Success," the Studio Guidebook says of this specialty candy shop. Plush M & M toys are also sold here.

L.A. PROP AND STORAGE – Guests can star in a video screen test here, as well as shop for Disney clothing, accessories, and movie/show memorabilia.

MICKEY'S OF HOLLYWOOD – This is the best place in the Studios to get Disney character merchandise, and Disney and Studio ready-to-wear, books, wallets, tote bags, and watches.

LAKESIDE NEWS – Comic books, movie magazines, and souvenirs are offered.

KEYSTONE CLOTHIERS – Disney jackets, jewelry, and fashions, all with a Hollywood twist, are sold here.

GOLDEN AGE SOUVENIRS – This shop, located alongside Echo Lake, sells radio and television program gifts plus Disney Channel memorabilia.

ENDOR VENDORS – Endor Vendors gets the nod as my personal favorite shop in the Studios. Anyone who enjoyed the Star Wars movies, Timothy Zahn's new trilogy, or just the Star Tours attraction that discharges passengers here will enjoy browsing this shop. Books, models, toys, games, gifts, and clothing are sold here, many of which bear the Star Wars or Star Tours logos. Be sure to notice Darth Vader's ominous body in the wall between Star Tours and here.

THE DISNEY STUDIO STORE – Located just outside the entrance to the Backstage Studio Tour and at the exit to Inside the Magic, this small shop sells clothing and collectibles with the Touchstone, Hollywood, and Walt Disney Studios logos. Film can be dropped off here for two-hour development.

ANIMATION GALLERY – At the end of the Magic of Disney Animation attraction, this shop sells original Disney animation cels, exclusive limited edition reproductions, books, and figurines, including an exclusive commemorative cell.

THE LOONY BIN – This shop is right out of Who Framed Roger Rabbit?, with the boxes that produce animal sounds, laughter, and street sounds when opened, a hole in the wall shaped like Roger, the Dipmobile used in the movie, and other props. The merchandise here includes gag gifts, plush toys, and Roger Rabbit stuff. This is also a drop-off point for two-hour photo development.

FOTOTOONS – Here, you have an opportunity to pose in photographs with famous cartoon characters. Finished Fototoons can be picked up here, or after closing, at Cover Story.

THE VILLAIN'S SHOP – This unique boutique is where you can pick up gifts celebrating the great villains from Disney animated classics, from Snow White's Wicked Witch to Aladdin's Jafar.

STAGE ONE COMPANY STORE – Items sold here include gifts, gadgets, and mementos highlighting everything from Mickey Mouse to Miss Piggy.

DISNEY AFTERNOON STORE – Gifts and souvenirs from Chip'n'Dale Rescue Rangers, Disney's TaleSpin, Darkwing Duck, and Goof Troop, the shows that make up the Disney Afternoon programming in syndication across the country.

INDIANA JONES ADVENTURE OUTPOST – Alongside the amphitheater that houses the Epic Stunt Spectacular!, this shop sells "adventure gear" and "artifacts" with the Indiana Jones logo.

TEENAGE MUTANT NINJA TURTLES CART – The Turtles' fans among you will love this portable shop selling all things TMNT, from tee-shirts to action figures.

ENTERTAINMENT IN THE DISNEY-MGM STUDIOS

There's some great entertainment in the Disney-MGM Studios complex. Below you'll find a brief list of the possibilities:

CHARACTERS – The Disney characters can be seen mingling on Mickey

Avenue and in the Studio Courtyard throughout the day. Muppets, Star Wars characters, and the Dinosaurs can often be found at their respective attractions.

FILMING – Crews may be producing shows at any given time, many of which welcome a studio audience. If you are interested in being in the house for one of these or want information on filming currently going on, visit the Production Information Window or Guest Services, both at the main entrance.

The Studios' resume includes, for television: Adventures in Wonderland, Body by Jake, Wheel of Fortune, and You Asked For It; for theaters: Beauty and the Beast, Honey, I Blew Up the Kid, and Flipper: The Movie.

"SORCERY IN THE SKY" – A pyrotechnic display based on the movie *Fantasia*, Mickey Mouse stars as the Sorcerer's Apprentice and conjures up a magical display from behind the Chinese Theater, all to the accompaniment of themes from motion pictures like Star Wars, Indiana Jones, and Gone with the Wind, played by a 100-piece symphony orchestra.

STAR TODAY – Some days, a celebrity visits the Studios and is available for interviews, photos, and autographs. Contact Guest Services at the Main Entrance or WDW information (tel. 824-4321).

STREET SHOWS – On Hollywood Boulevard, the Screen Extras Band, Tubafours Quartet, and Streetmosphere characters entertain daily. In the Studio Courtyard, the Disney characters are on hand daily, while the Toon Town Trio plays five days a week. On the Backlot, a piano player plunks the ivories on weekdays and the Teenage Mutant Ninja Turtles and the Hollywood Hitmen Band perform daily.

DISNEY-MGM STUDIOS MISCELLANY

Experience These Early
The Great Movie Ride, Star Tours

Scary? And Why?
   • **FRIGHTENING RIDE, VISUALLY INTENSE:** Star Tours.
   • **VISUALLY INTENSE:** The Great Movie Ride, Indiana Jones Epic Stunt Spectacular!

Memorable Shopping
   • Oscar's Classic Car Souvenirs, Sid Cahuenga's One-Of-A-Kind,

Endor Vendors, Animation Gallery, The Villains Shop.

Beat the Heat

All the attractions not listed below are indoors. Those listed directly below are outdoors, but in the shade:

• Backstage Studio Tour, Indiana Jones Epic Stunt Spectacular, Inside the Magic (partially outdoors.)

The attractions listed below are outdoors and offer no shade:

• Beauty and the Beast, Dinosaurs Live, Honey, I Shrunk the Kids Movie Adventure, Teenage Mutant Ninja Turtles.

Outta my WAY, I Gotta GO!

The Studio's least crowded bathrooms are located:

• At the kennel.
• At the Catwalk Bar.
• Adjacent to Superstar Television.
• At the 50's Prime Time Cafe.

13. OTHER DISNEY ATTRACTIONS

INTRODUCTION

Few people realize until they arrive at the Vacation Kingdom or until they read it somewhere that there's more than the three major theme parks to Walt Disney World. There's a pleasant outdoor marketplace, two water parks, a nighttime entertainment complex, a bona fide zoological park, and several educational programs. There is also a strip mall, although it is not technically part of Walt Disney World, but it falls within the 43-mile confines, and, opening in 1994, another entertainment complex called **Disney's Boardwalk**. Also, the **Team Disney** building is worth a look if you happen to be in the area.

DISNEY VILLAGE MARKETPLACE

The marketplace is considered part of **Disney's Village Resort**, and its cedar-sided buildings, gardens, twinkling lights, and music make it a pleasant place just to walk through, even if you weren't to enter any of the shops. However, the wide variety of merchandise sold in the stores here makes that a less-than probable possibility.

GETTING AROUND – The bus station is located in front of Mickey's Character Shop. To get to the Disney Village Marketplace from:

Magic Kingdom, Contemporary Resort, Polynesian Resort, Grand Floridian Resort: Take the monorail (or from the MK, the ferry) to the TTC and take the red-flagged bus.

TTC, EPCOT Center, or Typhoon Lagoon: Take the red-flagged bus. Or, from Typhoon Lagoon, take the orange-and-white-flagged, purple-and-gold-flagged, or pink-and-green-flagged buses, all marked with a V.

Disney-MGM Studios Theme Park and Disney's Village Resort: Take the green-and-gold-flagged bus marked STV. Depending on the location of your villa at the Village Resort, it may be easier to walk.

Pleasure Island: Take the footpaths to the Village.

Fort Wilderness: Take the blue-flagged bus to the TTC and switch to the red-flagged bus.

Disney Inn: Take the green-flagged bus to the TTC and switch to the red-flagged bus.

EPCOT Resorts: Take the purple-and-gold-flagged bus marked V.

Caribbean Beach Resort: Take the orange-and-white-flagged bus marked V.

Port Orleans, Dixie Landings, and Vacation Club Resorts: Take the pink-and-green-flagged bus marked V. Or, from the first two, take the water taxi.

The Hotel Plaza: It's easiest to walk or drive yourself, but if you intend to travel by bus, take the red-and-white-flagged bus marked V.

Off-site hotels in Lake Buena Vista: Take S.R. 535 to Hotel Plaza Blvd. and go straight to the Marketplace.

Off-site hotels via I-4: Take interchange 26B (EPCOT Center / Disney Village) into WDW, the exit for the Marketplace is the first one, turn right after getting off and follow the signs about a quarter of a mile. It'll be on your left.

PARKING – Parking at the Marketplace is free and plentiful. Valet parking is available by the Empress Lilly and by Village Spirits.

ADMISSION – Entry to the Disney Village Marketplace is free.

MONEY – There is a branch of the Sun Bank located in the Marketplace, offering cash advances, traveler's check services, personal check cashing, arrange for a wire transfer of money from a guest's home bank to the Sun Bank, and exchange foreign currency. Disney Resort ID is accepted for purchases.

PHONES – Located alongside EUROSPAIN, outside the Lakeside Terrace restaurant, by the Gourmet Pantry, Board Stiff, the Empress Lilly, and Chef Mickey's Village Restaurant.

RESTROOMS – Found at EUROSPAIN, Guest Services, Lakeside Terrace, Minnie Mia's Italian Eatery, the Empress Lilly, and Chef Mickey's Village Restaurant.

GUEST SERVICES – The building adjoining You and Me Kid offers information, brochures, magazines, gift certificates, gift wrapping, stroller and wheelchair rental, film, special event tickets, and two-hour photo processing.

VITAL STATISTICS

Location: Walt Disney World Village, P.O. Box 10,150, Lake Buena Vista, FL 32830-0150. *Phone:* 828-3058. *Hours:* 10 AM to 10 PM daily. Hours at restaurants differ. *Admission:* Free. *Parking:* Free. *Time to See:* Two hours. *When to See:* Anytime.

PRACTICAL INFORMATION – Alcoholic beverages: Allowed, sold at the Gourmet Pantry, Village Spirits, and most eateries. **Baby strollers:** Available for rental at Guest Services. **Cigarettes:** Available at Village Spirits. **Delivery:** The Gourmet Pantry will deliver telephone orders to the Village Resort. If you're not in your room, the deliveryman will even put the groceries in your refrigerator. Dial 31 on your room phone or call 828-3886. **Dress Code:** Shirts and shoes must be worn at all times.

Information: A directory of Pleasure Island and the Marketplace is available at Guest Services and most shops. **Reservations:** Accepted at the Empress Lilly (828-3900) and Chef Mickey's Village Restaurant (828-3723). **Wheelchair guests:** All areas of the Marketplace are wheelchair accessible. To get onto the dock, use the ramp by Chef Mickey's. Wheelchair rental is available at Guest Services.

Shopping
EUROSPAIN (828-8013) – This interesting shop features a variety of handcrafted gifts and decorative articles from prestigious European artisans and designers. Demonstrations are held daily.

PERSONAL MESSAGE (828-3388) – Electronic mechanisms, phones, radios, watches, clocks, cards, briefcases, pens, desk sets, calculators, and a good selection of books. The shop will personalize any gift with embroidering or engraving.

CHRISTMAS CHALET (828-3759) – To my knowledge, Orlando has never had a white Christmas. Shoppers here may think differently. It's yuletide season year round here, as a 24-foot tree towers over the festivities here. Caroling bells chime in the background. The fare consists mainly of American and European trim-a-tree ornaments, decor, nutcrackers, Snow Villages, collectibles, and character merchandise. A truly charming shop.

YOU AND ME KID (828-3875) – This whimsical shop has tables full of Legos and elaborate dollhouses that kids can play with. Toys, trains, clothing, and accessories for children of all ages, from infants to teenagers, are all sold here, and all items can be personalized.

GREAT SOUTHERN CRAFT CO. (828-3864) – The air at this lively shop is scented with potpourri and resonating with the sounds of banjos and hammered dulcimers. The stock here is Old South; Victorian hats, pottery, jewelry, antiques, furniture, quilts, stained glass, Alex Haley figurines, and David Winter cottages. A potter and silversmith are on hand to demonstrate their crafts. Also, at Lilly Langtry Photo Studio, you can get your photo taken in an Edwardian suit or a Victorian gown.

CRISTAL ARTS (828-3616) – It's a memorable experience to watch the crystal cutters at this small store adjoining Mickey's Character Shop. Glass sculpting and custom engraving of initials, messages, or pictures onto merchandise is done on the premises. The wares include cut-glass bowls and vases, clear glass mugs, glass sculptures, and other items. Similar to Crystal Arts and La Princesa de Cristal in the Magic Kingdom.

MICKEY'S CHARACTER SHOP (828-3191) – If you came to Florida vowing not to leave until you had a Mickey jacket, a Goofy hat, a Donald t-shirt, and a Pluto tie, do your one-stop shopping here. The **Character Shop** is the largest shop in the Marketplace and has the biggest and best selection of character merchandise in the World. Those skeptical about the store's size will soon have a change of heart as they enter to see a huge hot-air balloon soaring inside the shop, with Mickey, Minnie, Donald, Dumbo, Jiminy Cricket, Chip, Dale, and more of the characters riding.

The Disney creations can be found on clothing or as plush toys, ceramic collectibles, or as ink in a coloring book. Shirts are custom-made by a robot at one station, and other personalized items are in stock from A to Z. If there's an item that you would love to have personalized, but your name is Darren, Aloysius, or anything else that's somewhat unusual, the Disney people can special order it for you. This shop opens at 9:30 AM.

SIR EDWARD'S HABERDASHER (828-3821) – Boys' and men's apparel of all kinds is sold here. Lines offered include Ralph Lauren, Izod, and Baxter, in addition to Disney's own private label.

GOURMET PANTRY (828-3886) – Specialty housewares, accessories, cookbooks, and culinary gifts are offered here, in addition to groceries ranging from sundry to exotic, including Godiva chocolates, specialty sandwiches, salads, pastries, and gourmet coffees. Staples found here include orange juice, breads, cereals, yogurt, beer, and soft drinks. Delivery is available (see above). This shop opens at 9:30.

CONCHED OUT (828-1967) – The unique gifts here "capture the spirit of nature." Wind chimes, t-shirts, crystals, books, and gifts related to gardening, wildlife, and the environment.

BOARD STIFF (828-1992) – Surfers will be hard pressed to find a pipeline here, an hour from the ocean, but they can visit the next best thing: a surf shop. Boards, equipment, shoes, swimwear, and resortwear from Quiksilver, Billabong, Ocean Pacific, Vuarnet, and more.

RESORTWEAR UNLIMITED (828-3844) – Women can find the latest in lightweight, vivid fashions, plus sportswear and swimwear, all from famous labels like Liz Claiborne and Catalina. Jewelry, hats, handbags, and other accessories are also sold.

WINDJAMMER DOCK SHOP (828-3971) – Luggage, books, cards, and merchandise with a nautical theme is sold along with stock bearing the logo of the adjacent Captain Jack's Oyster Bar.

24KT PRECIOUS ADORNMENTS (828-3878) – Jewelry ranging from electroplated Mickey Mouse charms to diamonds, rubies, and sapphires. Watches from Lorus, Seiko, and Christian Dior are also featured.

COUNTRY ADDRESS (828-3860) – This shop offers moderately priced women's clothing, jewelry, and accessories.

VILLAGE SPIRITS (828-3868) – Wines from America and Europe are featured here, ranging from inexpensive table wines to rare vintages. Snacks, soft drinks, tobacco, souvenir wine glasses, acrylic barware, and crystal. A renowned wine festival is held here each February.

TEAM MICKEY'S ATHLETIC CLUB (828-3661) – Clothing and accessories bearing the logos of professional sports teams, and items like balls, gloves, shirts, and hats with Mickey, Minnie, Goofy, or the Disney University logo. Also, an extensive line of Mickey bowling items, baseball figurines, fashions, and collectibles.

Services & Entertainment
DOCK STAGE – Entertainment and special events at the water's edge.

MARINA – Go boating on 35-acre Buena Vista Lagoon. Craft available for rent include Water Sprites, small, one-man speedboats, rented for $11 a half hour (minimum rental age: 12); pedalboats, for $5.50 a half hour or $8 an hour; pontoon boats, for $35 an hour; and 16-foot, V-hulled canopy boats that can accommodate six, for $35 an hour. To rent, you must show a resort ID, driver's license, or passport. Open until dusk.

CAPTAIN'S TOWER (828-3862) – The landmark of the Marketplace, this often plays host to special promotions and events. Changed three to four times annually, depending on special event themes and the latest trends in merchandise.

Special Events
DISNEY VILLAGE WINE FESTIVAL – Held in February of each year, sixty wineries from Europe, California and the rest of the U.S. put their best grape forward.

BOAT SHOW – Central Florida's largest in-water boat show features 200 boats in and around Buena Vista Lagoon. Held in October.

HALLOWEEN – Local youngsters dress up for a costume contest, and the atmosphere is spiced up by "halloween-ifying" the Captain's Tower with cobwebs, Halloween merchandise, and the presence of villains from Disney flicks.

FESTIVAL OF MASTERS – Held at the beginning of each November, this is one of the biggest events of the year at the Marketplace, and the hype is decidedly worth it. This art show draws award-winning artists from around the country and is attended by locals and tourists with equal and ample enthusiasm, as one can see from the parking lot, packed to capacity.

THE GLORY AND PAGEANTRY OF CHRISTMAS – This is truly a sight to behold. This nativity pageant takes place in the Village Marketplace and is based on a French pageant dating back to the 13th century. Three dozen actors, all dressed in period costumes, participate in this beautiful event. The production goes up every Thanksgiving and lasts until New Year's. It would be a shame to visit Walt Disney World during this time of year and miss this.

PLEASURE ISLAND

In 1989, Disney opened a nighttime entertainment complex to rival downtown Orlando's Church Street Station. According to legend, **Pleasure Island** is the former home of a 19th century Pittsburgh ship merchant named **Merriweather Adam Pleasure**. Merchant sailing was on a downturn during Pleasure's heyday, but the advent of private yachting more than made up for the loss in his business, Pleasure's Canvas and Sailmaking, Inc. Pleasure Island was a community developed to advance his business as well as yearning for adventure.

The legend goes on. In 1939, Pleasure put the Island into the hands of his children as he went to circumnavigate the globe. He was lost at sea. The place fell into disrepair and remained that way until Disney "discovered" it in 1986 and transformed it into a paradise of nightclubs, restaurants, and shops.

GETTING AROUND – The bus station is located by the AMC Pleasure Island 10 Theatres. To get to Pleasure Island from:

Magic Kingdom, Contemporary Resort, Polynesian Resort, Grand Floridian Resort: Take the monorail (or from the MK, the ferry) to the TTC and take the red-flagged bus.

TTC, EPCOT Center, or Typhoon Lagoon: Take the red-flagged bus. Or, from Typhoon Lagoon, take the orange-and-white-flagged, purple-and-gold-flagged, or pink-and-green-flagged buses, all marked with a V.

Disney-MGM Studios Theme Park and Disney's Village Resort: Take the green-and-gold-flagged bus marked STV. Depending on the location of your villa at the Village Resort, it may be easier to walk.

Disney Village Marketplace: Take the footpaths to the Island. Fort Wilderness: Take the blue-flagged bus to the TTC and switch to the red-flagged bus.

Disney Inn: Take the green-flagged bus to the TTC and switch to the red-flagged bus.

EPCOT Resorts: Take the purple-and-gold-flagged bus marked V.

Caribbean Beach Resort: Take the orange-and-white-flagged bus marked V.

Port Orleans, Dixie Landings, and Vacation Club Resorts: Take the pink-and-green-flagged bus marked V. Or, from the first two, take the water taxi.

The Hotel Plaza: It's easiest to walk or drive yourself. But if you plan on riding a bus, take the red-and-white-flagged bus marked V.

Off-site hotels in Lake Buena Vista: Take S.R. 535 to Hotel Plaza Blvd. and turn left at the Marketplace. The Pleasure Island parking lot is about a tenth of a mile on your right.

Off-site hotels via I-4: Take interchange 26B (EPCOT Center/Disney Village) into WDW, the exit for the Marketplace is the first one, turn right after getting off and follow the signs about a quarter of a mile. It'll be on your left.

PARKING – Parking at Pleasure Island is free and plentiful. Valet parking is available by the Empress Lilly.

ADMISSION – Before 7 PM, admission to the Island is free. After 7 PM, the clubs open and guests pay $11.95 to gain admission to all parks. After

7 PM, guests under 18 years of age must be accompanied by a parent who understands that the entertainment is geared to adults. The five- and six-day Super Passes include admission to Pleasure Island for seven days, starting with the first time you use the pass. A 4-Season Salute pass allows unlimited admission for 146 days over the course of the year and costs $15. Annual passes to Pleasure Island are $34.95. When purchased with an Annual Passport to the 3 major parks, they cost $26.

DRINKING – You must be 21 years old to drink here. There is no drink minimum or pressure to drink, but if you choose to imbibe, expect to pay about $5 for most drinks, about half that for the drink of the day.

MONEY – There is a branch of the Sun Bank located in the adjacent Marketplace, offering cash advances, traveler's check services, personal check cashing, arrange for a wire transfer of money from a guest's home bank to the Sun Bank, and exchange foreign currency. Disney Resort ID is accepted for purchases.

PHONES – Located at the AMC Pleasure Island 10 and Mouse House.

RESTROOMS – Found at the AMC Pleasure Island 10 and Mouse House.

VITAL STATISTICS

Location: Walt Disney World Village, P.O. Box 10,150, Lake Buena Vista, FL 32830-0150. *Phone:* 934-7781. *Hours:* Shops, 10 AM to midnight daily. Clubs, 7 PM to 2 AM. Hours at restaurants differ. *Admission:* Free before 7 PM. $11.95 after 7. *Parking:* Free. *Time to See:* One evening. *When to See:* Anytime.

PRACTICAL INFORMATION – **Alcoholic beverages:** Allowed, sold at all table-service eateries and clubs. **Dress Code:** Shirts and shoes must be worn at all times. **Information:** A directory of Pleasure Island and the Marketplace is available at most shops. **Wheelchair guests:** All areas of Pleasure Island are wheelchair accessible.

Nightclubs

NEON ARMADILLO MUSIC SALOON – The legend says that Pleasure collected exotic plants from his travels here, in what used to be a greenhouse. Now, the Neon Armadillo plays host to some of the best country and western bands around. The decor is upscale Southwestern, and mixed drinks, beer, wine, and soft drinks are served. Two fajita bars offer chicken fajitas, chili, nachos, sausages, pickled eggs, and fresh pepperoni. The Saloon is more relaxed than the other dance clubs here.

This is a good bet for passing time before a show at the nearby Comedy Warehouse.

ROCK & ROLL BEACH CLUB – Originally planned as the XZFR (say zephyr) Rockin' Rollerdrome, a dance club with a futuristic theme and roller skating, this club was extensively revamped to create a beach party atmosphere and arguably the best dance club on the island. Supposedly, this was a wind tunnel in which Pleasure developed a flying machine. The first level holds the dance floor, which is a little bit diminutive, but there is plenty of seating. The second and third floors hold billiards tables and games.

There are often live bands here, and they are always top-notch. Oldies and current rock music is played here, loud. The bands play about 45 minutes every hour, and a disc jockey takes over during breaks to offer nonstop dancing. The Orbiter Lounge, on the first floor, offers alcoholic beverages, soft drinks, and snacks. Spinners, on the third floor, sells potato straws, pizza, burgers, chicken, and ice cream.

MANNEQUINS DANCE PALACE – The warehouse where Pleasure kept the materials for his business is no more. Now, it is the premier over-21 dance club on the island. The name of the club is taken from the mannequins who stand watch across the dance floor, which happens to be a rotating turntable. There are several dressed as felines from the Andrew Lloyd Webber musical "Cats," others representing Yul Brenner and Deborah Kerr performing the musical number "Shall We Dance" in the movie version of The King and I.

Special effects are king here. There is a collection of 70 robotically controlled lighting instruments, plus machines that can cause it to shower confetti, bubbles, or even snowflakes inside the club. The music is mainstream contemporary, Top 40, and recorded. However, the disc jockeys are excellent and the sound system is mindblowing. Carts throughout the club offer seafood, chicken, steak, and potato chips. Bars scattered throughout sell specialty cocktails, beer, wine, and soft drinks. No one under 21 years of age admitted.

8 TRAX – This one club has undergone more metamorphosis than any of the others. It started life in 1989 as Videopolis East, a club for the 13-to-20 set, selling no alcohol and taking its name from the Videopolis attraction in Disneyland. For reasons including a too-complicated ticket system, underage drinking, and the whole image of Pleasure Island, Imagineers scrapped Videopolis East, replacing it with CAGE!. Now, it has been changed yet again, this time to 8 Trax, a dance club featuring classic rock from the 1970's.

ADVENTURER'S CLUB – A plaque at the entrance presents the credo of the club, and of Merriweather Adam Pleasure: "Explore the unknown, discover the impossible." Inside, there are stuffed animal heads who turn to one another and begin talking (Audio-Animatronics, of course), eccentric characters, cast members who mingle with guests, and knick-knacks from wall to wall, all supposedly collected by Pleasure during his journeys.

This is the only true Disney creation on the island, modeled after a British explorer's club. It's actually a sort of a comedy presentation, but since there is neither a posted schedule nor any announcement that there is a show, many people walk in, check it out, and leave, missing the best part. Sit at the bar, order a drink from one of the bartenders, all of whom happen to be named Nash, and wait. Once every thirty or forty minutes, all guests present are ushered into library for the comic show. Exotic food and drink are served up here, ranging from Shrimp Trinidad to Lebanese steak tartare. Wine, beer, specialty drinks, and soft drinks are also offered.

THE COMEDY WAREHOUSE – Once, energy for the activities on the Island was produced here. Now, energy is produced by a troupe of five improvisational comedians and a musician who, five times nightly, partake in skits based on audience suggestions, including a riotous spoof of Walt Disney World. The contents include waiting and waiting to ride Space Mountain, a Disney plot to pilfer tourist dollars, and other hilarious subjects. Also, the comics have been known to make phone calls in the middle of the show, usually to the phone by the last seat in the fifth row. Avoid this seat if you're at all inhibited.

Guests sit on stools packed like sardines in a tiered arena, so everyone has a good view. Each show is different and equally entertaining, and this is the most popular club on the Island. If you don't plan to see the first or last show, expect a 30 to 45 minute wait in line. This is the only club that you can not come to and go from as you please. Popcorn, soft drinks, cocktails, beer, and wine are served.

PLEASURE ISLAND JAZZ CO. – The idea for this recently-opened jazz club was fueled by the popularity of "N'awlins" jazz at the Port Orleans, Dixie Landings, and Baton Rouge Lounge.

NEW YEAR'S EVE STREET PARTY – Throughout each evening, live bands and/or dancers entertain on the West End Stage, on the end of Hill Street. At a designated time each night (11 PM on Sunday-Thursday, midnight Friday and Saturday), a countdown begins: 10... 9... 8... As you reach zero, everybody is encouraged to shout "HAPPY NEW YEAR" at the top of his or her lungs, dance around, and revel in fireworks, search lights, music, dance, and a rain of confetti. The Island Explosion Dancers cavort on rooftops and the street party rages. Be sure you're outside at the designated time. It's New Year's Eve every evening here, and the party is a highlight of any visit to the Island. Guests are encouraged to get party hats, noisemakers, and even champagne to celebrate the occasion.

Shopping

AVIGATOR'S (934-7685) – Winged alligators mug on the label created exclusively for Pleasure Island. The "avigator" and the logo of the Adventurer's Club can be found on mugs, shirts, and magnets. Also, expedition wear, lightweight clothes of natural fabrics, leather jackets, and accessories are in stock.

JESSICA'S (934-7777) – Toontown's favorite torch song singer, the wife of Roger Rabbit, the one and only Jessica Rabbit, has her own boutique on Pleasure Island, where she sells accessories, gifts, and movie-related merchandise.

THE MOUSE HOUSE (934-7641) – Character merchandise is sold here in a more limited quantity and selection than in Mickey's Character Shop. Items include the usual array of t-shirts, sweatshirts, stuffed animals, mugs, keychains, books, gifts, and accessories.

CHANGING ATTITUDES (934-7692) – Everything is black and white at this unique shop. I don't mean that everything is clearly something, I mean that every item sold in the store is black and/or white. As trendy as stuff in SoHo or Melrose Place, the "new age" stock includes men's and women's apparel, electronics, jewelry, t-shirts, accessories, gifts, and specialty items.

HAMMER AND FIRE (934-7773) – An excellent place for handcrafted items, all unique, including jewelry, some of which is made of titanium, stoneware, platters, wall hangings, and decorative gifts. This shop has gained tremendous popularity among Floridians looking for a special, unusual gift.

DOODLES (934-7696) – Pleasure Island's self-proclaimed "party head-quarters". You can buy confetti, noisemakers, party hats, horns, and graphic t-shirts and memorabilia bearing the logos of the various clubs.

YESTEREARS (934-7680) – A nostalgic mix of Disneyana from the 30's and 40's, including character merchandise, dolls, puppets, posters, clothing, and figurines.

SUSPENDED ANIMATION (934-7683) – Original and reproduction posters, prints, lithographs, cels, and other animation art.

Other Entertainment

AMC PLEASURE ISLAND 10 THEATERS (827-1300) – A cinema multiplex is situated just west of the island, and you don't have to buy Pleasure Island admission or be over 18 to go. Ten first-run films are shown at once, call the number above for showtimes.

FRONT PAGE – You can appear on the cover of various national magazines for a fee. All needed accessories are provided.

SUPERSTAR STUDIOS – Lip sync to your favorite songs and star in a music video or use a karaoke machine to record your voice on tape.

STREET GAMES – Hill Street is peppered with midway-style games and folks who are willing to bet that they can guess your age, height, and weight. Also, street vendors sell everything from fruit-flavored ices to champagne, from t-shirts to noisemakers.

PROPELLOR HEADS – Pleasure Island's arcade features a good selection of video games and is open from 11 AM until 2 AM.

TYPHOON LAGOON

Once upon a time, on a tropical resort village, not so long ago, life was great. Then, a huge and terrible typhoon roared across the ocean and smashed into the village with all of its might. An earthquake and volcanic eruption turned bad to worse. Then, the clouds cleared, the cobwebs were cleaned, and **Typhoon Lagoon** was created. Flumes cut paths into once-impenetrable rock and formerly elegant buildings were now rubble. But most amazing of all was the sight of the Miss Tilly, a shrimp boat out of Safen Sound, Florida, atop 85-foot-high Mount Mayday. Every few minutes, the impaled craft attempts to free itself by sending a 50-foot stream of water into the air.

And there is the legend of Typhoon Lagoon, the most spectacular blend of water and imagination ever, and measuring 56 acres, it's the world's largest water park. Mount Mayday, incidentally, is the world's largest manmade watershed mountain.

GETTING AROUND – The bus station is located at the main entrance. **Magic Kingdom, Contemporary Resort, Polynesian Resort, Grand Floridian Resort:** Take the monorail (or from the MK, the ferry) to the

TTC and take the red-flagged bus.

TTC, EPCOT Center, Pleasure Island, or the Disney Village Marketplace: Take the red-flagged bus. Or, from the Marketplace or Pleasure Island, take the orange-and-white-flagged, purple-and-gold-flagged, or pink-and-green-flagged buses, all marked with a V.

Disney-MGM Studios Theme Park and Disney's Village Resort: Take the green-and-gold-flagged bus marked STV to the Marketplace and switch to one of the buses listed above.

Fort Wilderness: Take the blue-flagged bus to the TTC and switch to the red-flagged bus.

Disney Inn: Take the green-flagged bus to the TTC and switch to the red-flagged bus.

EPCOT Resorts: Take the purple-and-gold-flagged bus marked V.

Caribbean Beach Resort: Take the orange-and-white-flagged bus marked V.

Port Orleans, Dixie Landings, and Vacation Club Resorts: Take the pink-and-green-flagged bus marked V.

The Hotel Plaza: It is easiest to drive yourself or walk. But to get from the Plaza to Typhoon Lagoon by bus, take the red-and-white-flagged bus marked V to the Marketplace and switch to one of the buses listed above.

Off-site hotels in Lake Buena Vista: Take S.R. 535 to Hotel Plaza Blvd. and turn left at the Marketplace. The park will be on your left.

Off-site hotels via I-4: Take interchange 26B (EPCOT Center/Disney Village) into WDW, the exit for the Marketplace is the first one, turn right after getting off and follow the signs about a quarter of a mile. It'll be on your right.

PARKING – Parking at Typhoon Lagoon is free, but often on hot days, the lot fills up quickly.

ADMISSION – A one-day ticket costs $19.50 for adults and $15.50 for children between the ages of 3 and 9. Two-day passes are $31.80 for adults, $25.44 for kids. An annual pass is $75. With an Annual Theme Park Passport, it's $60. Added on to the Four Seasons Salute pass, it's $40.

Admission is included in five-and six-day Super Passes. After 4 PM in the summer, adults only pay $14.50, while a child's admission goes for $11.25.

RESTROOMS AND PHONES – Located at Typhoon Tilly's, Leaning Palms, and Ketchakiddie Creek.

VITAL STATISTICS

Location: Walt Disney World, P.O. Box 10,040, Lake Buena Vista, FL 32830-0040. *Phone:* 560-4100 or 560-4141. *Hours:* Opens 10 AM daily, closes at 9 PM in the summer, at 5 PM during the rest of the year. The park may close during January. *Admission:* $19.50 adults, $15.50 child. *Parking:* Free. *Time to See:* Four to six hours. *When to See:* From least to most crowded, Sunday, Friday, Monday, Tuesday, Saturday, Wednesday,Tuesday.

PRACTICAL INFORMATION – Age restriction: You must be 10 years of age to enter without an adult. **Alcoholic beverages:** You may not bring alcohol into the park. However, you can purchase it at Leaning Palms and Typhoon Tilly's. **Changing Rooms:** Located at Leaning Palms. **Dress Code:** Swim attire with buckles, rivets, or exposed metal is not allowed on water attractions. **First Aid:** Located at Leaning Palms.

Information: A park map is available at the entrance. **Lifeguards:** Highly trained and qualified, on hand at all attractions. **Life jackets:** Available for free at High and Dry Towels. A deposit is required, though. **Lockers:** Located near Shark Reef. **Lost and Found:** Located at High and Dry Towels. Due to the nature of some rides, glasses, jewelry, and loose articles should be removed beforehand. **Lost Children:** Report to High and Dry Towels. **Picnicing:** Allowed, as are coolers, however, glass bottles and alcohol may not be brought into the park.

Resting: There are hammocks and lounge chairs scattered throughout the beach. **Showers:** By Singapore Sal's. **Towels:** May be rented at High and Dry Towels. But it may be easier to bring your own. **Tube Rentals:** Available at Castaway Creek Raft Rental for use in bobbing wave pool, all tube ride attractions, and castaway creek. Tubes are not allowed in the surf pool. **Volleyball:** Nets are set up on the beach.

Attractions

TYPHOON LAGOON – The foremost attraction in Typhoon Lagoon is the one with the same name. This is a huge (2.75 million gallon) wave pool, pure and simple, and covers two acres. The waves here, released every ninety seconds, are either bobbing waves or the kind of waves adored by surfers and dreaded by landlubbers. It switches every hour. During the bobbing periods, tubing is allowed on the 2´ to 3´ foot waves. However, when the waves switch, ditch your tube and bear down for a 4´ to 6´ wave. I can personally vouch for the size of these waves. Only bodysurfing is allowed at the Lagoon during these times, and this is how you do it.

Watch several waves from onshore to get an idea of how to handle them. Then, hop in and swim about three fourths of the way to the wall from whence the waves come. When the machine lets one rip – you'll know by a buzzer, the crash of water, the screams of surfers, and the feeling that you get when your life flashes before your eyes. Now, swim towards the beach as fast as you can. The waves were created so that they will not slam you down on your face but either carry or bypass you.

WARNING: The biggest danger in the Lagoon is collisions. So, to avoid getting nailed, swim out past the crowd. Also, the lagoon's waves are known for their ability to remove everything from your body except your suit. Take off the glasses and watches, empty your pockets before jumping in. If you are more keen on swimming than surfing, go to Blustery Bay or Whitecap Cove, on either side of the surf pool.

CASTAWAY CREEK – If the excitement of the surf lagoon and the body slides has left you sapped, you will adore **Castaway Creek.** Just wade into the water from any one of the entrances, find a vacant tube floating by, and plop in. You can ride all the way around the 2,100-foot circuit or get out at any entrance point. There's never a line, and cruising along the 3-foot deep, 15-foot wide waterway is extremely placid. In the relaxing orientation tour of Typhoon Lagoon, you will travel under six bridges, through the **Water Works**, a mess of dripping pipes that overlooks the river, into the dark **Forgotten Grotto**, and through a delightfully misty and dense rain forest. A round trip takes about 30 minutes.

KETCHAKIDDIE CREEK – This area is open only to those of the under-four-feet persuasion. There are watered-down (no pun intended) slides, boats, fountains, waterfalls, a rapids ride, raft rides, bubbling jets, and assorted floating toys. Children must be accompanied by an adult.

RAFT RIDES – Three flumes on the south side of Mount Mayday offer the chance to board a small inner tubes for a journey down a river. All three rides measure about ten miles an hour. **Keelhaul Falls** allows you to spiral down a 400´ slide at a tame pace. **Gangplank Falls** puts you and up to three others on a six-foot-wide tube for a trip down a 300´ slide. In **Mayday Falls**, the most exciting of the three, the beginning is quick, then you slow down in a catch pool, then speed up for the rest of the 460-foot voyage. You must be four feet tall to ride Keelhaul and Mayday Falls.

HUMUNGA KOWABUNGA – Since they outlawed bungee jumping in Florida, the biggest thrill in the area is to stand at the center of Mount Mayday, look down on the action below, lay down in the rapidly flowing water streaming down the mountainside, wait for the attendant to raise the bar, and push off. You then drop like a rock, falling 51 feet down the 214-foot slide. The thrill is intense and the sensation of speed is greater than in roller coasters, because you are making the 30 mph journey with no car, no train, only your swimsuit. You must be four feet tall to ride. Pregnant women and those with back or neck problems are advised against riding. A wild ride, the view is a little bit sobering and the sight of the drop is scary, but it's over before you can shout "I haven't written my will!" – all too soon for many.

STORM SLIDES – These three wild adventures go by the names of Stern Burner, Jib Jammer, and Rudder Buster and put guests in a 20 mph downhill corkscrew. All three rides load from the same line and all take in pretty much the same route and the same sights. All are about 300 feet long and feature waterfalls, forests, caves, rocky crags, and other great scenery.

SHARK REEF – This is a chance to dive into the Living Seas. Here, you are equipped with fins, mask, snorkel, and wetsuit (you may not bring your own), then showered, and finally, instructed on your dive. You then plunge into the 72-degree salt-water pool, chock full of some 4,000 creatures, including nurse and bonnethead sharks, rays, and others, all clustered around the coral reef and the sunken tanker in the center of the pool.

Visit this attraction first thing in the morning, because the lines here build fast, and as an added bonus, when you dive early, often with very little in the way of fellow divers, attendants are more lenient when it comes to spending extra time in the pool and turning from the path. Otherwise, the attendants rush you through the pool and make the often hour-long investment of time seem unworthy.

MOUNT MAYDAY SCENIC OVERLOOK – You can take a path to the top of the mountain, where the view is exceptionally breathtaking.

SINGAPORE SAL'S SALEABLE SALVAGE – This building houses all the souvenirs sold in Typhoon Lagoon, mainly character merchandise, suntan lotion, film, swimsuits, sunglasses, hats, thongs, chairs, souvenirs, and clothing for men, women, and children. The atmosphere here is funky, with items displaced in the typhoon all over.

FORT WILDERNESS ATTRACTIONS

Fort Wilderness consists of a campground and resort with a Wild West theme, a zoological park, and a water park. The scenery is exceptionally beautiful here, and recreational choices abound. Streams and canals cut through the 740-acre swath of scrubby pine and cypress forest, and the air is thick with the sounds of cicadas and crickets. This is one of the most pleasant and overlooked spots in Walt Disney World.

GETTING AROUND

Magic Kingdom, Discovery Island: Take the green-flagged boat to the Fort Wilderness dock.

EPCOT Center, Disney Village Marketplace, Pleasure Island, and Typhoon Lagoon: Take the red-flagged bus or from EPCOT, the monorail, to the TTC and switch to the blue-flagged bus.

Disney-MGM Studios, Pleasure Island, Contemporary Resort: Take the gold-and-black-flagged bus marked STE. TTC: Take the blue-flagged bus.

Disney Village Marketplace: Take the red-flagged bus to the TTC and switch to the blue-flagged bus.

Polynesian Resort, Contemporary Resort, and Grand Floridian: Take the monorail to the Magic Kingdom and switch to the green-flagged boat or take the monorail to the TTC and switch to the blue-flagged bus.

Disney Inn: Take the green-flagged bus to the Magic Kingdom and switch to the green-flagged boat.

EPCOT Resorts: Take the purple-and-gold-flagged bus marked MK to the Kingdom and switch to the green-flagged boat.

Caribbean Beach Resort: Take the orange-and-white-flagged bus marked MK to the Kingdom and switch to the green-flagged boat.

Disney's Village Resort: Take the green-and-gold-flagged bus marked MK to the Kingdom and switch to the green-flagged boat.

Port Orleans, Dixie Landings, and Vacation Club Resorts: Take the pink-and-green-flagged bus marked MK to the Magic Kingdom and switch to the green-flagged boat.

Hotel Plaza: Take the red-and-white-flagged bus to the Magic Kingdom and switch to the green-flagged boat. Off-site hotels via U.S. 192: Take World Drive to Vista Boulevard. Turn right and take it to Fort Wilderness Trail, about a mile past, on your left.

Off-site hotels from Lake Buena Vista and I-4: Exit from I-4 at S.R. 535 North. Take it to Vista Blvd. (about ¨ mile past the entrance to the Grand Cypress Golf Club) and turn left. Take Vista Blvd. to Fort Wilderness Trail, about 2 miles.

PARKING – Parking at Fort Wilderness costs $4 per car.

RIVER COUNTRY

Before Typhoon Lagoon, there was **River Country**. Opened in 1976 at Fort Wilderness on the shores of Bay Lake, this was designed as the archetypical swimming hole, the kind of place where Huck Finn and Tom

Sawyer would frequent. There are fewer slides and rides here, making for longer lines, but there's not as much in the way of crowds. Relaxation is stressed more than excitement here.

ADMISSION – A **one-day ticket** costs $12.50 for adults and $10.00 for children between the ages of 3 and 9. **Two-day passes** are $18.82 for adults, $14.58 for kids. An **annual pass** costs $50. A **combination River Country-Discovery Island ticket** costs $15.75 for adults, $11.50 for children. Annual combination passes, when purchased with a Four Seasons Salute Pass, are $20. With an **Annual Passport**, it's $30. Admissions to both are included in five-and six-day Super Passes.

VITAL STATISTICS

Location: Walt Disney World, P.O. Box 10,040, Lake Buena Vista, FL 32830-0040. *Phone:* 824-2760. *Hours:* Opens 10 AM daily, closes at 8 PM in the summer, at 5 PM during the rest of the year. The park closes from January to mid-February. *Admission:* $12.50 adults, $10.00 child. *Parking:* $4. *Time to See:* Three to four hours. *When to See:* Anytime except summer weekends.

PRACTICAL INFORMATION – **Age restriction:** You must be 10 years of age to enter without an adult. **Alcoholic beverages:** You may not bring alcohol into the park. However, you can purchase it at Pop's Place and Waterin' Hole. **Dress Code:** Swim attire with buckles, rivets, or exposed metal is not allowed on water attractions. Information: A park map is available at the entrance. **Lifeguards:** Highly trained and qualified, on hand at all attractions.

   Lockers: Located near the entrance. **Picnicing:** Allowed, as are coolers, however, glass bottles and alcoholic beverages can not be brought into the park. **Resting:** There are hammocks and lounge chairs scattered throughout the beach. **Towels:** Small towels can be rented. But it may be easier to bring your own.

Activities
BAY COVE – This, a roped-off section of Bay Lake, is the main part of River Country. Swimming here is delightful, as is riding a tire swing or jumping off a ship's bow.

OL' SWIMMIN' HOLE – There is a kidney-shaped, 330,000-gallon heated swimming pool and the adjacent **Ol' Wadin' Pool**, perfect for the young'uns.

SLIPPERY SLIDE FALLS AND WHOOP'N'HOLLER HOLLOW – These two waterslides feature similar rides down a hillside on your back, one flume 260 feet long, the other, about 100 feet less. Both spit you out into Bay Cove.

WHITE WATER RAPIDS – You board an innertube for a pleasant, tame journey down a winding stream about ten feet wide from Raft Rider Ridge to Bay Cove. It's not as exciting as the flumes, but some people consider it a better ride.

UPSTREAM PLUNGE – Here, you plunge down one of two slides into the Ol' Swimmin Hole. As you fly out of the chute, seven feet above the water, the sensation is as close to flight as man gets.

RIVER RELICS – This is the place where you can buy film, sundries, and souvenirs of River Country.

DISCOVERY ISLAND

Discovery Island is best described as a decompression park for the hype, excitement, and glitter of the rest of the Vacation Kingdom. The 11-acre oasis, right in the middle of Bay Lake, was originally planned as a recreation of the scene from **Treasure Island**. But the theme was replaced by that of a cage-free aviary, with no evidence of the former plans save the lush scenery and the wrecked sailing ship on the beach.

ADMISSION – A ticket costs $8.00 for adults, $4.50 for children. A combination River Country-Discovery Island ticket costs $15.75 for adults, $11.50 for children. Admission to both is included in a five- or six-day Super Pass. An **annual combination pass** costs $30 with a Annual Theme Park Passport, $20 with a Four Season Salute pass.

PHONES – Located at the Thirsty Perch and next to Seaside Sparrow Study.

RESTROOMS – Found next to Seaside Sparrow Study and Eagle's Watch.

VITAL STATISTICS
Location: Walt Disney World, P.O. Box 10,040, Lake Buena Vista, FL 32830-0040. *Phone:* 824-3784. *Hours:* Opens 10 AM daily, closes at 7 PM in the summer, at 5:30 PM during the rest of the year. *Admission:* $8.00 for adults, $4.50 for children. *Parking:* $4 at Fort Wilderness. *Time to See:* Two hours. *When to See:* Anytime, but morning is best.

PRACTICAL INFORMATION – **Age restriction:** You must be 7 years of age to enter without an adult. **Alcoholic beverages:** You may not bring alcohol into the park. However, you can purchase it at the Thirsty Perch. **Baby Services:** There are changing tables in all restrooms. **Information:** A park map is available at the entrance. **Picnicing:** Allowed, as are coolers, however, glass bottles and alcoholic beverages can not be brought into the park. **Strollers and Wheelchairs:** Available for loan at the dock.

What to Do

There are over 90 species of animals at Discovery Island, plus 250 species of plants. The animals include hornbills, Caribbean flamingos, brush turkeys, kookaburras, scarlet ibis, trumpeter swans, toucans, ravens, bald eagles, brown pelicans, snowy egrets, great blue herons, American alligators, Galapagos tortoises, Patagonian cavies, miniature deer, golden lion tamarins, and ring-tailed lemurs. The last two are endangered primates. The tamarins are especially beautiful. The exotic animals, many facing extinction, others permanently injured and unable to survive in the wild, thrive in the tropical haven, which is devoted to man's love and respect for nature as well as to research and preservation.

Discovery Island, a certified zoological park, often exchanges animals with other zoos. The American Association of Zoological Parks and Aquariums has designated Discovery Island as the species manager of the rare Scarlet Ibis. Even if you live near the Philadelphia, Bronx, National, or other zoos, visit Discovery Island: it's in a class by itself.

DISCOVERY ISLAND KIDVENTURE – Kids 8 to 14 can explore Fort Wilderness and Discovery Island on four-hour guided tours daily during June, July, and August, sporadically during the rest of the year.

The cost is $25 and includes lunch, transportation, craft materials, and a souvenir photo. Reservations can be made by calling 824-3784.

DISNEY'S BOARDWALK

Opening Spring 1994, the **Boardwalk** will be a entertainment, shopping, and dining complex that pays homage to the glory days of boardwalks in places like Coney Island and Atlantic City. The 30-acre project can be found just west of EPCOT Center between the International Gateway and the Swan Hotel.

Robert A. M. Stern, creator of the Yacht and Beach Clubs, is the project's architect, which includes a 530-unit, all-suite hotel; **Under the Sea**, a 900-seat indoor aquatic dinner show starring Ariel and Sebastian from The Little Mermaid; **Disney Magic**, a dinner show that incorporates the Disney characters with magic; **Family Reunion**, a 300-seat environmental dinner show that literally puts performers in the audience's laps; **Walt's Attic**, a family-style restaurant featuring rare Disney memorabilia;

an antique carousel; a lighted Ferris wheel; saltwater taffy vendors, jugglers, and mimes entertaining passers-by on the boardwalk; two night clubs; various midway-style games; and several shops, including a new Disney department store.

WONDERS OF WALT DISNEY WORLD

These are **educational programs** for children 10 to 15 years old. Each program costs $75 and includes a book, classroom materials, access to the parks and backstage areas, lunch, a rental camera with free film, a completion certificate, and a book of follow-up activities. All three tours meet at the Wonders Greeting Area at the TTC. For reservations, call 345-5860 as soon as you make your hotel reservations. The first of the six-hour programs is **Art Magic**, which features a visit from a Disney animator and tours of the art studios inside EPCOT and the Magic Kingdom.

The climax is a drawing workshop, and participants take home a sketch book. In **Exploring Nature**, the participants listen to a discussion and film on the delicate balance of the Florida ecosystem followed by trips to Discovery Island and the 7,500-acre tract of land set aside for conservation. The third program, **Show Biz Magic**, is a "behind-the-scenes look at the hard work, dedication, and pixie dust it takes to put on a great show every time." You first watch an audition and rehearsal at the Studios, then head under the Magic Kingdom, yes, UNDER. There, you check out the Costuming and Wig and Make-up departments, participants watch a performance of the Diamond Horseshoe Revue.

After the show, they meet a cast member and see how lighting, props, sets, and costumes are mixed to create the show. *HINT:* Students who travel to WDW during the school year may be able to earn classroom credit by taking one or more of the Wonders programs. Ask your teacher or principal for details.

If you're over fifteen years old, don't fret: Disney has several programs for you. The Disney Learning Adventures include **Gardens of the World**, in which you head to World Showcase and learn about the various forms of horticulture around the Lagoon, explained to you by a Disney staffer; and **Hidden Treasures of World Showcase**, which details the art, architecture, costumes, landscape, and entertainment in each of the World Showcase pavilions. Both plans are $20 plus park admission, and each lasts about three hours.

For business and convention travelers, special programs are available, including **Innovation in Action** (in which guests are given a full tour of the underground tunnels beneath the Magic Kingdom), **Art and Science of Gardening** (in which guests visit the topiaries and nurseries of WDW), **Disney Approach to People Management**, **Disney Approach to**

Quality Service, Building Positive Images, Making Magic: Communicating your Message, The Show Behind the Show (similar to the "Show Biz Magic" Wonders program), and the **World Showcase Fellowship Program**, in which guests participate in a seminar that discusses the lifestyles of college students from the nations represented in the Showcase nations.

For information on all the programs discussed above, call 828-1500 or 345-5860, or write **Walt Disney World Seminar Productions**, Box 10,000, Lake Buena Vista, FL 32830.

14. SEA WORLD OF FLORIDA

INTRODUCTION

Central Florida's other World is devoted to marine life, and is the most popular marine attraction in the world, with over 4 million visitors each year. **Sea World**, with more than 200 acres, has a completely different feel to it than WDW. The pathways are wider, the pace of things more leisurely, more Floridian. Oh, did I mention that there are no Audio-Animatronics here? Every animal is real.

When seen towards the end of your vacation, Sea World serves almost as a decompression chamber, to allow you to recover from the vacation. Most of the attractions are shows held in stadiums big enough to accommodate several thousand people at once, so waiting and lines are rare. Also, snacks and beverages are sold in the bleachers where the shows are performed. Smoking is prohibited in all stadiums, gift shops, and restaurants. Sea World celebrated its 20th anniversary in 1993.

GETTING AROUND – To get to Sea World from:

Walt Disney World: Take I-4 east to exit 27A. The park will be on your right. Or, take EPCOT Center Drive, which will turn into International Drive. Take I-Drive to the Central Florida Parkway, and turn left.

Kissimmee: Take I-4 east to exit 27A. The park will be on your right.

Lake Buena Vista: Take I-4 east to exit 27A. The park will be on your right. Or, take S.R. 535 south to International Drive, turn left, and take I-Drive to the Central Florida Parkway, turn left.

International Drive, Sand Lake Drive: Take International Drive south to Central Florida Parkway, turn right.

Orange Blossom Trail: Take the Trail to the Central Florida Parkway, go west past I-Drive.

Downtown: Take I-4 to Exit 28 (Beeline Expressway). Take the first exit from the Beeline (International Drive). Turn left, go under the highway, and turn right at the Central Florida Parkway.

PARKING – The parking lot at Sea World is large; parking costs $5 per car and $7 per RV. Be sure to write down where you park.

ADMISSION – Sea World tickets are available in several incarnations, being the one-day pass, week-long pass, annual pass, and annual Busch Parks pass. The latter includes one year's admission to Busch Gardens, Cypress Gardens, and Sea World plus parking. Don't forget, prices are subject to change.

SEA WORLD PRICES		
	Adults	Kids 3-9
One-Day Admission	$32.95	$28.95
Two-Day Admission	$37.95	$33.95
Annual Admission	$59.95	$49.95
Annual 3-Park Admission	$115.95	$105.95

Admission includes all shows and rides except the Sky Tower, radio-controlled boats, guided tours, and luaus.

MONEY – There is a currency exchange service at the Special Services window at the main gate. There is also a 24-hour Cirrus automated teller machine at the entrance. Mastercard, and Visa are accepted in the park.

VITAL STATISTICS
Location: 7007 Sea World Drive, Orlando, FL 32821. *Phone:* 351-3600, 363-2200. *Hours:* Park opens at 9 AM. Closing hours vary. *Admission:* $32.95 for adults, $28.95 ages 3-9, kids under 2 free. *Parking:* $5. *Time to See:* One full day. *When to See:* Monday, Tuesday, or Wednesday. *Don't Miss:* Mission: Bermuda Triangle, Manatees: The Last Generation, Shamu: New Visions, Terrors of the Deep, Penguin Encounter, Shamu Night Magic, Gold Rush Ski Show.

PRACTICAL INFORMATION – **Alcoholic Beverages:** Allowed, sold at Bimini Bay Cafe and many counter-service eateries. **Baby Services:** Diaper changing facilities are located adjacent to most ladies' restrooms. Nursing facilities are located next to Penguin Encounter. **Baby Strollers:** Available for rental at the Information Center. **Banking:** An ATM machine is located at the entrance.

Cameras: Available for loan at Shamu Emporium. **Dress Code:** Shirts and shoes must be worn at all times. **First Aid:** Registered nurses are on duty. In an emergency, ask the nearest Sea World employee to contact one. **Information:** When you arrive, visit the Information Counter on the left side of the plaza. You will receive a personalized, computer-prepared map and show schedule designed to help you see as much of the park as possible without conflicts. This service is free, yet valuable. **Kennel:** Free, self-service, south of main entrance.

Lockers: By the Information Center by the main entrance. **Lost and**

Found: Report to or claim at the Information Center by the main entrance. **Lost Parents:** If you find yourself lost from your children, report to the Information Center by the main entrance.

Picnicing: Tables can be found in Atlantis Plaza, by the Atlantis Theater. However, it is wise to call ahead, as this may be reserved for private company events. **Same Day Reentry:** Get your hand stamped at the entrance. **Wheelchair Guests:** Wheelchair rental is available at the Information Center. Wheelchair ramps and facilities are located throughout the park and at all show areas. Sea Lion and Otter viewing area has a special entrance. Viewing areas are inside the other attractions.

Shows
CLYDE AND SEAMORE
Rating: 8. *Location:* At the Sea Lion and Otter Stadium. *Duration of Show:* 30 minutes.

This is a fun show starring two sea lions, **Clyde and Seamore**, plus an otter who drinks Pepsi while dancing to Michael Jackson's "Bad." The sea lions dart around a stunning set which conveys the hotel setting, and also play tricks on the humans in the show: **Harry** and **Foible**, animal trainers dressed as hotel managers. This show is enjoyable and well worth your time. *HINT:* Arrive 15 minutes before showtime and you will be able to watch a white-faced mime taunt audience members.

GOLD RUSH SKI SHOW
Rating: 10. Not to be missed. *Location:* Atlantis Stadium. *Duration of Show:* 35 minutes.

This show is a well-done blend of comedy, thrills, American history, and pure energy that rarely ceases to amaze. In this show, the good guys and the bad guys square off in a battle of skis, ending with the climactic duel in which skiers perform aerial somersaults at 90 MPH. Remember "The Devil Went Down to Georgia?" – the duel scene is a take-off of the classic Charlie Daniels Band song. The finale of the show is a 13-person human pyramid. After the show, you can meet the skiers, who pose for autographs and photos.

HAWAIIAN RHYTHMS
Rating: 4. *Location:* Hawaiian Village Theater. *Duration of Show:* 25 minutes.

What exactly is the purpose of this show? No other attraction in Sea World has anything to do with Hawaii. **Hawaiian Rhythms** consists of a three-man band and three dancing women. Many in the crowd leave before the show ends.

SHAMU: NEW VISIONS

Rating: 10. Not to be missed. *Location:* At Shamu Stadium. *Duration of Show:* 25 minutes.

The world's most famous killer whales star in this show, which features a handful of trainers, a quartet of video cameras, and a DiamondVision-like monitor. James Earl Jones narrates this presentation, in which **Shamu, Baby Shamu,** and **Baby Namu** cavort around the pool. If you have doubts about the intelligence of the whales, they will vanish when the whales interact with the audience and trainers. One of the most heart-warming moments is when Shamu sits on a platform and lets a child selected from the audience sit on his back. This show is not to be missed.

KILLER WHALE WORKOUT

WHALE & DOLPHIN DISCOVERY

Rating: 7. *Location:* At the Whale & Dolphin Stadium. *Duration of Show:* 30 minutes.

This endearing show features whales and dolphins from around the world, and you will be surprised by the grace and agility of the beasts. Whales respond to trainers orders to dance or take a bow, all in tune to the music. Dolphins take trainers water-skiing by letting him put each foot on a dolphin's back and let them cart him around the stadium.

WINDOW TO THE SEA

Rating: 8. Not to be missed. *Location:* At the Fantasy Theater. *Duration of Show:* 20 minutes. *Comments:* This show only plays during daylight.

This multi-media presentation offers an overview of Sea World. The show opens with "dancing waters" synchronized with music. Then, the curtain goes up, revealing aquariums, consoles, and monitors. The film section of the presentation includes comprehensive interviews and narratives. It is well-done and not to be missed.

NIGHT MAGIC

Rating: 9. Not to be missed. *Location:* Throughout the park. *Duration of Show:* Not applicable. *Comments:* This only occurs during peak seasons.

When the park is open late, Shamu stars in a new show at Shamu Stadium, with a festive atmosphere all over the park. There is a special magic show at the Fantasy Theater, plus a spectacular fireworks ballet, complete with lasers and dancing waters. There is also live entertainment.

Exhibits
PENGUIN ENCOUNTER

Rating: 9 1/2. *Location:* Next to Sea Lion and Otter Stadium.

A moving sidewalk carries you past over 200 penguins, plus puffins and other Antarctic sea birds. The indoor, glassed-in "penguin pen" is so Antarcticly chilly that it actually snows. "It's ninety-five in the shade out here, and those penguins get a ski slope," summer visitors often lament.

TERRORS OF THE DEEP

Rating: 8 1/2. *Location:* Sea World Theater.

Here, you travel down a moving sidewalk in a tunnel through an aquarium featuring the deadliest creatures to ever roam the oceans. That's right, through the aquarium. There's 500 tons of sea water above and around you along with creatures like the surgeon-fish, sharks, lionfish, puffer-fish, scorpion-fish, and more. But "Terrors" is a little of an exaggeration. It won't scare the pants off of anyone (just remember that six inch pane of acrylic all around you when staring down a shark), but it affords enough fright for the truly chicken-hearted.

TROPICAL REEF
Rating: 7 1/2. *Location:* Sea World Theater.

The Reef is a 160,000-gallon pool illuminated by neon coral bigger than a house. The exhibit's inhabitants include raccoon butterfly-fish, morey eels, lobsters, surgeon-fish, clownfish, Florida alligators, fanged baby sharks, and more. This exhibit is to conventional aquariums what Space Mountain is to conventional roller coasters. It's something special, one of the reasons people spend thirty bucks to get in.

STINGRAY LAGOONS, DOLPHIN COMMUNITY POOLS, SEA LION AND SEAL COMMUNITY POOLS
Rating: 7 1/2. *Location:* Between main entrance and Cap'n Kids' World.

Where else do you get the chance to come nose-to-soggy-nose with a dolphin, seal, or stingray? You can feed them, pet them, touch them, and learn about their species.

Play Areas
SHAMU'S HAPPY HARBOR
Rating: 8 1/2. *Location:* By Shamu Stadium. *Comments:* Closes at dusk.

This is an all-new, 3-acre play area, kind of a souped-up Cap'n Kids'. The equipment includes four stories of cargo netting, steel drums that guests can smash away on, a water maze, radio-controlled cars, an air bounce, slides, crow's nests, ball crawls, and vinyl mountains. Like at Cap'n Kid's, there are restrooms and an abundance of shaded seating. **Boogie Bump Bay**, a smaller area, is intended specifically for kids 3' 6" or less and features scaled-down versions of most of the equipment.

Rides
MISSION: BERMUDA TRIANGLE
Rating: 10. Absolutely not to be missed. *Location:* By Shamu Stadium.

In this ride, guests board flight simulators similar to those found in

Body Wars and Star Tours for a trip to the bottom of the 440,000-square mile section of the Atlantic that has spelled the doom of hundreds of ships and planes over the years. The "divers" board one of three, 59-seat "subs" and head off on the adventure with a high-definition, undersea film, which with the flight simulation, is as close as many will ever come to the Triangle and live to tell about it. "Riders will feel acceleration, increased g-forces, and other sensations of speed," Busch Entertainment Corporation vice president Joe Peczi explains, likening the experience to flight. This simulator is comparable to those in EPCOT and the Studios, and this one has more realism. See it before 11 AM if you can.

SKY TOWER
Rating: 6 1/2. *Location:* A landmark. *Comments:* Costs $3.18 extra per ride, per person.

For a few bucks, you can buy a ticket, then ride an elevator up a 400-foot tower to a superb vantage point from which you can see not only all of Sea World, but most of International Drive, the airport, and even Walt Disney World. One of only two real rides at Sea World, waits for this 15-minute ride seldom exceed a quarter of an hour.

ANHEUSER-BUSCH HOSPITALITY CENTER – This new, 5 1/2-acre center offers guests a chance to relax and enjoy the natural beauty of the park. The facility includes a 17,000-square foot **Hospitality House** and a **Clydesdale Hamlet**.

The Hospitality House is a prime example of Florida architecture, the white-steel structure featuring floor-to-ceiling glass walls, giving the entire house an open-air feeling. An outdoor terrace offers a splendid view of waterfalls, gardens, and the Clydesdale Hamlet. It's a relaxing spot to enjoy a snack or sample complimentary Anheuser-Busch products, including Michelob and Bud.

Guided Tours
In the **Backstage Exploration Tour**, a 90-minute backstage tour, guests are given the chance to see the park's breeding, research, and training facilities, see the working side of the marine life park, learn how Sea World cares for endangered and beached animals, observe the Penguin Incubation and Laboratory Facilities. The other, the **Animal Training Tour**, offers a chance to see an actual training session, learn how important trainer-animal relationships are forged, and meet a Sea World trainer.

The cost for one tour is $5.95 for adults, $4.95 for children. Both tours will set adults back $10.50 each, $9.50 for kids. Tour costs are in addition to park admission, and their worth is dependant on your interest in the subject. Reservations can be made at the Information Counter by the entrance.

"ALOHA" POLYNESIAN LUAU – At 6:35 each night at the **Luau Terrace**, a troupe of talented Polynesian singers, dancers, and musicians practice their craft to the accompaniment of tropical food and drink. The cost is $29.63 for adults, $20.09 for juniors, $10.55 for children. For reservations or information, call 351-6000, ext. 2559, 363-2559, or 800/ 227-8048.

Shopping

Sea World has many shops within its confines, some of them worthwhile and some of them worthless. Some of the better places to stop in are **Sandcastle Toys-n-Treats** for toys, games, and electronics; **Fashionations** and **Florida Gifts** for sportswear, swimwear, and Florida-themed gifts; the **Flamingo Point** for Polynesian curios and clothing; the **Shell Shop** for all things exoskeletal; **Ocean Treasures** for nautical gifts and shark items;photo keepsakes can be made at **Key Hole Photo, Sea Search Photo** or **Amazing Pictures**; and **Shamu's Emporium** for sundries, sportswear, gifts, candy, cigarettes, and souvenirs.

15. UNIVERSAL STUDIOS FLORIDA

INTRODUCTION

Universal is probably the single best-known name in studio tours. And that was before 1990, when it opened its new theme park in Kirkman Road south of downtown Orlando. The tram tour at Universal Studios California had experiences with earthquakes, giant apes, great white sharks, and more. Each of these, and more, have received entire attractions. So the person who decides not to visit Universal Florida because he's already been to Universal on the left coast is akin to someone skipping Disney World because he went to Disneyland.

Not so long ago, planning an Orlando vacation was merely intricate, but it's now as complex as a can of worms with the introduction of this park, the baby of MCA Inc. and Rank Organization PLC, especially if you have limited time in the area. Universal opened to generally good reviews in July 1990. But the $630 million question is, "Should my family visit Universal or MGM?" The decision depends on a lot of factors. But you may ask which a subjective question like, "Which park is better?" Let's check out the tale of the tape.

GETTING THERE – From Disney, Lake Buena Vista, and Kissimmee hostelries, MGM is infinitely more accessible. Universal is closer to the downtown and International Drive areas. Parking is about $4 at both places.

ADMISSION – If you are purchasing a multi-day Disney passport, then by all means, check out MGM. However, if you're buying individual tickets, and this is interesting, MGM will set you back $34 plus tax for an adult ticket and $27 plus tax for a child 3 to 9 years old; Universal will run you $33 for an adult and $26 for a kid.

TOURING TIME & OTHER BASICS – To see all that MGM has to offer, it takes somewhere in the neighborhood of six hours. Universal takes about nine hours.

• **Lines** – Lines are much quicker-moving in the Disney-MGM Studios.

• **Size** – Universal covers more than 440 acres, more than double the size of MGM. If you think you can't handle the walking, MGM will be more foot-friendly.

• **Children** – Disney-MGM is more family-oriented in most of its presentations, while Universal is somewhat more adult.

• **Attractions** – The studio tour is exponentially better at Disney-MGM. The stunt shows are comparable, and Universal gets the hands-down victory in the thrill ride department, by virtue of the number and quality of the rides there. Universal's interactive areas are far greater in number than MGM's. Disney-MGM alone has a nostalgic look at movies through the ages (Great Movie Ride), a 3D film (Muppet*Vision 4D), and an animation studio. Universal alone has a make-up show (Gory, Gruesome, and Grotesque Make-up Show), an animal show (Animal Actors Stage), and a children's playground (Fievel's Playland).

• **Food** – Without a question, Universal has better, more varied menus.

If you are a movie buff, or a theme park buff, check out both parks. Each is worthwhile, and you will definitely enjoy yourself at either. As far as the presentations go, Disney's are more comprehensive, educational, and seamless, while Universal is flawed in this department.

GETTING AROUND – To get to Universal Studios from:

Walt Disney World, Kissimmee, Lake Buena Vista: Take I-4 east to Exit 29. Turn left onto Sand Lake Drive, take it to Turkey Lake Drive, and go 1.6 miles to the entrance.

International Drive (Sand Lake Drive and south): Turn left on Sand Lake Drive, take it to Turkey Lake Drive, and go 1.6 miles to the entrance.

International Drive (North of Sand Lake Drive): Take I-Drive north to Kirkman Road, turn left. Take Kirkman 1.1 miles to the entrance.

Downtown and points northeast: Take I-4 west to exit 30B. Take Kirkman Road to the entrance.

PARKING – The Universal lot contains 7,100 spaces. The cost is $4; $6 for RV's and trailers. There is no cost for leaving and returning on the same day. Keep your receipt and WRITE DOWN where you parked.

ADMISSION

An admission ticket includes the use of all attractions. Listed below are the ticket options. Note that Universal tickets are available at discounts at several locations throughout the city. Children under 3 years of age are admitted free.

See the chart on the following page for prices:

> **One-Day Ticket:** $33 adult, $26 kids 3-9.
> **Two-Day Ticket:** $53 adult, $42 kids 3-9.
> **Annual Celebrity Pass:** $85 adult, $67.50, kids 3-9.
> (unlimited admission for a year)

MONEY – A branch of the Southeast Bank is located just inside the main entrance, offering full financial services. American Express, Visa, Mastercard, and Discover are accepted.

PACKAGE PICKUP – This service lets you send your packages to Guest Relations, where you can pick them up at the end of the day.

DRESS CODE – Shirts and shoes are required.

> ### VITAL STATISTICS
> *Location:* 1000 Universal Studios Plaza, Orlando, FL 32819-7610. *Phone:* 363-8200, 363-8210, 363-8220, 262-8182. *Hours:* Opens at 9 AM. Closing hours vary. *Admission:* $33 adults, $26 kids 3-9. *Parking:* $4. *Time to see:* A full day. *When to see:* From least to most crowded, Sunday, Friday, Monday, Saturday, Wednesday, Tuesday, Thursday. *Don't Miss:* Back to the Future...The Ride!, E.T. Adventure, Kongfrontation, The FUNtastic World of Hanna Barbera, "Alfred Hitchcock: The Art of Making Movies."

PRACTICAL INFORMATION

Alcoholic Beverages: Allowed, sold at most table-service establishments. **Baby Relations:** Located at Guest Relations and First Aid. Changing tables are available in all restrooms. **Baby Strollers:** Can be rented next to Southeastern Bank. **Banking:** There is an automated teller machine next to the Production Information Window at the Main Entrance. **Cameras:** Lights, Camera, Action! offers video cameras for rent, still cameras for loan, and film and tape for sale. Photos can be developed in one hour at The Darkroom. **Cigarettes:** Available at most shops throughout the park.

First Aid: Located By Louie's Italian Restaurant. **Foreign Language Assistance:** Foreign language maps and assistance are available at Guest Relations. **Guided Tours:** A VIP Tour is available for groups up to 15 people. For $91 apiece, you can roam the park with your own tour guide. Each tour consists of a maximum of 15 people who roam the park and receive the invaluable (in peak seasons) privilege of being able to bypass any line. If you've got $900 burning a hole in your pocket, you can get an exclusive tour with a guide and whoever you choose, whereas the VIP Tour consists of you and 14 other people who you may or may not know.

If you visit during peak season and have the extra cash, the tour can save you hours of waiting. Whether or not it's worth the price tag, it's a matter of opinion.

Hearing-impaired Guests: A Telecommunications Device for the Deaf (TDD) is available at Guest Relations. **Information:** To get facts about attractions, shows, and dining, visit the Guest Relations office. Also, information booths are located at Amblin Ave. and 57th Street and elsewhere in the park. Also, the board in front of Mel's Diner lists which attractions have the longest and shortest waits. **Kennel:** Pets are not allowed in Universal Studios. There is, however, an air-conditioned kennel next to the Toll Plaza. Reservations are not needed.

Lockers: Available for 50¢ per use, located next to the park exit and by the group entrance. **Lost Children:** Report to Guest Relations. **Reservations:** Accepted at Lombard's Landing and Studio Stars. Make in person as soon as possible. **Smoking, eating, and drinking:** For the enjoyment of other guests, smoking, eating, and drinking are not allowed in any attractions. **Wheelchair guests:** Wheelchair rentals are available in limited quantities next to Southeastern Bank.

Ride the Movies
BACK TO THE FUTURE... THE RIDE!
Rating: 10!!!!! *Arguably the single best theme park ride in Florida.* *Location:* Expo Center, between the Animal Actor's Stage and the Amity side of the Lagoon. *Duration of Ride:* 4 1/2 minutes. *Comments:* Riders must be 3'10". As this is a very rough ride, it will sometimes induce motion sickness. Switching off and child swapping is available. This ride is not recommended for those with back or neck problems, heart conditions, or claustrophobia, also not recommended for pregnant women. *Frightening?* Yes. The effects are visual — very visual, and physical — very, very physical.

This ride can be summed up in one word: **WOW!** The **Back to the Future** trilogy was one of the most popular series in the past decade, and the ride almost serves as yet another sequel, except that it stars you as the intrepid time travelers. You will wander the halls of the Institute of Future Technology to reach a pre-show area where Doc Brown (Christopher Lloyd) informs you that he has completed a batch of faster, more efficient, eight-passenger Deloreans-turned-time machines. He also glumly tells you that Biff Tannen (Thomas Wilson) has broken into the Institute and is plotting something not quite kosher. You have to hop into your time machine (which bears Florida license plate OUTATIME) and set off into a hemispherical, seven-story Omnimax theater with incredible flight-simulation effects. The liquid-nitrogen fog, the perfectly-timed hydraulic jolts, the 70mm film, and the multi-channel stereo surround sound all enhance the astonishing realism of the production.

On your journey, you chase Biff back past Leonardo da Vinci, the Wright Brothers, and over waterfalls, cliffs, and canyons, eventually into the mouth of a Tyrannosaurus Rex, over the lip of a volcano, and... well, let's just say that this is a quite intense ride from beginning to end. Kids over eight will usually love this ride, however, with younger kids, the fright potential is very high.

This ride is perpetually crowded, as it is THE ride of rides, and appropriately, the wait is THE wait of waits. Up to two hours in peak seasons. By contrast, Back to the Future is usually all but empty as closing time approaches. But in an optimum situation, a guest would get to the park before opening and as soon as the gate drops, rush to The FUNtastic World of Hanna-Barbera and then E.T. Adventure, this way bypassing the first-ride rush that it experiences each morning, and then being able to experience it during a relative hiatus. The ride is unlike anything else in Orlando, so if you only had one ride to experience in Orlando, you should make Back to the Future that one ride.

KONGFRONTATION

Rating: 6. An excellent ride adventure, well done. *Location:* New York, off 5th Avenue. *Duration of Ride:* 4 1/2 minutes. *Comments:* Riders must be 3'4". Children under 3 and expectant mothers are not allowed to ride. *Frightening:* Yes. Kong is extremely realistic, the ride is compellingly intense.

Another one of the premier attractions in Universal, **Kongfrontation** sets the tone immediately as you wander through a queue area designed after a subway terminal. As you wander through the area, notice the graffiti on the walls. Some of it was applied by artists prior to the attraction's opening. As for the majority of them, let's just say that some guests brought their own writing utensils. As you walk through the area, overhead television monitors tell of King Kong's rampage via news broadcast.

You finally reach the boarding area, where you are put on an aerial tram to Roosevelt Island. As you rise over the city, you can sense that something is wrong. Everywhere you look are fires, crushed buildings, broken water lines, and aerial trams-turned-scrap metal. Finally, you reach the Queensboro Bridge and there he is, all six tons of him. He grabs your tram and as he is about to smash it, a helicopter starts shooting at him and well, prepare to drop at 1.75 Gs. The tram somehow manages to get back to the ground intact, and a TV in the tram shows a news clip about your close call. The ride is very popular, but can be seen with a minimum wait in the first hour the park is open and after 6 PM.

E.T. ADVENTURE

Rating: 9. Well done, not to be missed. *Location:* Expo Center, between the Hard Rock Cafe and Hollywood. *Duration of Ride:* 4 1/2 minutes. *Comments:* Handicapped guests and those who are put off by the idea of sitting on a bike can ride in a gondola that follows the bikes.

Many people consider *E. T.* to be Steven Spielberg's crowning achievement, even though it lost the Best Picture Oscar to *Gandhi*. Nevertheless, it serves as the basis for this spectacular ride adventure in which you board a bike or a gondola and set off through a redwood forest to E.T.'s home planet. Once there, you meet E.T's playmates, including mini-E.T.'s, dancing flowers, and other exotic flora and fauna. At the end of the ride, E.T. thanks you by name.

How does he do this? Well, let's rewind here for a second. As you enter the ride, you are given a special pass in exchange for your name when you are "cast." Then, you walk through a dim, dark forest. Right before you board, you give the card to an attendant. The cards have your name computer-coded on them, so the ride knows who's on the ride at any given time. Another little touch that makes this ride so special is the original music, composed by John Williams (*Star Wars, Indiana Jones, Home Alone*). To avoid crowds, which can really bottleneck at this attraction, ride it second thing of the day, right after Hanna-Barbera.

EARTHQUAKE: THE BIG ONE

Rating: 7. Almost too realistic. *Location:* San Francisco, on the Embarcadero. *Duration of Show:* 23 minutes, total. The ride itself is only a fraction of that. *Frightening:* Possibly. The visual effects are intense, and anyone who has lived through the horror of the real thing may want to skip this.

Earthquake first puts you in a queue area surrounded by photos of the aftermath of the 1906 San Francisco quake. You then enter a theater to watch clips from Earthquake, the movie, and to see some of the miniature buildings used in the production of the movie. After that, you go into a display in which six volunteers show how the stunts in movies like Earthquake are filmed, demonstrating with a child dumping foam rocks on the adults' heads. Finally, you board a real BART train for a trip from Oakland and San Francisco.

But no sooner do you set off than an 8.3 earthquake hits, triggering buckling concrete, falling tanker trucks, flash floods, and fires, much like what happens in Catastrophe Canyon in the Disney-MGM Studios.

HINT: The best view during the ride can be had in the secondcar from the front (on your left). Try to sit in the middle of the car, as the view from the front is somewhat obstructed.

THE FUNTASTIC WORLD OF HANNA BARBERA

Rating: 9. Hilarious, exciting, not to be missed. *Location:* Production Central, at the corner of Plaza of the Stars and Nickelodeon Way. *Duration of Ride:* 4 1/2 minutes; 3 1/2 minute pre-show. *Comments:* May induce motion sickness. Those prone to motion sickness, those with back or neck problems, pregnant women, the elderly, and the very young are advised to sit in the front row of the auditorium, which does not move. *Frightening:* Yes. The physical effects are extremely intense, may be too much for some.

This is a flight simulation adventure that uses the technology of Body Wars and splices it with the lovable characters of eight-time Emmy Award and seven-time Oscar winners Bill Hanna and Joe Barbera. The storyline goes something like this: Dick Dastardly kidnaps Elroy Jetson, and Yogi and Boo Boo set off on a rocket to chase after Elroy, with pit stops in Bedrock and the future to pick up the Flintstones and Jetsons. Scooby Doo gets picked up along the way, and in the ensuing chase, the good guys win and the bad guys get their just desserts. Funny, original, and altogether a great experience, this not-to-be-missed attraction features long lines most of the day. See this as soon as you enter the park or right before leaving.

JAWS – Jaws was one of the original attractions here, but it suffered from constant mechanical problems, and it failed to entertain. In the ride, you had set out from Amity Harbor on a pontoon boat, being chased by the famous Great White himself. But the captain chucks a grenade at the shark, blowing him up. If it sounds lame, that might be some reason why the ride was closed and dismantled. However, it has been redesigned and was reopened in summer 1993.

Live & Interactive Shows
"MURDER, SHE WROTE" MYSTERY THEATRE

Rating: 6. Funny, a pleasant change of pace. *Location:* Production Central, 8th Avenue and South Street. *Duration of Show:* 40 minutes.

In this segmented show, guests are introduced to the components of post-production: dubbing, sound effects, editing, and everything else that goes on after the director shouts "That's a wrap." Guests are chosen from the audience to demonstrate each step of the process, and the results are shown on the big screen. Other guests choose the music, takes, guest stars, villain, and even the murder weapon. The total experience is a little bit like Monster Sound at the Disney-MGM Studios. If there's a long line for this attraction, skip it and come back another time.

"ALFRED HITCHCOCK: THE ART OF MAKING MOVIES"

Rating: 9. Amazing, not to be missed. *Location:* Production Central, 8th Avenue and Plaza of the Stars. *Duration of Show:* 40 minutes. *Frightening:* Some portions are extremely graphic and inappropriate for younger children.

This spectacular attraction is a fitting tribute to **Alfred Hitchcock**. You start off in a 3-D theater in which you will view a montage featuring his most famous films. The tribute's highlights are a scene from *Dial M For Murder* and the attack scene from *The Birds*, all done in three dimensions. It's frighteningly real.

You then go to a soundstage in which audience volunteers and professional actors combine their talents to reenact the most famous scenes, including *Vertigo*, *Rear Window*, *Strangers on a Train*, *Saboteur*, *Spellbound*, and the infamous *Psycho* shower scene (which was originally shot with 78 takes). After the visit to the soundstage, the tour deposits you in an interactive area where you can witness other famous scenes from Hitchcock's thrillers. Not to be missed.

GHOSTBUSTERS: A LIVE-ACTION SPOOKTACULAR

Rating: 6 1/2. Pure, unadulterated fun. *Location:* New York, at 57th Street and Amblin Avenue. *Duration of Show:* 15 minutes.

In this fun show, the **Ghostbusters** go up against Gozer, the Stay-Puft Marshmallow Man, and other assorted specters. The show is accentuated by Ray Parker Jr.'s rock theme. The special effects are a highlight of the show, which is best seen in the early afternoon.

THE GORY, GRUESOME, & GROTESQUE HORROR MAKE-UP SHOW

Rating: 7. Lively and fast-paced. *Location:* Hollywood, on Hollywood Boulevard. *Duration of Show:* 25 minutes. *Frightening:* Visually intense.

This well-conceived, well-done show focuses in on the make-up effects that make films like *Beetlejuice*, *The Fly*, and *The Exorcist* so successful. The humor is tongue-in-cheek, and there's more than enough gore to satisfy anyone's craving for it. The best thing about this worthwhile show is the fact that it is pretty much a sleeper, thus receiving few of the gigantic herds that plague many of the other attractions.

THE ANIMAL ACTORS SHOW

Rating: 6. Warm and happy. *Location:* Expo Center, by the Hard Rock Cafe. *Duration of Show:* 20 minutes.

The actors who entertain you here aren't quite human. In fact, they're really a bunch of animals. Literally. Mr. Ed, Benji, Lassie, Jerry Lee, and 45 other animal actors put on a show here with their trainers. Part of the fun comes from the spontaneity of an animal not doing what a trainer tells it to do, an element of risk not found in shows starring humans.

DYNAMITE NIGHTS STUNT SPECTACULAR

Rating: 7. Dazzling, impressive. *Location:* On the Lagoon. *Duration of Show:* 20 minutes. *Frightening:* Explosions and other visually intense effects may put off a few.

In this stunt show, cigarette boats zoom across the Lagoon, one filled with drug smugglers and their loot, the other carrying the good guys. The ensuing chase and pyrotechnic display is comparable to the vehicle stunts in the Indiana Jones Epic Stunt Spectacular in the Disney-MGM Studios. This show is usually held at 7 PM. *HINT:* The most comfortable viewpoints when the weather is especially hot can be had in San Francisco's Lombard's Landing and Chez Alcatraz restaurants.

THE WILD, WILD, WILD WEST STUNT SHOW

Rating: 7. Exciting. *Location:* By Amity, on the far edge of the park. *Duration of Show:* 18 minutes. *Frightening:* Explosions and other violent acts areshown. Visually intense.

The other half of the Universal stunt show duo, **the Wild West** has Clod and Cole Hopper, a pair of fictitious cowboys, duking it out with bad guys, falling off buildings, running into buildings, blowing up buildings, etc. This show runs continuously and features clips from old Westerns and trade secrets. See it at your leisure.

AN AMERICAN TAIL

Rating: 5. Boring for anyone over the age of 8. *Location:* San Francisco, on the Embarcadero. *Duration of Show:* 10 minutes.

Fievel, Tony, Tanya, and Bridget cavort around a small stage in this ten-minute musical revue that younger kids seem to love; teenagers and adults seem disenchanted.

ROCKY AND BULLWINKLE SHOW – This new show, which opened in July 1992, features the goggled aviator and his tall, antlered companion have landed their bi-plane in Hollywood, where "enormoose" star Bullwinkle has to choose a script for his next movie. His choices include "The Sound of Moo-sic" and "Raging Bullwinkle." Now that the Soviet Union has collapsed, Boris and Natasha have come to Hollywood seeking fame and fortune. But to get it, they will have to "off" their biggest competitors ... moose and squirrel! The comical Snidely Whiplash and Dudley Do-Right each also put in cameos.

THE BEETLEJUICE GRAVEYARD REVUE – Another new live show, this one follows in the footsteps of the Dead, with the dead. **Beetlejuice** has started up a band, whose members include Dracula, Frankenstein and his bride, and Wolfman. The 20-minute show is spooky and irreverent, the band straight from a Catskills gig. Dracula is reportedly the sixth New Kid on the Block, and he's the songwriter for the motley crew; the Bride of Frankenstein performs Carole King's "You Make Me Feel Like a Natural Woman;" the Phantom of the Opera sings "Great Balls of Fire," showing off his past associations with Chuck Berry, Jerry Lee Lewis, and Little Richard; and Frankenstein preforms "When a Man Loves a Woman."

Tours
PRODUCTION STUDIO TOUR
Rating: 4. Disappointing, far below guests' expectations. *Location:* Production Central, next to Nickelodeon Studios. *Duration of Tour:* 20 minutes.

Guests who board the tram for a behind-the-scenes look at Universal like what they get on Disney-MGM's tram tour will be sorely disappointed. In fact, so will anyone who hopes to get an inkling as to how the movie and television process works. Those purposes would be better sated in Alfred Hitchcock; Murder, She Wrote; and the Gory, Greusome, and Grotesque Horror Make-Up Show.

What this tour consists of is a whirlwind jaunt through vacant soundstages and closed-access post-production rooms and then a tram ride through the many street sets which you will see as you tour the park yourself. The narration is dull for the layman, and only marginally interesting for those who want to find out about set design and construction.

NICKELODEON STUDIO TOUR
Rating: 5 1/2. A letdown unless there is a taping. *Location:* Production Central, a landmark. *Duration of Tour:* 25 minutes.

Here, you walk through Nickelodeon's hair, makeup, and dressing rooms, soundstages, wardrobe, and prop departments. This tour is unmemorable compared to the Disney-MGM Studio Tour, unless a show is in production when you visit. To find out whether a show will be in production at the time of your visit, call 363-8000 or inquire at Guest Relations. *HINT:* If your kids have ever lamented about wishing to appear on Double Dare so they could get a taste of toxic-sounding substances like gak or slime, this is the only spot in Orlando to can fulfill that wish! The kitchen at Nick Studios dishes out the stuff. Yum???

HOW TO MAKE A MEGA MOVIE DEAL

Rating: 3. Not worth the time or space. *Location:* Hollywood. *Duration of Show:* 25 minutes.

This advertisement for AT&T products masquerades as a movie stressing the value of communication. On this sequential video presentation, you are shown a series of films documenting a young man's (Jack Archer) rise from mailroom flunky to movie executive. It's confusing and not terribly worthwhile. Spend your time elsewhere.

Be a Star

SCREEN TEST HOME VIDEO ADVENTURE

Rating: 6 1/2. Good fun, a nice keepsake. *Location:* New York, next to Kongfrontation. *Duration of Test:* 15 minutes. *Comments:* Costs $29.95 for 1 to 6 people.

Here, you step in front of a blue screen for more of that ChromaKey technology demonstrated in Dreamfinder's School of Drama in EPCOT's Future World. The difference is in the finished product: in this case, it's a 8- to 10-minute souvenir VHS video cassette depicting your test. You can choose one of two films: a Star Trek adventure or a butchered account of your day at Universal. You and your family or friends don costumes and through the use of sets, blue screens, and other authentic video technology, you are put on the Enterprise or inside Earthquake, Kongfrontation, and the other Universal attractions. The extra cost for this attraction tends to keep crowds at a minimum.

See a Star

Here at Universal, you may run into characters as diverse as Marilyn Monroe and Popeye. Animated characters roaming the park include Yogi and Boo Boo Bear, Scooby Doo, the Flintstones, Rocky & Bullwinkle, and Fievel Mouskewitz. Celebrity lookalikes include Groucho, Harpo, and Chico Marx, W.C. Fields, Charlie Chaplin, Stan Laurel, Oliver Hardy,

Ricky Ricardo, Beetlejuice, the Phantom of the Opera, and Wolfman Jack.

Street Entertainment
STREETBUSTERS – The Ghostbusters and Slimer go up against Beetlejuice outside the New York Public Library in this song-and-dance revue throughout the day.

HOLLYWOOD HI-TONES – These singers roam Hollywood Boulevard and its environs throughout the day.

BLUES BROTHERS – Two lookalikes of the R&B men perform in Chicago Bound each day on New York's Delancey Street.

UNIVERSAL SCIENCE BAND – Find these musicians wandering around the park.

Interactive Entertainment
NICKELODEON GAME LAB – This is where the Nick tour culminates, in a room filled with games that the network is testing out for use on their game show programs in the future. Kids have an opportunity to experience the Kid Wash and the One Ton Human Hamster Wheel and other games.

LUCY: A TRIBUTE – America's queen of comedy, **Lucille Ball**, enjoyed a career that spanned the vaudeville stage, classic motion pictures, and the golden age of television. And Universal honors the zany redhead with Lucy: A Tribute, which features never before seen memorabilia of life both in front of and away from the public's adoring eye. A special screen presentation takes highlights from "I Love Lucy," "Here's Lucy," and "The Lucy Show".

Also available for viewing are slides and rare home video footage with Lucy, Desi, and their family, props and costumes from Lucy's performances in "Mame" and "Sally Sweet." Other items on display include fan letters, Emmys, jewelry, magazine articles, and scrapbooks. There's also a scale model of the "I Love Lucy" soundstage, complete with Little Ricky's bedroom, the Tropicana, and the famed living room set. Also, a trivia game called "California Here We Come" tests aficionados' knowledge of the series as they "travel" with the Ricardo and Mertz families on their way to California for the first time.

AN AMERICAN TAIL: FIEVEL'S PLAYLAND – Another new attraction, this one inspired by the two **American Tail** movies in which the Mouskewitz clan emigrates to the U.S. and heads westward. Guests who enter will immediately be transported to a mouse-sized world populated by Fievel the mouse and Tiger, a two-story tall cat who will start a conversation with anyone who approaches. A 200-foot water ride towers over the 18,000-foot playground. You careen down curves in a sardine can, winding through oversized sewer pipes and finally into a strongbox.

Gigantic movie props are everywhere, including campfire skillets big enough for kids to play in, a 1,000-gallon cowboy hat, a 15-foot high canteen with a tendency to leak, a 30-foot spider web, and enormous gramophones and harmonicas which double as slides.

HANNA-BARBERA INTERACTIVE AREA – At the FUNtastic World of Hanna Barbera's back door, guests have the chance to color cartoons via computers and light pens, to try their hand at sound effects, use props like the Flintstones' pterodactyl piano, Pebbles' dollhouse, and create their own cartoon. You can enter this playground of the mind from the attraction or the Hanna-Barbera shop, the latter of which lets you enter without waiting in line.

HITCHCOCK INTERACTIVE AREA – Guests re-enact and witness dramatic scenes from Hitchcock's thrillers, including the apartment building scene in *Rear Window*, the Statue of Liberty scene in *Saboteur*, and more, your guides for this being John Forsythe, Norman Lloyd, and James Stewart, among others. This area is also accessible through a shop and the attraction. You need not wait to visit the interactive area, just enter through the Bates Motel shop.

THE BONEYARD – Some of Hollywood's most memorable props can be found here, including the houseboat from *Cape Fear*, the Love Rock from *Problem Child 2*, and the Great White himself from *Jaws*.

AT&T AT THE MOVIES – Here, you have the opportunity to test out some computers similar to those found in EPCOT Center's CommuniCore complex.

MCA RECORDING STUDIOS – Here, you can sing on your own record or a music video.

CARICATURE ARTISTS – Skilled artisans vend very personal souvenirs.

PITCH & SKILL GAMES – Amity's waterfront has a boardwalk-type midway with games including Short Shot basketball, Shark-Banger, Milk Can Menagerie, Hoop Toss, Dolphin Dash, and Muffin Tin.

KODAK TRICK PHOTOGRAPHY PHOTO SPOTS – Here, you can line up your camera, line up your subject, and click, you have a picture of whoever, except they're standing in Hollywood Hills, the Big Apple, or the Space Shuttle. Yeah, it's kitschy, but in a good way.

Shopping

Universal has twenty-six shops, many of them not warranting any particular interest, but there are some interesting marketplaces. The **Hanna-Barbera Shop** offers animation cels and memorabilia. The **Bates Motel Gift Shop** is a must for anyone with a Mother. **Safari Outfitters, Ltd.** offers (among other things) a chance to pose for a picture in the fist of one King Kong for $5. At **E.T.'s Toy Closet**, you can pose with everyone's favorite alien and get souvenirs bearing his likeness. **Golden Gate Mercantile** offers souvenirs from Earthquake! and the city's sets. **Quint's Nautical Treasures** purveys New England- and nautical-theme gifts. **San Francisco Imports** offers Oriental items.

Set Streets

One of Universal's foremost assets is the presence of these open-access **sets** of locales as varied as Little Italy, the Upper East Side, the Theater District, Gramercy Park, Coney Island, Battery Park, and Central Park in New York; Ghirardelli Square, Fisherman's Wharf, the Embarcadero, and the SFRT Subway Station in San Francisco, Boston Bay, Amity Village, New England Street, and Amity Harbor in New England; Hollywood Boulevard, Beverly Hills, Rodeo Drive, Sunset Boulevard, and the Walk of Fame, all in Hollywood, and other assorted scenes like Angkor Wat, the Bates Motel, the Psycho House, and Doc Brown's Science Center.

16. OTHER ORLANDO ATTRACTIONS AND EXCURSIONS

INTRODUCTION

Flip back to 1845 for a minute. Picture a soldier named **Orlando Reeves**, part of a party scouting for the Florida Indians in a Mosquito County settlement called Jernigan, after Georgian settler Aaron Jernigan. One night, Reeves was on duty, and some Indians disguised as pine tree logs infiltrated the camp. He fired his gun and woke the camp, saving their lives. Unfortunately, in the ensuing battle, Reeves was shot with an Indian arrow and died on the spot. Soon thereafter, the area was referred to as Orlando. The name just stuck. Later that year, Mosquito County became Orange County, and the city of Jernigan officially became Orlando in 1857.

Earlier in this century, the area immediately south of where Walt Disney World sits today, known as Kissimmee (Seminole for Heaven's Place), was a cow town (and still is, as is evidenced by its many farms and cattle auction houses). It's main drawing cards were the bars where cowboys could get a drink without dismounting. The whole community was a sleepy little place with virtually no tourist interest.

Enter **Walt Disney**. He came onto the scene and purchased the 28,000-acre tract of land known as the Reedy Creek Improvement District and changed the face of Florida. Orlando's population has more than doubled. In a true test of being on the scene, Orlando was awarded, in 1990, an expansion franchise of the NBA, the Orlando Magic. The team went platinum, selling out every home game in three seasons.

Orlando treats its new-found stardom the same way a working-class friend would treat winning $25 million in the lottery. The city is a little shy about it, more than a little surprised, but still friendly and approachable. It bears little resemblance to New York, Chicago, Washington, or even Tampa or Miami. The city is sparkling, almost everything less than 25 years old.

And since Disney, other attractions have sprung up. Most notably, Sea World and Universal Studios Florida. But other small, worthwhile spots exist, and this chapter delves into them.

THEME PARKS

BUSCH GARDENS TAMPA

Location: P.O. Box 9158, Tampa, FL 33674-9158. *Phone:* 813/987-5171, 813/987-5082, 813/987-5000. *Hours:* 9:30 AM until 6 PM, extended in the summer and holiday periods. *Admission:* $26.95 for adults, $22.95 for kids aged 3 to 9. Kids under 3 free. *Parking:* $3. *Credit Cards:* Visa, Mastercard, Discovery. *Time to See:* Six to nine hours. *When to See:* Weekdays. *Don't Miss:* Questor, The Scorpion, Python, Monorail, Congo River Rapids, and Myombe Reserve.

Next to Walt Disney World, **Busch Gardens** is Florida's most popular attraction. And with good reason. Busch Gardens is one part theme park, that theme being a trip across Africa, and one part accredited zoo. At the theme park end of it, Busch Gardens features two thrilling roller coasters, a flight simulation adventure, and three water rides. As a zoo, Busch Gardens has received a myriad of awards, including certificates for the first North American captive breedings of thirteen species and thirteen Gold Propagator Certificates for breeding 50 of a species, all awarded by the American Association of Zoological Parks & Aquariums.

Zoological habitats are found in all areas of the park, but is concentrated in several sections: Myombe Reserve: The Great Ape Domain, the Bird Gardens, Nairobi, the Serengeti Plain, the Koala Habitat, the Clydesdale Hamlet, and the Elephant Habitat. All told, the collection houses 3,436 creatures representing 359 species. Special features include the Zoo Kitchen, with dieticians and veterinarians ensuring that park animals receive the proper nutrition; the Hospital, with operating rooms, x-rays, laboratories, recovery areas, and brooder rooms for birds; the Nairobi Field Station Animal Nursery, reminiscent of a turn-of-the-century African hospital, offering ample viewing space, skylighted playrooms, heated floors, and pens equipped with oxygen and 12 computerized isolettes (adapted human incubators) for newborns' health care.

Busch Gardens is divided into **eight themed sections**, the Bird Gardens, Crown Colony, Morocco, Nairobi, Serengeti Plain, Stanleyville, The Congo, and Timbuktu.

To get to Busch Gardens from Orlando, Kissimmee, Walt Disney World, and other Central Florida areas, take I-4 west to the exit for I-75 north. Take I-75 to exit 54, Fowler Avenue, and follow signs to Busch Gardens and Adventure Island. It's about an hour and a quarter drive.

Bird Gardens

This area was one of the original areas when the 300-acre park opened in 1959. The title attraction of the **Bird Gardens** still boasts lush foliage and nearly 2,000 exotic birds and birds of prey. There is also a koala habitat with three females and one male. Many of the birds can be seen in the **World of Birds** show as well as **Eagle Canyon**, a walk-through, free-flight aviary featuring golden and bald eagles. **Dwarf Village** is a newly expanded playground for the younger set. Last, but to some, definitely not least, is the Anheuser-Busch Brewery Tour.

While in the Bird Gardens area, stop in at the Hospitality House (L,D, $3 to $5.50) for pepperoni and chef's combo pizzas, and something called the Tampa Sandwich: salami, turkey, cheese, and salad, all on a roll.

Crown Colony

This is a mock-up of a British colony in Africa, and possesses one of the park's top rides: **Questor**. This is a flight simulation adventure in which you join Sir Edison Fitzwilly on a thrilling, wild, and occasionally wacky journey in search of the mystical Crystal of Zed. The trek, whose technology is similar to that used in Star Tours and Body Wars, sends guests through the core of the earth and over waterfalls. Other attractions include the Clydesdale Hamlet, in which six of the magnificent corporate symbols of all time mug about, the Sky Ride puts you in an open-air gondola for a placid journey over Timbuktu, the Serengeti Plain, Congo, and Crown Colony, and a Monorail station. You can board the monorail for a silent, ten-minute journey that takes you over the Serengeti. It offers an excellent (not to mention air-conditioned) opportunity to get close to the animals, so have your camera ready.

Crown Colony boasts the **Crown Colony House** (L,D, $7 to $13), one of the finest restaurants in Busch Gardens. No reservations are accepted, and the twelve prime tables that look out onto the veldt go fast. To increase your chances of getting a table with a view, show up before noon or after 4.

Morocco

The **Jewel of Africa** is represented as a beautiful walled city featuring lots of shops that emote a bustling medina feel and restaurants, with a few entertainment venues. Foremost among these is the **Moroccan Palace Theatre**, which hosts "Around the World on Ice," a dazzling display of skating prowess. The 1,200-seat theatre fills up about 20 minutes before midday shows, check an entertainment schedule for details. The **Marrakesh Theater** puts on two shows daily: the new (May 1992) "Latin, Latin!", which features hot salsa, rhythmic mamba, and flamboyant costumes, and "Listen to a Country Song," a revue of country music ranging from the early days of country gospel to the present.

If the munchies hit while in Morocco, pay a visit to Boujad Bakery

(B,S, $2 to $3) for pastries including gigantic muffins, Zagora Cafe (B,L,D,S, $3.50 to $5.50) for an assortment of sandwiches and burgers, or the Ice Cream Parlor (S, $1 to $3) for you-know-what.

Nairobi

The primary draw of this area of Busch Gardens is the brand-new **Myombe Reserve: The Great Ape Domain**, a stellar attraction paying tribute to man's closest relatives. Six lowland gorillas and eight common chimpanzees roam the simulated rain forest. Also in the area is the aforementioned **Nairobi Field Station**, with its baby birds and other animals frolicking around. **Nocturnal Mountain** is where the wild things are and where it is always after dark. The **Nairobi Station of the Trans-Veldt Railroad** is also located here. Hop on the train for views of the animals on the **Serengeti Plain**. Younger kids love the petting zoo and the elephant wash here.

Serengeti Plain

No big-name rides, no flashy shops here, only a wide-open, 80-acre tract of land, home to 800 African animals. Guests can observe animals from the railroad, sky ride, monorail, or from a promenade that winds through the park. Of interest is the fact that the Serengeti Plain also has a successful breeding and survival program for animals like the black rhino and Asian elephant.

GREVY ZEBRAS GRAZING WITH MONORAIL IN BACKGROUND - BUSCH GARDENS

Stanleyville

Feeling a little hot, sticky, icky, and sweaty? Visit **Stanleyville**, a bustling African village named for the distinguished explorer Sir Henry Morgan Stanley. Ride the **Stanley Falls Log Flume** through winding foliage and eventually over a 43-foot cliff. Still feeling a bit dry? Lose that arid feeling for good on the **Tanganyika Tidal Wave**, where you can get into a large raft for a climb up a 55-foot high track, surrounded by luxuriant scenery, and then you will reprove that what goes up must come down. Then, after the ride, you are given the opportunity to stand on a bridge right in the path of the impending splash. You may never dry out again.

The **Stanleyville Variety Show** includes serialists, jugglers, acrobats, and specialty acts. The show rotates so there are several different exhibitions over the course of the year. The **Congo Comedy Corps** will split sides in an audience-participation improv in the Zambezi Pavilion.

The **Stanleyville Smokehouse** (L,D, $5 to $7.50) offers barbecue which is considered some of the best take-out food in the park. Chicken and ribs are served with french fries and cole slaw. Also, the **Bazaar Cafe** (L,D, $2 to $5) is a good place for salads and sandwiches.

The Congo

This is the thrill ride nerve center of Busch Gardens, with the **Python**, a 1,200-foot roller coaster with a 360° double spiral that cars travel at speeds up to 50 miles an hour; the **Congo River Rapids**, in which 12 riders in a gigantic inner tube set off on a wild journey punctuated by geysers; leaky caves, white water, drops, rapids, and other wet wonders, made even more exciting by the fact that the ride is never the same twice. The rafts drift in different patterns, so you could sit in the same seat twice and get soaking wet once and not feel a drop the second time around. Also, there's the **Monstrous Mamba** octopus ride, **Ubanga-Banga Bumper Cars**, and stations of the railroad and the sky ride.

With technology similar to that of Universal's Screen Test Adventure, **Congo Cal's Video Ventures** gives you an opportunity to record a VHS video tape starring you in various positions throughout Africa for about $20. One of the truly beautiful spots in the park is **Claw Island**, which features white Bengal tigers in their natural setting.

Timbuktu

Timbuktu is themed after an ancient desert trading center, and contains several major attractions: **The Scorpion**, a looping roller coaster almost as intense as The Python; **The Phoenix**, a ride in which centrifugal force puts you through a 360° loop in a boat; **The Sandstorm**, an aerial whip ride; and **Carousel Caravan**, a unique merry-go-round complete with camels and Arabian horses. One of the park's most intriguing shows, **Dolphins of the Deep**, has two bottle-nosed dolphins named Bud and Mitch, who with their sea lion friend and their trainers, make for a fast-paced show at Dolphin Theater.

For a combination dinner and musical revue, grab a table at **Das Festhaus** (L,D, $4 to $6), a 1,200-seat restaurant that combines authentic German fare with two rousing shows that alternate daily, the International Show, and Bavarian Colony Dancers and Band.

CYPRESS GARDENS

Location: P.O. Box 1, Cypress Gardens, FL 33884. *Phone:* 813/324-2111, 800/237-4826, 800/282-2123. *Hours:* 9 AM to 6 PM, daily. *Admission:* $18.95 for adults, $12.95 for kids aged 3 to 9. Kids under 3 free. *Parking:* Free. *Credit Cards:* Visa, Mastercard, Discovery. *Time to See:* Four to six hours. *When to See:* Anytime.

Cypress Gardens is a 223-acre, family-style theme park known worldwide for its ski revues, botanical gardens, and its old-fashioned Southern hospitality. The park is located in Winter Haven, 40 minutes from Walt Disney World. Take I-4 west to exit 23. Take U.S. 27 south to S.R. 540 and turn right. Wheelchairs, strollers, lockers, first aid, and a kennel are all available.

Cypress Gardens' attractions include **When Radios Were Radios**, a permanent exhibition of antique memorabilia commemorating the nostalgic years of radio with hundreds of different vintage radios from the 20's through 50's. **Feathered Follies** is an exotic revue with a colorful cast of performing birds combining entertainment with education.

Cypress Gardens is sometimes called the **"Waterski Capital of the World."** Nowhere is this more evident than at Ski! Ski! Ski! Everybody's Skiin' Caribbean, the exciting water-ski show combining the sights and sounds of the tropics with the feats of Cypress Gardens' Greatest American Ski Team, including barefooting, free-style jumping, swivel skiing, and Delta Wing kite performances.

Carousel Cove is a children's ride area with eight rides and a beautiful carousel. **Captain Robin's Flying Circus** features trapeze, web, spinning ladders, and tumbling acts, all blended with old-fashioned circus entertainment and trampoline performances. **Kodak's Island** in the Sky puts guests on a revolving platform for a 153-foot ascension, from which point you can see for miles around. **Cypress Junction** is an elaborate model railroad system with 1,100 feet of track and up to 20 trains traveling on it at once. **Cypress Roots** is a museum telling the story of the first Florida attraction, including a display of cameras from the 20's to the 70's, the waterskis used in original Cypress Gardens shows, and photos of celebrities who visited the park. Electric boats wind through a maze of landscaped canals with pleasant scenery.

There is also an accredited zoo and botanical garden. The original gardens feature 8,000 varieties of plants from 75 different countries. The zoo contains a free-fly aviary, gator show, and the **Critter Encounter petting zoo**. The park also features several annual floral festivals, including the Spring Floral Festival, with ten uniquely designed topiaries shaped as various animals, plus a variety of spring flowers (March 15 to May 15); the Chrysanthemum Festival, with more than two million colorful blooms, the nation's largest exhibition of this kind (Mid-November); and the Poinsetta Festival (December 1 to Mid-January), with 35,000 blooms creating a holiday wonderland.

The park has several eateries: **Crossroads Restaurant**, a full-service restaurant featuring Southern specialties; **Village Fare**, a food court with Southern, Italian, Mexican, and dessert counters. Also, there are over 15 shops selling everything from country furniture to skis.

GATORLAND

Location: 14501 S. Orange Blossom Trail (U.S. 441), Orlando, FL 32837. *Phone:* 855-5496 or 800/393-JAWS. *Hours:* 8 AM until dusk daily. *Admission:* $9.95 for adults, $6.96 for kids aged 3 to 11. Kids under 3 free. *Parking:* Free. *Credit Cards:* American Express, Visa, Mastercard. *Time to See:* Three to four hours. *When to See:* Anytime. *Don't Miss:* Gator Wrestlin' and Gator Jumparoo shows.

This is a zoo named for and starring the famed Florida carnivores. Alligators, crocodiles, and snakes are everywhere in this zoo, you even walk through a grotesquely large pair of gator jaws to enter the park. When inside, you can stroll along the boardwalk, watching for the reptiles sunbathing in swamps on either side. You've probably already seen **Gatorland**, provided that you've seen Indiana Jones and the Temple of Doom, Ernest Saves Christmas, Survival, Nickelodeon's Total Panic, Late Night with David Letterman, or National Geographic. Gatorland or its inhabitants have been involved in those projects and more.

There are three headliner shows here: the oldest being the famed **Gator Jumparoo**, in which reptiles leap out of the water for slabs of meat being dangled over the water! Who knew that gators could jump?!? Also, the **Snakes of Florida** show provides an entertaining and educational look at the 69 varieties of snakes native to Florida. **Gator Wrestlin' "Cracker Style"** disproves the myth that only Seminoles tangled with alligators, as men dressed as Florida Crackers (cowboys) go to battle.

A train ride carries guests around and affords photo opportunities, as do the **Swamp Walk, Observation Tower,** and **Alligator Breeding**

Marsh walk. **Pearl's Smokehouse** sells gator ribs and gator nuggets, and several snack bars offer more traditional theme park fare. Also, for souvenirs, visit the gift shop at the main entrance. For those of you who aren't revolted by the thought of **Gatorland Zoo** selling alligator leather, there's a boutique at the main entrance as well.

To get to Gatorland from Walt Disney World or Kissimmee, take U.S. 192 east until you reach U.S. 17-92-441, the South Orange Blossom Trail. Turn left, the zoo will be on your right. The S.O.B.T. can also be accessed by the Beeline Expressway, Florida's Turnpike, the Central Florida Parkway, Sand Lake Drive, or I-4 (exit 33A).

KENNEDY SPACE CENTER/SPACEPORT USA

Location: TWRS, Kennedy Space Center, FL 32899. *Phone:* 452-2121. *Hours:* 9 AM until dusk daily except Christmas. *Admission:* Free. Several attractions require admission. *Parking:* Free. *Time to See:* Six to nine hours. *When to See:* Weekends. *Don't Miss:* Astronauts Memorial, The Boy From Mars.

Kennedy Space Center's visitor center is **Spaceport USA**, featuring a variety of exhibits, films, and tours, many of which are free. The remainder are priced so that a family of four could experience everything in Spaceport USA for less than the cost of a ticket to Disney World.

The attractions at the Spaceport include **Satellites and You**, a 45-minute exhibit utilizing animatronics and stunning audiovisual effects to show the uses of satellites in our everyday life. **The Boy from Mars** is a funny, heartwarming tale of the first American colony on the Red Planet and the first child born on Mars as he returns to Earth. The **NASA Art Gallery** is a surprising collection of more than 250 paintings and sculptures created by artists commissioned by the NASA Art Program.

The Rocket Garden and **Outdoor Exhibits** is highlighted by authentic rockets tracing America's space program, an Apollo access arm, tracking antennas, a lunar module, and a "moon tree." The **Gallery of Spaceflight** offers guests a chance to view an actual moon rock, spacecraft, and other exhibits. The **Astronauts Memorial** is a stunning, somber tribute to the 15 astronauts who died in the line of duty. The massive granite "space mirror" is computerized so it rises and sets with the sun. After dark, it is illuminated so the names engraved on the memorial are reflected to the sky.

Then, enter the 5 1/2 story IMAX theater for one of two films: *The Dream Is Alive* (37 minutes) and *Blue Planet* (42 minutes), both of which feature film taken from the Space Shuttle. The footage is incredible, the sound system impressive. Tickets to each cost $2.75 for adults, $1.75 for children 3 to 11. Children under 3 are admitted free.

There are two bus tours available, each lasting two hours. Each costs $6 for adults and $3 for children 3 to 11. The **Red Tour** features a simulated launch from the site where the Apollo astronauts trained, inspection of the Saturn V rocket, viewing of the Crawlers that carry the shuttles to the launching pad, and a close-up look at the launch pads from which all the Apollo moon missions and space shuttle flights end. The **Blue Tour** features a visit to Cape Canaveral Air Force Station, where the history of the early space program unfolds, visits to the launch sites for the Mercury and Gemini programs, the current launch pads, and the Air Force Space Museum. The double-decker buses are air-conditioned and feature live and taped narration. The tours leave throughout the day and exact routes are subject to change due to launches.

For souvenirs, visit the **Gift Gantry** or call 800/621-9826 for a catalog. For sustenance, visit the **Orbit Cafeteria** for a variety of dishes, The **Lunch Pad** for chicken, fish, and barbecued ribs, and outdoor kiosks for hot dogs, pizza, sandwiches, ice cream, beer, and soda.

A RARE NIGHT LAUNCH OF THE SHUTTLE ATALNTIS

Information Central, located at **Spaceport Central**, is the place to get answers as you plan your visit. Free pet facilities are located at the Administration Building, though they ask that you furnish a water dish. Cameras and wheelchairs are provided at no charge, a deposit of a credit card and driver's license is required. To get to the Space Center from Orlando, take the Beeline Expressway east ($1.10 toll) to S.R. 407 north. From there, follow signs for Kennedy Space Center or Kennedy Spaceport Center Spaceport USA.

SILVER SPRINGS

Location: P.O. Box 370, Silver Springs, FL 32688. *Phone:* 904/236-2121, 800/234-7458. *Hours:* 9 AM to 5:30 PM, 365 days. *Admission:* $19.95 adults, $14.95 for kids age 3 to 10, combination ticket to Silver Springs and Wild Waters, $24.90 adults, $18.90 kids. Children under 3 admitted free. *Parking:* Free. *Credit Cards:* American Express, Visa, Mastercard. *Time to See:* Six to nine hours. *When to See:* Anytime.

Silver Springs might be called Florida's oldest attraction, claiming to have drawn visitors for 10,000 years. Whether this bit is true or misinformation, Silver Springs makes a lovely place to spend a day, if you have the time. Like Sea World and Cypress Gardens, Silver Springs is a blessedly calm attraction that can serve to repose and recover from the frenetic pace of a normal WDW vacation.

There are five major attractions, the first of which is the **Jungle Cruise.** Unlike the Jungle Cruise at the Magic Kingdom, all the animals you will encounter on this boat jaunt are real. Six continents are represented by the animal population of this placid river voyage. The **Glass Bottom Boats** take you through waters of the largest artesian spring in the world, actually 14 springs so clear that sunlight can penetrate to depths of 83 feet. And now for something completely different, the **Jeep Safari** puts you in a convertible, tiger-striped Jeep Wrangler for an exciting venture through the jungles where the original Tarzan movies were filmed. On your safari, you may see deer, zebras, monkeys, macaws, and deer, with absolutely nothing coming between you and the animals, not even a cage, not even a pane of glass.

The **Lost River Voyage** takes you back thousands of years into a pristine Florida ecosystem, home to wild boar, deer, gators, osprey, wild turkeys, hawks, eagles, and 29 varieties of waterbirds. **Doolittles Petting Zoo** would make its namesake proud. Younger kids also seem to enjoy this section of Silver Springs. Several different **Animal Shows** are performed daily as well. Finally, a museum of nostalgic knick-knacks, antique cars, and phonographs, on display.

Silver Springs' boats are all covered, and free parking, kennels, camper parking, and handicap facilities are available. Picnic areas are available as well. Silver Springs is 72 miles north of Orlando. Take Florida's Turnpike north to I-75 north. From I-75, take exit 69, S.R. 40 east. The national landmark is one mile east of Ocala.

WEEKI WACHEE SPRINGS

Location: U.S. 19 at S.R. 50, Weeki Wachee, FL. *Phone:* 904/596-2062, 800/678-9335. *Hours:* 9 AM to 5:30 PM, 365 days. *Admission:* $13.95 adults, $9.95 for kids age 3 to 10, combination ticket to Weeki Wachee Spring and Buccaneer Bay, $17.95 adults, $13.95 for kids. Children under 3 admitted free. *Parking:* Free. *Credit Cards:* American Express, Visa, Mastercard. *Time to See:* Four to six hours. *When to See:* Anytime.

Weeki Wachee Springs is a beautiful enclave located on the state's west coast, about 45 miles north of Tampa. Known as "**Mermaid City**," the attraction features the world's only live underwater theater. Hans Christian Anderson's classic novel "The Little Mermaid" is performed several times daily. Don't expect any Disney animation, all the actors in this are living, breathing (well, sort of) creatures. Also, the **Wilderness River Cruise** takes you down the pristine Weeki Wachee River, abundant with native foliage and wildlife. A highlight is the **Pelican Preserve**, a refuge where disabled and injured birds are either nursed back to health or given a home for life. The **Birds of the World** and **Exotic Bird Shows** feature various feathered creatures that awe and amuse. Finally, the **Animal Forest Petting Zoo** lets children get up close and personal with llamas, pygmy deer, emus, and sheep.

All boat rides and shows are covered for all-weather comfort. Free parking, kennels, and picnic grounds are provided. Weeki Wachee is something of a drive from Orlando, but if you're headed to the left coast, it's worth a look-see. From Orlando, take I-4 north to Colonial Drive and take that west to U.S. 19. It's about an hour and a half.

AMUSEMENTS & DIVERSIONS

ALBIN POLASEK GALLERIES

Location: 633 Osceola Ave., Winter Park, FL 32789. *Phone:* 647-6294. *Hours:* 10 AM to noon and 1 PM to 4 PM, Wednesday through Saturday, 2 PM to 4 PM Sunday. Closed Monday and Tuesday and from July to October. *Admission:* Free.

Albin Polasek's Winter Park home, located on the shores of Lake Osceola, features a stunning collection of the sculptor's works, as well as paintings. As you enter the grounds, you are greeted by **Man Carving His**

Own Destiny, a statue of a man holding a chisel in his hand and carving his body out of stone. Guided tours of the house are given and you can roam the 3-acre gardens freely.

ALLIGATORLAND SAFARI ZOO

Location: 4580 W. Irlo Bronson Mem. Hwy., Kissimmee. *Phone:* 396-1012. *Hours:* 8:30 AM until dusk. *Admission:* $5.95 adults, $4.50 for children 4 to 11, children under 3 admitted free.

Alligators and unusual animals from around the world make this one of Central Florida's largest exhibits. Featured are animals indigenous to Florida, exotic cats, primates, birds, and much more.

BOK TOWER GARDENS

Location: Box 3810, Lake Wales. *Phone:* 813/676-1408. *Hours:* 8 AM to 5 PM. *Admission:* $3 adults, children under 12 free.

Bok Tower Gardens is Florida's highest point, a whole 324 feet above sea level. Rising out of this hillside is a lovely 200-foot carillon tower that rings out every half hour, and features a daily 45-minute recital at 3 PM. The tower is made of coquina and pink and grey marble, with latticework and copper doors depicting Bible scenes. To get to Bok Tower Gardens take I-4 west to exit 23 (U.S. 27 and Cypress Gardens). Take U.S. 27 south about 5 miles past the Cypress Gardens exit, turn onto Route 17A and take it to Alt. U.S. 27. Follow signs through Lake Wales to the park.

BRAVE WARRIOR WAX MUSEUM

Location: At Fort Liberty, 5260 W. Irlo Bronson Mem. Hwy., Kissimmee. *Phone:* 351-5151 or 800/776-3501. *Hours:* 10:30 AM to 8:30 PM daily. *Admission:* $4.00 adults, $2.00 for children 4 to 11, children under 3 admitted free. Ft. Liberty dinner show ticketholders get 50% off.

The **Brave Warrior Wax Museum**, at Fort Liberty in Kissimmee, is part of the entertainment complex's $25 million expansion. In it, the savage beauty of the western plains of America is recreated in lifelike panoramas. A dramatic synchronized soundtrack accompanies each visitor through the tour.

The entertaining and history-filled trip through the museum begins with the famous Lewis and Clark expedition to explore the Mississippi River. The tour continues walking amid tableaus featuring scenes depicting lifestyles of six Native American Indian nations, including the classic tribal sundance tribal initiation ceremony. The tour ends with a visit to General George Custer and his wife Libby during a session with world-famous photographer David Berry. Authentic replicas of clothing, utensils, and other props are used to recreate the scenes.

CARTOON MUSEUM

Location: 4300 S. Semoran Blvd., Suite 103, Orlando. *Phone:* 273-0141. *Hours:* 10 AM to 6 PM Monday through Saturday, 11 AM to 4 PM Sundays. *Admission:* Free.

Located in the downtown area, the **Cartoon Museum** contains 70,000 vintage comic books, from Superman to Batman and more. Cartoon drawings and political cartoons are also on display. Much of this art was created by owner Jim Ivey, who once drew political cartoons for Mad Magazine, the San Francisco Examiner, and the now-defunct Washington Star. It's nostalgic and beguiling, and it's free. Anyone whose mom ever threw out their comic book collection ("and now it's worth thousands") would enjoy the museum. However, note that the museum contains no Ninja Turtles or Saturday morning cartoons, and is not recommended for children under 11. Take I-4 north to the East-West Expressway (toll). Take it east to Semoran Blvd., turn right.

CORNELL FINE ARTS MUSEUM

Location: Rollins College, 633 Osceola Ave, Winter Park. *Phone:* 646-2526. *Hours:* 10 AM to 5 PM Tuesday through Friday, 1 PM to 5 PM weekends. Closed Monday. *Admission:* Free.

The **Cornell Museum**, located on the campus of Rollins College, sponsors four or five special exhibits annually, plus works of the students and faculty of the college. The entire collection, which may include at any time traveling exhibits and art on loan from other museums, is somewhat small but classy. Educational tours and lectures are available. Take I-4 east to Fairbanks Avenue. Take Fairbanks east to Park Avenue and turn right.

ELVIS PRESLEY MUSEUM

Location: Old Town, 5770 W. Irlo Bronson Mem. Hwy., Kissimmee. *Phone:* 396-8594. *Hours:* 10 AM to 11 PM daily. *Admission:* $4.00 adults, $3.00 for children 7 to 12 and senior citizens, children under 7 free.

The King is alive! At least in this museum in the Old Town shopping center, he is. The **Elvis Presley Museum** is called the largest collection of Elvis memorabilia outside of Graceland. The collection, licensed by the Elvis Presley Estate, includes his jumpsuits, bed, original birth records, jewelry, wardrobe, furniture, karate ghi, awards, concert belts, "TCB" reading glasses, guns, pianos, Rolls Royce, Cadillac, Mercedes 600 limo, gold records, and more — 300 items in all. There's also a gift shop where you can purchase all things Elvis. From I-4 or the WDW main entrance, Take 192 east 2 miles past I-4, Old Town will be on the right.

FLORIDA CITRUS TOWER

Location: 141 North U.S. 27, Clermont. *Phone:* 904/394-8585 or 800/ CITRUS 1. *Hours:* 8 AM to 6 PM daily. *Admission:* $5 adults, $3 for children 10 to 15, kids under 10 admitted free.

A scant 20 minutes from Walt Disney World, the **Florida Citrus Tower** serves as an excellent and informative introduction to Florida's famed citrus industry. On a clear day, the three observation decks on the tower afford views of nearly 2,000 square miles of citrus groves. The narration of the tram tour tells about the entire process of citrus cultivation, from planting to harvesting.

Also part of the Citrus Tower complex is the packing house, where you can sample the succulent fruit in season. You can also purchase bags and boxes of fruit for the folks back home. The basket shop offers a behind-the-scenes look at the production of gift baskets. Not surprisingly, you can purchase them as well. The candy kitchen is where a company called Carolyn Candies produces coconut patties, citrus candies, and pecan rolls. Samples are always available, and nobody will stop you from buying some of the product. The marmalade house features marmalades and jellies of all citrus varieties and combinations. You can sample and/ or purchase the wares here as well.

If you scoff at coconut patties and fresh grapefruit but jump at the chance to buy Sunshine State cigarette lighters, you'll want to make a stop at the gift shop. You can get more to eat here than free samples of citrus products. There's the **Ice Cream Patio** (L,S), a snack bar offering hot dogs, frozen yogurt, popcorn, ice cream cones, sundaes, floats, and banana splits. The **Citrus Tower Restaurant** (B,L) is for those who prefer sit-down dining.

The Florida Citrus Tower is particularly easy to get to. From the downtown area, the Orange Blossom Trail, or International Drive, take I-4 north to S.R. 50 (Colonial Drive). Take Colonial Drive west to U.S. 27. Turn right. Or, from Kissimmee, Lake Buena Vista, and Walt Disney World, take U.S. 192 west to U.S. 27 north. The Tower is on the right, one mile past the junction of U.S. 27 and S.R. 50.

FLYING TIGERS WARBIRD AIR MUSEUM

Location: 231 N. Airport Road, Kissimmee. *Phone:* 933-1942. *Hours:* 9 AM to 6 PM (5 PM Sundays). *Admission:* $6 adults, $5 kids 6 to 12 or seniors, kids under 6 admitted free.

This charming museum by the Kissimmee Municipal Airport offers an opportunity to see World War II aircraft restored or under restoration. The planes are not just restored on the outside, they are repaired and made flightworthy. At any given time, one or more of them may be buzzing about over your head.

FUN 'N WHEELS

Location: 6739 Sand Lake Drive, Orlando, and 3711 U.S. 192, Kissimmee. *Phone:* Orlando: 351-5651; Kissimmee: 870-2222. *Hours:* Monday to Friday: 6 PM to 11 PM. Saturday and Sundays: 10 AM to 11 PM. Summer hours: 10 AM until midnight. *Admission:* Free. Tickets are $1.25 each or 30 tickets for $30. Rides are 1 to 4 tickets each.

The two **Fun 'N Wheels** parks, owned by Orlando Entertains (the folks who brought you the Hard Rock Cafe, King Henry's Feast, and Fort Liberty), are collections of usual carnival and amusement park attractions run on a pay-per-ride basis.

Both the Orlando park, at the corner of Sand Lake Road and International Drive, and the Kissimmee Park, at Osceola Square Mall, have three go-cart tracks of varying skill levels. The **Fun Track** and **Family Track** are more for the inexperienced go-carters, while seasoned drivers zip around the **Fast Track** at speeds up to 24 miles an hour. There are also bumper boats, kiddie bumper cars, ball pits, arcades waterslides, tank tag, skee ball, bumper cars (Kissimmee only), mini golf (Orlando only), and a ferris wheel (Orlando only). Both locations have gift shops and snack bars.

GREEN MEADOWS CHILDREN'S FARM

Location: 1368 S. Poinciana Boulevard, Kissimmee. *Phone:* 846-0770. *Hours:* 9:30 AM until 5 PM. Last tour leaves 3 PM. *Admission:* $8, children 2 and under free.

Are your kids at that age when they think the coolest thing in the world would be living on a farm? Then take them to the **Green Meadows Children's Farm**, located in rural Kissimmee. For the price of admission, you receive a two-hour guided tour of the farm, with more than 200 animals. Everyone gets to milk the farm's cow, and the kids get pony rides.

Picnic areas, souvenirs, snacks, and beverages are all available. From I-4, take exit 25A (U.S. 192 east). Take it 3 miles and turn right on Poinciana Blvd. Take Poinciana 5 miles, on your right. Before you decide to visit Green Meadows, realize that the ride is in a tractor-drawn hay wagon. If you are allergic, you might want to reconsider.

MEDIEVAL LIFE

Location: 4510 W. Irlo Bronson Mem. Hwy., Kissimmee. *Phone:* 396-1518, 800/327-4024, and 800/432-0768. *Hours:* 1 PM to 9 PM daily. *Admission:* $7 adults, $5 kids 3 to 12, kids under 3 free.

Described as a "step back in time," **Medieval Life** is the only permanent medieval village in the United States. Wander the cobblestone streets of "**Raymondsburg**," lined with thatched-roof buildings and observe faithfully-clothed artisans — potters, blacksmiths, millers, carpenters, glassblowers — working their trade with the materials and techniques of their ancestors. You can explore homes furnished with cooking utensils and housewares of the period, and even taste medieval fare in the kitchen. Sadomasochists in the crowd will appreciate a visit to the jail and dungeon, where torture devices and explanations of their uses await. The village square hosts a "birds of prey and hunting dog" demonstration.

MORSE MUSEUM OF AMERICAN ART

Location: 133 Welbourne Ave., Winter Park. *Phone:* 644-3686. *Hours:* Tuesday through Saturday: 9:30 AM to 4 PM. Sunday: 1 PM to 4 PM. Closed Mondays. *Admission:* $2.50 adults, $1 children.

The **Charles Hosmer Morse Museum of American Art** is 9,000 square feet of Tiffany stained glass, art nouveau, and pottery. The Tiffany glass, mainly some of the stuff that Louis Comfort Tiffany made for himself, furniture, pottery, vases, lampshades, and windows. A small souvenir shop is located in the museum, and guided tours are available for groups of twelve or more. To get to the Morse gallery, take I-4 east to Fairbanks Avenue. Take Fairbanks east to Park Avenue and turn left. Take it to Welbourne and turn right.

MYSTERY FUN HOUSE

Location: 5767 Major Drive, Orlando. *Phone:* 351-3355. *Hours:* 10 AM to 11 PM. *Admission:* Varies, see below.

The **Mystery Fun House** is a three-part attraction. Admission can be purchased for one, two, or a combination of all three parts. There's the **Mystery Fun House** ($7.95) itself, with 15 chambers, including an Egyptian Tomb and the Forbidden Temple. Also, there's 18 holes of **Mini-Golf** ($2.95), and **Starbase Omega** ($5.95), a laser game in which you cavort about a "foreign planet" with a laser blaster and a computer belt-pack and try to blow everything in sight away. A combination ticket can be purchased for $11.85.

There is also an arcade, a shooting gallery, gift shop, restaurant, ice cream parlor, play area, and portrait painting area.

To get to the Mystery Fun House, take I-4 to exit 30B, Kirkman Road north. Turn right on Major Blvd., the Fun House will be on the right. Or, from International Drive, turn left on Kirkman Road, past I-4. The Fun House also operates a trolley that cruises International Drive. It stops at all major tourist attractions, hotels, restaurants, and shopping malls continuously from 10 AM to 10 PM. A round-trip to the Mystery Fun House is free. A round trip to any other location is $1.50 round trip.

ORANGE COUNTY HISTORICAL MUSEUM
Location: 812 East Rollins Street, Orlando. *Phone:* 898-8320. *Hours:* Tuesday through Friday, 10 AM to 4 PM. Weekends, 1 PM to 5 PM. Closed Mondays. *Admission:* $2 for adults, $1 for kids.

The **Orange County Historical Museum**, located in downtown Loch Haven Park, attracts 100,000 visitors a year to tour the displays of central Florida's heritage. There's exhibits on alligators, Orange County aviation, Florida Indians, folk medicine, the pioneer days, and a historic photo gallery. It's an edifying experience for anyone who wonders about life in Orlando before Disney.

ORLANDO INTERNATIONAL TOY TRAIN MUSEUM
Location: 5253 International Drive, Orlando. *Phone:* 363-9002. *Hours:* 10 AM to 10 PM. *Admission:* $6 adults, $4 children.

The brand-new **Toy Train Museum**, located at International Station, features the largest indoor toy train layout operating in America. There's also a full-sized steam train that you can ride, a display of toy trains dating from the turn of the century to the present. For memorabilia and souvenirs, there's a gift shop.

ORLANDO MUSEUM OF ART
Location: 2416 N. Mills Ave., Orlando. *Phone:* 896-4321. *Hours:* Tuesday through Saturday, 9 AM to 5 PM. Sunday, noon to 5 PM. Closed Mondays. *Admission:* By required donation, minimum $3 adults, $2 kids 6 to 18. Kids under 6 admitted free.

Another of the three Loch Haven Park museums, the **Orlando Museum of Art** offers a diverse schedule of exhibitions along with permanent collections of 19th and 20th century American, Precolumbian, and African works. Exhibitions in 1992 included **The Southern Black Aesthetic**, with works of over 20 African-American artists living in the south; **Light, Air, and Color**, a celebration of American impressionism;

a Californian art display; **Collaborations in Contemporary Art**, with current works created at Graphicstudio since its opening in 1968; **Artists' Views of the American West**, a collection of late 19th and 20th century Western art; and **Frontier America**, comprised of over 100 works providing a brilliant chronicle of the Western frontier.

The **Museum Shop** offers a wide variety of art-related books, posters, t-shirts, jewelry, cards, and gifts. The **Orlando Museum of Art Cafe** (L,S, $3.50 to $7.50) offers a medley of salads, sandwiches, and entrees for lunch and varying tea service and desserts.

ORLANDO SCIENCE CENTER

Location: 810 E. Rollins Ave., Orlando. *Phone:* 896-7151. *Hours:* Monday through Thursday 9 AM to 5 PM. Friday 9 AM to 9 PM. Saturday noon to 9 PM. Sunday noon to 5 PM. *Admission:* $4 adults, $3 children 4 to 11. Planetarium $1.50 additional. Laser shows $4, general admission. Kids under 3 admitted free.

The Science Center features laser light and planetarium shows, plus hands-on activities and exhibits.

ROMANCE RIVERCRUISE LINES

Location: 433 N. Palmetto Ave., Sanford. *Phone:* 321-5091, 800/423-7401 (FL), 800-225-7999. *Hours:* See below. *Admission:* See below.

The **Riverships** *Romance* and *Grand Romance* offer seven different cruises up the St. John's River. The idyllic, paddlewheel-style *Grand Romance* offers the **River Visit** (11 AM to 2 PM, Wed/Sat/Sun; $27.83 adults; $17.83 kids under 12), a luncheon cruise with live entertainment; the **River Escape** (11 AM to 3 PM, Mon/Tue/Thu/Fri; $36.32 adults; $26.32 kids), a cruise with a light brunch and an early dinner, live entertainment, and 25 miles of scenery; the **Showtime Spectacular** (7:30 AM to 10 PM, Tue/Wed/Thu; $33.02 adults; $23.02 kids), a dinner cruise and musical revue, and the **Moonlight Magic Dinner-Dance** (7:30 PM to 11 PM, Fri/Sat; $37.74 Fri, $42.45 Sat), with musicians, hors d'oeuvres, dinner, drinking, and dancing. The modernistic **Rivership Romance** offers one-, two-, and three-day cruises ($79, $247.20, $377, respectively) up the St. John's to Deland, Palatka, Jacksonville, or St. Augustine.

To get to the Monroe Harbour Marina in Sanford, where the cruises all leave from, take I-4 east to exit 51. Go east five traffic lights (approx. 5 miles) and turn left on Palmetto. Call for required reservations.

SCENIC BOAT TOUR WINTER PARK

Location: 312 E. Morse Blvd., Winter Park. *Phone:* 644-4056.

Hours: 9AM to 5 PM daily (ex. Christmas). *Admission:* $5 adults, $2.50 children 2 to 11. Kids under 2 admitted free.

Winter Park's lakefront contains some of the area's most prized real estate, with more than a few million-dollar estates. The lakes are navigated by boats that leave every hour on the hour. The guides point out the sites from Lakes Osceola and Virginia, making for a unique perspective of the little hamlet. Exit I-4 at Fairbanks Avenue, go east past Orlando Ave., amd turn left on Park Ave. and right on Morse.

TUPPERWARE MUSEUM
AND INTERNATIONAL HEADQUARTERS

Location: 3175 N. Orange Blossom Trail, Kissimmee. *Phone:* 847-3111, ext. 2695, 826-5050, ext. 2695, 800/858-7221. *Hours:* 9 AM to 4 PM weekdays. *Admission:* Free.

This may sound like a strange premise for an attraction, and it is. But if it intrigues you, enter and receive a guided tour that includes explanation of the manufacturing process through narration and photographs, a walk through a "home" in which Tupperware products are utilized, and a gallery of historic food containers. At the end of the tour, you can order Tupperware to be delivered anywhere in the continental United States.

This is also the company's corporate headquarters, and includes the **Tupperware Convention Center and Auditorium**, where orchestral, choral, dance, and theatre companies may be performing at any time. A highlight is Ballet Orlando's annual performance of The Nutcracker. Call up 826-4450 for details.

XANADU

Location: 4800 W. Irlo Bronson Mem. Hwy., Kissimmee. *Phone:* 396-1992, 239-4335. *Hours:* 10 AM to 10 PM daily. *Admission:* $4.95 adult, $3.95 senior, kids under 9 free.

You want to talk about strange tourist attractions? Here's another one for the "things that make you go hmm" file. **Xanadu** calls itself the house of the future, with 15 rooms, 6,420 square feet of bizarre technology that may be used in homes in the future. The hearth and art gallery are electronic, one bathroom has a whirlpool bath, solar sauna, and a saltwater float tank. You can wander the house on your own or hook up with the tour groups that form periodically.

Nighttime Attractions

No other place in America has the concentration of dinner shows as the Orlando metropolitan area, with a total of 18 of these attractions. Also, there are two entertainment complexes and numerous nightclubs. Unless otherwise stated, dinner shows last for between two and three hours, and all accept reservations. Make them as early as possible.

"ALOHA" POLYNESIAN LUAU

Location: Sea World, 7007 Sea World Drive, Orlando. *Phone:* 363-2195 and 800/227-8048. *Admission:* $27.95 adults, $18.95 for kids 8 to 12, kids 3 to 7, $9.95. Kids under 3 free.

Sea World's nightly Polynesian luau consists of salads, seafood, pork and chicken, rice, vegetables, and dessert, plus unlimited beer, island cocktails, and soft drinks. The entertainment includes fire-dancers and hula girls.

ARABIAN NIGHTS

Location: 6225 W. Irlo Bronson Mem. Hwy., Kissimmee. *Phone:* 239-9223 or 800/553-6116. *Admission:* $29.95 adults, $16.95 for kids 3 to 11, kids under 3 admitted free.

Arabian Nights is a dinner show about the exploits of a princess who searches for her true love, guided through time and space by a magical genie. Over 100 spectacular horses (eight different breeds) and performers dazzle audiences in 25 acts. The four-course meal consists of prime rib, garden salad, vegetable soup, dinner rolls, baked potato, dessert, and Miller Genuine Draft beer, wine, and soft drinks.

ASIAN ADVENTURE

Location: 5225 International Drive, Orlando. *Phone:* 354-0880 or 800/944-ASIA. *Admission:* $27.95 for adults, $19.95 for kids 3 to 11. Kids under 3 admitted free.

One of the two brand new dinner shows in the International Drive area, **Asian Adventure** uses architecture, food, and entertainment to bring guests a taste of Oriental culture. The architecture of the building imitates that of a Chinese palace, and the entertainment, which has been referred to as a "Chinese Ed Sullivan Show"' includes acrobats, jugglers, magicians, rope tricks, ninja battles, and a dragon dance. The four-course meal includes soup, Oriental tossed salad, Five Spice Chicken, Chinese spare ribs, Parisian potatoes, stir-fried vegetables, and Oriental orange cake for dessert.

BACKSTAGE

Location: Clarion Plaza Hotel, 9700 International Drive, Orlando. *Phone:* 352-9700.

The **Backstage Lounge**, a $400,000 "danceterium," features a Happy Hour from 3 PM to 8:30 PM daily, a live band Wednesdays through Sundays, and DJ's and VJ's nightly.

BOB CARR PERFORMING ARTS CENTRE

Location: 401 W. Livingston St., Orlando. *Phone:* 423-9999.

The **Carr Centre**, located in the downtown area, features orchestral, choir, dance, and acting touring companies throughout the year. Full-scale Broadway musicals hit the Carr Centre every so often as part of the **Orlando Broadway Series**, which has in recent months included stops from Cats, Les Miserables, Grand Hotel, and more.

BRAZIL CARNIVAL

Location: 7432 Republic Drive, Orlando. *Phone:* 352-8666. *Admission:* $27 for adults, $18 for children 3 to 12. Kids under 3 admitted free.

Brazil Carnival rounds out the duo of new dinner shows in the International Drive area. This show captures all the flavor and excitement of the rythmic music and famous dances native to Brazil, including the Samba and Lambada. Other entertainment includes a filmstrip highlighting some of Brazil's most memorable locales.

BROADWAY AT THE TOP

Location: Disney's Contemporary Resort, PO Box 10000, Lake Buena Vista. *Phone:* 934-7639. *Admission:* $44.50, adults. $19.50, children 3 to 11. Kids under 3 admitted free.

Broadway at the Top takes place in the Contemporary Resort's Top of the World Supper Club, fifteen stories above the Magic Kingdom. During the four-course meal, with entree choices of prime rib, seafood fettucine, cornish game hen, roast marinated duckling, catch of the day, and the Contemporary Duo (fresh catch and filet), diners are serenaded by the six-piece Top of the World Orchestra. After dinner, a cast of singers and dancers perform over 50 show-stopping songs from Broadway musicals including Cats, Phantom of the Opera, Funny Girl, and The Music Man.

CHURCH STREET STATION

Location: 124 West Church Street, Orlando. *Phone:* 422-2434. *Admission:* Free until 5 PM. Afterwards, $15.95 adults, $9.95 children 4 to 12. Kids under 4 free. Special passes available, see below.

Long before Pleasure Island, there was **Church Street Station**, a more adult nighttime entertainment complex. Where the dilapidated Orlando Hotel once stood, there is now a spectacular experience waiting to happen. In fact, the restoration of Church Street Station was a catalyst in the revitalization of downtown Orlando. In the daytime, Church Street Station is open, but features little in the way of entertainment or excitement. After the sun sets, though, the place explodes. There are five clubs here offering a variety of musical entertainment.

Church Street Station Showrooms

Rosie O'Grady's Good Time Emporium was what started it all. The club, built on the remains of the circa-1904 Orlando Hotel, calls itself "75 years behind the times and darn proud of it." It's the home of Rosie's Banjo Man, who performs in the afternoons, and in the evenings, Rosie's Good Time Jazz Band with the torchy "Last of the Red Hot Mamas". The club is a throwback to the era of strummin' banjos, Dixieland bands, Can-Can girls, Charleston dancers, and singing bartenders and waiters. Those with an eye for detail will notice the antiques lining the walls and ceiling, including the chandeliers (from Boston's First National Bank, circa 1904).

The Cheyenne Saloon and Opera House celebrated its tenth anniversary in June 1992. The club, which took 2 1/2 years to construct, is something of an antique museum, with hundred-year-old chandeliers from the Philadelphia Mint, pool tables from 1885 San Francisco, antique gun collections from the Stagecoach Museum in Shakopee, Minnesota, wooden Indians, pictures depicting the Wild West, buffalo and moose heads, even a stuffed brown bear from Kodiak Island, Alaska. The dining room seats, interestingly, are pews from an old Catholic church. The featured music is C&W, Grand Ole Opry style. James and the Cheyenne Stampede Band perform nightly, and big-name talent is not foreign to the Cheyenne.

Apple Annie's Courtyard features house band "Triple Action" and other folk and bluegrass artists in a Victorian garden atmosphere. Many of the items of furniture in the club came from churches and cathedrals across the east and south.

The Orchid Garden Ballroom is light bulbs, lattice, and tuxedoed waiters and barkeeps. The Ballroom's decor is dominated by Marilyn Monroe, at least one of a Belgian artist's exact reproductions of her stance over the subway grating in *The Seven Year Itch*. Dancing is done here to rock and roll from Chuck Berry and Elvis Presley to the Eric Clapton and U2. Blackjack is big here as well, despite the fact that card gambling is illegal in Florida. Gamblers rent scrip and compete for the title of Nightly Blackjack Champ.

In a mood to dance the night away? **Phineas Phogg's Balloon Works** can accommodate that desire with high-energy dance music. "Phogg's" is one of the more popular clubs with both locals and tourists. And in addition to a disco, it's also a ballooning museum of sorts. There's pictures and artifacts from some of the world's most historic balloon flights, including those made by Colonel Joe Kittiger of Rosie O'Grady's Flying Circus. You must be 21 to enter.

Commander Ragtime's Midway

On the third floor of Church Street Station Exchange is Commander Ragtime's, an arcade with NAMCO pinball and video games, surrounded by turn-of-the-century London circus memorabilia. And suspended from the ceiling is 1,400 feet of model railroad track on which six electric trains zoom through the Midway. A sports bar in the Midway features pool tables, electronic dart games, and a big-screen television for watching major sporting events. Bar fare is served, including peanuts, hot dogs, wings, sausage, and milkshakes.

Carriage Rides

There are several hitching posts outside Church Street Station, and from this location, horse-drawn carriages depart for scenic tours of the downtown area and Lake Eola. The trip lasts about 30 minutes and the cost is $20 for a couple, $25 for a group of three or four. Call 855-2900 for information.

Historic Railroad Depot

If you walk around Church Street Station, you will come upon the railroad depot for which the entertainment complex is named. The station has its own steam engine, the **"Old Duke,"** which was "borne" in 1912 at Baldwin Steam Engine and Iron Works in Baldwin, Ohio. The engine, found in Pensacola, was restored and is now available for viewing. Pushcart vendors also occupy the depot, and there are several shops, including **Sunshine Sportswear**, **Totally Unique T-Shirts**, and the **Remedy Store.**

Church Street Station Shopping

The **Bumby Gift Emporium** features T-shirts and glassware from Rosie's, Apple's Lili's, Phogg's, Ragtime's, Cheyenne, and the Orchid Garden. Videotape tours, albums by house artists, garters, jackets, belt buckles, playing cards, ashtrays, charms, and more. The **Church Street Station Exchange** has over fifty shops in a Victorian setting. For more information on this shopping center, see the section on "Shopping Centers" later in this chapter.

Street Parties

For locals, Church Street Station's eight annual street parties make an excellent excuse for buying a membership card. In January, there's the **Boola Bowl**, a post-Citrus Bowl party; in March, there's a **St. Patrick's Day** party; in April, the **Island Fest** kicks off summer, Bahamas style; in May, the **Golden Oldies** party features rock legends; the **Oktoberfest** in September features oom-pah-pah and beer; the **Italianfest** and **Halloween Party** in October make for unique fun; and the **New Year's Eve** party is a very sought-after ticket.

Weekly Specials

Sunday: Ladies Night at Phogg's: 50¢ beer and frozen drinks for ladies. 7 PM to 2 AM.

Monday: Red Hot Monday at Rosie's: $1.50 beer, cocktails, and deli sandwiches. Live entertainment, free peanuts and popcorn. 4 to 7 PM.

Wednesday: Nickel Beer Night at Phogg's: Draft beer for 5ō. 6:30 PM to 7:30 PM.

Thursday: Longneck Night at Cheyenne: 95¢ Longneck beer and wine coolers, $1.50 BBQ sandwiches, live C & W music. 4:30 to 7:30 PM.

Friday: S.O.B. Party at Crackers: Shrimp, Oyster and Beer for a buck. 4 to 7 PM. Blues Attic at Phogg's: Live blues and drink specials. 4 to 9 PM.

Church Street Station Memberships

Four different membership cards are available. The **single membership** is $24.95 and will get you in until the end of the year. A **double membership** lets you and a guest in for $39.95. A **VIP pass** lets you and three guests in for $69.95. A **corporate membership** lets in any four people for $99.95. To get to Church Street Station, take I-4 east to the Anderson Street exit. Follow the blue signs to the complex. Pay parking is available at the Sun Bank building, the Church Street Garage, and the Church Street Market garage. Metered parking is available under I-4.

CAPONE'S

Location: 4740 W. Irlo Bronson Mem. Hwy., Kissimmee. *Phone:* 397-2378. *Admission:* $29.50 adults, $14.75 kids 3 to 12.

Capone's Dinner and Show, a 1992 addition to the U.S. 192 landscape, features a 15-item unlimited Italian buffet, unlimited Budweiser,

Bud Lite, Sangria, soda, or "Al's Rum Runners" to the accompaniment of a show taking place in 1931 Chicago's gangland that resembles a Guys and Dolls set.

CRAZY HORSE SALOON
Location: 7050 Kirkman Rd., Orlando. *Phone:* 363-0071.

The **Crazy Horse Saloon** features country and western music provided by the house's Rosebud Creek Band and others. Live entertainment is featured six nights a week, and dancing lessons are given on Tuesdays, Thursdays, and Fridays.

THE CRICKETERS ARMS
Location: Mercado, 8440 International Drive, Orlando. *Phone:* 354-0686.

The **Cricketers Arms**, calling itself "the oldest and newest English pub," offers 15 imported British stouts, lagers, and bitters served in 20 oz. mugs. Domestic beer, wines, ports, and sherries are also available, as are breakfast and an English lunch and dinner menu. Live entertainment is featured Tuesday, Wednesday, and Saturday nights, and a satellite dish will show English soccer and other sports on a big screen television.

CUDA BAY CLUB
Location: 8510 Palm Parkway, Orlando. *Phone:* 239-8815. *Admission:* $5.

Located in Vista Centre, this snazzy new club is decorated by neon pink flags and backed by a runoff pond known as Cuda Bay. The sound and light systems are impressive and there's a 30' by 30' stainless steel dance floor. A DJ plays Top 40 hits, and there's an occasional live band.

FAT TUESDAYS
Location: Mercado, 8445 International Drive, Orlando. *Phone:* 351-5311.

Fat Tuesdays makes its eighth appearance in the Southeast here. The bar offers over fifty different flavors of frozen drinks ranging from simple strawberry daquiris to concoctions like 190 Octane, Nuclear Fallout, and Group Mind Eraser. Free samples of all the flavors are available, and food is served until midnight. Beer, wine, and spirits are also available, and there is live music every Thursday.

HOOP-DEE-DOO REVUE
Location: Disney's Fort Wilderness Resort, PO Box 10000, Lake Buena

Vista. *Phone:* 934-7639. *Admission:* $32 for those 21 and over, $24 for ages 12 to 20, and $16 for ages 3 to 11. Kids under 3 admitted free.

The Hoop-Dee-Doo Revue is the absolute favorite among WDW veterans as far as fun and food are concerned, and performances often book up weeks in advance. At **Pioneer Hall** three times a night, the immensely popular show is full of song, dance, and slapstick comedy.

The food is nothing to sneeze at either, with all-you-can-eat fried chicken, barbecued ribs, corn on the cob, baked beans, and strawberry shortcake with unlimited beer, wine, and soda. Reservations are required and can be made up to 30 days in advance.

J.J. WHISPERS
Location: 5100 Adanson Street, Orlando. *Phone:* 629-4779, 629-BONK for Bonkerz. *Admission:* Varies.

"**Whispers**" was once a Woolco, but now it's a wild and wooly nightclub complex. The clubs include the **Bonkerz Comedy Club**, regarded as one of the best places in the area for yuks. Show times vary, and reservations and information can be acquired by calling 629-BONK. Whispers features a band playing Top 40 music. The **Game Room** has pool tables and video games. **City Lights** is a disco with five dance floors. The **VIP Room** is a quiet bar overlooking the main stage. Mondays at J.J. Whispers are Teen Night. Those over 16 can enjoy the clubs and no alcohol is served. Tuesdays are Ladies Nights, and Wednesdays and Sundays are progressive music nights.

KING HENRY'S FEAST
Location: 8984 International Drive, Orlando. *Phone:* 351-5151, 363-3500, or 800/776-3501. *Admission:* $29.95 adults, $19.95 for kids 3 to 11, kids under 3 admitted free.

King Henry's Feast isn't difficult to find. It's the only medieval fortress at Plaza International. Inside the 14,000-foot castle, you celebrate King Henry VIII's birthday with a search to find the monarch a seventh wife. This is accomplished through song, dance, magic, and comedy.

King Henry is played by Jacob Witkin, who has performed with the Royal Shakespeare Company and West End theaters in England. His herald is Gerald Martin, who has performed in musical theatre, film, and television, including the stage and movie versions of "Oliver!". Henry Miller dazzles with his magic, Linda Edelston with her aerial "ballet", and Marek and Krystyna Dudek with their balancing acts and feats of danger. Last, but not least, is the comical Max Burton as the court jester.

As for the food, it's fit for a royal appetite, with all-you-can-eat soup, salad, whole wheat rolls, roast chicken and ribs, vegetables, and pie a la mode. Unlimited beer, wine, and soda are also included. Full bar service is available. King Henry's Feast is located just north of the Orange County Convention/Civic Center.

MARDI GRAS

Location: Mercado, 8445 International Drive, Orlando. *Phone:* 351-5151 or 800/776-3501. *Admission:* $29.95 adults, $19.95 for kids 3 to 11, kids under 3 admitted free.

Mardi Gras, located inside the Mercado shopping center on I-Drive, takes diners on a two-hour tour of all the world's hottest carnivals. The tour will take you from Latin America to the Caribbean and finally, to Bourbon Street. The sets and costumes make for a flashy accompaniment to the song-and-dance cabaret. The menu includes vegetable soup, buttered rolls, Caesar salad, baked chicken breast with herb dressing, steamed broccoli, roasted new potatoes, and meringue Key lime pie, and unlimited beer, wine, and Coca-Cola. The children's menu consists of fruit cocktail, vegetable soup, chicken nuggets with french fries, and meringue Key lime pie.

MARK TWO DINNER THEATER

Location: 3376 Edgewater Drive, Orlando. *Phone:* 843-6275 or 800/726-6275. *Admission:* See below.

Mark Two is one of the only "true" dinner theaters in Orlando, using Actor's Equity Association (AEA) performers in Broadway musicals and comedies. The cost of a show includes performance and a buffet featuring prime rib or beef sirloin tips.

The prices and times are as follows: Wed, Thu, and Fri matinees, $28; doors open 11:30 AM, curtain time is 1:15 PM; Wed and Thu evening, $30; doors open 6:00 PM, curtain time is 8:00 PM; Sun twilight, $30; doors open 4:30 PM, curtain time is 6:30 PM Fri; and Sat evening, $32; doors open 6:00 PM, curtain time is 8:00 PM.

For tickets or more information, call or write the Mark Two. To get there from points south, take I-4 east to exit 44, Par Avenue. Turn left and take it to Edgewater.

MEDIEVAL TIMES DINNER & TOURNAMENT

Location: 4510 W. Irlo Bronson Mem. Hwy., Kissimmee. *Phone:* 396-1518, 239-0214, 239-8666, 800/432-0768 (FL), 800/229-8300. *Admission:* $28.00 adults, $20.00 for kids 3 to 12, kids under 3 admitted free.

Does the name of this attraction sound familiar? It should, if you live in the vicinity of Lyndhurst, NJ; Buena Park, CA; Chicago; or Dallas. **Medieval Times** dinner shows are located in those four cities as well. But what's the hype is all about?. Just the single most exciting dinner show in the state, that's all. The year is 1093 AD, the place is the court of His Grace, Count Don Raimundo II. Six brave knights compete in swordplay, falconry, sorcery, romance, and even a real joust. Which of the six knights do you root for? Well, your seat bears the same emblem on the shield of one of the knights. Find that one and keep an eye on him, because he's yours.

The menu includes appetizers, vegetable soup, whole roast chicken, spare ribs, herb-basted potato, pastries, coffee, beer, wine cocktail, and soft drinks.

MEMORY LANE
Location: Hotel Royal Plaza, 1905 Hotel Plaza Boulevard, Lake Buena Vista. *Phone:* 846-3355, ext. 3111 or 827-3111. *Admission:* $26.95 adults, $19.95 for kids 3 to 11, kids under 3 admitted free.

Memory Lane is a song-and-dance revue featuring 35 songs from the turn of the century up to the 1950's. The four-course meal includes choice of entree and beverages.

MICKEY'S TROPICAL REVUE
Location: Disney's Polynesian Resort, PO Box 10000, Lake Buena Vista. *Phone:* 934-7639. *Admission:* $27 for those 21 and over, $21 for ages 12 to 20, and $12 for ages 3 to 11. Kids under 3 admitted free.

Mickey's Tropical Revue is a junior version of the Polynesian Revue (see below), with Polynesian dancers and Mickey, Minnie, and other Disney characters doing the hula. Full dinner and dessert is served.

MULVANEY'S IRISH PUB
Location: Dansk Plaza, 7220 International Drive, Orlando, and 27 W. Church Street, Orlando. *Phone:* 352-7031 (I-Drive) and 872-3296 (Downtown).

Mulvaney's, styled after a real Irish pub, features live entertainment, traditional Irish fare (including Irish breakfast, served all day), and six imported beers on tap.

MURDERWATCH MYSTERY THEATRE
Location: Grosvenor Resort, 1850 Hotel Plaza Blvd., Lake Buena Vista.

Phone: 828-4444, ext. 6117. *Admission:* $25 adults, $12 for kids 3 to 12. Kids under 3 admitted free.

Held every Saturday night in Baskerville's Restaurant, this, like Sleuths, puts you in the shoes of Sherlock Holmes and Angela Lansbury to figure out "whodunnit" while enjoying an unlimited prime rib buffet. Successful detectives receive prizes at the end of the evening. Reservations are required.

PLANTATION DINNER THEATRE

Location: Orlando Heritage Inn, 9861 International Drive, Orlando. *Phone:* 352-0008. *Admission:* $35.95, Tue, Wed, Thu. $25.95, Fri, Sat. kids under 12, $12.

The **Plantation Dinner Theatre** offers light dramas five nights a week in the Orlando Heritage Inn, by the Orange County Convention/Civic Center.

POLYNESIAN REVUE

Location: Disney's Polynesian Resort, PO Box 10000, Lake Buena Vista. *Phone:* 934-7639. *Admission:* $29 for those 21 and over, $23 for ages 12 to 20, and $15 for ages 3 to 11. Kids under 3 admitted free.

The **Polynesian Revue**, held twice each evening in **Luau Cove**, features authentic Polynesian dancing and specialty acts, many of which are performed by artists who have studied at the Polynesian Cultural Center in Honolulu. The meal includes Luau Barbecued Ribs, seafood moana, spit-roasted Hawaiian chicken, grilled Mahi-Mahi in herb butter, Oriental vegetables, fruit salad, fried rice, and flaming volcano ice cream dessert. Also included are unlimited soft drinks, beer, Mai Tais, melon coladas, and pina coladas. Like the Hoop-Dee-Doo Revue, this show requires reservations and accepts them up to 30 days in advance.

SHOOTER'S WATERFRONT CAFE U.S.A.

Location: 4315 N. Orange Blossom Trail, Orlando. *Phone:* 298-2855.

Shooter's, located on the shores of Lake Fairview, attracts a crowd of under-30 Floridians and features Top 40 music, a swimming pool, boat dock, and volleyball court, making this one of the liveliest nightspots around.

SLEUTHS MYSTERY DINNER SHOW

Location: 7508 Republic Drive, Orlando. *Phone:* 363-1985 or 800/244-

6042. *Admission:* $29.95 adults, $19.95 for kids 3 to 11, kids under 3 admitted free.

Be forewarned. Every night at **Sleuths**, somebody dies. But don't worry, because this is International Drive's only murder mystery dinner theater. Four shows alternate through the week, but in all of them, the audience mingles with the actors, and it's up to them to solve the crime. The successful sleuth who cracks the case receives a prize.

The dinner includes hors d'oeuvres, crackers and cheese, rolls, honey glazed Cornish game hen, vegetable medley, mashed potatoes and gravy, herb stuffing, fruit garnish, "mystery" dessert, and unlimited beer, wine, and soft drinks.

From Kissimmee, Lake Buena Vista, and WDW, take I-4 east to exit 30A (Republic Drive). Go past International Drive and Wet'n Wild. It's four doors past the cinema, on the right. From Sea World and the International Drive area, take I-Drive north to Republic and turn right.

TERROR ON CHURCH STREET
Location: 135 S. Orange Ave., Orlando. *Phone:* 649-FEAR. *Admission:* $10.

A new entry into the Orlando nightlife scene, **Terror on Church Street** is based on a 1987 production by a troupe of Argentinian actors, called Pasaje del Terror (Passage to Terror). They toured Mexico and Spain and Mexico, and the first permanent location opened in Bilbao, Spain in 1988.

Internationally recognized magician Ignacio Brieva came to Orlando and created the first American installment of the attraction, in two floors of the old Woolworth's building. The attraction combines the use of live actors, theatrical sets, cinematic special effects, microchip technology, and 23 individual soundtracks in an attempt to scare the pants off of you. They even promise to frighten you or refund the ticket price. Theatrical use of sound, light, and the element of surprise, along with actor improvisation, ever-changing scripts, and audience participation are incorporated into the production to make each journey unique.

And just in case they manage to frighten you out of your mind, there's constant surveillance, two "chicken out" exits, and first aid assistance for those who need it. The **Little Shop of Terror** is open from 5 PM to closing and offers gifts and memorabilia, and the adjacent **Moorefield's Restaurant** (tel. 872-6960) offers enjoyable dining and entertainment.

WILD BILL'S WILD WEST DINNER SHOW AT FORT LIBERTY
Location: 5260 W. Irlo Bronson Mem. Hwy, Kissimmee. *Phone:* 351-5151

or 800/776-3501. *Admission:* $29.95 adults, $19.95 for kids 3 to 11, kids under 3 admitted free.

One of the mainstays in the come-and-go world of Orlando dinner shows, **Wild Bill's**, formerly "Fort Liberty," is considered one of the best non-Disney dinner shows around. Themed after an 1876 citadel called Fort Liberty, the 12-character show features Bob Hope-style entertainment for the soldiers of E Troop. Your hosts for the evening, the lovely Miss Kitty and Wild Bill, guide you through specialty acts including the Comanche Dance Group, who perform the Hoop Dance and Eagle Dance; Texas Jack Fulbright, an eighth-generation cowboy who performs tricks including gun spinning and roping; and Cetan Mani, who combines archery and knife throwing with humor. Audience participation is also a big part of the show.

The 22-acre, $29 million attraction can seat 600 people, and the menu includes fried chicken, barbecued pork ribs, corn on the cob, vegetable soup, baked potato, biscuits, salad, apple pie a la mode, and unlimited beer, wine, and Coca-Cola. Full bar service is available.

WOLFMAN JACK'S ROCK & ROLL PALACE

Location: Old Town, 5770 W. Irlo Bronson Mem. Hwy., Kissimmee. *Phone:* 396-6499, 239-2823. *Admission:* $8.50 after 5 PM.

Nostalgic to the max and irresistably cool, **Wolfman Jack's** takes you back in time to the 1950's. Classic cars, hula hoops, poodle skirts, and a 24-foot high door shaped like a jukebox all carry out the theme. 50's artists like Fabian, Herman's Hermits, the Shangri-Las, and the Drifters perform, and live music from the 50's to 70's is performed nightly. There's a nightly Happy Hour and dancing to great music. Memberships are available.

ZANZI-BAR

Location: 6308 International Drive, Orlando. *Phone:* 363-5251.

Zanzi-Bar features dancing, dining, and drinking in a tropical atmosphere indoors and a pleasant outdoor deck. The menu includes British favorites and American standbys. Live music is featured nightly.

Shopping

Orlando, like most major cities, has a handful of large shopping centers and malls. Orlando, like most tourist traps, has truckloads of chintzy souvenir shops offering keychains, t-shirts, mugs, and cigarette lighters. Factory outlets are big here too for some reason. The largest

variety can be found in **Belz Factory Outlet World** and along U.S. 192 and International Drive.
Listed below are major shopping centers in the area:

192 FLEA MARKET OUTLET, INC.
Location: 4301 W. Vine Street, Kissimmee. *Phone:* 351-5311.

This flea market, located towards downtown Kissimmee, has over 400 dealer booths and is open seven days a week.

ALTAMONTE MALL
Location: 451 Altamonte Avenue, Altamonte Springs. *Phone:* 830-4400.

Altamonte Mall, located in the northern suburb of Altamonte Springs, is anchored by **J.C. Penney's, Burdines, Maison Blanche,** and **Sears.** There's also a General Cinema and 160 specialty stores. The Treats Food Court has fifteen different eateries offering everything from gyros to pizza to hot dogs to tacos. Rounding out the other eateries in the mall are **Ruby Tuesday's, Perry's Restaurant,** and **Baskin Robbins.** Take I-4 east to S.R. 436. and go east half a mile.

BELZ FACTORY OUTLET WORLD
Location: 5401 W. Oakridge Rd., Orlando. *Phone:* 352-9611.

The Belz Mall, as it is commonly referred to, is a collection of over 160 factory outlet stores, including **Bass** and **Capezio** shoes, **Calvin Klein, Guess, Pfaltzgraff, Corning Revere,** and more, in two malls and three annexes. A food court in Mall 2 has six eateries, Mall 1 has a **Sbarro's Italian Eatery, David's Cookies,** and **Sub City.** Take I-Drive to its northern terminus or take I-4 east to 30B, Kirkman Road, and turn left on I-Drive and take it to the end.

CHURCH STREET MARKET
Location: 55 W. Church Street, Orlando. *Phone:* 872-3500.

Church Street Market, located in Orlando's historic downtown, has shops and restaurants including the **Olive Garden, Pizzeria Uno, Haagen-Dazs,** and more in a neat, brick-lined bulding.

CHURCH STREET STATION EXCHANGE
Location: 124 W. Pine Street, Orlando. *Phone:* 422-2434.

The **Church Streeet Station Exchange**, located inside the Church

Street Station entertainment complex, features more than forty shops in a pleasant, streamlined, Victorian setting. A food court offers six different cuisines.

COLONIAL PLAZA MALL

Location: 2560 E. Colonial Drive, Orlando. *Phone:* 894-3601.

Orlando's very first mall, on the scene since 1956, and is anchored by **Dillard's, Belk Lindsey, J. Byrons,** and **Lille Rubins.** There are about 100 smaller shops in the mall.

CROSSROADS OF LAKE BUENA VISTA

Location: I-4 & S.R. 535, Exit 27, Lake Buena Vista. *Phone:* 827-7300.

Crossroads may or may not be technically a part of Walt Disney World, depending on whom you ask. I have consulted with several Disney employees who seemed to differ on that point. Regardless of whether or not it's inside the boundaries, it contains something that guests at the area villa hotels would look upon as a boon: the contemporary, chic **Gooding's Supermarket,** open 24 hours a day. Other shops in the plaza include **Beyond Electronics,** for personal electronics, toys, games, and watches, **Camp Beverly Hills, Ken Done, Mojo's Surfin' USA, Sunworks, Vacanza Shoes, Chico's,** and **Foot Locker** for apparel for men, women, and children, **Disney's Character Connection** for character merchandise, **Mitzi's Hallmark** for cards, stationery, and gifts, and **White's Books** for reading material.

Services in the shopping center include **Buena Vista Vision Center** for eyeglasses, contact lenses, and examinations, **Hudgeon's Cleaners** for dry cleaning, the **Lake Buena Vista Post Office,** and a branch of the **Sun Bank.** One of the Orlando area's three **Pirate's Cove Adventure Golf** 36-hole complexes is located here as well.

There are ten restaurants in Crossroads. **Expresso's Liquors & Pizza** offers wines, beers, and spirits plus Italian dishes for eat-in and take-out. **Larry's Old Fashioned Ice Cream, McDonald's,** and **Taco Bell** offer counter-service eats, while **Jungle Jim's, Pebbles, Perkins Family Restaurant, Pizzeria Uno, Red Lobster,** and **T.G.I. Friday's** offer more relaxed, sit-down meals.

FLEA WORLD

Location: U.S. Hwy. 17-92, Sanford. *Phone:* 647-3976.

Located northeast of Orlando, **Flea World** calls itself America's largest flea market. With over 1,600 dealer booths, it just might be. On a tract of land bigger than the Magic Kingdom, the market includes 14 concessions and parking for 4,000 cars.

Fun World, located in the same complex as Flea World, is a family fun park with 2 miniature golf courses, go-carts, bumper cars and boats, a ferris wheel, batting cages, and midway rides. A pizza/burger restaurant and 350 game arcade round out the offerings. The park is open from 10 AM to midnight every Friday, Saturday, and Sunday as well as school holidays. For info on Fun World at Flea World, call 628-2233. To get to Flea World and Fun World, take I-4 east to exit 50. From there, go east 1 mile on U.S. 17-92.

THE FLORIDA MALL
Location: 8001 S. Orange Blossom Trail, Orlando. *Phone:* 851-6255.

The biggest mall in the entire state, the **Florida Mall** encompasses 170 specialty stores, a food court with nineteen restaurants, and four full-service restaurants: **Ruby Tuesday's**, **Friendly's**, **Morrison's**, and **Sassy's**. The mall, whose decor ranges from Art Deco to Mediterranean to Victorian, is anchored by **Belk Lindsey**, **JC Penney**, **Maison Blanche**, **Sears**, and the **Sheraton Plaza Hotel**. The Florida Mall is easy to get to, as it is on the corner of the S.O.B.T. (U.S. 17-92-441) and Sand Lake Road (S.R. 482). Take exit 29 from I-4 and turn east. The mall is a can't-miss sight, the first corner after the Turnpike bridge.

FORT LIBERTY TRADING POST
Location: 5260 W. Irlo Bronson Mem. Hwy., Kissimmee. *Phone:* 351-5151, 363-5000, 800/776-3501.

Fort Liberty features a dinner attraction, wax museum, and this, a Western-themed shopping village with 20 unique shops.

KISSIMMEE MANUFACTURERS' MALL
Location: 2517 Old Vineland Rd., Kissimmee. *Phone:* 396-8900.

Many factory outlets also found at the Belz Mall are also located here, including **Nike**, **Van Heusen**, **London Fog**, **Book Publishers' Outlet**, **Totes**, and **American Tourister**.

THE MARKETPLACE
Location: 7600 Dr. Phillips Blvd., Orlando. *Phone:* 679-9301.

The Marketplace is a strip mall at the corner of Dr. Phillips and Sand Lake Road, and is more popular among locals than tourists. For necessities, there's an ultramodern **Gooding's**. Several of the area's best restaurants are also located here, in **Chatham's Place**, **Christini's**, and **Darbar**.

MERCADO MEDITERRANEAN VILLAGE

Location: 8445 S. International Drive, Orlando. *Phone:* 345-9337.

Mercado is one of those special places that brings a smile to your lips every time you see it. And you'll know it when you do. It's International Drive's only Spanish mission. As if the stucco-and-Spanish tile building weren't distinctive enough, there's a jungly tangle of waterfalls, lakes, streams, palms, hills, and golf next door at Pirate's Cove Adventure Golf.

Make Mercado the very first place you go during your vacation if you're staying at an International Drive hotel. At the front of the village is the Visitor Information Center. Here, you can pick up brochures from all area attractions, hotels, restaurants, and services, purchase discounted tickets to attractions, and pick up coupon-laden publications like SEE Orlando, International Drive Bulletin, Enjoy Florida Magazine, and more. This simple task can save a family of four hundreds of dollars over the course of a week's vacation. Also, ask for a Mercado coupon book with over $200 in savings.

Some of the fifty-some specialty shops in Mercado include **The Village Corner** and **Exclusively Mickey's** for licensed Disney, MGM, and Universal souvenirs; **Hello Dolly** for teddy bears and collector dolls; **One for the Road** for eveything for the car enthusiast; **Conch Republic** for tropical clothing, and jewelry; **The Looking Glass** for crystal and engraved glass; **Space 2000** for air and space related gifts; and **The Magic Shop** for novelties and magic tricks.

Interestingly, Mercado is does not have any department stores as anchors. Instead, it uses restaurants. **Damon's: The Place for Ribs**, features excellent barbecue. **Charlie's Lobster House** has fresh, simply prepared seafood. **Bergamo's Italian Restaurant** offers "a taste of Italy — New York style!" The **Mardi Gras Dinner Attraction** offers a four-course meal with a side order of song and dance. **The Butcher Shop Steakhouse** features big steaks and prime rib. **Jose O'Day's Mexican Restaurant** offers fajitas, quesadillas, and seafood and steak specialties, "South of the Border" style.

Also located in the complex are nightspots **Fat Tuesday's** and **The Cricketer's Arms**, and a food court with counters offering Italian, Greek, Chinese, Latin American, American, Tex-Mex, and more. Live entertainment is provided in the attractive courtyard each evening, usually musicians who serenade guests with sounds of the 50's, 60's, 70's, 80's, and 90's.

For the kids, not-so-live entertainment is provided by **Mugsy's Merry**

Medley, a hokey little songfest with crude animatronic birds. Also, if you're the kind of person who eats up the legends of attractions like Pleasure Island and the Haunted Mansion, follow signs for a self-guided walking tour of Mercado's fictional history. As you stroll the quaint streets of the Mercado, you will notice many murals, watercolors, and sculpture handcrafted and designed by Florida resident Don Reynolds.

OLD TOWN

Location: 5770 W. Irlo Bronson Mem. Hwy., Kissimmee. *Phone:* 396-4888, 800/843-4202, 800/331-5093 (FL).

Similar in decor and motif to the Magic Kingdom's Main Street, USA, **Old Town** offers Victorian splendor as a backdrop for seventy specialty shops, plus **Wolfman Jack's Rock and Roll Palace** and the **Elvis Presley Museum**. 1920's Florida nad 1950's rock and roll may seem like odd bedfellows, but who cares? It works.

ORLANDO FASHION SQUARE MALL

Location: 3201 E. Colonial Drive, Orlando. *Phone:* 895-1131.

Fashion Square is one of Orlando's older, quieter malls, with 100 specialty stores plus **Sears, Maison Blanche, Burdine's, Piccadilly Cafeteria**, and **Ruby Tuesday's**.

OSCEOLA SQUARE MALL

Location: 3831 W. Vine St., Kissimmee. *Phone:* 847-6941.

Kissimmee's only enclosed, climate-controlled shopping center, anchored by **Wal-Mart, J. Byron's, Ross**, and **Eckerd Drugs**, contains 40 specialty shops, an international food court, and Cobb's 12-plex cinema. Also located at Osceola Square Mall is the **Kissimmee Fun'n Wheels**. For eats, try **Friendly's** or **Morrison's Cafe**.

PARK AVENUE

Location: PO Box 11, Winter Park, FL 32790. Shopping district runs from Fairbanks to Canton. *Phone:* 671-5845.

Like its Big Apple namesake, **Park Avenue** in Winter Park offers upscale, chic shopping at antique stores and boutiques like **Williams-Sonoma, Banana Republic, Victoria's Secret, Limited Express, Talbot's**, and **The Gap**. If the urge strikes you, and it will, stop for an ice cream cone at **Haagen-Dazs, Thomas Sweet**, or **Brandywine's**.

QUALITY OUTLET CENTER

Location: International Drive, one block east of Kirkman Road, Orlando. *Phone:* 423-5885.

The **Quality Outlet Center** is a collection of twenty-some factory outlet shops between Kirkman Road and Oakridge Road, including **Corning-Revere**, **Perfumania**, **Linens'n Things**, **Totes**, **American Tourister**, **Mikasa**, and **Royal Doulton**.

Special Shops

CITRUS CIRCUS

Location: 6813 Visitor's Circle, Orlando. *Phone:* 351-1694.

This gaudy shop, located across from Wet'n Wild, offers an excellent selection of citrus fruit and citrus wines, candies, jellies, fresh-squeezed orange juice, t-shirts, souvenirs, shell jewelry, and gifts. Shipping to all parts of the U.S. and Canada is available. To get there, take I-4 to exit 30A and make two quick rights.

DANSK FACTORY OUTLET

Location: Dansk Plaza, 7000 International Drive, Orlando. *Phone:* 351-2425.

Dansk is a well-known name among kitchenophiles. This outlet offers dinnerware, cookware, crystal, flatware, teakwood, stemware, linens, barware, silver gifts, and cutlery at discounts up to 60%.

EDWIN WATTS GOLF SHOPS

Location: Dansk Plaza, 7220 International Drive, Orlando, and 7297 Turkey Lake Dr., Orlando. *Phone:* 352-2535 and 345-8451.

The Turkey Lake location is the largest **Edwin Watts** factory store in the country, and both shops offer an excellent selection of golf apparel and equipment including brands like Wilson, MacGregor, Dunlop, Mizuno, and more.

ORLANDO MAGIC FANATTIC & SPORTS CENTER

Location: 715 North Garland, Orlando. *Phone:* 649-2222.

This shop offers **Orlando Magic** merchandise, including sweats, jackets, t-shirts, basketballs, and models of Stuff, the Magic Dragon. Other sports teams are represented as well.

RON JON SURF SHOP

Location: 3850 S. Banana River Rd., Cocoa Beach. *Phone:* 799-8888.

Ron Jon deserves an entry here, even though it's an hour east of Orlando. Quite simply, Ron Jon calls itself the "East Coast Surfing Capital." It is, with 42,000 square feet of beachwear, surfboards, t-shirts, and everything for everybody who ever rode a wave, or dreamed of it. And that includes a stretch of clean, uncrowded beach. To get to Ron Jon from Orlando, take the Beeline east to A1A south. It's at the corner of A1A and S.R. 520. The shop never closes.

SHELL WORLD

Location: 4727 and 7550 W. Irlo Bronson Mem. Hwy., Kissimmee, and 6464 International Dr., Orlando. *Phone:* 396-9000, 396-4544, 351-0900.

If you've been to Sea World and Disney World and even Flea World, and you still crave yet another world, check out **Shell World**. These odd shops offer seashells, coral, seashell jewelry and souvenirs, and coral and mother-of-pearl jewelry.

GENERAL INDEX